By Water and the Word

By Water and the Word

The Scriptures of Baptism

Daniel B. Stevick

 CHURCH

Church Publishing Incorporated, New York

The Scripture quotations contained herein are from the New Revised Standard Version Bible, copyright © 1989 by the Division of Christian Education of the National Council of the Churches of Christ in the U.S.A., and are used by permission. All rights reserved.

The text of the hymn "Baptized in water" is by Michael Saward, copyright © 1982 by Hope Publishing Co., Carol Stream IL 60188. All rights reserved. Used by permission.

Library of Congress Cataloging-in-Publication Data

Stevick, Daniel B.
     By water and the word: the scriptures of baptism / by Daniel B. Stevick.
       p. c.m.
   Includes bibliographical references and index.
   ISBN 0-89869-296-2 (pbk. : alk. paper)

     1. Baptism—Biblical teaching. 2. Baptism—Episcopal Church. 3. Baptism—Anglican Communion. 4. Baptism (Liturgy) 5. Episcopal Church—Liturgy. 6. Anglican Communion—Liturgy.   I. Title.

BS2545.B36S74   1997   97-29870
234' . 161—dc21   CIP

Church Publishing Incorporated
445 Fifth Avenue
New York NY 10016

5 4 3 2 1

Contents

Water and the Word together constitute one baptism.

Martin Luther, *Large Catechism*, IV.46

Introduction

In the flow of the Prayer Book initiatory rite, a service of scripture and preaching leads to baptism and the eucharist. The biblical message precedes, informs and interpenetrates the initiatory action. The scripture passages that are appointed for use at the baptismal occasions add up to a rich source for sacramental understanding.

Yet the readings go by rapidly, and worshipers may be excused if they wonder what these varied portions of the scriptures have to do with one another or with Holy Baptism.

Preachers, for their part, are often called by the liturgy to look at the scriptures for Sundays and several of the great feast days of the year as scriptures for baptism. They are scriptures to be preached, and the sermon will be followed by baptism. Can a preacher, with a candidate, a family, and a congregation in mind, take a fresh look at the baptismal texts?

Further, *The Book of Occasional Services, 1994* asks persons preparing for baptism, along with their teachers and sponsors, to reflect on the appointed biblical readings with baptism and the baptized life in mind. *The principal curriculum for each catechetical session is reflection on the respective readings of the Sunday eucharistic lectionary as these illumine the faith journey of catechumens, sponsors and catechists* (p. 114).

This book is intended to direct all such persons—worshipers, preachers, catechumens and catechists, members of study groups—to the extensive biblical resource that is now in hand to inform baptismal occasions and the seasons that precede and follow them.

This inquiry goes beyond the lectionary readings and considers also the biblical allusions that unobtrusively pervade the Prayer Book rite. We shall look, too, at the accounts of baptism in the book of Acts, for even though the lectionary does not use them all, they tell us all we know of what was being done at baptism by the church that wrote the gospels and explained itself in the epistles.

The biblical material that is discussed here is organized largely by the rites and lectionary readings of the Prayer Book and *The Book of Occasional Services*. The disadvantage of this method may be that the biblical passages are taken out of their settings in the text, but they may also fall here in the configurations in which they are met in the liturgy, in catechesis, and in preaching.

When a biblical passage is used in more than one location in the lectionary, as several are, I give my principal comments in connection with what I take to be the most important occurrence and cross-reference to those comments when the passage appears elsewhere. I have used the NRSV translation of the Bible and the Prayer Book Psalms.

This inquiry began as a unit of study material which I prepared for the Catechumenal Process Committee of the Diocese of Pennsylvania and which was used widely in Lent of 1996. As I wrote it I found myself drawn into this biblical material, and persons who followed this Lenten study reported that they, too, found it rewarding to examine at first hand the scriptures for baptism. This text has now grown far beyond the dozen typed pages of that original study guide. I send it out, praying that through it others may be inwardly engaged by this body of biblical material, as I have been.

This book is much more substantial than it would have been otherwise, because at an early stage it received a careful reading and many constructive suggestions from the Rev. Byron Stuhlman. I am grateful for his suggestions and encouragement.

Daniel B. Stevick
Lent 1997

Baptism and Experience

Even in the midst of our careless, self-absorbed, self-sufficient lives, people do become Christians. A life which is not their own touches them and becomes their own. A distant story meets them and becomes their story. A new presence engages them in forgiveness and support and in firm but gentle leading and correction. A glory beyond their conceiving illuminates their lives.

Baptism is the act which outwardly—in water, a few words, human hands, and a company of believing people—signifies and conveys this new life.

Historically, Christian baptism breaks on the scene in the New Testament, coincident with the faith and the church. The book of Acts, our first account of the life of the church, tells of the Good News of Christ moving into new places and encountering new groups which pose new challenges for the gospel. Preaching, faith and baptism are the signs of its advance—reaching deep into existence, breaking up old patterns of loyalty, extending new claims, and opening new promise.

Today, baptism, in the power of the Spirit, still can divide and unite, judge and redeem. The living divine Word has forever allied itself with baptism.

Yet to speak of baptism in terms of a vital encounter with God—terms that are taken for granted in the New Testament and the early church—can seem strained in the light of the generally reduced meaning that baptism has come to have in much of present-day church and society.

The baptismal rite was for a long time generally carried out in the church in ways that diminished it—making it very often a hole-in-a-corner affair with a small child, a family and a few friends, and a single minister, gathered at a font in an otherwise empty church. Individual Christians could

be excused if they did not think it very important. They were simply inter-
nalizing what they saw and heard. This inattention to baptism is changing,
but habits in spiritual matters change slowly. Virtually all American churchgoers have been baptized, often in infancy. But too often their baptism has
remained in their past as little more than a social fact, unremembered and
uncreative. In words that might well be ours, Martin Luther complained
that in his society, sixteenth-century Germany, everyone was baptized, but
hardly anyone thought or did anything about their baptism: "There are
scarce any who call to mind their baptism and still fewer who glory in it."[1]

It would take a long book (and a book different from this) to inquire
how the Christian movement got from where it began to where it was for a
long time, and from there to where we are now. (We need a good social
history of baptism.) But if we are to move ahead confidently from where
we are, we shall, in the odd way of the Christian community, move forward and move backward at the same time. It is not that we can or should
replicate our first-century past (nor our fourth-century nor our sixteenth-
century past). No past situation was our situation, and no past way of doing
things can be our way. Yet as we move forward we must allow ourselves to
be confronted afresh with our always determinative, always elusive starting place. Hence this inquiry goes directly to the biblical witness—to New
Testament baptism, in its immediacy, its power, and its mystery.

In the second half of the twentieth century many traditions, seeking to
repossess this deep past, have addressed freshly their initiatory theology,
liturgy, and pastoral practice. A significant recovery can be observed in
the service books of the churches, Catholic and Protestant. This recovery
has not yet reached all churches equally nor all parts of any church to the
same extent. It is easier to revise liturgical texts than to address tired practices or understandings. Yet the momentum for baptismal renewal continues—and with it profound personal discoveries.

Several perceptions—ultimately biblically derived perceptions—have
been important in this renewal, and if we cite them briefly here in general
terms it may orient us to the inquiry that lies ahead:

The act of baptism is foundational, for it brings believing persons into
a relation with God in Christ which God does not retract. The church comes
to birth through baptism, an act which signifies a bond, imparted to humanity and secured in the faithfulness of God. Baptism brings the individual within the redemptive life that has been won in principle for all in
the work of Christ and to which the church is witness-community.

Despite its outward simplicity, baptism carries theological and spiritual depth. In it persons speak and act, and they seek to act responsibly. But beyond, before, and through the actions of ministers, sponsors, parents, and friends, the initiative in baptism is taken by God, who is the principal actor and speaker. It is as though in baptism God were saying to each person who is baptized, *I will never leave you or forsake you* (Heb. 13:5, citing Deut. 31: 6, 8 and Josh. 1:5). The sacrament is an outward, bodily sign of the divine self-investment in humanity. *He who did not withhold his own Son, but gave him up for all of us, will he not with him also give us everything else?* (Rom. 8:32).

For the individual Christian, baptism declares at the beginning all that can be declared on one's behalf by the Christian gospel. It enacts the whole gospel, not part of the gospel. Baptism engages us not in part, but in our wholeness. It is a divine pledge that nothing can separate us from the love of God in Christ Jesus. Baptism stands, though all else should fall.

While baptism often touches us deeply, expressing a venture of faith and calling forth serious commitments, the reality of baptism does not depend on our awareness, our faith, or our understanding. We are not baptized into our experience or our conversion, but into the death and resurrection of Jesus Christ. The new life which is signified and conveyed in baptism is first of all from God; it meets us as gift, grace. It is not so much that we are seeking that new life, as that the new life makes itself known when we are busily looking in another direction or for something else. We do not congratulate ourselves on a discovery, but we are awed that we have been found.

Although in one sense baptism is a single fairly compact event, in another sense *baptism continues.* The sacrament is objectively complete; it is not repeated and cannot be added to. Yet it signifies and initiates an interpersonal relationship, and relationships must grow or die. In baptism we are linked, by name, with God. Then, after baptism, it is the work of a lifetime to discover what, through grace, is already true of ourselves. That discovery does not, however, carry us beyond our baptism, but into it. The Swedish theologian Gustaf Wingren has said, "Nothing can be added to baptism, and all that we receive after baptism is the means by which the work of baptism is continued."[2]

Although baptism stands at the beginning of our life in Christ and the church and is never repeated, that baptism is, in our own experience, validated by what follows it—hence the serious commitments we make in The

Baptismal Covenant (BCP, pp. 304f, 416f). We must continue to have dealings with the fact of our baptism, to touch it or be touched by it, to draw on it and to repossess it. We know our baptism, not as a more or less interesting fact in our biography, but as a determining event which is known from within—as all the important things about ourselves are known. We can come to know our baptism in this way as we bring it out of the past and into relation with what we understand now of the love and purpose of God. Our deep past engages our present. The New Testament scholar C. K. Barrett has said, "As a rite, baptism is not repeated; but unless it is in substance continually renewed it might as well not take place at all."[3]

Since baptism lies in one's past, it is only accessible by *the human act of remembering*. Yet, persons who were baptized as small children, as most baptized persons were, will have no specific recollection of the event. Those who were baptized as somewhat older children are likely to have actual but quite indistinct memories of what took place. And even those who were baptized as adults no doubt grasped at the time only a little of what the act would come to mean. When we speak of remembering baptism, we must consider the depth and mystery of what we remember, and how we remember.

Memory is thick, layered, and complex. It is flexible and full of surprise. Recent things can be less vivid and certain than earlier things. Memory is never literal or exact, but is affected by later experience. To remember is always to interpret. We can remember things in one sense which we cannot remember in another. How many of our earliest memories are events we can picture in our mind's eye, confident that we have them right, and how many are vague scenes supported and informed (if not, in fact, entirely produced) by family stories and pictures that go as far back as anything we can recover in our personal histories? Do we remember these things or do we not? In some senses, no; but in the emotional sense that matters most, yes.

When we remember the past that is determinative for us, it ceases to be past, and becomes contemporaneous. This presentness and accessibility of the past is made plain in the memories that skilled counselors help us to recover and articulate on our way to fuller self-knowledge or in the way in which eyes fill when we remember past joys and griefs.

The Bible is fully aware of the contemporaneity of the remembered past. In biblical religion past events and their potency are or can be present. We are like Jews at the Passover who in every generation are as though they themselves came out of Egypt. On Good Friday we ask with trembling, "Were you there when they crucified my Lord?"

The point is relevant for baptism, in that whenever and however our baptism happened, we can know that it happened, and as we grow in the life in faith, we can understand more of what it meant than we did at the time it took place. Our baptism is a given act of God's grace; but on our part it is also a latency, waiting in the recesses of our consciousness. Remembering it does not mean bringing the circumstances of it to mind as though we were present at the occasion, looking on like a family photographer. Rather, our remembering is an updating, a repossession. Our baptism will forever remain uncreative unless we make it a subject for reflection, a part of our present self-awareness. It must be brought into relation with our present understanding of God, redemption, Christian faith, and Christian service. It may be recalled as an anchor of the soul in times of struggle, crisis, or despair. When we let our baptism lie dormant, we are something like the people one reads about in news stories, who lived for years in poverty but are discovered after their death to have kept a fortune hidden away somewhere unutilized.

Our understanding of baptism—which is incomplete at the time of our baptism, whether we were baptized as a child or as an adult—can grow by reason of our membership in *a baptizing, preaching, and eucharistic church.* The church's liturgical life might be thought of as a system of acts and words which holds our baptism before us and assists us in living into its implications. Our unrepeated baptism is renewed in the often repeated eucharist—as the life that is begun in our physical birth is sustained by frequent feeding. It is renewed when we are present at the baptism of someone else and touch again the grace and the pledges of the act. Preaching puts us in touch with our baptism, drawing on it for present Christian faith and ministry. As J. G. Davies once put it, "Preaching. . .begins from the experience of baptism and proclaims the renewal of that experience in the eucharist. It. . .enables us to become through the eucharist what we are through baptism."[4] Our present touches our baptismal beginning, not only in every weekly eucharist, but at every confession and absolution, at every proclamation of the gospel, and in every commitment to service for others.

The Prayer Book provides occasions for expressly renewing the promises of baptism. Some of them belong to one's individual biography—as at Confirmation, Reception or Reaffirmation (BCP, pp. 303, 309f, 413-19).[5] Some occasions belong to the ordered life of worship, as the corporate

Renewal of Baptismal Vows at the Great Vigil and on the other baptismal days (BCP, rubric on p. 312).

While considering experience, it would be unrealistic not to recognize that much experience of baptism is negative. While it is true that baptism is a sign of an interior renovation which must continue and be remembered and renewed, it is also true that in many cases baptism signifies very little at the time it is administered, does not continue in any meaningful way, and, indeed, is hardly ever thought about afterward. As a matter of observation, many baptized persons, expressly or by practice, repudiate their baptism. Some simply drift away, while others openly reject it, sometimes feeling that they should not be held to something to which they gave such minimal consent. Some quite exploitative things are done in the church's practice of evangelism and baptism, and pain can be inflicted at a point which should stand for divine mercy and the community's welcome. In modern society, faith is fragile, there are many competitors for the place in life that belongs to God, and attachment to the church is inconstant. Persons who begin life in the Christian community either at infancy or at a later life stage may leave it. Still later, some of those who leave may return. (Of course, it is not all a story of loss. Persons who are products of a deeply secularized culture often come to faith in adult years with a sense of discovery and surprise.) There can be no certainty that what is promised in baptism will be carried out with unflagging dedication over a lifetime. We are considering in this study what baptism means and what the church at its best intends when it brings persons to the water. Insofar as baptism is an act of God through the church, baptism stands in the faithfulness of God. When we drift from it or reject it, it stands. When we return to it, it is there for us.

When we touch our baptism, we touch our past, but also our present and our future. Whenever and however our baptism took place, and however much or little regard has been paid to it since, it is a sign in our flesh of the enduring love of God. However dormant it may have been, it is indefinitely awakenable.

CHAPTER 2

The Scriptures and Baptism

At Christian baptism a sacramental action and the scriptures meet. They should meet fruitfully. Baptism is an action rooted in the redemptive message of the Bible, and the biblical message is enacted in baptism—a performative word and a declarative act. Parish clergy and congregations stand several times a year at this meeting-place of scripture and sacrament.

The appointed biblical passages form an indispensable foundation for this sacrament of the gospel and for catechetically oriented seasons that surround it. While Christian initiation can be thought of usefully in categories drawn from anthropology, social psychology, or cultural history, a Christian understanding of baptism begins with the scriptures, and it always returns to them. Baptism is a very human act, and, perhaps because it often centers on children, it seems to invite sentimentality, triviality, and an emphasis on the non-essential. But all that the church properly means by baptism derives from the realism and evangelical promise of the scriptures.

While today we begin with the scriptures, it was not so at first. The church was a baptizing community before it was a gospel-writing and an epistle-writing community. The sacramental life of the community was from the first supported by customs that stemmed from its founding events and in some sense from Jesus, by traditions that were handed on orally, and by a Christian use of the Jewish scriptures. When in the second half of the first century Christians committed their faith to writing, they wrote in and for a community which had from its beginning been bonded by baptism and the Lord's Supper.

Thus the New Testament writers take baptism for granted. It was not that they thought baptism unimportant, but since it occasioned little dispute, they seldom needed to speak about it directly, and never at length.

For the most part they talk about the reality that baptism signifies, and they presuppose the baptismal act. Yet deep levels of our minds are evident in the things we take for granted. One scholar remarks that apart from specific references, a "baptismal pattern" pervades the New Testament.[1] All that the church meant by its gospel was brought to expression in the primal, essential rite which marked one's becoming a Christian. This act was the gospel in water.

Since the apostolic generation, however, Christians have had the New Testament, and their doctrinal, ethical, and cultic life has been informed and corrected by the gospels, the Acts, and the epistles. The New Testament writers were not persons standing outside the redemptive events, describing them and reflecting on them; rather, they and their writings were caught up in those events and were part of the gospel to which they bore witness. Whatever the church in subsequent generations means when it baptizes has its source and must seek its ultimate verification in the primary testimony of the New Testament scriptures.

The Service of the Word.   The primacy of the scriptures is witnessed in the liturgy itself, where a service of readings, psalms, and preaching precedes and informs the baptismal act. Before the church is a baptizing church, it is a listening church. When the community turns to the candidates, the sponsors, and the water, it has first heard the Word of God (BCP, pp. 299-301). Before, behind, and in the baptismal act stands the self-expressive, self-imparting redemptive activity that arises from divine freedom and is witnessed in the scriptures.

In baptism the articulated Word of God does not stand apart from the water, as though to explain the water. Rather, it leads to the water; it is a Word bound up with the water, a Word that declares itself in and through the water. In the initiatory event, the Word is acting in the water.

Baptism is not simply something done, it is a declaration of evangelical meaning. It needs to be a focus for theological reflection and for instruction, and it needs to be a subject for preaching. However, if baptism is to be preached, there must be moments when it grips a preacher with a fresh sense of its grace and wonder. Preachers will be gripped if they open themselves to their charter documents, looking at familiar scriptures in new ways, making new connections, and discovering new depth and relevance.

The lectionary and typology.   Quite expectedly, the Prayer Book appoints for the baptismal occasions the principal passages from the New

Testament epistles, the gospels, Acts, and Revelation that speak of baptism. However, passages which do not expressly mention baptism are found appropriate as well. Since the early church was a community of converts, the New Testament writers often speak of the life of faith in ways that contrast the old life with the new. *You were going astray like sheep, but now you have returned to the shepherd and guardian* [episcopos] *of your souls* (1 Pet. 2:25). They express the reality that is enacted in baptism, which is the sacrament of conversion.

However, the baptismal lectionary also includes a great deal from the Jewish scriptures. Candidates and congregations hear the primal myths of Genesis, stories from the patriarchal narratives, the account of Israel's calling and liberation, extensive passages from the prophets, the varied comment of the psalms, and some excerpts from the intertestamental literature. Obviously the church assumes that there is a significant unity in the Bible, that ancient event illuminates subsequent experience, and that Moses and the prophets hold authority for Christians. We must give at least summary attention to why and how the scriptures of Israel are used in the church's liturgy.

The initial Jewish context.   The church's distinctive ways with the Jewish scriptures began with the first Christians, who drew inevitably on their experience as synagogue Jews who sang the psalms and out of lifelong habit turned to the scriptures *for teaching, for reproof, for correction, and for training in righteousness* (2 Tim. 3:16). From the scriptures which have *been read aloud every sabbath in the synagogues* (Acts 15:21), the Christians found vocabulary and concepts by which to name, understand, and communicate the thing that had happened in Jesus Christ. Since the Good News that had overtaken them was God-given, it must be continuous with, and indeed it must have been anticipated in, the God-given history and literature of Israel.

Although those Jews who came to believe in Jesus as Messiah continued to read their scriptures as they always had and to use the psalms for prayer and praise, the momentous event in Christ and the Spirit had such an impact that in the light of it they, devout Jews, came to read their sacred literature in a different way, finding in it new meanings and a new organizing factor. The earliest Christians saw Christ as the fulfillment of promises or foreshadowings in the scriptures. He was a new Moses, indeed a new Adam (Rom. 5:12-21; 1 Cor. 15:45-49), the healing brass serpent (Jn. 3:14f), *our Paschal Lamb* (1 Cor. 5:7b), the rock in the wilderness (1 Cor. 10:4), the Son (i.e. Israel) who was called out of Egypt (Mt. 2:15b), the corner-

stone of God's temple (1 Pet. 2:1-10), the true vine (Jn. 15:1-8), the Great
High Priest (Heb. 4:14—5:10)—and scores of similar scripture-derived
images.

Jesus belonged to Israel, and it was inevitable that he would see himself and that his followers would understand his redemptive significance
through the scriptures of his people. God who had spoken in the past had
spoken freshly and definitively in Christ (Heb. 1:1-2a); the ancient word
and the new word interacted and interpreted one another. Moses and the
prophets in some sense spoke of him (Jn. 5:39). Even the resurrection came
to be understood through the prophets (Lk. 24:25-27), and the basic description of the ascended Christ as the one at the right hand of the heavenly
throne (Heb. 8:1; 12:2; Rev. 5:7) traces to a Christian reading of the opening verse of a royal psalm (Ps. 110:1). Paul, in setting forth justification by
faith, secured his doctrine in the prophet Habakkuk (Rom. 1:17, citing Hab.
2:4). In the story of Christ and the church, new realities took on depth and
nuance as they touched the story of Yahweh and Israel.

The typological reading of Israel's past was not invented by Christians
and imposed on the Jewish scriptures, but echoes of the old within the new are
found within the strata of the Jewish writings. The exodus stands as a paradigm by which to tell and interpret events that came both before and after the
escape from Egypt. The stories of Abraham's call (Genesis 12) and of the
entry of the Hebrews into Canaan (Joshua 1-3) are told to the exodus model,
and the prophets describe Israel's restoration following the exile as a new
exodus (as Isa. 11:12-16; 43:19-21; 51:9-11; 52:4-5) and indeed as a new
creation (as Isa. 65:17; 66:22). The prophets envision the future in terms of the
past; Isaiah foresees a new Eden (Isaiah 35), Jeremiah a new covenant (Jer.
31:31-34), and Ezekiel a new temple (Ezekiel 40). The Christians understood
their present through a past, as the Jews had before them.[2]

It seems inevitable that any community which began in foundational
events that were then followed by a continuous history will interpret new
experience through the paradigmatic actions and words that marked its
origin. Especially when the community's life is given written form, the
stories and even the phrases of a book—stories and phrases that are recited
at moments of importance and are taught to children—fill the minds of
each generation. Members of a "community of the book" have no direct
access to either the past or to their own present, but reality is mediated
through the interpreting, imagination-forming written record. The past will

echo in the present, and the present will be validated as it is seen to replicate patterns from the past.

However, typology is not just a matter of finding correspondences in two literatures. While the Christian authors did write with their minds saturated with Moses and the prophets, they were not playing Joycean language games. Rather, the re-coining of old images in the early church expressed a conviction that the ways and character of God are and have been consistent. The God of Abraham, Isaac and Jacob—the God who took people by surprise, who summoned people from old, defined ways to a life of pilgrimage, the God who disregarded the orders of society and showed a preference for the poor and the oppressed, the God who stood with those in hopeless situations as presence and promise—had again been demonstrated in Jesus and the gospel. Typology provided a way to trace continuity and identity in the midst of change and newness.

For the most part, these correspondences were discovered after the fact. At the time of the event, even devout people were taken by surprise. After the event, they wondered how anything so obvious as these biblical anticipations could have been missed.

The scripture-derived images that the earliest Christians found to illuminate the gospel seem somewhat random, as though each had been observed independently, perhaps in a specific moment of insight. However, quite soon the exodus story of the calling and forming of Israel—the story that was basic to Israel's identity—gave the early Christians a presiding, unifying mythic narrative by which to speak of redemption, sacraments, and existence. The central story of Israel—the historic/mythic story of Egypt, the Red Sea, Sinai, the wilderness, and the land of promise—interpreted the central story of the Christian faith—the story of Christ, the Spirit, and the church.

As they appropriated the exodus event, the early Christians spiritualized and universalized it. Using the large sweep and many details of the story, the Christians saw themselves as:

◆ a new Israel, leaving, under a new Moses, an old, alienated condition and its oppressive power, and leaving it dramatically, as Israel had, by way of water;

◆ standing before Sinai and entering into a new covenant with God, through a new sacrifice, where they were made kings and priests;

◆ wandering now through the wilderness, sustained as they went by the bread from heaven;

◆ drawn on by the assurance of the promised land.[3]

As Christian liturgy and theology developed, the exodus story came to speak simultaneously of Israel, Christ, the church, and the individual Christian. This "layering" of meanings meant that for Christian readers, the Jewish Bible, no less than the apostolic writings, spoke of Christ and redemption.

The two testaments interpenetrated, the old echoing in the new, and the new taking mythic dimension and nuance from those echoes. G. W. H. Lampe argued that typology contributed a necessary depth to the Christian message: "It would be difficult for the Church to have come to any full understanding of the Gospel events if it had not been able to interpret Christ in terms of, and by reference to, the traditional imagery of Hebrew religious thought, imagery taken from Old Testament history."[4] As seen through the redemptive saga of Israel, the story of Jesus is set in the eternal purpose of God and becomes not an account of a remarkable individual, but a gospel of divine action, carrying universal significance.

Typology sustained. The typological use of the Jewish scriptures, which began early, continued in the following centuries. Moses and the prophets, as much as the apostolic writings, provided material for interpreting Christ, the Christian life, and the church and its sacraments. In varying degrees, typology was incorporated in early Christian preaching, in biblical exposition, in popular devotion, and in structures and phrases of the liturgy.

We may take Cyril of Jerusalem (early fourth century) as an example. In the days after Easter, he explains the baptismal actions to the newly baptized. Rather than giving a systematic account of sacramental meanings, he moves through the ritual actions slowly, telling the new Christians that the redemptive saga of Israel's exodus had been made their story through their baptism into Jesus Christ:

> Now turn your mind from past to present, from symbol (*tupos*, type) to reality(*aletheia*, truth). Of old Moses was sent into Egypt by God, but in our era Christ is sent into the world by the Father. As Moses was appointed to lead his afflicted people from Egypt, so Christ came to deliver the people of the world who were overcome by sin. As the blood of the lamb served to avert the destroyer, so the blood of Jesus Christ, the blameless lamb, had the effect of routing demons. That tyrant of old pursued the ancient Jewish people as far as the sea, and here and now the devil,

bold and shameless, the source of all evil, followed you up to the waters of salvation. Pharaoh was submerged in the sea, and the devil disappears in the waters of salvation.[5]

This practice of reading one story and one literature in terms of another had some obvious strengths for the Christian tradition. Since the saga of Israel spoke immediately to Christians through a fabric of spiritual meanings, the outline of the biblical story was held in mind and remained familiar. The names of Abraham, Moses, David, and Jeremiah were known to Christians as they were to Jews. In the Middle Ages, some stained-glass windows had matching panels showing Old Testament types and New Testament antitypes. The Christian memory was informed by both. The Bible was read theologically and as a unity, for all parts of it referred—albeit in their different ways—to a divine redemptive work which included Israel, the gospel of Christ, the Christian church, and the one destiny of the whole creation.

However, this Christian reading of the story of Israel also had weaknesses. While the typology of the earliest Christian writings was modest and fairly controlled, in some later times it invited the fanciful extremes of allegorism. Obscure correspondences were identified, and a premium was put on ingenuity. Allegory tends to reduce a text to an illustration of a meaning outside itself, which usually seems to be the interpreter's real interest. Sometimes a spiritual meaning helped to deal with a difficulty in the text—as when Cyril, in the passage quoted above, softens the harshness and chauvinism of the exodus story by equating Egypt with sin and Pharaoh with the devil, minimizing the shock of God's rescue leaving those literal Egyptians dead on the seashore. But what could seem like a relief from a difficulty to some readers might seem to others to be an evasive dodge. Moreover, it could and can be objected that the reading of the Jewish scriptures in search of types can drain the historical events which are read as types of their own meaning and remove the permanent religious significance they have in their own right. For many centuries the force of such objections to typological interpretation was not felt in the Christian tradition, and the conviction that the Bible contained two testaments, both of which told the same story, although each in a different way, persisted from the early generations, through the Middle Ages and into the Reformation period and after.

Typology in question, historicism.   The modern mind, shaped by Renaissance humanism, the Enlightenment, and nineteenth-century historicism and scientism, has for many generations raised sharp questions about this way of handling the scriptures. With the rise of historicism, typological reading (which its critics did not distinguish from allegorism) was discredited, for it tended to make all parts of the Bible say much the same thing. Modern canons of interpretation have required that texts be read in the context of their historical situations, for what they really mean is what they originally meant. Non-historical readings obscure the pastness of the past. As investigation made known more material from early cultures and religions, biblical texts came to be interpreted by that which preceded them. Scholars became fascinated with sources and influences.

As a result of generations of historical-critical study, the biblical literature and the life it reflects are no longer isolated, as for most of church history they had been; but they have been set in the culture, thought, literary genres, the land, and the movement of people in the ancient world. Readers have been made aware of the variety of thought and form in the Bible, and they have been warned of the danger of conflating or homogenizing, and of the historical sin of anachronism. Moreover, the objectivity that historical interpretation requires has meant that scholars of many confessions and religious traditions have been able to work together with mutual respect in their common task of understanding the scriptures.

A divided mind. During the period in which historicism has held authority in academic biblical studies, older, pre-critical ways of using the Bible have persisted in such deeply traditioned expressions of faith as liturgy, hymns, and some popular devotion and preaching. The result has been a split in the way in which the Bible is used in the modern church—and a split in the consciousness of some Bible readers. Persons who would ordinarily think that Israel means Israel and the Red Sea means the Red Sea, yet on Easter sing themselves into the exodus story, "God has brought his Israel through the Red Sea waters."

Only a perverse literary insensitivity would disallow an extended meaning to old texts. The Bible is deeply self-referential. Imaginative, oracular words can and do leap out of their own time and serve purposes, perhaps multiple purposes, that their authors could not have envisioned. That is the way of profound insights, poetically expressed. A people with a long, continuous history informed by an authoritative literature will find patterns of life reproducing themselves in new situations. Persons of insight will see the old in the new with a "shock of recognition."

Moreover, human life, if it is to be intelligible, requires comprehensive structures of meaning which, if they are to be grasped at all, must be grasped by the imagination. Christian imaginations have taken their fundamental informing myths from the Bible, the whole Bible. The stories, pictures, and images of the scriptures are so bound up with the gospel that one cannot really have it without having them. The life-interpreting myths of creation, election, incarnation, redemption, and destiny, while they incorporate time-space events, are meta-historical, and hence their truth is not subject to criticism by historical methods. Over the generations they have been—and remain—variously understood in the light of changing worldviews; but Christians cannot dispense with them. Historical criticism can trace the history of a myth; it cannot say anything about its truth or value.

Historicism in question. The historical-critical style of interpretation has held the field (in the academy at least) for many generations, but for some time questions have been raised about its adequacy. Strict historical interpretation seeks to place texts in their own settings, and it asks that interpreters see them as they would have been seen in the original writing/ reading situation. It is claimed that historical interpretation is objective and does not impose meanings on texts, as unhistorical ways of reading do. If one can just go directly to the text itself in its linguistic and cultural background, one can, by rigorous analysis, discover its true, i.e. its original, meaning.

However, as much present-day analysis of reading and interpretation indicates, the scientific, historical interpretation of documents is not presuppositionless, and it does not yield certainty. To be sure, such interpretation does not begin with a dogmatic set of religious beliefs which the text is required to support. Nevertheless, it does carry the pre-understanding of nineteenth- and twentieth-century scientism. It is important for a community of faith to note that historical inquiry always relativizes; it can only yield probabilities. One need not read long to discover that critics who are equally committed to historical-critical reading often differ markedly in what they make of the text. Historical integrity is important, but it cannot be the final determiner of faith.

Moreover, pure historical interpretation by intention leaves out the reader and the reader's situation and prior understanding. But any texts that are read seriously are read by someone, in a social context, and for a purpose. One who is committed to the rules of historical interpretation must deal with a large question: Once one has situated a text in its own time as well as one can, what can a text which is thoroughly embedded in a past time say to anyone today? If it belongs to its time, and we, the readers, belong inescapably to ours, can anything bridge between it and us?

This methodological question is urgent for a community which seeks authority for its present-day faith in an ancient literature. However, in this matter, historicism creates a problem which in itself it does not answer.

The Bible in the church.   A reader who seeks to hear the scriptures (Old Covenant or New) as Word of God must step outside the role of the historian and read and respond as a fully engaged human being who necessarily brings to the act of interpreting a great deal that was not present in the experience of the writer or the first readers. Twentieth-century Christians do not go to the Bible directly, but they stand within the church, its present and its past. They must read and inquire, not only from within the community of belief, but also from within the faith and doubt, the spiritual hungers, and the openness and the closedness to God of twentieth-century experience.

Today's methodological questions indicate that interpretation is entering a new era whose outlines have not yet fully established themselves, but which will in some measure affect the ways in which the Bible is read for all purposes, including its reading in the liturgy.

The Christian reading of the Bible is impacted by our shaking of the cultural foundations in the late twentieth and early twenty-first centuries. If the community of faith is to make sense to itself or to the world in which it serves, it must be a participant in its own time, its insights and its trauma. Yet at the same time, Christians read the scriptures as people of the church— a community which is always and necessarily passionately engaged with the Bible.

Several observations:

1. In worship, as in private study, Christians will read the Bible, all of the Bible, with Christian eyes—not only as historians, but also as believers. They want to know all they can about it as a complex literature from an ancient Jewish and the early Christian past, but principally they read it for its witness to God and the ways of God. They seek a structure of meaning adequate to the chaos and un-meaning that surrounds them and that in some measure invades them. They need not be defensive about reading as persons of the church who have an urgent concern for what they read, for everyone reads the Bible through an interpreting tradition. There is a Jewish midrash, but there is also a Christian midrash, an Islamic midrash, and a historical-critical midrash.

Everyone must reckon with the insights and the limitations that are given by the community in which one stands and by the point of view from which one interprets. Christians should not be expected to read the Bible as though they were not Christians.

2. Since the Prayer Book lectionary guides the public reading of a Christian church, it is necessarily governed by the New Testament story—the accounts of Jesus from the synoptic gospels, distributed over the weeks, seasons, fasts, and feasts of the Church Year. But the Christian scriptures do not stand alone. The minds of the first generation of Christians who gave us the New Testament, were, as we have seen, saturated in the Jewish scriptures; and they interpreted both Jesus and themselves through the Bible-derived words and phrases, pictures and thought forms, paradigmatic persons, and archetypal patterns they held in store. Their story of Jesus and the church was given depth and overtone by being interwoven with the story of Yahweh and Israel. The substructure of the earliest christologies was provided by the interpreting images that were taken from the Bible of Judaism. Scores of New Testament texts which do not say "as it is written" yet contain echoes or allusions to the Jewish Bible which filled the minds of their authors. In short, the very first Christians began the enduring tradition of understanding Jesus Christ through the Jewish scriptures and of reading the Jewish scriptures in the light of Jesus Christ.

   When we organize a program of Bible reading around the New Testament story, we may properly seek to read our Christian sources in the spirit in which they were written. What the apostolic writers gave us, in its unique fusion of new and old, is the gospel which Christians still believe and by which they live. The practice of using the Jewish scriptures to interpret the Christian story is almost unavoidable in a lectionary that is governed by the Church Year and the gospels, as the eucharistic lectionaries are. Moreover, one may argue, as the literary critic Northrop Frye does, that such a reading is true to the text:

   This typological way of reading the Bible is indicated too often and explicitly in the New Testament itself for us to be in any doubt that this is the "right" way of reading it—"right" in the only sense that criticism can recognize, as the way that conforms to the intentionality of the book itself and to the conventions it assumes and requires.[6]

3. The way in which the Jewish scriptures are read in the Sunday lectionary from week to week is to a great extent non-continuous, episodic, and

selective. Passages are appointed because in some way or another they illuminate the Christian story and offer some guidance for Christian faith and life. The result of this Christian selectivity is that whole sections—most of the wisdom literature and large portions of the histories and even the prophets, for example—are left out. The integrity of the Jewish scriptures tends to be compromised, in that they are used insofar as they point to something outside themselves. They are reduced to "Old Testament." Yet the intention of the Sunday lectionary is not to provide a course of reading in the Jewish scriptures, but to present the fabric of the Bible as it would have been seen by the apostolic witnesses.[7]

No one lectionary can do everything, and if the Sunday and Feast Day selections have inevitable limitations, the Prayer Book also contains the Daily Office Lectionary (pp. 933-1001), which is organized to provide more complete and continuous readings. Although only a few communities and individuals follow this lectionary, it addresses some of the questions that have been raised about the three-year ecumenical lectionary for Sundays and Holy Days.

4. We have not considered typology here in order to establish how we should interpret the Jewish scriptures today. We cannot read Moses and the prophets as they were read by Christians in the first or the fourth century—just as Christians from those periods could not have written the *Anchor Bible* commentaries. We do not take note that some first-century Christians saw Jesus prefigured in the brass serpent in the wilderness (Jn. 3:14) in order to strain to read Moses in that same way today. What we do seek is a sympathetic reading of the imaginative construction which was created in the early Christian generations and which we still inhabit. The persons who gave us the first expressions of Christian faith thought easily in terms of types. They gave form to their thought in the Christian scriptures and in the fundamental shapes of liturgy—forms which have endured, giving us the ways in which we still believe, preach, and worship. We do not simply cite the words from those creative generations; we seek to interpret them for a different age. But in order to interpret, we must, to the extent we can, enter their mode of consciousness, think in their way and in some measure find it convincing.

CHAPTER 3

The Scriptures for the Easter/Pentecost Complex

While baptism enacts the Christian gospel in a ritual event that requires only a few words, a few actions, and a few minutes, the Church Year uses a dramatic shaping of time to carry the church through an extended celebration of that same gospel, spacing events over the seasons, fasts and feasts of a calendar year. Since both of these liturgical forms present the same story, albeit in different ways, the yearly high points of the redemptive saga illuminate baptism, and baptism illuminates the great days of the Church Year.

The Church Year centers on Easter, the yearly celebration of Christ's victory over sin and death, by which he inaugurated a new age and a new people. By the fourth century, Easter was the principal time for baptism. It was not thought of not as a day, but as a celebratory period of fifty days, and baptisms might also be performed on the Day of Pentecost, the end of Easter. Thus the church's yearly celebration of the redemptive crisis in which it originated was also the time at which new persons were brought from death and sin and incorporated into Christ, his victory and his people.

However, over the generations the connection between baptism and liturgical time broke down. The observance of the Vigil largely lapsed in the West, and baptism came to be observed at any time of the year, usually without a congregation present.

In the liturgical changes of the sixteenth century, the Church of England sought to address the matter. In the first rubric of the service of Public Baptism in the 1549 Prayer Book, Cranmer judged that it was impracticable to restore Easter and Pentecost as baptismal occasions, even though he knew those to have been the early baptismal days.

It appeareth by ancient writers, that the Sacrament of Baptism in the old time was not commonly ministered, but at two times in the year, at Easter and Whitsuntide, at which times it was openly ministered in the presence of all the congregation: Which custom (now being grown out of use) although it cannot for many considerations be well restored again, yet. . . .

However, he sought to make baptism no longer a private or family event taking place in an otherwise empty church, but to have it observed only on Sundays and holy days, with a congregation present. The rubric continued:

. . .yet it is thought to follow the same as near as conveniently may be: Wherefore the people are to be admonished, that it is most convenient that baptism should not be ministered but upon Sundays and other holy days, when the most number of people may come together. As well for that the congregation there present may testify to the receiving of them, that be newly baptized, into the number of Christ's Church, as also because in the Baptism of Infants, every man present may be put in remembrance of his own profession made to God in his Baptism. For which cause also, it is expedient that Baptism be ministered in the English tongue. Nevertheless (if necessity so require) children ought at all times to be baptized, either at the church or else at home.

Cranmer would no doubt have been distressed to know that the reduced practice which he only allowed because of necessity, was in time further reduced when in the normal custom of his tradition baptisms came to be held on any convenient day with only family and friends present and a single minister officiating.

This diminished, late-medieval baptismal practice continued widely throughout the churches of the West well into the twentieth century. Individualistic modern culture found no reason to question it. However, dissatisfaction with the observance of baptism as an act for the individual in the family, rather than as an act of the individual and the family in the church, had been growing, and during the fifties many congregations developed ways of holding baptism at a congregational service on Sunday and involving the people actively in the celebration of new divine life and of expressing communal welcome.[1] When, in the sixties and seventies, the church began active steps toward the revision of its initiatory rites, the process could take advantage of several years of serious pastoral reconsideration of the place of baptism in the church.

In the Prayer Book which emerged from the process of revision, an opening rubric of the baptismal rite speaks to the time, the place, and the communal setting of baptism, saying that *Holy Baptism is appropriately administered within the Eucharist as the chief service on a Sunday or other feast* (BCP, p. 298). This direction brings three actions or events into significant relation: (1) Each *baptism* is a celebration of life in the living Christ; (2) hence *Sunday*, the church's basic resurrection day, is an obvious time for observing it. This rubric opens any of the Sundays of the year as a proper occasion for baptism (see chapter 6). The rubric sets baptism (3) within *the eucharist*, for the two great sacraments are related, as birth is related to feeding. As they stand on the Prayer Book pages, the rite of baptism ordinarily leads directly to the eucharist (BCP, p. 310).

However, in another rubric (p. 312) the Prayer Book suggests that as baptismal occasions, some Sundays are more appropriate than others. It commends that as far as possible baptisms be ordered so that they fall on important moments in the church's year-long kerygmatic shaping of time: *The Easter Vigil*, which speaks of death and resurrection, Christ's and ours, is cited first and occupies a preferred place. The Prayer Book lists also the First Sunday after Epiphany which observes the *Baptism of Our Lord*; it lists *Pentecost*, which marks the gift and power of the Holy Spirit; and it includes among the baptismal occasions *All Saints' Day* (or the Sunday following it), which speaks of the Great Church. A day when a bishop is present is also named as suitable for baptism, for the bishop, as chief pastor and sacramental leader, is a strong sign of Christians bound to one another in community.

A comparison of Cranmer's rubric of 1549 and the 1979 rubric on the same subject suggests that the Episcopal Church in the late twentieth century has been able to carry out his intentions better than he could himself in the mid-sixteenth century.

The Prayer Book rubric directs that when a baptism takes place on one of these commended occasions, *the lessons are properly those of the Day* (p. 300). Thus the scripture readings for baptism will usually be the readings for Sundays or for the great occasions in the year-long celebration of redemption. When a baptism occurs at a time other than a Sunday or one the baptismal days, readings *are selected from "At Baptism"* (BCP, p. 300)—referring to a group of readings which the lectionary provides among the votives (p. 928; see chapter 8 below).

Congregations are seeking to comply with the intent of this rubric. Some of them observe baptisms only on the commended days. Others make an effort to have baptisms on the days specified in the rubric, even if on occasion they must schedule baptisms on other Sundays as well. A rubric (BCP, p. 312) says, *If on the four days listed above there are no candidates for Baptism, the Renewal of Baptismal Vows, p. 292, may take the place of the Nicene Creed at the Eucharist.* Through this verbal gesture of remembering and renewing, Christians touch again their common sacramental beginning-point on the baptismal days, even when no baptism takes place. On these days important baptism-related scriptures are read and preached, and the liturgy holds before the church the baptismal reality in which its life is grounded.

The Easter Complex

For a time, Easter was the church's only yearly festival. Easter, however, was not so much a day as an extended ritual event, the Paschal season of fifty days. In the early Christian generations, Easter did not focus narrowly and somewhat biographically on Jesus' rising from the tomb, but spoke broadly of the cosmic Christ and of the church as witness to the new order that was inaugurated by his resurrection and pledged for the future. It marked in ritual time the passage from the old aeon to the new.

Christian Easter grew from Jewish Passover. (The two days still fall close to one another, and in some years they virtually coincide.) As a matter of record, the Passion events in Jerusalem had taken place at Passover, Israel's great yearly festival of its emancipation from Egypt. After that, for Jesus' followers, Passover could never again be as it had been. Each year, the first Christians (who were themselves practicing Jews) celebrated the heart of their new faith at the same time that they recalled the heart of their Jewish faith. The two could not be separated. In one event in ritual time Christians observed (1) Israel's escape from oppression in Egypt and its entry into a new covenant existence, and (2) Jesus' passage from death to life and the passage in him of the redeemed community from sin to salvation. At quite an early time, Easter became the church's occasion for bringing new Christians into the shared life, as the death and resurrection of Jesus were replicated in the baptismal passage of converts from sin and death to righteousness and life. Thus at the yearly Paschal observance the whole church was caught up in the anamnesis (the remembering) of redemption and touched again collectively its inmost reality.

The church made skillful use of times of anticipation and times of fulfillment. The period before Easter was devoted to preparing the catechumens for their baptism. The community (many of whose members had themselves been through this initiatory process at an earlier Easter) identified with these Christians-in-training, sharing their austerities and their eagerness. After Easter Day, the celebratory tone was sustained through Pentecost—the Great Fifty Days of the risen Jesus living among his people. During the post-Easter days the newly baptized were given special instructions based on the ritual events they had experienced.

We shall consider in sequence the scriptures of the Easter/Pentecost complex, giving special attention to the relation of the lections to Christian initiation.

A. The Lenten Scriptures

In the first Christian generations one who sought baptism was enrolled in a preparatory period of instruction and formation, called the catechumenate (from the Greek *katechein*, to instruct), which often lasted several years, although the time was variously shortened and extended. A candidate's way of life, occupation, and family life were examined. If one's work involved compromise with idolatry, as many occupations did, it would have to be changed, or one would be refused. Three things marked the months of preparation: (1) The catechumens were under instruction, for there was much they had to learn and to unlearn. The biblical story would henceforth be their story, and men and women who knew Homer and Virgil had to learn Moses and the prophets. (2) During this time the catechumens were performing works of mercy—learning to do the sorts of thing Christians do. And (3) they attended the Sunday eucharist regularly, but only for the instructional portion of the liturgy; they were dismissed with a blessing after the scripture readings and the sermon. The catechumens were believers, perhaps quite informed and courageous believers. But they were not yet baptized. The community was always kept aware of Christians-in-the-making in its midst. As Easter drew near, the catechumens who were judged to be adequately prepared were selected for special austerities and advanced instruction. The baptized Christians, remembering their own baptism, caught the eager seriousness of the candidates. Baptism was an event that involved the faithful community.

In time, with the Christianization of society, most of the persons who were brought to baptism were no longer converts from paganism, but the children of Christian parents; and the catechumenate disappeared. Influenced by the appalling commonness of infant mortality and in the West by the Augustinian definition of original sin, baptism came to be observed within a few days of the birth of a child and hence at any time of the year. With the fall of the Roman Empire and the ensuing disorganization of society, a mood of despair settled over Europe. The weeks leading up to Easter, instead of being a time of getting the catechumens ready for baptism at the Pasch, became a time to think about and to repent the sins of Christians. Pleasures were restricted, and disciplines were assigned. To a great extent, a penitential tonality, centered on the cross, dominated Lent through modern times.

The liturgical revisions of the twentieth century have sought to restore to Lent its place in the initiatory sequence, making it again a season of instruction and self-scrutiny that points toward Easter and baptism. Where there is an active catechumenate, in the weeks before Easter the church is once again preparing candidates for baptism. Whether or not there are catechumens in any year, the baptized community prepares for Easter by learning again the basic lessons and commitments which no Christian ever outgrows.

When baptism takes place at the Easter Vigil, Lent is generally the period of candidacy, during which *The Book of Occasional Services* says, *"The principal curriculum for each catechetical session is reflection on the respective readings of the Sunday Eucharistic Lectionary as these illuminate the faith journey of catechumens, sponsors and catechists"* (p. 114). The Lenten scriptures have been chosen for their suitability for Christians-in-training.

Certain emphases, patterns, and clusters of material run through the Lenten readings in all three lectionary years, giving the season a consistent character:[2]

The first Sunday in Lent always tells the story of Jesus' solitary *temptation in the wilderness*, using Matthew, Mark, and Luke in years A, B, and C respectively. The accounts of Jesus' temptation in Matthew and Luke are full and vivid; that in Mark is short and summary. The story may remind Christians who are thinking about their own baptism that Jesus' baptism, with its declaration of his divine sonship was followed at once by a severe testing, requiring him to discern and reject false courses.

In Year A, the Matthean story of Jesus' temptation (4:1-11, see p. 30) is matched with the account of the Fall in Genesis. Jesus' successful holding off of the tempter begins the undoing of the mischief of which the primal yielding of Adam and Eve is a symbol. The second reading is Romans 5:12-19 (20-21), where Paul contrasts two human solidarities, one in disobedience and death, the other in righteousness and life, which he describes under the names of two representative figures, Adam and Christ.

In Year B, Jesus' temptation is told in Mark's summary account (1:9-13). The first reading (Gen. 9:8-17, see p. 88) tells of God's covenant with Noah (and with physical nature as well) following the destruction of the flood. The second reading is the difficult passage from 1 Peter 3:18-22 (see pp. 47, 133, 236, 276) in which baptism is spoken of as prefigured by Noah's deliverance from the flood.

Luke's story of the temptation (4:1-13) in Year C is preceded by Paul's account of salvation in Romans 10:5-13. The two passages may be linked by Paul's theme "the word is near," which suggests Jesus putting down the tempter with the Word of God. The first reading is Deuteronomy 26: (1-4) 5-11, the recital of God's bringing Israel from bondage in Egypt to freedom in its own land, a recital that connected the people with the land and that was to be made at the presentation of firstfruits.

No other Sunday in the season has a theme that runs through all three years. Rather, the scripture material for Lent falls into clusters, reflecting common sources or common themes:

On three Sundays in Lent in Years A and B, the church appoints a group of seven *readings from John,* all of which have a clear relation to baptism:

◆ Jesus speaks with Nicodemus of being born again (3:1-17; Lent 2, Year A). (See p. 31.)

◆ At the well, Jesus tells the Samaritan woman that he is the living water (4:5-26 [27-38] 39-42; Lent 3, Year A). (See p. 32.)

◆ The evangelist interprets Jesus' body as the true Temple, which, if it is destroyed, he will rebuild in three days (2:13-22; Lent 3, Year B).

◆ Jesus heals the man who had been born blind and declares himself to be the light of the world (9:1-13 [14-27] 28-38; Lent 4, Year A). (See p. 33.)

◆ After feeding the multitude, Jesus explains that he is not just the giver of bread, but is himself the true Bread from heaven (6:4-15; Lent 4, Year B).

◆ The raising of Lazarus witnesses that Jesus is the resurrection and the life (11: [1-17] 18-44; Lent 5, Year A). (See p. 34.)

◆ Jesus sums up his public claims, speaking of grain that does not multiply until it "dies" (12:20-33; Lent 5, Year B).

Jesus' signs of transformation and his christological affirmations conduct the church into the heart of the Johannine presentation of the enfleshed Word. They interpret baptism as birth from above, as passage from blindness to sight and from death to life. Through faith in Jesus, one drinks the water of life and eats the bread from heaven.

Jesus' life was one of self-giving, which led him to the cross. The life of the baptized is on the pattern of Jesus. On Lent 2 in Year B, the gospel reading brings realism into the preparation for baptism by appointing Mark 8:31-38, in which *Jesus speaks of his coming passion* and makes it clear that those who would come after him must take up their cross and follow him.

The first reading for this day is *the story of Abraham's testing* by God, who summons him to sacrifice his son Isaac, Genesis 22:1-14. This difficult and troubling passage tells of Abraham, a person of great faith, acting under severe testing. Indeed, the testing is the worst imaginable, for it comes through a demand of God—but a demand which seemed to go against all that God had previously pledged. Everything that God had promised to Abraham hinged on Isaac, his only and loved son. But now Isaac's life was demanded by God. God seemed to be contradicting God. When in this situation Abraham trusts, it is in the absence of reason for trust. But Abraham does trust, and his trust is vindicated. The terrible command is withdrawn.

The original intention of this story may have been to urge substitute offerings rather than the sacrifice of the firstborn (see the law in Ex. 34:19). But if so, the psychological depth of the narrative takes it beyond such a purpose. The suggestions that lurk in the story led very early to a Christian typological interpretation. (And the juxtaposition of this story with the gospel reading of Jesus' prediction of his passion may suggest that such an interpretation be developed.) But the matter calls for some judgment. Typology has long been a way of avoiding difficulties in the scriptures. To see this reading as somehow an anticipation of the gospel and Isaac as a type of Christ can minimize the human terror of the account. Abraham is not depicted in the story itself as a picture of God the Father, as the typological reading would have him, but as a man tormented by the demand of God. Walter Brueggemann remarks that the story confronts us with the inscrutability of God: "We do not know why God claims the son in the first place nor finally why he will remove the demand at the end."[3]

However, this story of Abraham and Isaac is also read at the Easter Vigil and may be read on Good Friday; in those contexts, when typology is in the air, Isaac might well be interpreted as prefiguring Jesus. (See the notes on the Vigil reading, p. 48.) Would it not be best if in Lent the passage were read and preached in its stark ambiguity, strangeness, and suggestion?

In Year C, *the gospel readings for Lent all come from Luke*, beginning, of course, with Luke's story of the temptation on Lent 1 (4:1-13). On the whole, they are hard sayings.

◆ On Lent 2, Jesus makes a severe statement about the narrow door and the few who enter, which is followed by his lament over Jerusalem, *"I desired. . .and you were not willing,"* (13: [22-30] 31-35). The reading may suggest that baptism, while it represents the invitation of divine grace, is still, in a sense, *the narrow door.*

◆ On Lent 3, Jesus speaks of the urgency of repentance, *"Unless you repent, you will all perish,"* (13:1-9). Those preparing for baptism are coming to terms with sin.

◆ On Lent 4, Jesus tells his well-known parable of the wastrel son, the self-righteous and petulant brother, and the forgiving father, *"This son of mine was dead and is alive again; he was lost and is found,"* (15:11-32). Baptism is the merciful restoration of a lost child to the divine family.

◆ On Lent 5, Jesus tells his story of the wicked tenants (20:9-19). Jesus' parable is not a remote incident of rural life, but a Galilean gothic tale, worthy of a Conrad, a Faulkner, or a Flannery O'Connor. It is followed by Jesus' comment (vss. 17-19), citing Psalm 118:22, about the reversal of human judgment.

Over the three years of Lenten lessons, the church reads seven *passages from Romans, chapters 4-8,* Paul's great sustained description of life in Christ.

◆ Abraham believes God's promise and is reckoned righteous on that account (4:1-17; Lent 2, Year A).

◆ Christ, the obedient one, is the answer to the universal condition, whose sign is Adam and his transgression (5:12-21; Lent 1, Year A).

◆ Christians are justified by faith in Christ (5:1-11; Lent 3, Year A).

◆ Those who were slaves of sin and were paid by death have become servants of God and have the gift of life (6:16-23; Lent 5, Year A).

◆ Paul describes a sinner's inner self-contradictions and asks, *Who will rescue me?* He answers his own question, *Thanks be to God through Jesus Christ our Lord!* (7:13-25; Lent 3, Year B).

◆ Through Christ we are more than conquerors (8:31-39; Lent 2, Year B).

These readings from the heart of Romans speak of redemption in Christ, its rootedness in faith, and the glory which it pledges. This is catechetical material of first-rank importance. Persons preparing for baptism need to hear it; all Christians need to hear it again.

Converts are stepping into a new life in which they are given a new history—a history that remembers Moses and the prophets as well as Jesus and the apostles. For Lent the lectionary provides a rich group of *readings from the Jewish scriptures*:

◆ Persons preparing for baptism are supported by *two "call stories"*—God's call of Abraham to leave his land and people (Gen. 12:1-8; Lent 2, Year A; see p.155) and God's call of Moses at the burning bush to lead Israel out of Egypt (Ex. 3:1-15; Lent 3, Year C).

◆ They are entering a life of covenant, and they hear the *accounts of God's covenants* with Noah after the flood (Gen. 9:8-17; Lent 1, Year B) and with Abraham as God promises much and asks much (Gen. 15:1-12,17-18; Lent 2, Year C). A new and inward covenant—a covenant of a different kind—is described in the reading from Jeremiah 31:31-34 (Lent 5, Year B).

◆ The reading for Lent 3, Year A (Ex. 17:1-7) tells the baptismal candidates of God's provision of *water from the rock* for the thirsty Israelites in the wilderness.

♦ A covenant community lives under discipline, and Exodus 20:1-17 (Lent 3, Year B) tells of the giving of *the Ten Commandments,* long a staple of pre-baptismal ethical instruction.

♦ The story of *Abraham's willingness to sacrifice Isaac* (Gen. 22:1-14, which is read on Lent 2, Year B, and was commented on above) says that a life called by God and lived in covenant will have moments of bewilderment and painful testing.

♦ Baptism pledges a future of God's appointment, and Lent 4, Year C, tells of Joshua leading the people into *the land of promise* (Josh. [4:19-24]; 5:9-12).

♦ On Lent 1, Year C, the reading is the passage in which the devout Israelite observes the harvest by rehearsing before the Lord *the saga of redemption,* which brought the people out of slavery and into their own land (Deut. 26: [1-4] 5-11).

♦ Christians at baptism will be anointed, as kings were anointed, and on Lent 4, Year A, the lectionary appoints the story of *Samuel anointing David,* not Jesse's oldest son, but his youngest (1 Sam. 16:1-13). (See p. 126.)

♦ Baptism is understood on the exodus pattern, and on Lent 5, Year C, Isaiah 43:16-21 (see p. 124) envisions the return of Israel from Babylon as *replicating the exodus* from Egypt. Under the influence of the analogy, the people's trek through the desert is described as God's making a path in the mighty waters.

♦ Baptism is a sign of *life out of death,* and on Lent 5, Year A, Ezekiel's vision of life returning to the dry bones in the desolate valley is read (Ezek. 37:1-3 [4-10] 11-14). (See p. 58, 266.)

♦ On Lent 4, Year B, the lectionary appoints 2 Chronicles 36:14-23, the account of King Cyrus' authorizing *the exiles to return and rebuild the temple,* with his blessing—a good reading for baptism, in which one who is made by and for God returns from exile.

The Lenten weeks include important readings from the New Testament epistles, some of which have already been identified. For the most part they are non-consecutive.

1 Corinthians 10:1-13, Paul's warning, is read on Lent 3 in Year C. All the Israelites *passed through the sea, and all were baptized into Moses,* yet many of them displeased God. Paul tells his readers, as the church tells the baptized, that they should not presume.

Ephesians provides two lections for Lent 4. *Ephesians 2:4-10* (Year A) describes believers as alive in Christ. Appropriately for persons coming to baptism, *5:1-14* (Year B) speaks of passing from one way of life to another, from darkness to light.

Philippians is the source of two readings, both of them appropriate for baptismal candidates. In *3:8-14* (Lent 5, Year C), Paul, speaking confessionally, says that for him Christ is worth the loss of all things. And *3:17—4:1* (Lent 2, Year C) speaks of a Christian's true commonwealth being in heaven.

Hebrews 5:1-10, which is read on Lent 5, Year B, speaks of Christ as heavenly high priest, emphasizing that he is a compassionate priest because he himself knew human struggle and suffering.

These pre-Easter and pre-baptism readings set a tone by which God's faithful people can "prepare with joy for the Paschal feast" (second Preface for Lent, BCP, p. 379).

The gospels for Year A

A rubric in *The Book of Occasional Services* directs that when there are catechumens to be baptized at the Great Vigil of Easter, *it is appropriate in any year with the consent of the Bishop to use the Sunday Lectionary for Year A during Lent and during the Great Fifty Days of Easter* (p. 128). These are for the most part the readings designated for these Sundays in the early Western lectionaries. Since they are especially commended for the weeks leading up to baptism at the Vigil, we shall look at them more fully, particularly at the gospels:

Lent 1—Matthew 4:1-11. Jesus' temptation follows immediately after his baptism and before the opening events of his public ministry. It seems to speak of a process of sorting out. If Jesus is God's anointed, i.e. the Christ, as the baptism had declared, what sort of Messiah is he going to be? Since Jesus is alone in the wilderness, there was no one to witness or report; all that happens is interior and is described in highly symbolic terms. Readers are to understand that (not only in one event at the start, but throughout his public life) he entertains and dismisses real, attractive, but mistaken directions. (1) The proposal that Jesus *command these stones to become loaves of bread* suggests that he could gain a following by providing everyone with enough to eat. (2) The temptation to *throw yourself down* from the pinnacle of the temple and land unharmed suggests that Jesus could win loyalty by spectacular acts which would test God but in which he would be vindicated. Or (3) the offer of *all the kingdoms of the world and their splendor. . .if you will fall down and worship me* is the enticement of glittering and successful political leadership. Jesus rejects these appeals—although not all those who have claimed his name have done so. He cites the scriptures, specifically Deuteronomy, for his priorities. Jesus will, with integrity, take the way of obedience, which will eventually lead him to a cross.

This gospel is matched with Genesis 2:4b-9, 15-17, 25—3:7, which contains the second Genesis account of creation and the story of the Fall. Where Adam and Eve, in a garden, were tempted and failed, Jesus, in the barren wilderness, was tested, and was victorious. The epistle reading is Romans 5:12-21, which develops Paul's contrast of Christ with Adam. The deeply penitential Psalm 51, which Samuel Terrien describes as "the most profound analysis of sin and renewal to be found in the Hebrew Bible,"[4] is appointed to open the Sundays of Lent.

Lent 2—John 3:1-17. A Jewish leader, Nicodemus, comes to Jesus, recognizing his spiritual authority. At once, Jesus begins to speak of being "born from above." Although the passage contains no express reference to baptism, the phrase about being *born of water and the Spirit* suggests that this discourse is John's indirect account of the meaning of Christian baptism.

When Jesus speaks paradoxically of living persons who must be born, his words suggest that people, as they are, are alive, but in a pseudo-life— a life so defective that it does not simply need correction or adjustment, but something much more radical, something so discontinuous with itself as to be like one's initial, unrepeated passage from non-life into life; like being "born again." Persons (even a good person like Nicodemus) must be freshly born.

Jesus' term can be translated "born from above" (as in the NRSV) or "born anew" or "again." "Born again" is a time image, while "born from above" is a space image. The author may have intended this suggestive double meaning. In the NRSV translation, Nicodemus' misunderstanding is based on this ambiguity. Jesus speaks in space-terms, *No one can see the kingdom of God without being born from above.* While Nicodemus' commonsense request for explanation takes these words to be time-terms, *How can anyone be born after having grown old?*

Jesus is not simply talking about starting over, but about birth into another kind of life. Since what he speaks of can only be described indirectly, he uses suggestion—which literal-minded Nicodemus finds difficult (vs. 4).

The gospel promises that a radical, God-given newness can, and indeed must break in upon our oldness. Baptism is the effective sign of that new birth. The times when we get a fresh start in the midst of life's tired continuities and say, "I feel like a new person," give Jesus' metaphor about divine action something within us with which it can work. We tend to prefer self-improvement to the grace of new birth, or we cheapen being "born again" to some certifiable experience. As Nicodemus vaguely gathered, the birth from above of which Jesus speaks is not in our control—an experience that we can work up to or bring down. Being born of the Spirit is a divine mystery (cf. vss. 7b-8).

The first reading for this Sunday is the Call of Abraham in Genesis 12 (see p. 155). The epistle is Romans 4:1-5 (6-12) 13-17, in which Paul (4:3, citing Gen. 15:6) speaks of Abraham's faith by which he was justified. The Psalm is 33:12-22 (see pp. 50, 118).

Lent 3—John 4:5-26 (27-38) 39-42. As Jesus passes through Samaria, he meets a woman at a well and asks her to draw water for him to drink. Then, in a puzzling way, he begins to tell her of "living water" which he has. The woman understands him to be talking about some source of ordinary water, so Jesus explains that he is talking about a different kind of water: *Everyone who drinks of this water will be thirsty again, but those who drink of the water that I will give them will never be thirsty. The water that I give will become in them a spring of water gushing up to eternal life.* The water that Jesus gives quenches thirst forever, and anyone who receives it becomes a source of water. Paradox upon paradox! The woman, who is not good at paradoxes, wants this water so that her endless trips to the well can come to an end.

The conversation has not revealed much about either Jesus or the woman, but suddenly Jesus shows a knowledge of her that startles her. Perceiving him as a prophet she begins to ask the sort of question that prophets should know about: Is the Samaritan Mount Gerizim or the Jewish Jerusalem the right place of worship? The interview which had begun by remarking that a Jewish man could talk to a Samaritan woman advances to saying that neither Jewish nor Samaritan cult is the determining thing; true worship is not validated by being done in the right place, but is worship in spirit and in truth (vss. 21-24). This point is followed by the woman's remark that the Messiah, when he comes, will pronounce on such things. Jesus tells her, *"I am he, the one who is speaking to you,"* (vss. 25f)— more than a prophet.

Others enter the scene, and influenced by the woman's testimony concerning Jesus, come to believe *that this is truly the Savior of the world* (vss. 27-42). As the story has progressed, the perception of Jesus has advanced from *"you, a Jew"* (vs. 9) to *"I see that you are a prophet"* (vs. 19), to *"Messiah"* (vs. 25), and to *"the Savior of the world"* (vs. 42).

The pertinence of this reading for baptism lies principally in the passage concerning *living water* (vss. 10-15). The term is almost playful. It means moving, rather than still water—water that seems to live. Symbolically such water is capable of imparting life. Whereas baptism is a ritual washing, or perhaps a drowning, which uses water externally, most of the water imagery in John's gospel speaks of drinking, of taking water internally. But those who think in symbols revel in multiple meanings. These two uses of water are hard to separate (see, for example, 1 Cor. 12:13). The water in Jacob's well was in one place, to which users needed to come repeatedly; the well was deep; and those who drank from it in time grew thirsty and had to return. Jesus offers water of another sort, which yields eternal life and satisfies thirst forever. Baptism signifies such a salvation.

The first reading for the Sunday is Exodus 17:1-7, the miraculous provision of water from the rock, an event to which Paul gives a christological meaning (see 1 Cor. 10:4). And the second reading is Romans 5:1-11, Paul's description of the results of justification. The Psalm is 95.

Lent 4—John 9:1-13 (14-27) 28-38.   Jesus and his disciples encounter a man who had been blind from birth. When the disciples try to relate his blindness to sin—asking whether it was due to his own or his parents' sin—Jesus says that his condition was to provide an occasion to reveal the works of God. He speaks of his own ministry as daylight that has blazed up in the darkness, but night will return (vs. 4), adding (in the central christological disclosure of the episode), *As long as I am in the world, I am the light of the world* (vs. 5). Then he puts mud on the man's eyes and sends him to wash in a nearby pool, and when he comes back he is able to see (vss. 6f).

The rest of the episode is occupied with controversy: The act took place on the sabbath, and could one who broke the sabbath have such power from God? Was this sighted man the very one who had formerly been blind? The man's parents verify his identity and the fact of his having been healed, but they are afraid to say much about Jesus. The man himself says that although he knows little about Jesus, he can bear witness to his healing, *"One thing I do know, that though I was blind, now I see."* But the man's unassailable testimony is put down, and he is expelled from the synagogue. Jesus later meets the man (who until then had never seen him), and when he knows who has healed him he says, *"Lord, I believe."* The narrator adds that *he worshiped him.* In a concluding bit of paradox, Jesus speaks of the two-sided effect of his revelatory work, saying, *"I came into this world for judgment so that those who do not see may see, and those who do see may become blind"* (vs. 39).

This incident is one of the Johannine stories of transformation. An old condition is, through the action of Jesus, replaced by a new condition— hence its appropriateness for baptism. Moreover, since the early Christians thought of baptism as the illumination of the darkened soul, this story of a man who had been blind from birth being given his sight (and by washing in a pool) seemed to them to speak of baptism.

The other readings for this Sunday are 1 Samuel 16:1-13, the anointing of David (which is also appointed for the Vigil of the Baptism of Jesus, see p. 126), and Ephesians 5: (1-7) 8-14, in which the renunciation of old ways of life and the imagery of light in (vss. 8, 13-14) suit this reading to persons preparing for baptism. The Psalm is 23, which has long associations with baptism (on which see p. 251).

Lent 5—John 11: (1-17) 18-44. Jesus' friend Lazarus has died. After a deliberate delay, Jesus goes to Bethany, where Lazarus has lived with his sisters Mary and Martha. When Jesus arrives, Martha says to him that if he had come earlier, her brother would not have died. Jesus replies, *"Your brother will rise again."* Martha, a good Jew in the tradition of the Pharisees, believes in a future general resurrection, and she gives a textbook comment, *"I know that he will rise again in the resurrection on the last day."* But is her textbook religion adequate? Can a future resurrection comfort a loss that is now? Can a general resurrection heal a pain that is particular? Jesus replies with a startling self-revelation, *"I am the resurrection and the life."* Setting aside textbook answers, he speaks of himself, saying "I am." (*"I* am." Not a doctrine, but me. "I *am.*" Not then, but now.)

It is a certainty of the human condition that life passes over into death, from which there is no recall. We watch, with care and reverence, that inevitable, one-way passage. Yet Jesus does not recognize such inevitabilities. He works by other laws to bring life out of death. Jesus calls into the dark tomb, *"Lazarus, come out!"* Lazarus comes out, bound in his grave wrappings. He is freed. And there, despite our wish to hear more, the gospel story ends.

The passage says in vivid terms that Jesus is a power greater than our human dying—able to call the dead to life. As a Lenten gospel, the Lazarus story of life brought out of death is a picture of baptism. It is as though, at the coming Easter baptism, one who is hopelessly enclosed in a grave and out of touch with everything that lives and breathes unexpectedly hears a commanding voice, speaking one's own name, saying, "Come out! You were not made for death!" And one who is dead is awakened into life. Everyone meets death, but one who is baptized meets it, being already in touch with the One who relativizes death and overcomes that "last enemy," and who will not let us go.

This gospel is the climax of the series of stories of transformation—old life to new (Jn. 3), water that leaves one thirsty again to water that satisfies forever (Jn. 4), blindness to sight (Jn. 9), and death to life (Jn. 11). These stories are christological disclosures, speaking of a transformation given in Jesus Christ, dying and living. They give us images for a transformed life and for baptism, the central sign of personal transformation.

This gospel follows Ezekiel 37:1-3 (4-10) 11-14, the vision of the valley of dry bones (on which see pp. 29, 58, 266), and Romans 6:16-23, in which Paul says that those who had been slaves of sin are now servants of righteousness. Psalm 130 is appointed (see p. 97).

B. The Easter Vigil and Easter Day

The accounts in the book of Acts describe baptism as administered whenever a convert gave a clear indication of faith.[5] However, as the church's developing liturgical life came to incorporate and exhibit the structures of the redemptive life, the liturgical occasion that celebrated Jesus' resurrection and the birth of the new age and of the church—the people of the new age—seemed a fitting time for bringing new Christians to birth. Easter became the preferred time for baptism.

The earliest clear evidence of baptism at Easter is in Tertullian's *On Baptism*, written about 210 CE, which is the first extended Christian writing on a sacramental subject. Tertullian says: "The Passover provides the day of most solemnity for baptism, for then was accomplished our Lord's passion, and into it we are baptized."[6]

While the Jewish Passover fell on a specific date on the Jewish calendar, that calendar did not coincide with the way in which other cultural groups reckoned time. As the church became more distanced from the synagogue and its customs, Christians made their yearly celebration of the resurrection fall always on a Sunday. The liturgical observance of the Christian Passover (the *Pasch*) would begin on the Eve of Easter, which was reckoned as the beginning of the day. Before Easter daybreak, the candidates for baptism were taken to the water. At first the church used whatever water was available, having a preference for water that flowed—"living water." At the water, each candidate disrobed, was led into the water, and facing west, renounced Satan and his works. The candidate then turned to the east and was baptized in a three-part act at which each candidate made the threefold confession of faith which in time came to be the Apostles' Creed. In many places (but not in all), each person was then anointed with chrism. The newly baptized resumed their clothing and were brought to the eucharistic room.

While the baptismal candidates, sponsors, ministers, and attendants were at the water, the baptized Christians had been in the eucharistic room preparing to celebrate the in-breaking of the new life in Jesus' resurrection and to welcome the new Christians. When the newly baptized joined the worshiping community, they took part in three powerful gestures of incorporation: For the first time they joined in the prayers of the people, they shared the kiss of peace, and they received the body and blood of Christ. In the days that followed, the bishop gave them counsel for the life they had entered, especially explaining the sacraments to them.

By these acts, the entire Christian community was caught up in a quietly powerful ritual event in which the individual was brought from death to new life against the background of Jesus' death and resurrection, and the whole church was renewed in the redemptive reality which defined its life, while exodus/Passover motifs informed it all, and the natural world passed from darkness to dawn.

These practices continued for several centuries, but in time they weakened. The Vigil—with its dramatic use of darkness and light and its rehearsal of the mighty acts—lapsed. Baptisms came to be performed at any time of the year, and by the Late Middle Ages in the West they came to have no connection with the eucharist. Easter became an especially festal Sunday, rather than every Sunday being a repeated part of the plenary christological-sacramental-experiential event of the Easter Vigil.

The Roman Catholic Church in 1951 restored the Easter Vigil, an important step in the modern liturgical revival. In the ecumenical liturgical renewal of the mid-twentieth century, the Great Vigil of Easter has commended itself in many churches by its own convincing character as the church's fullest liturgical enactment of the redemptive message and the organizing center of the economy of ritual time. Each year, at the Vigil and the first eucharist of Easter, the church reorients itself to the basic realities from which its life derives.

The Vigil begins with a service of light: The church is in darkness; the Paschal candle is lit; and the *Exsultet* is sung (BCP, pp. 285-87). Then follows a series of readings, with a psalm and collect set for each (BCP, pp. 288-91). The readings are followed by Holy Baptism (BCP, pp. 301-8), or, if there are no baptisms, by The Renewal of Baptismal Vows (BCP, pp. 292-94). The church bursts into light, and, with the acclamation of the resurrection, the liturgical action moves to the first eucharist of Easter. The rubrics permit variations, and the liturgical sequence is handled differently in different churches, but by rubric (BCP, p. 284) the rite has a general structure of light, word, baptism, and eucharist.[7]

Light: the Scriptures in the Exsultet

After a bidding to the congregation and a prayer, the Paschal candle is lighted. While the candle moves through the church, "The light of Christ" is sung or said three times. Other candles are lit from the Paschal candle. Then a deacon (if a capable deacon is on hand, otherwise a cantor), standing near the candle, sings or says the *Exsultet* (BCP, p. 286f). This lengthy, evocative canticle seems to have grown from the prayers that accompanied lamp-lighting. It dates from the early sacramentaries that stand at the head of the Western liturgical tradition. Its text has varied, but its character has remained fairly constant. This song of praise of the night and the candle gathers many scriptural allusions, giving the Service of Light and all the liturgical events that follow a setting in the biblical saga.

[The *Exsultet* will be described here as though the Prayer Book text were in sections, numbered from section 1 (p. 286) to section 12 (p. 287).]

The first three sections are calls to rejoice, directed to the *heavenly hosts and choirs of angels*, to *all the round earth*, and to *Mother Church*. This imagery echoes the psalms (such as Ps. 148) which speak of the heavens and the earth as engaged in the praise of God. The creatures of earth, by being what they are and doing what they do, are praising God. More immediately, it draws on the great picture from Revelation 4 and 5 of the cosmos engaged in praise for the divine being, for creation, and for the redemption won by Christ. In this canticle the whole cosmos sings because of Christ's victorious work.

The canticle describes redemption in terms of "Christus Victor": *the victory of our mighty King* (section 1), *darkness has been vanquished by our eternal King* (section 2), and the theme returns later, *Christ broke the bonds of death and hell* (section 7). This way of describing Christ's work, which marked the preaching, teaching, and liturgy of the church's early generations, thinks of human life as held in bondage by forces such as sin and death, the world, the devil, hell, and judgment. Christ stepped into the situation of the oppressed and broke the power of these enemies, and the church lives by that victory. This theological idiom has its roots in the Jewish sense of the victory of God—told in the exodus story, but repeated praisefully in the psalms. This divine triumph is sometimes celebrated as a past deed, and sometimes it is longed for as yet to come in fullness. The New Testament proclamation builds on this idiom, speaking of Christ overcoming the world (Jn. 16:33), and death (1 Cor. 15:54f), and his triumphing over the adversarial powers in the cross (Col. 2:15, and see Eph. 1:20-23). His conquest is shared, and through him Christians overcome Satan (Rom. 16:20; 1 Jn. 2:13f), and the world (1 Jn. 4:4f). The description of Christ as victor is not so much a theory of the atonement as it is a proclamation which finds a place in the preaching and hymns of the early church. This theme is so basic to the Christian message that when it becomes obscured, it is rediscovered.

The fourth section of the *Exsultet* calls the congregation—*all you who stand near this marvelous and holy flame*—to pray for grace *to sing the worthy praise of this most holy light.* Thus the light of the Paschal candle in the church, *this holy flame*, and the radiant light which now fills the court of the church (section 3) are connected with Christ's vanquishing of darkness (section 2).

The deacon bids, *Let us give thanks to the Lord our God*, and the congregation responds, *It is right to give him thanks and praise.* Then the deacon resumes (section 5) with praise of the divine being, *the invisible, almighty, and eternal God* (a suggestion of 1 Tim. 1:17). Turning to Christ, the Son, the text enlarges. Christ is *the true Paschal Lamb, who at the feast of the Passover paid for us the debt of Adam's sin.* There are clear allusions to Paul's *Our paschal lamb, Christ, has been sacrificed* (1 Cor. 5:7) and to his Adam-and-Christ parallel in Romans 5. These allusions and the language about deliverance through Christ's blood speak of redemption in terms of sacrifice.

Sections 6 through 8 begin *This is the night.* The idiom derives from the Jewish sense, expressed at the Passover and often in Jewish liturgy, that when a determinative past event is remembered, it is no longer past, but in being celebrated it becomes present. The time between then and now vanishes. The past event is now, and we are participants in it.

This is the night of the exodus, *when you brought our fathers, the children of Israel, out of bondage in Egypt.* The Christian church sets itself in continuity with *our fathers, the children of Israel.* Their emancipation was our emancipation.

This is the night when Christ's people *are delivered from the gloom of sin, and are restored to grace and holiness of life.* The emancipation from Egypt is affirmed, but at the same time universalized and spiritualized. The Christians' exodus is the passage in Christ from sin to grace.

This is the night of Christ's triumph, through resurrection, over humanity's ancient oppressors: death and hell. The words restate the Christus Victor motif of section 2, and the following section also speaks of conflict ended and enemies overcome.

The next three sections (9-11) are exclamations, *How wonderful. . .How holy. . .How blessed!* The divine sacrifice put wickedness to flight and unites humanity with God in peace and reconciliation.

The *Exsultet* concludes (section 12) with a prayer that God will accept the offering of *this candle,* asking that its light (participating as it does in the light of Christ and his work) may *shine continually to drive away all darkness,* and that Christ, *the Morning Star who knows no setting may find it ever burning.*

The candle shining in the church, seeking *to drive away all darkness,* suggests the eternal Word, the divine light *that shines in the darkness, and the darkness did not overcome it* (Jn. 1:5, and see 1 Jn. 2:8-11).

The *Morning Star,* as an image, referred initially to the planet Venus. However the Christian tradition, beginning very early, read messianically as an anticipation of Christ an oracle of Balaam in Numbers 24:18 which speaks of a "star out of Jacob" who shall rule (see Rev. 22:16). The star at

Jesus' birth in Matthew's story of the Magi was widely said to be Balaam's star. The poetic use of the image in the *Exsultet* may have been suggested most directly by 2 Peter 2:19, *be attentive. . .until the day dawns and the morning star rises in your hearts,* referring to Christ at his anticipated appearing.

This canticle weaves together, in words of beauty, many themes: the trumpets and shouts of praise of heaven and earth; a sense of humanity's condition, *the gloom of sin*; God's emancipation of Israel from bondage in Egypt through the Red Sea; the redemptive work of Christ which vanquished darkness and broke the bonds of death and hell; the new life of cleansing, joy, peace, and concord opened for the church by Christ; and finally a community gathered on this occasion on this night around this *marvelous and holy flame.*

Word: the rehearsal of the mighty acts

The heart of the Liturgy of the Word at the Vigil has always been a series of scripture readings. Over the generations, the number and the selection of the readings has varied, although certain readings have held their place quite consistently. The series of readings from the Jewish scriptures which the Prayer Book rite uses (pp. 288-91) run in a broad sequence from the deep past to visions of the future. They appeal to the imagination, holding before the church the mythic structure under which it, along with the Jewish community, lives and interprets life.

Thus the series is dramatistic. The Jews were and are a story-telling people. They do not find their account of reality in systems or speculative ideas that speak of timeless truths so much as in revelatory events: *A wandering Aramean was my ancestor* (Deut. 26:1-11). The Jews have kept their identity by continuing to tell their shared story, and their liturgy provides ordered ways of keeping the story before them and carrying them through it ritually. In each generation the story becomes one's own.

Christians, too, are a story-telling people. As a community of shared memory, the church situates itself in its remembered past through acts of collective recalling. As it does so, its past becomes present to itself, and the community of faith rediscovers its identity and purpose. Up to a certain point the Jewish and the Christian traditions tell the same story. The early Christians were Jews who confidently attached their special story of Jesus, the Spirit, and the church to the story of Abraham, Moses, David, and

Jeremiah, exile and return, and the brave Maccabean revolt. The first believers saw Jesus' death and resurrection as the fulfillment of the long-laid purpose of God which had been carried out in a history which centered on Israel and which was witnessed in the scriptures. Even though the epochal act of God in Christ had for the most part been unexpected, through the eyes of faith it was seen to have been profoundly anticipated. It was an act of God continuous with God's former acts. Thus, at this central celebration of their own gospel, Christians—in awe and gladness—read the Jewish scriptures.

The Christian community, poised to enter the newness in the living Christ, recalls the past that was given to it through the mighty creative and recreative acts of God. Through the structures of the Vigil, the church rehearses its story. But the story is unfinished, and in some of the visionary material of the liturgy, the church also shares by anticipation in the future that lies in God's promise.

The Prayer Book rite (pp. 288-91) provides nine lessons. A rubric requires that at least two of them be read, one of which must be the exodus story. Sometimes these scripture units are told or acted or sung. A psalm is appointed for each of them, and an appropriate collect is printed, with a period of silence commended before it is spoken. Special music is often associated with these readings. Usually these scriptures are not preached as they are read, a sermon coming *"at the Eucharist"* (BCP, p. 295). However, a rubric on p. 292 says that a homily may be preached after any of them.

The story of creation: Genesis 1:1—2:2

In the beginning when God created the heavens and the earth, the earth was a formless void and darkness covered the face of the deep, while a wind from God swept over the face of the waters. Then God said, "Let there be light"; and there was light. And God saw that the light was good; and God separated the light from the darkness. God called the light Day, and the darkness he called Night. And there was evening and there was morning, the first day.

And God said, "Let there be a dome in the midst of the waters, and let it separate the waters from the waters." So God made the dome and separated the waters that were under the dome from the waters that were above the dome. And it was so. God called the dome Sky. And there was evening and there was morning, the second day.

And God said, "Let the waters under the sky be gathered together into one place, and let the dry land appear." And it was so. God called the dry land Earth, and the waters that were gathered together he called Seas. And God saw that it was good. Then God said, "Let the earth put forth vegetation: plants yielding seed, and fruit trees of every kind on earth that bear fruit with the seed in it." And God saw that it was good. And there was evening and there was morning, the third day.

And God said, "Let there be lights in the dome of the sky to separate the day from the night; and let them be for signs and for seasons and for days and years, and let them be lights in the dome of the sky to give light upon the earth." And it was so. God made the two great lights—the greater light to rule the day and the lesser light to rule the night—and the stars. God set them in the dome of the sky to give light upon the earth, to rule over the day and over the night, and to separate the light from the darkness. And God saw that it was good. And there was evening and there was morning, the fourth day.

And God said, "Let the waters bring forth swarms of living creatures, and let birds fly above the earth across the dome of the sky." So God created the great sea monsters and every living creature that moves, of every kind, with which the waters swarm, and every winged bird of every kind. And God saw that it was good. God blessed them, saying, "Be fruitful and multiply and fill the waters in the seas, and let birds multiply on the earth." And there was evening and there was morning, the fifth day.

And God said, "Let the earth bring forth living creatures of every kind: cattle and creeping things and wild animals of the earth of every kind." And it was so. God made the wild animals of the earth of every kind, and everything that creeps upon the ground of every kind. And God saw that it was good.

The God said, "Let us make humankind in our image, according to our likeness; and let them have dominion over the fish of the sea, and over the birds of the air, and over the cattle, and over all the wild animals of the earth, and over every creeping thing that creeps upon the earth."

So God created humankind in his image,
in the image of God he created them;
male and female he created them.

God blessed them, and God said to them, "Be fruitful and multiply, and fill the earth and subdue it; and have dominion over the fish of the sea and over the birds of the air and over every living thing that moves upon the earth." God said, "See, I have given you every plant yielding seed that is upon the face of all the earth, and every tree with seed in its fruit; you shall have them for food. And to every beast of the earth, and to every bird of the air, and to everything that creeps on the earth, everything that has the breath of life, I have given every green plant for food." And it was

so. God saw everything that he had made, and indeed, it was very good.
And there was evening and there was morning, the sixth day.

Thus the heavens and the earth were finished, and all their multi-
tude. And on the seventh day God finished the work that he had done, and
he rested on the seventh day from all the work that he had done.

The Vigil's account of the mighty acts begins with the sweeping story
of the days of creation with which the Bible opens. The passage is a poem,
with unity, design, and climax—its orderly account speaking of an ordered
creation. First the dark chaos is stirred by *a wind from God,* or *the spirit
(breath) of God* (NRSV margin). The powerful divine word brings light.
Then God separates things, distinguishes them, and sets them in their proper
places. Light is separated from darkness, and the waters below the earth
are separated from those above. (This act of the second day draws on an
ancient water cosmology. The earth and sky exist in an opening between
waters below and waters above. The earth floats on deep waters, and over-
head there are waters, some of which occasionally fall to earth. The two do
not unite because God maintains a "dome" between them.) The sea is separated from the land; day is marked from night. The earth is then populated
with living things, plants and animals, each according to its kind. Then
humankind is created in the divine image, and finally God rests—signifying that God who is in the world, is more than the world, beyond the world.

The poem creates rhythm by several refrains: *there was evening and there
was morning. . . .and God said. . . .and it was so. . . .God saw that it was good.
. . . after its kind.* This creation story took its present form from the priestly
school of Israel, among persons accustomed to ceremony. Alan Richardson
remarks:

> Once we have imaginatively grasped the Priestly conception of all cre-
> ated things as ceaselessly fulfilling their appointed "liturgy" (service) to
> the greater glory of God, we shall come to hear these stylized refrains
> almost as liturgical "responses"—antiphons in the great offering of praise
> and thanksgiving that continually ascends from the creation to the Cre-
> ator.[8]

The instrument of the creation is the divine word—*and God said.* The
Bible came from a largely oral culture in which words were either heard
and held in the memory or else they were gone as soon as they were spoken. In an oral culture, words are acts; they are spoken from one person
and to another, conveying challenge, rebuke, compassion, or support. The
spoken word carries the force of the speaker. The Bible portrays God as a

speaking God and God's word as powerful, performative. God's word is an act, effecting what is said.

In the creation of humanity (unlike the second creation account in 2:4-25) both sexes arrive on the scene at once, suggesting the complementarity and mutuality of male and female. The image of God comprises the two together (1:26f). As the story is told, when human beings appear, God speaks *to* them (vss. 28-30). God has spoken *about* the rest of the creation, declaring it good; but only in human beings is there a self able to enter into personal relation with God—a relation carried by speech.

The inclusion of the creation story in the readings of the Vigil brings the unfolding events of salvation history—the subject of the later readings—into a cosmic setting. The redeeming God of the exodus and of the cross and resurrection is also the Creator of heaven and earth. This affirmation of God as Creator and ourselves as creatures of the sixth day reminds us of our bonds with physical and biological nature. Set as we are within the creation story, we stand related to God, first of all, not by our faith or through our religious awareness, but by reason of our fundamental humanity, made in God's image (1:26). Our dependence on the material creation is our dependence on God. Alexander Schmemann rooted sacramental reality in creation memorably when he remarked that the first concern of newly created humanity is something to eat (1:29-30). Our food, Schmemann said, is given us by God *as communion with God*: "All that is exists as God's gift to humankind, and it all exists to make God known to humankind, to make human life communion with God."[9]

Biblical religion clearly affirms creation. Physical nature is God's work, and it is good (1:10, 12, 18, 21, 25); indeed, after humanity is brought in, God sees that everything that has been made is very good (1:31). God blesses the animate creation (1:22) and the human creation (1:28). Persons who live in this biblical tradition are—or should be—life-affirming. We do not draw near to God by escaping from the world, or from the body, or from historical-societal existence. Rather, we meet God and we respond to God in the support and provision, but also in the strangeness and indifference of nature, in the goodness of created things, in our interaction with other persons, in our embodiedness, in our experience of eating and drinking, of work, of rhythm, sex, and play.

The radical newness in the primal creation gave later biblical writers terms by which to speak of radical newness in the midst of history. A prophet could speak of Israel's return after the exile as a new creation, as in Isaiah 48:6ff: *"From this time forward I will make you hear new things, hidden things you have not known. They are created now, not long ago: before today you have never heard of them, so that you could not say, 'I already knew them.'"* (See also Isa. 43:18-19; 65:17ff.) A later Christian apostle, using creation imagery, can say, *If anyone is in Christ, there is a new creation: everything old has passed away; see, everything has become new!* (2 Cor. 5:17). The Christian message sees Christ as a new Adam, the beginning of a new humanity, and individual Christians as set within that new humanity by baptism. The biblical story looks forward to *a new heaven and a new earth* (Rev. 21:1). This story of creation, standing first in the Vigil readings, is foundational to the biblical panorama that follows.

The creative impulse begins with the Spirit stirring over the waters (1:2). While the Hebrew authors did not speak of the Holy Spirit in the sense that the New Testament knows—the Spirit of Christ—the imagination of the church has not worried about chronology, but has freely read its fuller knowledge into this early anticipation, convinced that God who works through the Spirit has always worked through the Spirit. The Creator Spirit who was agent of the first creation and of the new creation is at work in baptism, the sign of the new creation—and again the creative work is associated with water.

[The creation story is also read on Trinity Sunday in Year A.]

With Psalm 33:1-11 or Psalm 36:5-10

Psalm 33:1-11 speaks powerfully of God as creator, emphasizing (as the Bible often does) the divine word as agent of the creation: *By the word of the LORD were the heavens made. . .He spoke and it came to pass.* Psalm 36:5-10 uses images from nature and its dimensions of height and depth to speak of God: *Your love, O LORD, reaches to the heavens. . .Your justice is like the great deep.*

The Flood: Genesis 7:1-5, 11-18; 8:6-18; 9:8-13

The LORD said to Noah, "Go into the ark, you and all your household, for I have seen that you alone are righteous before me in this generation. Take with you seven pairs of all clean animals, the male and its mate; and a pair of the animals that are not clean, the male and its mate; and seven pairs of the birds of the air also, male and female, to keep their kind alive on the face of all the earth. For in seven days I will send rain on the earth for forty days and forty nights; and every living thing that I have made I will blot out from the face of the ground." And Noah did all that the LORD *had commanded him.*

In the six hundredth year of Noah's life, in the second month, on the seventeenth day of the month, on that day all the fountains of the great deep burst forth, and the windows of the heavens were opened. The rain fell on the earth forty days and forty nights. On the very same day Noah with his sons, Shem and Ham and Japheth, and Noah's wife and the three wives of his sons entered the ark, they and every wild animal of every kind, and all domestic animals of every kind, and every creeping thing that creeps on the earth, and every bird of every kind—every bird, every winged creature. They went into the ark with Noah, two and two of all flesh in which there was the breath of life. And those that entered, male and female and all flesh, went in as God had commanded him; and the LORD *shut him in.*

The flood continued forty days on the earth; and the waters increased, and bore up the ark, and it rose high above the earth. The waters swelled and increased greatly on the earth; and the ark floated on the face of the waters.

At the end of forty days Noah opened the window of the ark that he had made and sent out the raven; and it went to and fro until the waters were dried up from the earth. Then he sent out the dove from him, to see if the waters had subsided from the face of the ground; but the dove found no place to set its foot, and it returned to him to the ark, for the waters were still on the face of the whole earth. So he put out his hand and took it and brought it into the ark with him. He waited another seven days, and again he sent out the dove from the ark; and the dove came back to him in the evening, and in its beak there was a freshly picked olive leaf; so Noah knew that the waters had subsided from the earth. Then he waited another seven days, and sent out the dove; and it did not return to him any more.

In the six hundred first year, in the first month, the first day of the month, the waters were dried up from the earth; and Noah removed the covering of the ark, and looked, and saw that the face of the ground was drying. In the second month, on the twenty-seventh day of the month, the earth was dry. Then God said to Noah, "Go out of the ark, you and your wife, and your sons and your sons' wives with you. Bring out with you every living thing that is with you of all flesh—birds and animals and every creeping thing that creeps on the earth—so that they may abound on the earth, and be fruitful and multiply on the earth." So Noah went out with his sons and his wife and his sons' wives. And every animal, every creeping thing, and every bird, everything that moves on the earth, went out of the ark by families.

Then God said to Noah and to his sons with him, "As for me, I am establishing my covenant with you and your descendants after you, and with every living creature that is with you, the birds, the domestic animals, and every animal of the earth with you, as many as came out of the ark. I establish my covenant with you, that never again shall all flesh be cut off by the waters of a flood, and never again shall there be a flood to destroy the earth." God said, "This is the sign of the covenant that I make between me and you, for all future generations: I have set my bow in the clouds, and it shall be a sign of the covenant between me and the earth."

The story of the flood is an ancient myth of divine judgment; the world had grown corrupt, and when the limits of divine patience were reached, God released the terrible waters to destroy everything except the inhabitants of the ark. The flood is described as a fundamental disruption of nature; the separation that God had established between the waters below the earth and the waters above it (Gen. 1:6-8) weakened, and the lower waters welled up, while "the windows of heaven" opened (Gen. 7:11; and see 8:2). At the end of the story, when the earth is restored, God makes a covenant not only with Noah, but with physical nature, pledging that nothing of the sort will ever be done again.

The flood story draws on the sense of water as threat and a sign of death. The flood is a demonstration that God is not indifferent to systemic evil. But the story does not emphasize destruction so much as a cleansing which allows for a fresh beginning. In the Genesis account, all emphasis is on the persons and the animals in the ark. Some Jewish sources looked at the Noah story as a story of redemption. In Isaiah 54:7-9 and in Sirach 44:17, Israel's restoration, an act of divine salvation, is compared to Noah's vindication and rescue and the renewed earth and the covenants that followed the flood.

Christians, beginning as early as 1 Peter 3:20-21, read the flood story subordinating the motif of judgment and destruction to the motif of preservation and redemption. Early Christians saw the ark as the church, and they made much of the dove of mercy. Christians of the earliest generations were a small movement in a society which they regarded as hostile, corrupt, Satan-dominated and destined for destruction. A "remnant," called by grace and identified by baptism, would be saved from the awful judgment. This typological reading of the flood story continued through the liturgy and preaching of the early church, the Middle Ages, and the Reformation era.[10]

Christians during much of the past have found divine judgment and redemption in this Genesis myth. The Vigil reading holds it before the church in its clarity and its mystery.

With Psalm 46

This Psalm speaks of the awesome stir of God in nature—*the earth's waters rage and foam.* God also stirs among the nations—*he breaks the bow, and shatters the spear.* In the tumult of nature and of history, God is the *refuge and strength* of his people.

Abraham's sacrifice of Isaac: Genesis 22:1-18

After these things God tested Abraham. He said to him, "Abraham!" And he said, "Here I am." He said, "Take your son, your only son Isaac, whom you love, and go to the land of Moriah, and offer him there as a burnt offering on one of the mountains that I shall show you." So Abraham arose early in the morning, saddled his donkey, and took two of his young men with him, and his son Isaac; he cut the wood for the burnt offering, and set out and went to the place in the distance that God had shown him. On the third day Abraham looked up and saw the place far away. Then Abraham said to his young men, "Stay here with the donkey; the boy and I will go over there; we will worship, and then we will come back to you." Abraham took the wood of the burnt offering and laid it on his son Isaac, and he himself carried the fire and the knife. So the two of them walked on together. Isaac said to his father Abraham, "Father!" And he said, "Here I am, my son." He said, "The fire and the wood are here, but where is the lamb for the burnt offering?" Abraham said, "God himself will provide the lamb for a burnt offering, my son." So the two of them walked on together.

When they came to the place that God had shown him, Abraham built an altar there and laid the wood in order. He bound his son Isaac, and laid him on the altar, on top of the wood. Then Abraham reached out his hand and took the knife to kill his son. But the angel of the LORD called to him from heaven, and said, "Abraham, Abraham!" And he said, "Here I am." He said, "Do not lay your hand on the boy or do anything to him; for now I know that you fear God, since you have not withheld your son, your only son from me." And Abraham looked up and saw a ram, caught in a thicket by its horns. Abraham went and took the ram and offered it up as a burnt offering instead of his son. So Abraham called that place "The LORD will provide"; as it is said to this day, "On the mount of the LORD it shall be provided."

The angel of the LORD called to Abraham a second time from heaven, and said, "By myself I have sworn, says the LORD: Because you have done this, and have not withheld your son, your only son, I will indeed bless you, and I will make your offspring as numerous as the starts of the heaven and as the sand that is on the seashore. And your offspring shall possess the gate of their enemies, and by your offspring shall all the nations of the earth gain blessing for themselves, because you have obeyed my voice."

This difficult story has stirred reflection and interpretation in the Jewish and the Christian traditions. (It is known among Jews as the *aqedah*, the "binding" of Isaac.) In the comments on its use on Lent 2 in Year B (see p. 26, 29 above), reference was made to a very old Christian typological reading of the story, warning that such interpretation can drain away the terror and moral dilemma of the incident by making it an illustration of another known story. When that is done, the story of Abraham is not really opened.

If it is advisable to avoid typology and deal with the story straight-on when it is read and preached at some times, at the Great Vigil this christological approach can fit the liturgical setting and the context of the other readings from the Jewish scriptures.

Jewish tradition had begun the broadening of this story. Some rabbinic sources identified the mountain of the *aqedah* with the temple mount in Jerusalem (2 Chr. 3:1), connecting the incident with the sacrificial system and especially with Passover and the Day of Atonement. Other rabbinic interpreters taught that Isaac was a willing victim, consenting to God's will, thus making him a prototype of martyrs. His sacrifice was thought to be effective for his posterity. Some exegetes spoke as if Isaac had returned from the dead—an idea which probably stands behind Hebrews 11:19. Although these interpretations pre-dated the church, it does not seem likely that they influenced Christian thought directly, for the New Testament makes only minimal reference to the sacrifice of Isaac. Yet they do show that the depth of suggestion in the story had gripped the Jewish mind.

In the early church the story of Abraham's sacrifice of Isaac is often pictured in mosaics and told in medieval church dramas, often closely associated with Jesus' sacrifice and with the Christian eucharist. As the Christians read this incident, Isaac was a type of Christ: the only and beloved son of his Father, carrying the wood to the place of sacrifice. The God-provided lamb of the story was suggestive.[11] This typological interpretation was not just a matter of finding ingenious parallels, but the story of Abraham's willingness to yield the son he loved seemed to illustrate the heart of God who *did not withhold his own Son, but gave him up for all of us* (Rom. 8:32). The Christian framework of meaning makes the story "a type of a sacrifice that God carries through with no reprieve."[12]

[This story is also appointed for the Second Sunday in Lent in Year B, and it may be read on Good Friday in all three years.]

With Psalm 33:12-22 or Psalm 16

Psalm 33:12-22 emphasizes that God sees and understands all who dwell on the earth, especially watching those who fear him, plucking them from death and feeding them in famine (see also p. 118).

Psalm 16 is an expression of trust, in life and death, in God, who will not abandon those who place their faith in him.

Israel's deliverance at the Red Sea: Exodus 14:10—15:1

As Pharaoh drew near, the Israelites looked back, and there were the Egyptians advancing on them. In great fear, the Israelites cried out to the LORD. They said to Moses, "Was it because there were no graves in Egypt that you have taken us away to die in the wilderness? What have you done to us, bringing us out of Egypt? Is not this the very thing we told you in Egypt, 'Let us alone and let us serve the Egyptians'? For it would have been better for us to serve the Egyptians than to die in the wilderness." But Moses said to the people, "Do not be afraid, stand firm, and see the deliverance that the LORD will accomplish for you today; for the Egyptians whom you see today you shall never see again. The LORD will fight for you, and you have only to keep still."

Then the LORD said to Moses, "Why do you cry out to me? Tell the Israelites to go forward. But you lift up your staff, and stretch out your hand over the sea and divide it, that the Israelites may go into the sea on dry ground. Then I will harden the hearts of the Egyptians so that they will go in after them; and so I will gain glory for myself over Pharaoh and all his army, his chariots, and his chariot drivers. And the Egyptians shall know that I am the LORD, when I have gained glory for myself over Pharaoh, his chariots, and his chariot drivers."

The angel of God who was going before the Israelite army moved and went behind them; and the pillar of cloud moved from in front of them and took its place behind them. It came between the army of Egypt and the army of Israel. And so the cloud was there with the darkness, and lit up the night; one did not come near the other all night.

Then Moses stretched out his hand over the sea. The LORD *drove the sea back by a strong east wind all night, and turned the sea into dry land; and the waters were divided. The Israelites went into the sea on dry ground, the waters forming a wall for them on their right and on their left. The Egyptians pursued, and went into the sea after them, all of Pharaoh's horses, chariots, and chariot drivers. At the morning watch the* LORD *in the pillar of fire and cloud looked down upon the Egyptian army, and threw the Egyptian army into panic. He clogged their chariot wheels so that they turned with difficulty. The Egyptians said, "Let us flee from the Israelites, for the* LORD *is fighting for them against Egypt."*

Then the LORD *said to Moses, "Stretch out your hand over the sea, so that the water may come back upon the Egyptians, upon their chariots and chariot drivers." So Moses stretched out his hand over the sea, and at dawn the sea returned to its normal depth. As the Egyptians fled before it, the* LORD *tossed the Egyptians into the sea. The waters returned and covered the chariots and the chariot drivers, the entire army of Pharaoh that had followed them into the sea; not one of them remained. But the Israelites walked on dry ground through the sea, the waters forming a wall for them on their right and on their left.*

Thus the LORD *saved Israel that day from the Egyptians; and Israel saw the Egyptians dead on the seashore. Israel saw the great work that the* LORD *did against the Egyptians. So the people feared the* LORD *and believed in the* LORD *and in his servant Moses.*

Then Moses and the Israelites sang this song to the LORD*:*
"I will sing to the LORD*, for he has triumphed gloriously;*
horse and rider he has thrown into the sea."

This reading (which is quite long, but very fast-moving and dramatic) tells the story of Israel's crossing of the Red Sea—the first major event after the people had left Egypt. It is told with tension and a sense of climax: the barrier of the sea, the advance of Pharaoh's army, the fear and complaint of the people, the confidence of Moses, the safe passage of the Israelites, the dramatic act of Moses followed by the panic and terrible destruction of the Egyptians, the victory songs of Moses (15:1-18) and of Miriam (15:20-21). The incident recounts the decisive passage of Israel out of slavery. The people were not free of Egypt until they had crossed the sea.

This story, in its highly interpreted, quasi-mythic form of telling, became central to Israel's sense of its identity and calling. The nation was who it was because God had loved it, despite itself, and brought it by divine power out of bondage and into the life of covenant and finally to its own land. The story of deliverance has continued to be sung and told and given ritual re-enactment and poetic retelling from generation to generation (see for example Ps. 105:23-45).

Moreover, the Jewish scriptures used the exodus as a paradigm by which to interpret other events, such as the call of Abraham (Gen. 12) and the entry of the Hebrews into Canaan (Josh. 1-3). The prophets describe Israel's restoration following the exile as a new exodus (as Isa. 11:12-16; 43:19-21; 52:4-5). Patterns such as a call to a new land or rescue from seeming hopelessness reproduced themselves in the biblical literature because they recurred in the life of the people, who kept encountering the familiar hand of the God of the exodus.

The exodus was originally a momentous event in one nation's history. Although the exodus story has been spiritualized and universalized by the Christian tradition, it has not been made so spiritual that it cannot touch society. It gives a powerful, messianic interpretation of history and existence, saying that God takes the part of the burdened and oppressed, calling them to freedom in covenant. This saga of oppression, emancipation, journeying, and arrival has captured the imagination of other people in bondage, and the exodus pattern remains a liberating force in modern society. "When Israel was in Egypt's land. . . .Let my people go." This ancient motif has not lost its power, but germinates in the human imagination and has remained into modern times a restless, potent shaper of history.[13]

The early Christians adopted the exodus story to speak of transformation in Christ. They saw the church as a new Israel and Jesus' death and resurrection as a new exodus passage through which the new Moses had carried his people. By baptismal dying and rising (passing through the water), one came to share in the life of this exodus-people. An old condition of bondage was left, and a new life of freedom in covenant was entered. David Stanley has said, "Israel, by leaving Egypt at Moses' word to follow Yahweh in the desert, took a step which, religiously speaking, is comparable to the Christian renunciation of the world and adherence to Christ through baptism."[14]

With Canticle 8 (The Song of Moses)

The text of this canticle is Exodus 15:1-6, 11-13, 17-18, the song that was sung by Moses and the Israelites when they had safely passed through the Red Sea. It is a quite stylized poem, retelling the story in a tone of celebration. It emphasizes repeatedly and in exuberant praise that the escape of Israel was solely God's doing. *In your steadfast love you led the people whom you redeemed.*

God's presence in a renewed Israel: Isaiah 4:2-6

On that day the branch of the LORD shall be beautiful and glorious, and the fruit of the land shall be the pride and glory of the survivors of Israel. Whoever is left in Zion and remains in Jerusalem will be called holy, everyone who has been recorded for life in Jerusalem, once the Lord has washed away the filth of the daughters of Zion and cleansed the bloodstains of Jerusalem from its midst by a spirit of judgment and by a spirit of burning. Then the LORD will create over the whole site of Mount Zion and over its places of assembly a cloud by day and smoke and the shining of a flaming fire by night. Indeed over all the glory there will be a canopy. It will serve as a pavilion, a shade by day from the heat, and a refuge and a shelter from the storm and rain.

Isaiah prophesies preservation and renewal for the Israelites who, during the exile, have managed to remain in Jerusalem. They are described as *the survivors of Israel* (vs.1b), expressing Isaiah's theme that a "righteous remnant" will carry on the nation's calling and covenant. A day will come when the land will be fruitful (vs. 2). The unfaithfulness that had brought judgment on the nation seems to the prophet like a pollution, a befoulment. But the people of Zion will be a purified people (vss. 3f), made so by God's washing and God's fire (vs. 4). (When the prophet says in vs. 3 that those who are in Jerusalem *will be called holy*, he means that they really will be holy.) The survivors are recorded in God's book of life (vs. 3)—a reference which early Christians assimilated to registration for baptism. God will set a protecting presence over Israel (vss. 5-6), a presence described in terms drawn from the exodus story as a cloud by day and fire by night. God will give *a refuge and a shelter from the storm and rain.*

With Psalm 122

This short psalm voices an Israelite's joy in going to Jerusalem. There one finds others who have also come *to praise the Name of the LORD.* It is a secure place where sound judgments are given. The concluding verses, 6-9, are the pilgrim's prayer for Jerusalem and its peace.

Salvation offered freely to all: Isaiah 55:1-11

Ho, everyone who thirsts,
come to the waters:
and you who have no money,
come, buy and eat!

Come, buy wine and milk
  without money and without price.
Why do you spend your money for that which is not bread,
  and your labor for that which does not satisfy?
Listen carefully to me, and eat what is good,
  and delight yourselves in rich food.
Incline your ear, and come to me;
  listen, so that you may live.
I will make with you an everlasting covenant,
  my steadfast, sure love for David.
See, I made him a witness to the peoples,
  a leader and commander for the peoples.
See, you shall call nations that you do not know,
  and nations that do not know you shall run to you,
because of the LORD your God, the Holy One of Israel,
  for he has glorified you.

Seek the LORD while he may be found,
  call upon him while he is near;
let the wicked forsake their way,
  and the unrighteous their thoughts;
let them return to the LORD, that he may have mercy on them,
  and to our God, for he will abundantly pardon.
For my thoughts are not your thoughts,
  nor are your ways my ways, says the LORD.
For as the heavens are higher than the earth,
  so are my ways higher than your ways
  and my thoughts than your thoughts.

For as the rain and the snow come down from heaven,
  and do not return there until they have watered the earth,
making it bring forth and sprout,
  giving seed to the sower and bread to the eater,
so shall my word be that goes out from my mouth;
  it shall not return to me empty,
but it shall accomplish that which I purpose,
  and succeed in the thing for which I send it.

The prophet speaks glowingly of the re-establishment of Israel. As the reign of the divine King is inaugurated, it is as though Israel were invited to a lavish free banquet. *Come, buy wine and milk without money and without price* (vss. 1-2). The tone resembles that of a hawker of wares in a market, but these goods are to be given away! It becomes clear that the substance of the banquet is the divine word, *Listen, so that you may live.* God will establish again with his people the covenant that was made with David (vss. 3-5). Israel should, at this time of favor, seek God with repentance, assured of divine pardon (vss. 6-7). God's gracious intentions for his people far exceed their conceiving: *For as the heavens are higher than the earth, so are my ways higher than your ways and my thoughts than your thoughts* (vss. 8-9).

Having mentioned the divine word, the prophet introduces a comparison (vss. 10, 11), which is spoken as though by God. Rain and snow, the divine speaker observes, move in one direction, from the sky down to the earth. They remain and produce an effect, making the barren earth fruitful and feeding its inhabitants. They are needed by the earth, but they are not produced by the earth; they come from heaven. They are sought and welcomed, but they are not under the earth's control, but arrive as gift or grace; they can only be received. This beneficial gift from heaven, God then says, is like the divine word: *So shall my word be that goes out from my mouth.* It will not return to the speaker empty, but will accomplish that for which it was spoken. "God's word is a word that does things."[15]

This passage, which describes Israel's restoration in terms of life-giving water and the divine word, obviously suits both the Vigil and baptism.

With Canticle 9 (The First Song of Isaiah) or Psalm 42:1-7

Canticle 9 (Isa. 12:2-6) is a song of deliverance. The singer speaks of "my salvation" (vs. 2). Then a voice says that *you will draw water from the springs of salvation* (vs. 3). The praise of those who are saved is spoken in verses 3b-6.

Psalm 42:1-7 opens with an image that has been associated with baptism from the earliest centuries: *As the deer longs for the water-brooks, so longs my soul for you, O God.* (On this psalm, see p. 244.)

A new heart and a new spirit: Ezekiel 36:24-28

I will take you from the nations, and gather you from all the countries, and bring you into your own land. I will sprinkle clean water upon you, and you shall be clean from all your uncleanness, and from all your idols I will cleanse you. A new heart I will give you, and a new spirit I will put within you, and I will remove from your body the heart of stone and give you a heart of flesh. I will put my spirit within you, and make you follow

*my statutes and be careful to observe my ordinances. Then you shall live
in the land that I gave to your ancestors; and you shall be my people, and
I will be your God.*

These words were written in exile. Ezekiel, a highly imaginative Jewish prophet, along with the leaders and many citizens of Judah, had been
taken into Babylon in 597 BCE. In this situation of almost unendurable loss,
Ezekiel prophesies hope. A purified and chastened people will return to its
own land.

The restoration, he says, will be an act of God. Speaking in the voice of
God, the prophet says "I will" eight times in five verses. The return will
not be because of the nation's strength or its wise policies, for it has lost
control of its own future. Its radical cause would be God, who remained
faithful to Judah even when Judah had been faithless, and who would vindicate the divine name which the nation had profaned. *"O house of Israel,
I am about to act"* (36:22).

Ezekiel does not describe this coming restoration circumstantially, but
in visionary terms, using a series of images:

(a) It will be a gathering of the scattered people. The Jews were deeply
attached to the land that was theirs by divine promise—*the land that I
gave to your ancestors* (vs. 28). It was the basis of their secure liveli-
hood and a sign of their identity and continuity in covenant with God.
When they were taken from it and carried into other nations, the loss
was all but unbearable. The prophet says that the people, even though
they are scattered, are known to God, who will bring them again to
their own land.

(b) The people's compromise with idolatry has brought about a kind of
impurity or contamination which must be dealt with (see 36:17). Water is an inevitable and powerful symbol for restoring something that
has become soiled. Ezekiel says that Israel's restoration will begin with
a ritual bath carried out by God on the nation. A divine cleansing by an
affusion of clean water institutes a new beginning for the whole people.

(c) The exile has revealed the flaws in the nation's soul. Simply to take
the same people back to their land might mean that the whole sad story
would be played over again. Inward renovation is required. God promises the gift of a new heart—describing the matter in terms somewhat
like surgery; a cold, lifeless heart of stone will be removed and replaced by a beating heart of flesh.

(d) God's own spirit (or "breath") will be within the people, transforming them, communicating divine life and power to them. The image suggests the creation story in which God breathes life into the dust of the earth and Adam becomes a living person (Gen. 2:7).

(e) God will turn the people from idols to a life of obedience, and they will live again in their land, free from idols and in covenant faithfulness. God's final pledge, *You shall be my people, and I will be your God,* expresses the mutual commitment of Israel to God, and of God to Israel, in covenant. This is a favorite phrase in Ezekiel (see Ezek. 11:20; 14:11; 34:31; 37:23).

The prophet described this restoration in terms that went below situations and circumstances and engaged the imagination. Hence his words remain to interpret more than he could possibly have had in mind when he wrote them. His images of the creation of a people, of divine cleansing, of water and the spirit, of inner newness, were held in the biblical tradition; and in the imagination of the early believers in Christ these images were made contemporary by new divine actions. Ezekiel's words became parts of the vocabulary by which Christians interpreted both redemption and baptism, which was the sign of redemption. As one commentator puts it, "Whatever the historical antecedents of Christian baptism, whether an initiatory cleansing of the Qumran type, or proselyte baptism, or a combination of different features, the basic pattern is already detectable in Ezekiel's promise to the deportees."[16]

The early Christians would have understood Ezekiel's images—gathering in a homeland, washing, life by God's own breath—to speak of spiritual renewal, of course. But at the same time they would have heard reference to concrete ritual actions, for at baptism the early church dramatized redemptive meanings by washing with water, anointing with oil, and in some liturgies even by a ceremonial breathing on the candidates. Ezekiel, as they saw it, had anticipated the gospel of Christ, and his water and spirit images described and interpreted the fundamental sign of the gospel, Christian baptism.

With Psalm 42:1-7
or Canticle 9 (The First Song of Isaiah)

This psalm and this canticle were also appointed for the previous reading, and both are commented on elsewhere.

The valley of dry bones: Ezekiel 37:1-14

The hand of the LORD came upon me, and he brought me out by the spirit of the LORD and set me down in the middle of a valley; it was full of bones. He led me all around them; there were very many lying in the valley, and they were very dry. He said to me, "Mortal, can these bones live?" I answered, "O Lord GOD, you know." Then he said to me, "Prophesy to these bones, and say to them: O dry bones, hear the word of the LORD. Thus says the Lord GOD to these bones: I will cause breath to enter you, and you shall live. I will lay sinews on you, and will cause flesh to come upon you, and cover you with skin, and put breath in you, and you shall live; and you shall know that I am the LORD."

So I prophesied as I had been commanded; and as I prophesied, suddenly there was a noise, a rattling, and the bones came together, bone to its bone. I looked, and there were sinews on them, and flesh had come upon them; but there was no breath in them. Then he said to me, "Prophesy to the breath, prophesy, mortal, and say to the breath: Thus says the Lord GOD: Come from the four winds, O breath, and breathe upon the slain, that they may live." I prophesied as he commanded me, and the breath came into them, and they lived, and stood on their feet, a vast multitude.

Then he said to me, "Mortal, these bones are the whole house of Israel. They say, 'Our bones are dried up, and our hope is lost; we are cut off completely.' Thus says the Lord GOD: I am going to open your graves, and bring you up from your graves, O my people; and I will bring you back to the land of Israel. And you shall know that I am the LORD, when I open your graves, and bring you up from your graves, O my people. I will put my spirit within you, and you shall live, and I will place you on your own soil; then you shall know that I, the LORD, have spoken and will act," says the LORD.

The prophet first describes a vision (vss. 1-10) and then explains it (vss. 11-14). The vision is so graphically told that when it is read at the Vigil, this lesson borders on humor; yet it is strangely moving.

In the spirit of the Lord, the prophet is set in a valley of dry bones—fragments of persons who once had lived; but living bodies had died; dead bodies had desiccated; and disconnected, irrational parts were all that was left. The scene (which suggests a battlefield) is one of sheer desolation; it is impossible that life should return.

Yet, bidden by God, the prophet does an unreasonable thing; he addresses this hopeless material: *O dry bones, hear the word of the LORD.* As he does, the bones rather noisily reassemble themselves; flesh comes upon the bones; and when Ezekiel prophesies again, breath comes to the bodies, and *they lived, and stood on their feet, a vast multitude.* The impossible has happened—and all because of the life-imparting word of God.

God gives the prophet an explanation: *These bones are the whole house of Israel.* God will bring the nation back from its virtual extinction, restore it to its own land, impart the divine breath to it, *and you shall live.* Nothing is more final than death—and the dryness and fragmentation emphasize its finality. Yet the prophet is saying that God is in the business of doing the impossible, bringing life out of death. The power of God at work in history should not be measured by ordinary human expectations. The vision concludes: *"Then you shall know that I, the LORD, have spoken and will act."*

The passage suits baptism and the Vigil by its depiction of passage from death to life. The prayer that follows this reading, echoing Eucharistic Prayer B, speaks of God's having *brought us out of sin into righteousness and out of death into life* (BCP, p. 291).

[This passage is also appointed for Lent 5, Year A, where the gospel reading is the Johannine story of Jesus raising Lazarus.]

With Psalm 30 or Psalm 143

Psalm 30 speaks the thanks of one who had once been in a position of security and prosperity and had been brought near to death. God has restored the psalmist, who expresses deep and lasting gratitude. This can be thought of as a psalm of a grateful individual or as a psalm of restored Israel—the people brought back from the grave.

Psalm 143 is a plea for help by one who pleads personal unworthiness (vs. 2), who is crushed to the ground (vs. 3), held in darkness (vs. 4), threatened with annihilation (vs. 7), and surrounded by enemies (vs. 9). In this condition the psalmist prays (vs. 1), recalls God's former deeds (vs. 5), stretches out his hands in entreaty (vs. 6), asking for words of love (vs. 8) and for guidance (vs. 8b, 10). *Let your good spirit lead me on a level path.*

The gathering of God's people: Zephaniah 3:12-20

> *For I will leave in the midst of you*
> *a people humble and lowly.*
> *They shall seek refuge in the name of the LORD—*
> *the remnant of Israel;*
> *they shall do no wrong*
> *and utter no lies,*

nor shall a deceitful tongue
      be found on their mouth.
Then they will pasture and lie down,
      and no one shall make them afraid.

Sing aloud, O daughter of Zion;
      shout, O Israel!
Rejoice and exult with all your heart,
      O daughter of Jerusalem!
The Lord has taken away the judgments against you,
      he has turned away your enemies.
The king of Israel, the Lord, is in your midst;
      you shall fear disaster no more.
On that day it shall be said to Jerusalem:
Do not fear, O Zion;
      do not let your hands grow weak.
The Lord, your God, is in your midst,
      a warrior who gives victory;
he will rejoice over you with gladness,
      he will renew you in his love;
he will exult over you with loud singing
      as on a day of festival.
I will remove every disaster from you,
      so that you will not bear reproach for it.
I will deal with all your oppressors
      at that time.
And I will save the lame
      and gather the outcast,
and I will change their shame into praise
      and renown in all the earth.
At that time I will bring you home,
      at the time when I gather you;
for I will make you renowned and praised
      among all the people of the earth,
when I restore your fortunes
      before your eyes, says the Lord.

The early parts of Zephaniah's prophecy are filled with severe judgments against Judah and Jerusalem, as well as against the surrounding nations. A coming *day of the Lord* (1:7, 14)) will bring destruction. *That day will be a day of wrath* (1:15). But the passage that is appointed for the Vigil reading comes from a later and quite different section of the book. In

3:12-13 the voice of God pledges that after the judgment has done its work, a chastened remnant of Judah will *seek refuge in the name of the* L*ORD*.

In 3:14-18a the prophet speaks, bidding the people to rejoice, for God has removed the judgments against them and turned away their enemies. They should not fear, for *The* L*ORD, your God, is in your midst*. Very strikingly, the prophet says that God, too, rejoices in the people's rejoicing (3:17-18a).

At verse 18 the voice of God resumes, making a series of pledges, concluding with the gathering of the people. *I will bring you home, at the time when I gather you.*

[This passage is also read on Advent 3 in Year C.]

With Psalm 98 or Psalm 126

Psalm 98 is a sustained burst of praise, calling for *a new song* in celebration of God's victorious deeds, which are obviously deeds in the field of history (vs. 3b). The whole earth is summoned to praise (vss. 4-9). Verses 5f speak as though the powers of earth played instrumental music.

Psalm 126 begins with a joyful recollection of liberation—a victory brought about by God. (Or it may be that the words speak of a future time when the people would look back with such rejoicing.) The second section (vss. 4-6) asks for deliverance from adversity, anticipating the joy that comes eventually. *May those who sow in tears reap with shouts of joy.*

At the Eucharist of Easter

In the early Christian generations, baptism led at once to communion. This unified ritual act, the Easter-baptism-eucharist, brought the two great sacraments of the gospel into significant relation to one another, and both of them stood in clear relation with the death and resurrection of Christ. For anyone who was baptized, the sequence of sacramental moments—catechesis, renunciation of the devil, affirmation of faith, water baptism, anointing with oil, incorporation in the new community through eucharist—was a ritualization of conversion.

It was clear in the ritual actions of the early Christians that the reality of Easter and the reality of baptism were bound together. They still are. Every baptism, whenever and however it is performed, enacts the truth of Easter. However, for a very long time the bond between them was hard to perceive, since in custom Easter came to be observed without baptism, and baptism could be at any time of the year, usually close to a child's birth.

Today, the liturgical churches have sought once again to bring these two central acts into clear relation with one another. At the Vigil, the readings from the Jewish scriptures pass to the service of Holy Baptism (or The Renewal of Baptismal Vows). Then the resurrection is announced (BCP, p. 294), and the church passes into full light. The eucharist follows, with special canticles and collects (BCP, p. 294f). (The actions of baptism or renewal of vows may be held until this place, where they follow the gospel reading [BCP, p. 295].)

The two readings from the Christian testament at the first eucharist of Easter are:

Romans 6:3-11

Do you not know that all of us who have been baptized into Christ Jesus were baptized into his death? Therefore we have been buried with him by baptism into death, so that, just as Christ was raised from the dead by the glory of the Father, so we too might walk in newness of life.

For if we have been united with him in a death like his, we will certainly be united with him in a resurrection like his. We know that our old self was crucified with him so that the body of sin might be destroyed, and we might no longer be enslaved to sin. For whoever has died is freed from sin. But if we have died with Christ, we believe that we will also live with him. We know that Christ, being raised from the dead, will never die again; death no longer has dominion over him. The death that he died, he died to sin once for all; but the life he lives, he lives to God. So you must consider yourselves dead to sin and alive to God in Christ Jesus.

When the resurrection is announced, the church at once turns to scriptures that are among the most important in the vocabulary of Christian baptism. Evidently Paul's readers already understand that their baptism is baptism *"into Christ Jesus."* They were also familiar with the traditional Christian proclamation that *Christ died for our sins. . ., that he was buried, and that he rose again,* a proclamation that Paul reminds his Corinthian readers of in 1 Corinthians 15:3f. Paul is more urgent and dramatic when he says here that by baptism each Christian is united with those saving events. *All of us who have been baptized were baptized into his death. . . .We have been buried with him by baptism into death. . . .We will certainly be united with him in a resurrection like his.*

These words come in a sustained argument that had begun in chapter 5. Before Paul speaks of a Christian's baptism as dying and rising with Christ, he has spoken about Christ, saying that his death and resurrection are basic to the Christian's new condition, for Christ, in what he did, acted for others—indeed, for all (5:6-11). For Paul's point to be persuasive, his readers must think of Christ not only as an individual, a moral hero, but as a representative figure, a single person who stands for a collective life (5:12-21). Paul describes two humanities or two contrasting human conditions which he identifies under two names: Adam is an old humanity, while Christ is a new Adam, a new humanity. Adam, who disobeyed, is a sign of sin, death, and judgment, while the obedient Christ is a sign of righteousness, forgiveness, and life. In Adam, death "exercised dominion" throughout humanity; but into the tragic continuities of sinning and dying came an obedient one, and in him there is a gift of righteousness which *exercises dominion in life through one man, Jesus Christ* (5:17). The parallel with Adam indicates that Christ—the righteous one who came, who died, and who rose again—marks the coming of a new age, the beginning of the renewal of all things; God was inaugurating a new humanity by a creative act in a new primal figure.

Thus, in the purpose of God, what happened in Christ, specifically in his death and resurrection, happened for the race, for sinners. He was the *one* who invested himself, in life and death, for *all*. He inaugurates a new humanity, a new human solidarity in grace, of which the church is the sign-community. His life beyond death demonstrates the newness of life which is open to others, not only as a future certainty, but as a qualitatively different life now. But what Christ did for others is not effective unless there is inward consent. One enters Christ and his benefits by an act of faith, and faith has its outward sign in baptism, which replicates in and for each Christian the redemptive crisis of the Savior; each Christian is *baptized into Christ* (6:3), that is, united with his dying and rising (6:3f), brought within that inclusive personality which he is. The New Testament scholar Rudolf Schnackenburg has said, "Through baptism we have been included in the destiny of our spiritual progenitor, Christ. We have undergone the same thing he has, and we have done so with him."[17]

Dying and rising is a drastic image. It says that for a sinner, self-reformation is not enough, for the self is precisely the problem. What is needed is not an external tidying-up, but a death and resurrection! Death speaks of that final negation, that reduction to nothingness of all that we seek to do from ourselves and for ourselves. But only such a dying in the creative death of Christ provides the openness to being rebuilt into the richness and security of a new life in Christ and his people.

The transformation by way of a death and resurrection, which is enacted in baptism, has moral consequences. The self that was dedicated to sinning has died in Christ (6:5-11). Yet one goes on living, but now in the new life in the risen Christ that is opened to one who believes. The new life which one enters on the other side of this sacramental death is a life of obedience, a life in the Spirit. As to sin and its power, one has effectively died. In another letter Paul speaks of the ethical meaning of dying with Christ when he says, *Those who belong to Christ Jesus have crucified the flesh with its passions and desires* (Gal. 5:24). He was speaking of a dramatic moment when, united with Christ's crucifixion, something in a Christian had been put to death so that something else, *the fruit of the Spirit* (Gal. 5:22f), might live.

This Pauline motif of life through death, of rising to a new quality of life, surely speaks to the widespread and at times almost desperate modern-day sense of inner weariness and a search for renewal. But it warns searchers not to settle for quick-fix offers of new life. Baptism, as described by Paul, asks for everything we are—it is about dying. But in it Christ offers everything he is—it is about newness of life.

Paul has argued that what happened in Jesus' death and resurrection is, in a sense, replicated in those who are united with him by baptism: *If we have been united with him in a death like his, we will certainly be united with him in a resurrection like his.* Christ's risen life, as shared by the baptized, is not just a matter of future promise, but also of the righteousness of life now. What died in the baptism by which a Christian shares in Christ's creative death is *our old self*, and those who have died are freed from enslavement to sin, for death cancels all. Christ who now lives *lives to God.* United with him and living in him, *you,* Paul says, *must consider yourselves dead to sin and alive to God in Christ Jesus.*

With Psalm 114

This psalm is virtually a fanfare of praise to God for the passage of Israel out of Egypt. In Jewish tradition it is sung before the Passover meal. Israel was brought out of a people who spoke a strange language to become the sanctuary of God (vss. 1-2). The psalm dwells on the natural wonders that accompanied God's stir in history: the Red Sea and the Jordan turned back (vs. 3, 6); the mountains engaged in something like a frolic (vss. 4, 6, no doubt referring to Sinai); the rock gave out water (vs. 8). Nature is taunted because it had to respond to the power of God (vss. 5-6). The first four verses are in past tense, speaking of history. The last four verses are in present tense; the past, with its feeling tone, is present.

Matthew 28:1-10

After the sabbath, as the first day of the week was dawning, Mary Magdalene and the other Mary went to see the tomb. And suddenly there was a great earthquake; for an angel of the Lord, descending from heaven, came and rolled back the stone and sat on it. His appearance was like lightning, and his clothing white as snow. For fear of him the guards shook and became like dead men. But the angel said to the women, "Do not be afraid; I know that you are looking for Jesus who was crucified. He is not here; for he has been raised, as he said. Come, see the place where he lay. Then go quickly and tell his disciples, 'He has been raised from the dead, and indeed he is going ahead of you to Galilee; there you will see him.' This is my message to you." So they left the tomb quickly with fear and great joy, and ran to tell his disciples. Suddenly Jesus met them and said, "Greetings!" And they came to him, took hold of his feet, and worshiped him. Then Jesus said to them, "Do not be afraid; go and tell my brothers to go to Galilee; there they will see me."

Moments after we have said in the liturgy, *Alleluia. Christ is risen*, we hear this passage, the first gospel of Easter Day. It is Matthew's story of the discovery by two women followers that Jesus has risen. On the Sunday after Jesus' crucifixion, *Mary Magdalene and the other Mary* went to the tomb. Then follows a series of supernatural events, which are unseen and are expressed much in the idiom of apocalyptic: There was a great earthquake. A shining angel in gleaming clothing rolled back the stone from the door of the tomb and sat on it. The guards were struck with terror. The angel speaks to the women. (His speech occupies about one-third of the narrative.) He tells them not to fear, for Jesus is risen; and he invites them to see where he had lain. The angel then charges them to go and tell the disciples, for Jesus will go ahead of them to Galilee.

The women leave the tomb *quickly with fear and great joy,* and as they go they are met by the risen Jesus. They worship him. He repeats the angel's message for them to go and tell his disciples to go to Galilee where they will see him (as they do, 28:16ff). In this account, it is remarkable how little the risen Jesus does or says.

In this gospel these women are the first witnesses to the resurrection, but they drop from the story, and Jesus' one further appearance in this gospel (vss. 16-20) is to the eleven disciples.

Two touches are repeated: (1) In this story, when the women saw Jesus, *they came to him, took hold of his feet, and worshiped him* (28:9), and later, when the eleven see him, *they worshiped him* (28:16). One overhears in this language an expression of first-century Christian conviction that Jesus, the Living One, is an object of worship. (2) The angel at the tomb tells the women to *go quickly and tell his disciples* (28:8); and when they encounter the risen Jesus, he tells them *go and tell my brothers* (28:10). He next encounters the eleven disciples (28:16ff). This emphasis says that Jesus' resurrection is the beginning of a new relationship with his followers. The risen Jesus is not an isolated figure, but is bound up with a people. He is not accessible to dispassionate, value-free inquirers, but is known in, bound up with, and is truly followed only in the community of faithful disciples.

This story in Matthew is not the earliest resurrection account we have, but is based on Mark's prior, somewhat stark narrative, with its abrupt ending. Matthew has interpreted the event as he received it, giving it an apocalyptic character by the touches we have observed. Matthew's *great earthquake* is not in Mark. Mark's "young man" dressed in a white robe (Mk. 16:5) has become Matthew's angel whose *appearance was like lightning, and his clothing white as snow.* But the earliest record we have of the Easter event and faith is neither Matthew nor Mark, but is from Paul in 1 Corinthians 15:3-8. This ringing witness to the resurrection makes no use of the tradition of the empty tomb and suggests no dazzling physical events. Readers and preachers must treat the New Testament witness as a whole and observe with care, sympathy, and integrity this evangelist's mixture of event and symbolic interpretation.

The Scriptures of Easter Day

In the centuries during which the Vigil had lapsed, there was always, of course, an Easter eucharist, for which propers were appointed and which was one of the high celebratory occasions of the year. Now most of the churches which observe the Vigil also have a well-attended eucharist on Easter Morning—often more than one. The rubric that specifies the preferred baptismal occasions mentions the Vigil. But the meaning and the festal tone carry over into all the services of the day, and baptism might appropriately be celebrated at any of them. We take brief note of the scriptures that are appointed for Easter Day, listed here in their biblical order:

Exodus 14:10-14, 21-25; 15:20-21 [Year A]

This story of Israel's deliverance at the Red Sea is also appointed at the Vigil. (See comments on p. 50.)

Isaiah 25:6-9 [Year B]

The day of salvation is envisioned as a banquet prepared by God for all people. Death and sorrow will be banished.

Isaiah 51:9-11 [Year C]

God is summoned to awaken and ransom Israel as God did in the events of the exodus. (There is some mingling in this passage of creation and exodus water imagery.)

Matthew 28:1-10 [Year A]

Two women followers of Jesus discover the empty tomb; an angel, dazzling in appearance, tells them to go and tell Jesus' disciples; as they go they are met by the risen Jesus. (See the comments on the gospel at the eucharist of the Vigil, p. 65)

Mark 16:1-8 [Year B]

In the startlingly abrupt ending of Mark, three women disciples go to Jesus' tomb; the stone has been removed from the entry; a young man with the appearance of an angel tells them that Jesus is risen. The women flee in terror and for a time tell no one. This is by far the shortest and plainest of the resurrection accounts. No one sees Jesus.

[A fuller ending that seems to be a composite was written at quite an early time and added to Mark. It is full of vivid material, but untrue to the intention of the evangelist, who is not trying to amass witnesses of the resurrected Jesus or make startling claims for the powers of the church. Rather, with great subtlety, he leaves the story where he does and leaves readers to explore his work again and to explore themselves.]

Luke 24:1-10 [Year C]

Women followers go to Jesus' tomb intending to anoint his body. The stone is removed from the entrance, and the body is gone. Two men in dazzling clothing tell them that Jesus is risen. They leave quickly and tell the other disciples.

John 20:1-10 (11-18) [Year A]

The empty tomb is discovered by Mary Magdalene who tells Peter and another disciple. The two men run to the tomb, enter it, and see the discarded grave clothing. The unnamed "other disciple" perceives what has taken place.

Acts 10:34-43 [Year A]

Peter is speaking at Cornelius' house. He sketches Jesus' ministry—his preaching and healing, his death, his resurrection by God's power, and his appearances to chosen witnesses, the command to his followers to preach, the witness of all the prophets, and the offer of forgiveness in him. As Peter is speaking, signs of the Spirit interrupt. (See pp. 134, 136)

Colossians 3:1-4 [all three years]

Christians have been raised with Christ (indicative mood) and hence are (imperative mood) to set their minds on things above. The new age has come in Christ, and by baptism Christians are admitted to it; yet the old age continues, and life remains firmly located on earth. In this situation, believers must identify wholly with Christ and his present, victorious life, for that is where they truly live. Union with the risen Christ pledges a future; Christians are destined for glory, but in their present life in history they have "died" to the ways of sin, and their life is hid with Christ in God.

C. EASTER TO PENTECOST

The Prayer Book sustains the celebratory tone of Easter throughout the Great Fifty Days. The seven Sundays until Pentecost are Sundays *of* Easter. In the early Christian generations, during this season no one fasted, and no one knelt for prayer.

In the early church, both the weeks before Easter and the weeks after Easter took their character from the part they played in the making of new Christians. Before Easter, as we have seen, the catechumens were being prepared for baptism. In the days after Easter the bishop gave the newly baptized special instruction, called *mystagogia*, to lead them more fully into the life they had entered. The bishop's mystagogic addresses usually included a step-by-step explication of the dramatic and closely packed ritual events of baptism and first communion which the new Christians had experienced. Things had been done and said which needed to be explained.

Chosen as they are, as *mystagogy*, the gospel readings for the weeks of Easter all speak, in their varied ways, of Jesus in and with his people. As Gordon Lathrop put it:

> In the fifty days, the preacher, faithfully using the material of the pericopes,
> leads those who have been baptized—at *pascha* or at any time, for the

The Scriptures for the Easter/Pentecost Complex ♦ 69

paschal baptism gathers to itself the remembrance and reality of all baptizing—deeper into the mystery of the resurrection and the mystery of
the identity of the church as these are known in the sacraments.[18]

The lectionary passages for the season can be thought of as falling in
seven clusters:

(1) Resurrection appearances.

On the days of Easter Week, and then on the first three Sundays of
Easter, in all three lectionary years, the liturgical gospels present all the
resurrection accounts from the four gospels. After the Day of Resurrection, the church—and now the newly baptized—live in the glow of the
present, living Jesus, bearing witness to himself and his triumph and establishing his followers in the life they now share with him. While the
gospel accounts describe past times, places, people, and events, they cannot be confined. They speak at the same time of realities which touch all
times, places, and people. The disciples on the road to Emmaus (Lk. 24)
and in the room in Jerusalem (Jn. 20:19-29) are the church. The living
Jesus is conferring his peace on present-day Christians, giving them the
Spirit and the authority to forgive, and commissioning them for mission to
the world.

There is some duplication and literary dependence among the New
Testament accounts of Jesus' resurrection appearances, and they do not fit
into a clear place-time sequence, so each story may be looked at in its
literary distinctness. Yet when these stories are considered as a group, several features stand out: (1) The appearances of Jesus are unexpected and
meet with some initial unbelief, as though to say that Jesus' followers were
not looking so hard for him that they persuaded themselves that they saw
him. (2) The appearances are entirely to his faithful followers, as Jesus
establishes a hidden and interior, yet real and powerful bond, between his
risen life and his community. The church, with all its failings, is the place
where the living Jesus is found. And (3) the appearances come to an end as
the relation with the living Christ passes to the mode of the church living in
the Spirit.

[The resurrection accounts from the gospels will not be commented on
here, for they were noted briefly in the readings for Easter Day, above,
and some of them are spoken of more fully elsewhere; see the index of
scripture passages.]

(2) The Good Shepherd.

The Fourth Sunday of Easter in all three years is "Good Shepherd Sunday," using for the gospel reading sections of John 10 in which Jesus presents himself in the vivid figure (vs. 6, *paroimia*) of the Good Shepherd. The image draws deeply on the Jewish heritage in which Abraham, Moses, David, and some of the prophets were shepherds, and on the biblical images which describe God as the true shepherd and Israel as God's flock (as Gen. 49:24; Ps. 23; 95:7; Jer. 23:3-4; Ezek. 34:11-31; Mic. 2:12).

The contrast in John 10 of the Good Shepherd with the thieves and hired hands suggests the denunciation in Ezekiel 34:1-10 of the shepherds who have fed themselves and not the sheep. God, the prophet says (34:11-31), is the true shepherd who will seek out his sheep and rescue them. Similarly, Zechariah 11:15-17 depicts worthless shepherds who are scorned by God. Terms like "pastor" and "flock" have become so much terms of the church that a present-day reader may not realize that these Hebrew prophets were talking about social justice. In Israel, as widely in the ancient world, rulers were spoken of as the people's shepherds or as shepherd-kings. When the prophets speak of false, self-serving shepherds who exploit the sheep, they voice their passion for justice and their righteous anger at kings and persons of power who prey on the poor and the weak. Israel longed for good shepherds, but it was usually disappointed. Jesus presents himself as the model, the ideal, the beautiful shepherd (*ho poimen ho kalos*).

Through Ezekiel, God speaks as Israel's shepherd, *"I myself will be the shepherd of my sheep. . .I will seek the lost. . .I will feed them"* (34:11-16). When Jesus presents himself as the true and faithful Shepherd, he fills the place in relation to his people that the Jewish scriptures assign to God.

John 10:1-10 [Year A]. In the first unit of the Good Shepherd passage, Jesus contrasts himself with a thief who must approach the sheep in their fold by a roundabout way, whereas the shepherd enters openly by the gate. He knows and cares for his sheep individually, and they recognize and respond to him, while they turn from strangers (vss. 1-6). Jesus' words are something of a riddle, and they are not understood, so he changes the figure, describing himself as the door for passage to and from the sheepfold. Speaking again of false leaders ("thieves"), he says that unlike those who deceive and destroy, his shepherding gives life to the sheep (vss. 7-10).

As always in John, there are levels of meaning. Against the background of the exploitative shepherds of Ezekiel 34, Jesus is casting himself in the role of God, as a true shepherd, and his opponents (that is generally the chief priests and scribes) as *strangers,* and *thieves,* who do not care for the interests of the sheep. His words are challenging, provocative. But at another level, in the sub-text of John, the prayer of Jesus speaks indirectly of the first-century Johannine church which was newly separated from the synagogue. The early Christians had become estranged from their former shepherds, but they are discovering their ties with their true Shepherd, the living Christ—ties which uphold them when they meet opposition and threat. Although they may have known uncaring shepherds, Jesus is the true shepherd who knows and cares for his sheep.

Jesus' words, read after Easter, give strength and comfort to the newly baptized who face a new future. They are under the care of a shepherd who gives them life, abundant life.

John 10:11-16 [Year B].   In these verses the sheep are no longer in the fold, but in the open where wild animals are a danger. The sheep are under attack. A hired hand has been asked to watch the sheep, but he cares very little for them, for they are not his. He runs from a wolf and leaves the sheep. But Jesus is the Good Shepherd, who knows his sheep and puts himself in jeopardy for their sake: *I lay down my life for the sheep.*

None of the passages in the Jewish scriptures that depict God as the true shepherd of Israel speak of the shepherd dying for his sheep. In this touch the evangelist is obviously laying creative hands on his sources and, knowing the story of Jesus' cross, he turns the image in a specifically christological direction.

When Jesus says *I know my own and my own know me, just as the Father knows me and I know the Father* (14-15a), he is speaking in the idiom of the farewell chapters (compare 14:20; 15:9-10; 17:21). The voice is now that of the living Christ speaking to and of the church. The mutual knowing of Jesus and "his own" is like the mutual and complete knowing that persists between himself and the Father.

This reading ends with a reference to *other sheep* who are Jesus' sheep and who must be brought into the one flock under one shepherd. Here, too, the reference moves beyond the setting in the gospel narrative and to the first-century Johannine church, in which converts may be Gentiles or at least persons beyond the social setting of the initial Johannine community. The concern for a "second generation" of followers of Jesus returns in

Jesus' prayer (17:20f), and both of these references express a desire for unity. Evidently in the Johannine church—as is likely to be the case in any rapidly growing community—there was some tension between "first generation" and "second generation" believers, and the evangelist addresses it through the voice of Jesus.

John 10:22-30 [Year C]. Jesus, who has put himself forward so boldly and challengingly, is questioned, *"Are you the Messiah? Tell us plainly."* He replies that his works, which he has done in his Father's name, have attested who he is. Yet many do not believe, because they do not belong to his *sheep.* Jesus seems to be saying that how he is perceived depends on where the questioner stands. Knowing him, like all important knowing, is "from the inside." But the sheep, for their part, do know the shepherd, and he gives them eternal life. Moreover, they cannot be snatched from his hand, for the hand is also the hand of the Father.

The reading ends with Jesus saying, *The Father and I are one* (vs. 30). The words will forever hold their mysteries, but it is clear that the evangelist is not talking ontology or trinitarian doctrine. Jesus, speaking in the thought idiom of the Fourth Gospel, says that he and the Father are one in mind, purpose, and action. His shepherding work is a concretization of the divine shepherding.

These readings for the Fourth Sunday of Easter speak to the baptizing church and to its newest members. The early church used shepherd and sheep imagery extensively to picture Jesus and believers, particularly new believers—the young lambs of the flock. In the earliest identifiable place of Christian worship, a now ruined house church in Dura Europos, a city on the eastern edge of the Roman Empire which was abandoned about 256 CE, there was a long room which had at one end a tub with an arch over it, which was obviously a baptismal pool. On the wall over this tub a crude scene was painted showing a shepherd with a lamb on his shoulders and a small flock moving with him. In this painting, the community was saying that to have been baptized was to have been brought into the flock of the Good Shepherd.

(3) Jesus' "Farewell."

On the fifth through the seventh Sundays of Easter, in all three years, the gospel readings turn to the "farewell" of Jesus in John's gospel (chapters 14-17). The usual pattern in John is *event,* followed by related *discourse*—as when Jesus meets the Samaritan woman at the well, and then speaks of living water (chapter 4), or after the sign of feeding, when he speaks of himself as the true bread from heaven (chapter 6). But the most important *event* in the Fourth Gospel, Jesus' crucifixion and resurrection (chapters 18-21), is interpreted by the *discourse* which precedes it, Jesus' farewell, the longest body of discourse in the gospel. Although Jesus speaks before the passion, he speaks of his departure (14:1-7, 28f; 16:28) and what lies beyond it. He describes the community of his followers living under the Spirit (14:16f, 26; 15:26f; 16:7-11, 12-15); doing the works that he has done, and greater works (14:12); praying in the name (14:13; 15:7; 16:26f); living in conflict with the world (15:18—16:4a)—but the community's members are deeply bound into the life that Jesus shares with the Father (14:18-24; 15:1-11; 16:27) and commanded to exhibit mutual love among themselves (13:34f; 15:12f). Clearly in chapters 13-16 Jesus is speaking about the post-Easter community of believers, and in chapter 17 he prays for it.

We shall sketch the portions of this farewell material which are used in the lectionary, but set them in their biblical order:

In *13:31-35 [Easter 5, Year C]*, Jesus opens his farewell with a highly compressed, almost poetic passage, speaking, first, of the exchange of glory between himself and the Father—an exchange in which his life and its coming climax are rooted (vss. 31f). He is glorified *now* (in the events that are beginning to unfold); and in his being glorified, God is glorified. He and the Father are so united that glory for either is at the same time glory for the other. Secondly, he speaks of his imminent departure, saying that he goes alone, although he will soon associate others with his "going" (vs. 33). And thirdly, the one who has just washed the feet of his followers leaves with them the "new commandment" that they love one another as he has loved them (vss. 34f).

Later Jesus will say that his followers (the baptized) are invited into the exchange of life and glory that persists between himself and the Father (14:21, 23; 17:22) and that the love among his disciples is a participation in the love that he shares with the Father (14:23; 15:9f; 17:26).

In *14:1-14 [Easter 5, Year A]*, Jesus' words about his departure have caused consternation, and he seeks to quiet his disciples' troubled hearts, saying that he is going to his Father's house, where he acts as a guest-master, preparing a place to which he will bring his friends. He will return and take his followers so that ultimately they will be with him where he has gone. This is a strikingly low-key revision of an eschatological pattern that appears in Paul's first extant writing. In 1 Thessalonians 4:16-18, Paul speaks in dramatic, apocalyptic terms of the return of Christ to take his people to be with him—the Lord descends from heaven with an archangel's cry; believers are caught up to meet him in the air. Although the large pattern of 1 Thessalonians 4:16-18 is reproduced in John 14:1-3, it is spoken from the point of view of the Johannine Jesus himself and in a quiet, almost domestic idiom. He is going to his Father's house, a place for which his followers are also destined. Although he goes alone, he has not forgotten his friends, but will return for them. The words are eschatology without trumpets.

Thomas, speaking for the group, tells Jesus that in order to be sure about the goal, they must know the way. He wants a map showing not only the destination but also the route. Jesus replies that he is the way—the true and living way—and to know him, as they do, is enough.

From language of going to the Father—language of movement—Jesus passes in verses 7-9 to non-spatial terms of *knowing* and *seeing*. Anyone who has seen or known Jesus has seen and known the Father. Jesus can say this about himself because of the mutual indwelling that persists between himself and the Father (vss. 10f). *Do you not know that I am in the Father, and the Father in me?* This indwelling comes to expression in Jesus' words and his works (vss. 10-11). Now, when Jesus goes to the Father, his own works and even greater works will be replicated in the works of his followers (vs. 12), but only through prayer (vss. 13f). In these verses Jesus assures the baptized that while in one sense he has departed, in another sense his life remains deeply shared with his people.

In *14:15-21 [Easter 5, Year B]*, in verses 15-17, Jesus introduces the figure of the Paraclete (translated "advocate" in the NRSV, with the reading "helper" in the margin). The Paraclete (who is identified as the Holy Spirit in 14:26) will be with the disciples permanently, as Jesus himself cannot be.

Then in an unexpected turn, Jesus, who has told his followers he is leaving them (13:33; 14:1-4), now says, *I will not leave you orphaned; I am coming to you* (14:18). His departure is real, but it cannot be understood apart from a countermovement, a *coming* to his people. His *going* is at the same time a *coming*; indeed, his *coming* depends on his prior *going*. Then Jesus sets aside his space metaphors and describes this "coming" in terms of "seeing" (vs. 19), "knowing" (vs. 20), "loving" (vs. 21), and self-revelation (vs. 21). All these terms describe a deep interpersonal relationship—a relationship which unites the disciples, Jesus, and the Father: *I am in my Father, and you in me, and I in you* (vs. 20). *Those who love me will be loved by my Father, and I will love them* (vs. 21).

[*14:8-17* is read on Pentecost, at the end of the Fifty Days, in years A, B, and C, and it will be discussed below. See p. 115.]

In *14:23-29 [Easter 6, Year C]*, Jesus in verse 23 makes the powerful affirmation, *Those who love me will keep my word, and my Father will love them, and we will come to them and make our home with them.* The one who has said, "I am leaving you and going to the Father's house, to which I will take you" (vss. 2f), now says, "The Father and I will come to you." The one who spoke of preparing a place (Greek *mone*) to which he would take his followers now speaks of his followers as the home (the same word, *mone*) in which he and the Father will come to dwell. Quite obviously, the movement that is Jesus' "going" to the Father is at the same time his (and the Father's) "coming." The evangelist subverts place images even as he uses them. This passage, read in Easter, says that Jesus, who is gone in one sense, is deeply present in another sense. Baptism opens one to be a place for the dwelling of God.

In these verses, the departing Jesus speaks of what he leaves with his people: his words (vs. 24), the Paraclete to teach (vs. 25), and his peace (vs. 26).

In *15:1-8 [Easter 6, Year A]*, Jesus uses the image of branches in a vine to speak of life in relation to himself. He himself is the vine; his Father is the careful vinegrower, and (although it is not said until verse 5) his followers are branches in him. The purpose of the vine is to bear fruit, and Jesus speaks of bearing and non-bearing branches. Otherwise Jesus is not interested in planting, tending and harvesting, or wine-making—unlike the vine images of the Jewish Bible or the agricultural parables of the synoptic gospels which speak of the life-history of a vine. Here Jesus speaks single-mindedly of the structure, the interconnectedness of the vine. Branches (baptized Christians) take their life from the vine (from Jesus). A detached branch is lifeless, fit only for the brush fire. The passage uses the word "abide" (simply "remain") seven times: *Abide in me as I abide in you.* The words dramatize the importance and the difficulty of remaining in the life that Jesus shares with his people and that is entered by baptism.

In *15:9-17 [Easter 6, Year B]*, Jesus links love with the keeping of his commandments, remarking that he keeps the Father's commandments (vss. 9-10). The obedience he requires, he models. Love, in the people of Christ, as in Jesus himself, is love in discipline. Having spoken of love, Jesus illustrates the quality of love by the supreme example, giving one's life for one's friends (vs. 13). Love is sacrificial.

As Jesus continues, he develops his own word, "friends." His followers are his friends, not his servants (vs. 15). He explains that a servant is commanded and must obey. But among friends it is otherwise. Friends listen to one another and share their minds with one another; the only consent one seeks from a friend is informed, willing consent (vs. 15). Read in Easter, this passage says that baptism admits us to a relationship in which we obey commandments, but we do so in a context of love, of sacrifice and of friendship.

[*16: (5-10) 12-15.* This lengthy passage about the Paraclete is not appointed for the Easter weeks, but is read on Trinity Sunday—appropriately, since, in the triadic language of the Discourse, the *Holy Spirit* comes because *Jesus* goes to the *Father.* The Paraclete, as described in this discourse, confronts and judges the world (vss. 7-11), but supports and nurtures the church (vss. 12-15).]

Chapter 17, Jesus' profound, but simply worded final prayer, is read on the last Sunday of the Easter season in all three lectionary years. The prayer, spoken in the unique voice of the Johannine Jesus, contains two kinds of material: Passages in which Jesus reviews his mission from the Father and his work on earth alternate with passages of petition, in which he asks things for himself or for his followers who remain in the world. The wording of the prayer fits Jesus' departure, but there is also a sub-text in which the evangelist is speaking about issues that were urgent in the first-century community.

Verses 1-11 [Year A] largely concern Jesus himself and his relation to the Father. Yet he always speaks in awareness of his work for others. *I glorified you on earth by finishing the work you gave me to do.* Jesus has glorified the Father and made the Father's name known (vss. 4, 6). He asks that those who belong to him (and to the Father as well, vss. 9f) be protected (vs. 11).

In *verses 11b-19 [Year B],* Jesus speaks of his followers, asking for their unity and for their protection in their encounter with the world's hatred—a world in which they live and serve, but from which they have been separated by the Father's word, which he has given them and by their faith in him: *They do not belong to the world, just as I do not belong to the world.* Hence they are in some peril.

In *verses 20-26 [Year C]*, the prayer widens to include the next generations of the church—*those who will believe in me through their word.* The urgent plea *that they all may be one* seems to refer in the prayer itself not to broad ecumenical issues (although it may be so applied), but specifically to friction between the original generation of the Johannine church and the second generation—the Christians at first hand and the Christians at second hand (vss. 21-23). Jesus ends by looking beyond history, praying that those who have been given to him may be with him to see his glory.

These farewell chapters of John do not mention baptism, and the images of water, bread and light, which have appeared in earlier chapters, and which some (but not all) interpreters take to be sacramental references, are missing from these discourses. Yet Jesus' final counsel is appropriate for the Easter-to-Pentecost period—the period of *mystagogia*—for in it he deals with the life into which one is brought by baptism. He describes an intimate exchange of life, love, and mutual knowing that persists between himself and his people. He shows himself to his followers and makes them his friends, with whom everything is shared. They are authorized to use his name in prayer. While he is no longer with them, they are supported and taught by the constant presence of the Holy Spirit. Indeed, Jesus and the Father make their home with and in them. For their part, they are to practice love for one another. Since the deepest mystery of the baptized life is the mystery of Christians' relation with their Lord, these chapters describe, perhaps more fully than anywhere else in the New Testament, the interiority of the life which the Christian lives in the church and the church lives in Christ.

(4) 1 Peter.

The entire book of 1 Peter, from which six post-Easter readings are taken in Year A, is so full of baptismal motifs and themes that it seems likely that it was written with a baptismal occasion in mind. The language sounds as though it were spoken rather than written, and the book (or at least 1:3—4:11) may have originated as a homily, giving encouragement to the newly baptized.[19]

Yet in 1 Peter, baptism is not described, and, indeed, it is only mentioned once (in 3:21). However, the thought of the book is permeated by suggestions of baptism. The English exegete, G. A. Beasley-Murray, says: "Does any other writing of the New Testament contain so much baptismal material in comparable proportions to that of 1 Pt.1:3—4:11? I doubt it."[20]

The homilist reminds his hearers, who may well be new converts, of the momentous thing that has happened to them: You have received *a new birth* (1:3) and are pledged a secure *inheritance* (1:4); you were *ransomed* (1:18); you have *purified your souls* (1:22); you have been *called out of darkness into. . .light* (2:9); you have *received mercy* (2:10); you are *called to follow in* Jesus' *steps* (2:21); you have been *healed* (2:24) and have *returned to the shepherd and guardian of your souls* (2:25).

The homily is full of contrasts—an idiom that is characteristic of converts who must talk about what they were and what by grace they have become. The hearers have been ransomed from slavery (1:18); brought from darkness to light and made a new people (2:9); brought from being no people to being God's people (2:10); healed from sickness (2:24); and returned from straying (2:25). Old ways of life have been left (1:14, 18; 4:3, 4), so much so that their former associates will wonder about them, 4:3f.

The passages that appear in the lectionary are:

1 Peter 1:3-9 [Easter 2].   The homilist begins in the praiseful prayer tone of the Jewish *berakah*, thanking God that his newly baptized hearers, with all Christians, have been given *a new birth* (1:3), a birth which promises *an imperishable inheritance* (1:4). The homilist says "now" twice and speaks directly to his hearers, saying "you" repeatedly, imparting a sense of immediacy; something important is happening *now* (see also 1:12; 2:10; 3:21, 25; 4:4). The speaker shares with his hearers the joy of an actualized redemption, saying at the very outset, *God. . .has given us a new birth into a living hope through the resurrection of Jesus Christ from the dead.*

1 Peter 1:17-23 [Easter 3].   As suits instruction for the newly baptized, the homilist mixes indicatives and imperatives. *You were ransomed. . .you have come to trust in God. . .you have purified your souls by obedience to the truth. . .You have been born anew.* Using the image of ransom, the homilist points to the one by whose blood his hearers have been bought into freedom (vss. 18-21). In another image, he says that his hearers' new birth is not *of perishable but of imperishable seed*; that is to say, their new birth is not from mortal, human generation, but from God (1:23). The *imperishable seed* from which they are born, he explains, is *the living and enduring word of God*, that is, the gospel which had been declared to them (1:25b). The powerful, active divine word which in the creation brought being from non-being and life from non-life has acted to bring these baptized persons to a new life through a new birth.

In the light of these things, the new Christians are to *live in reverent fear. . .*and *love one another deeply from the heart.*

1 Peter 2:19-25 [Easter 4].   Verses 18-25 are addressed specifically to Christians who are slaves, although the lectionary begins the reading with verse 19, allowing the homilist's counsel to slaves to be universalized. The homilist says that some of these Christians may suffer cruel and unjust treatment from their owners, but they must take care that if they suffer, it will not be for doing any wrong (vss. 19f). Then he develops the theme of innocent suffering by citing Jesus: *for to this you have been called, because Christ also suffered for you, leaving you an example, so that* you should follow in his steps (vs. 21). In a passage (vss. 22-25) which draws heavily on the Suffering Servant of Isaiah 53, the homilist weaves together two themes: Jesus' meekness and patience under suffering, and the redemptive effect of his sacrifice.

The homilist gives a context of meaning for a course of Christian passivity in the face of oppression, which may have been about all that his hearers, in their situation, could do. History at times offers Christians other situations which open other courses of action. But the power of the weak should not be underestimated.

[All the passages from 1 Peter are read in sequence except for this one. It is appointed for Easter 4 so that its reference to Christ as *the shepherd and guardian of your souls* will fall on the Sunday in which the gospel speaks of Jesus as the Good Shepherd.]

1 Peter 2:1-10 [Easter 5].   In a passage rich in ideas, the new Christians are urged to turn away from old ways of life and grow into salvation (vss. 1-3). In verses 4-8 the homilist plays with the word "stone." Christ himself is the cornerstone of God's building, although he is a stone over which some persons stumble and fall. New Christians have been built like living stones into *a spiritual house*—a temple in which they are (in a mixing of metaphors) at the same time not only building-stones which make up the temple, but holy priests who offer spiritual sacrifices within it. Drawing on the story of the making of the covenant between Yahweh and Israel (Ex. 19:6), the homilist tells his hearers that they are a holy nation, a nation of kings and priests, and heirs of the prerogatives of Israel. Drawing on Hosea 1:9; 2:23, the homilist describes his hearers as persons who had no identity as a people, but they have been made a people by God. The Christian community is not an ethnic identity, but a people shaped by a common call.

1 Peter 3:8-18 [Easter 6].   Baptism asks new commitments. Christians must exhibit traits suited for life in a new community of love and trust. The homilist has already said that his hearers must be holy (1:15f), and that they are to develop from the heart love for one another (1:22); dropping malice and guile (2:1), they are to love the family of believers (2:16), cultivating a gentle and quiet spirit (3:4). Now he says to the newly baptized that they should practice unity, sympathy, love, tenderness, and non-retaliation (3:8-10). Together the new Christians must be blameless before the world (3:13ff; cf. 2:11). The homilist enforces his point by citing a lengthy passage from Psalm 34 (3:8-12). Then in a piece of realism, he adds that even if you live so, you may suffer—only be sure that, like Christ, you suffer for doing good, not for doing evil (3:13-18). Baptism took persons out of their former collectivities and broke the terms that the society set for getting on in life. Loyalty to Christ could, and often did, make one a misunderstood outsider in one's own society. The baptismal life, the homilist says, is not an easy life.

[The important passage that speaks expressly of baptism, 3:15b-22, is omitted in this Easter survey of 1 Peter. It is appointed, however, for the Vigil for the Eve of the Baptism of Our Lord, and some comment is given below, pp. 133, 236, 276.]

1 Peter 4:12-19 [Easter 7].   The homilist is speaking to Christians who are suffering for their faith. They are *reviled for the name of Christ* (vs. 14). When this adversity comes upon them, they should not be surprised (vs. 12), but should rejoice, for as they share Christ's sufferings they will eventually share his glory (vs. 13). The Christians' suffering should never be for actual crime, but always innocent (vs. 15). In this suffering, they should *glorify God because you bear his name* (vs. 16). In this adversity, the Christians should *entrust themselves to a faithful Creator, while continuing to do good* (vs. 19).

During these weeks, in which the twentieth-century church is engaged in the task of *mystagogia,* it reads this New Testament call for courage— one that was surely written (or spoken) for new Christians, and perhaps for persons who had just been baptized.

(5) 1 John.

First John, which is read on the Sundays of Easter in Year B, has none of the marks of a letter and is more like a homily. While it has several recurrent themes, it has little structure and no sustained argument, but is made up of short passages. It seems to be written for young Christians who find their life in a hostile world bewildering. As elementary counsel for all Christians, but as especially suited for the newly baptized, it is used in the lectionary in the Easter-to-Pentecost weeks as follows:

1 John 5:1-6 [Easter 2].   To love God and to keep God's commandments are not opposites, but are in fact identified: *For the love of God is this, that we obey his commandments. And his commandments are not burdensome* (vss. 1-3). Those who, by believing that Jesus is the Christ, have been born of God are conquerors of the world: *And this is the victory that conquers the world, our faith* (vss. 4-6).

1 John 1:1—2:2 [Easter 3].   The human, tangible Jesus is identical with the divine Son of God. His death brings salvation. This is the true faith, given from the beginning, to which hearers should hold. Christian life is fellowship with God in faith and constant cleansing from sin.

Present-day readers who recall the promise in the Baptismal Covenant that, should one sin, one will repent and return (BCP, p. 304), may note that no book in the New Testament says more than 1 John says about sin among the baptized: *If we confess our sins, he who is faithful and just will forgive us our sins and cleanse us from all unrighteousness* (1:9).

1 John 3:1-8 [Easter 4].   Out of love, God has called Christians *children of God,* and the children of God are incomprehensible to the world (3:1). This divine calling, which creates tension with the world, at the same time pledges a future: *We are God's children now; what we will be has not yet been revealed* (3:2-3). The writer sees Christians set in a deep dualism (3:4-8). On the one side, *The devil has been sinning from the beginning,* and in something of a counter-family, the devil, too, has children—persons who commit sin, which is lawlessness. But on the other side, the sinless Christ was revealed in this deeply flawed situation *to take away sin.* Those who abide in him do not persist in sin.

1 John 3: (14-17) 18-24 [Easter 5].   Love for one's fellow Christians is a sign that one has *passed from death to life* (vss. 14-15). Love is on the model of Christ, who laid down his life for us. How can God's love abide in anyone who will not help a brother or sister in need (vss. 16-17)?

Love must be *in truth and action* rather than merely *in word or speech.* But one cannot love from a guilty, troubled heart. God, who knows everything, can overcome the heart that accuses itself (vss. 18-22). God's commandment is a dual commandment: *that we should believe in the name of his Son Jesus Christ and love one another.* All those who obey this commandment abide in God and God in them (vss. 23-24).

1 John 4:7-21 [Easter 6].   In a series of interwoven affirmations the author says: God is love (vss. 8, 16). God's love was revealed in the sending of the only Son into the world to be the atoning sacrifice for our sins (vs. 10). Everyone who loves is born of God, and those who are born of God ought to love one another (vss. 7-12).

This reading contains some of the sayings about love for which 1 John is best remembered: *God is love, and those who abide in love abide in God, and God abides in them* (4:16b). *There is no fear in love, for perfect love casts out fear* (4:18). *We love because he first loved us* (4:19). *Those who do not love a brother or sister whom they have seen, cannot love God whom they have not seen* (4:20).

1 John 5:9-15 [Easter 7].   Verses 9-12 are concerned with testimony, asking, "Who can validate Jesus Christ?" The author says often and in several ways that God gives testimony to his Son. In other words, the gospel is ultimate, self-validating. Nothing outside it is more convincing than it is. Nothing can make it convincing if the inner testimony of the gospel itself is not adequate.

The homily draws to a close speaking of answered prayer, a subject that appears several times in much these same terms in Jesus' farewell in John's gospel.

(6) Revelation.

The readings for the Sundays of Easter in Year C are from the book of Revelation.

Revelation 1: (1-8) 9-19 [Easter 2].   The authority of all that is to follow in this book is secured in the seer's opening vision of the living, reigning Christ (vss. 4f, 5b-6, 7, 8). Christ is seen in verses 9-19 as a figure of dignity, splendor, and authority. The prophet falls at his feet as though dead, but the stricken prophet is raised and commissioned (vss. 17-19).

Revelation 5:6-14 [Easter 3].   In a vision of heaven which begins in chapter 4, attention centers on a throne on which there sits a Lamb who is as though it has been slaughtered. Three hymns praise the worthiness of the Lamb. The first is sung by the heavenly elders, the second by many angels, and the third by *every creature in heaven and on earth and under the earth*. The idea of cosmic praise appears in the Jewish scriptures, but here it is given a dramatic visual setting, and it is all focused on the regal Lamb, i.e. the crucified, yet triumphant Christ. It is often thought that the components of this scene of ordered heavenly worship are projections of features of the worship of the first-century Christians.

Revelation 7:9-17 [Easter 4].   This passage is also read on All Saints' Day and is commented on below, p. 168.

Revelation 19:1, 4-9 [Easter 5].   The appointed verses use the word *hallelujah* (which means, "praise *Yah*," i.e., "praise the Lord") three times. The term is familiar from the Psalms and from the Christian praise tradition, but Revelation 19 is the only place in which it used in the New Testament. (Rev. 19:6b is one of the texts for Handel's "Hallelujah Chorus.") The scene is set in a heavenly throne room. A burst of praise comes from its inhabitants, and is answered by a voice *from the throne*, i.e. by the voice of God (vss. 4-5). Then a hymn is cried out by *the voice of a great multitude*, meaning all the redeemed, the fruit of the promise to Abraham. The hymn speaks fervently of *the marriage of the Lamb* for which the bride is made ready and favored guests are invited (vss. 7, 9). The words speak in metaphor of the union of Christ, as bridegroom, with the church, as bride. (The image also appears in Revelation 21:2, 9; 22:17; 2 Corinthians 11:2; and Ephesians 5:25-33—and in the Jewish scriptures, Israel is spoken of as the bride of Yahweh in Isaiah 54:5 and Hosea 2:19-20. In both the Jewish and the Christian uses, a large, continuing community is spoken of as a single individual.) The marriage itself is not described. The image signifies love and joyful union.

Revelation 21:22—22:5 [Easter 5].   The Christian visionary sees the New Jerusalem. It contains no temple, but (as was not true in the vision of the heavenly temple in Ezek. 40-43) God and the Lamb are the Temple; they are accessible to everyone everywhere. The city is full of light, not of the sun or moon, but of the glory of God. Through the city there runs a life-giving river. In contrast to the Jewish tradition in which no one can see God (Ex. 33:20; Deut. 4:12), the citizens of this city will see God's face.

Some of these passages from Revelation, read during the post-baptism weeks of Easter, suggest—in vivid, but not always easy symbolism—that by baptism one is introduced into a glory-filled life which participates now in the praise of heaven. Some of these visions also support Christians who now live in conflict with the world and must endure. These readings look, finally, beyond the present conflicts and seize the promised future.

(7) Acts.

On the days of Easter Week and on the seven Sundays following, in all three years, the lectionary appoints readings from Acts. Through them the present-day church encounters the church of the first years—its Spirit-given vigor and courage, its struggle with opposition, its growing insight into its own message and task, its geographical spread, its maturation, and its many colorful people.

In Prayer Books since the sixteenth century, the book of Acts had little place in the eucharistic lectionary, being used as the liturgical epistle only on Pentecost and on the feast days of persons who figured in the Acts narrative. Yet the book of Acts needs to be heard in the preaching and teaching life of the church, for without it there is no transition from the Palestinian world of the gospels to the context of the apostolic letters. When we read Paul's letters addressed to Corinth, if we did not have Acts, we would have to wonder, "Who is Paul, and how did there come to be Christians in Corinth?"

Many, but not all parishes celebrate the Holy Eucharist on the weekdays of Easter Week, but congregations, as a rule, are small. However, the passages from Acts that the lectionary provides as alternative first readings on the Sundays from Easter to Pentecost touch the people of the church directly.

When during the weeks following Easter, the twentieth-century church reads through the rapidly moving incidents in Acts, the appointed readings might be thought of as a vivid account of the "greater works" that Jesus in John 14:12 said his followers would do in the power of the Spirit because he was going to the Father. The church is the place in which the living Christ dwells, the instrument by which he acts in the world. Hence, in a season concerned with membership in Christ and his people, we read this record of the early events in the life of this concrete, flesh-and-blood community of faith.

In the Sunday lectionary which carries the church through the vivid episodes of Acts, there is little effort to match the readings from Acts with the liturgical gospels. We therefore note them briefly, not in their Sunday-by-Sunday groupings, but in their order in the book of Acts.

Before Pentecost

Two readings from the earliest section of Acts are appointed for the last of the Sundays of Easter. They serve as a preparation for the coming Feast of Pentecost.

Acts 1: (1-7) 8-14 [Easter 7, Year A].   The risen Jesus tells his disciples to wait for the promise of the Spirit. After Jesus ascends, his closest followers, with his family, wait in Jerusalem.

Acts 1:15-26 [Easter 7, Year B].   Matthias is chosen to replace Judas and to be, with the other associates of Jesus, a witness to his resurrection.

The community in Jerusalem

The coming of the Spirit (2:1-13) is read on Pentecost in all three years. Peter's speech and the events that follow it are read on Easter 2 and 3, Year A.

Acts 2:14a, 22-32 [Easter 2, Year A].   On the Day of Pentecost, Peter addresses the curious crowd, telling the story of Jesus. This story, told in summary or at length, will be the principal content of Christian preaching. The verses for this Sunday show Peter using Joel 2:28-32 to speak of the Spirit and Psalm 16:8-11 to speak of Jesus. The prophecies are being fulfilled.

Acts 2:14a, 36-47 [Easter 3, Year A].   Peter's sermon concludes, calling for a response. Peter says that *"the promise is for you, for your children, and for all who are far away, everyone whom the Lord our God calls."* Many are converted. The community lives quietly and harmoniously, having the regard of all.

Acts 3:12a, 13-15, 17-26 [Easter 2, Year B].   When people marvel at the healing of a lame man, Peter sets the act in the context of Jesus' mission, which he summarizes (vss. 12-15). Saying that God had *foretold through all the prophets, that his Messiah would suffer,* Peter cites Deuteronomy 18:15-20 and mentions Samuel and Abraham. Again, the saving (healing) events are interpreted as the fulfillment of divine promises.

Acts 4:5-12 [Easter 3, Year B].   Peter and John are arrested for giving witness to Jesus. Peter, speaking before the high priest and the council, says that the healing of a crippled beggar (3:1-9) was in the name of the Jesus who had been rejected by human judgment, but vindicated by God and appointed the savior of all. He secures his point by citing Psalm 118:22, which seems to have been a favorite Christian text.

Acts 4: (23-31) 32-37 [Easter 4, Year B].   The apostolic community (citing Ps. 2:1-2) prays that it might have boldness before hostile authorities. Among themselves, the Christians held everything in common; there were none who were needy.

Acts 5:12a, 17-22, 25-29 [Easter 2, Year C].   The apostles are arrested, but are delivered from prison and resume their preaching. When they are forbidden, on the highest authority, to speak further, Peter and the apostles answer, *"We must obey God rather than any human authority."*

Acts 6:1-9; 7:2a, 51-60 [Easter 4, Year A].   When the apostles are burdened with tasks that others could do, seven men are chosen to serve, one of whom is Stephen. Stephen is arrested, not for serving, but for his acts and his speech. His vigorous defense to the council, arguing that prophets have always been persecuted, is rejected angrily. He is seized, taken out of the city, and stoned to death. He is the first Christian martyr.

The work of Philip

The Christian movement spreads beyond Jerusalem.

Acts 8:26-40 [Easter 5, Year B].   Philip (one of those who had been set apart to serve) goes to Samaria, where he preaches and gathers eager converts. He later meets a god-fearing Ethiopian eunuch who is returning to his land in his chariot, reading Isaiah as he rides. He takes Philip as a rider and hears from him the story of Jesus. He is converted and baptized.

The conversion of Saul and the start of his work as a Christian

Acts 9:1-19a [Easter 3, Year C].   Saul, on his way to Damascus to apprehend the Christians there, is struck to the ground and blinded by a light from heaven. Saul, sensing that someone is trying to reach him, asks, *"Who are you, Lord?"* A voice, which identifies itself as *"Jesus, whom you are persecuting,"* sends him into the city. There he is visited by a Christian, Ananias, who baptizes him; and his sight is restored.

Acts 11:19-30 [Easter 6, Year B].   Because of persecution at Jerusalem, the church's spread extends further. Unnamed Christians gather a group of believers at Antioch. Barnabas, an admired Christian, is sent there. He finds Saul, who has understandably been distrusted, and puts him into a role of leadership. The outlying communities send help to the needy in Jerusalem.

The early missionary journeys of Paul and Barnabas

The wider spread of the gospel continues under Paul and his companion.

Acts 13:15-16, 26-33 (34-39) [Easter 4, Year C].   Barnabas and Saul set out on a missionary journey (during which "Saul" becomes "Paul," and "Barnabas and Paul" becomes "Paul and Barnabas"). Paul, now the spokesman, preaches in the synagogue at Antioch (another Antioch, Antioch of Pisidia), again telling the story of Jesus and the fulfillment in him of what was said in the Psalms and the prophets.

Acts 13:44-52 [Easter 5, Year C].   The Pauline mission, which has begun in synagogues, no longer seeks a hearing exclusively among Jews, but turns to welcome the Gentiles. As in the earlier stages of the mission, this development is justified by scripture (Isa. 49:6).

Acts 14:8-18 [Easter 6, Year C].   When, in Lystra, a lame man is healed, the crowds in the city want to treat Paul and Barnabas as gods in human form. The apostles protest, *"We are mortals just like you, and we bring you good news, that you should turn from these worthless things to the living God."* With some difficulty, the townspeople are dissuaded from offering sacrifice to the Christian missionaries.

The mission of Paul and Silas into Macedonia and Athens

Paul has a new associate, Silas, and their journeys carry them into Europe.

Acts 16:16-34 [Easter 7, Year C].   At Philippi, Paul and Silas challenge a necromancer, whose owners have them imprisoned. In prison, the Christian missionaries pray and sing at midnight. There is an earthquake, and the jailer, fearing that his prisoners may escape, rushes to Paul and Silas asking what he should do. They tell him the Christian message. He believes, and he and his household are baptized at once.

Acts 17:1-15 [Easter 5, Year A].   The missionary work of Paul and Silas at Thessalonica causes an uproar. When they escape to Beroea, they represent the gospel in the synagogue, with some response. But when those in Thessalonica hear of it, trouble pursues Paul and Silas there.

Acts 17:22-31 [Easter 6, Year A]. Paul in Athens, the seat of culture and thought, makes an address in which he seeks to establish some common ground between his gospel (and its Jewish presuppositions) and the thought world of his hearers. He speaks of universal religious hunger and of the one creator. Yet at the same time he must witness to Christ. His hearers listen interestedly until Paul mentions the resurrection. Then they turn away.

The passages from Acts that are read in the Sunday lectionary leave out some important incidents, such as Peter's visit to the house of Cornelius, the "council" at Jerusalem, and Paul's mission at Ephesus and his eventful voyages. But Acts is read consecutively in the Daily Office lectionary in the weeks of Proper 6 through 16 of Year One. Clearly the church of Acts is a baptizing community, but neither the lectionary readings for the Easter weeks nor the comments that are made here emphasize baptism. However, chapter 9, below, discusses the church of Acts as an evangelizing, baptizing community and deals with some of the emphases, as well as the complications, in the accounts. The lectionary readings for the Easter-to-Pentecost weeks provide a sense of the vitality of the early church. As *mystagogia*, they tell the newly baptized a great deal about the community into which they have recently come.

(8) Non-continuous readings from the Jewish Scriptures.

In all three lectionary years, readings from the Jewish scriptures are listed as alternatives to the readings from Acts, as the readings from Acts are listed as alternatives to the readings from the epistles. The passages from the scriptures of Israel are expressions of God's compassion, restoration, faithfulness, and promise.

Genesis 8:6-16; 9:8-16 [Easter 2, Year A]. After the flood, God makes a covenant with Noah and with physical nature. The creation depends on God, who pledges never again to overturn its order. (Gen. 9:8-16 is also the first reading for Lent 1, Year B.)

Exodus 28:1-4, 9-10, 29-30 [Easter 7, Year B]. The vestments of the high priest are prescribed, emphasizing the precious stones that carry the names of the tribes of Israel when the priest goes into the holy place. He acts as representative and intercessor.

Numbers 27:12-23 [Easter 4, Year C]. Joshua, *a man in whom is the spirit,* is appointed to lead the people into the promised land, as Moses cannot.

Leviticus 19:1-2, 9-18 [Easter 5, Year C]. Israel is to be holy, for God is holy. Holiness, primarily a cultic demand, also requires compassion, honesty, and truthfulness. *You shall love your neighbor as yourself: I am the LORD.*

Deuteronomy 4:32-40 [Easter 5, Year B]. The unique experience of Israel bears witness to the uniqueness and incomparability of God: *There is no other.*

Deuteronomy 6:20-25 [Easter 5, Year A]. Each generation of Israelites should be taught to acknowledge the divine laws by being told the story of God's emancipation of the people from slavery.

1 Samuel 12:19-24 [Easter 7, Year C]. Although the people have erred by seeking a king, God will not forsake them. They will be given spiritual leaders who will intercede for them and instruct them.

Nehemiah 9:6-15 [Easter 4, Year A]. In a long prayer of confession, Ezra recalls the goodness of God to Israel, retelling in the prayer the story of God's sustenance in the exodus.

Job 42:1-6 [Easter 2, Year C]. After God, from the whirlwind, has asked overwhelming questions, Job is humbled; he had spoken beyond his knowledge and will do so no more.

Isaiah 26:2-9, 19 [Easter 2, Year B]. God has defended Jerusalem and defeated its enemies, so it sings a processional song of victory.

Isaiah 43:1-12 [Easter 3, Year A]. God, who created Israel, will redeem Israel. God will gather the exiles. *Do not fear, for I am with you.*

Isaiah 45:11-13, 18-19 [Easter 6, Year B]. God created the world and humanity in it. God makes the great nations do his bidding. Israel was not made for chaos; its ways will be put in order by God.

Jeremiah 32:36-41 [Easter 3, Year C]. Although God's judgment brought about the fall of Jerusalem, God will restore. *I will give them one heart and one way that they may fear me.*

Ezekiel 34:1-10 [Easter 4, Year B].   God is against the false shepherds (the unjust rulers) who have exploited the people. *I will rescue my sheep from their mouths.* (The passage is matched with Jn. 10:11-16 about the Good Shepherd who rescues his sheep and even lays down his life for them.)

Ezekiel 39:21-29 [Easter 7, Year A].   Israel which went into captivity because of its iniquity will be restored to security in its own land. God says, *I will never again hide my face from them.*

Joel 2:21-27 [Easter 6, Year C].   After years of occupation and devastation, the land will be restored, with abundant rain and productive soil. God says, *You shall know that I am in the midst of Israel.*

Micah 4:1-5 [Easter 3, Year B].   The nations will be established under the God of Jacob in peace and security. *And no one shall make them afraid.*

The rubric in *The Book of Occasional Services* which commends the readings of Year A for use before Easter when there are adult baptisms at Easter (p.128), also recommends that when there are such baptisms, the Easter-to-Pentecost readings, regardless of the actual lectionary year, follow Year A as well. These readings have all been noted above, but set in the order in which they appear in the lectionary, they are:

Easter 2: John 20:19-31; Acts 2:14a, 22-32 *or* Gen. 8:6-16; 9:8-16;
      1 Peter 1:3-9 *or* Acts 2:14a, 22-32

Easter 3: Luke 24:13-35; Acts 2:14a, 36-47 *or* Isaiah 43:1-12;
      1 Peter 1:17-23 *or* Acts 2:14a, 36-47

Easter 4: John 10:1-10; Acts 6:1-9; 7:2a, 51-60 *or* Nehemiah 9:6-15;
      1 Peter 2:19-25 *or* Acts 6:1-9; 7:2a, 51-60

Easter 5: John 14:1-14; Acts 17:1-15 *or* Deuteronomy 6:20-25;
      1 Peter 2:1-10 *or* Acts 17:1-15

Easter 6: John 15:1-8; Acts 17:22-31 *or* Isaiah 41:17-20;
      1 Peter 3:8-18 *or* Acts 17:22-31

Easter 7: John 17:1-11; Acts 1: (1-7) 8-14 *or* Ezekiel 39:21-29;
      1 Peter 4:12-19 *or* Acts 17:1-11

D. THE PENTECOST VIGIL AND PENTECOST

The liturgical year developed in the church following the time-scheme of Luke/Acts, in which Jesus' resurrection is followed after forty days by his ascension (Lk. 24:50-53; Acts 1:3) and after seven weeks by the feast of Pentecost, on which the Spirit is given (Acts 2:1-42).

These three events, Easter, Ascension, and Pentecost, standing in a linear sequence, should not suggest that the redemptive realities of resurrection, ascension, and the Spirit are distinct. In the light of the total New Testament witness, they should be understood as moments in, or aspects of, a unified redemptive work. No other part of the New Testament literature follows this Luke/Acts time line. Matthew 28 identifies no period of time between Easter morning and the Ascension (although, since it does speak of a changed location, Mt. 28:16, perhaps a later time is implied). The Fourth Gospel, as we shall note more fully below, virtually identifies Jesus' death with his resurrection, ascent to the Father, and the giving of the Spirit. None of the epistles suggests any separation between the Christ-event and the Spirit-event, and none makes any reference to the Day of Pentecost events that Acts narrates so circumstantially.

Nevertheless, the Luke/Acts time-scheme which is held before us by the liturgical year says something important. In this sequence, Jesus, in his final encounter with his disciples, tells them to *"stay in the city until you have been clothed with power from on high"* (Lk. 24:49b), and the motif of waiting is repeated when, in the opening verses of Acts, at the time of his departure, Jesus directs his followers to wait for the baptism of the Spirit which will equip them to be witnesses (Acts 1:5, 8). At the end of the gospel narrative, Jesus is risen, and his community knows it. But something further must happen.

This holding back of the Spirit seems to be the Lukan way of saying that the church is not fully the church, equipped to do its work, apart from its endowment with "power from on high." The church is not an agency with a leader, a purpose, and a program, needing the Spirit as an empowerment to make its work successful. The church is not in charge of its own life, drawing on the Spirit for occasional bursts of fresh energy. Rather, without the Spirit, the church is nothing. Or perhaps it is less than nothing—only a deluded group setting about its work in the self-sufficient, self-important ways in which human groups tend to set about their work.

The Spirit does not come in to supplement such efforts, but to judge and reconstruct them. The event of Pentecost—coming after Jesus' earthly work is over, and following a period of expectant waiting—speaks of the Spirit as a power which is not of ourselves. Although it dwells in the church, it first comes to the church. The Spirit is, in John V. Taylor's fine phrase, "the beyond in the midst."[21] While the Spirit takes up into its work the created life it has made, it is not properly understood as an immanent force—as the human spirit writ large, or the spirit of the times or of the community or the culture. It has its origin in the transcendent. It breaks and refashions the material that the Christian community derives from the culture. It takes its rise from the free initiative of God. It is *power from on high* (Lk. 24:49).

Liturgical time was handled in the early church in a way that indicated the deep connection between the reality of the risen Christ and the reality of the Spirit. As we have had occasion to note, in the early church Easter was not regarded as a day, but as a period of fifty days, celebrating the risen Christ living among his people. Easter Day was not an end and climax so much as it was the beginning of a celebratory season signifying a new age that had dawned in Christ; and Pentecost marked the end of the days of Easter. When the early church began to baptize at Easter, baptisms which could not be observed at the Easter Vigil, the beginning of the Fifty Days, were held for the end of the period at Pentecost. We noted earlier that Tertullian commended Easter, or "Passover," as the preferred day for baptism. But in the same passage, he says, "After that, Pentecost is a most auspicious period for arranging baptisms."[22]

Pentecost as a time for Christian initiation reinforces the theological connection between baptism and the inner agency of the Holy Spirit and underlines the strong emphasis on the Spirit within the baptismal rite itself. Since baptism is *full initiation by water and the Holy Spirit into Christ's Body the Church* (BCP, p.298), it, and not some act or experience beyond or in addition to it, ministers the Spirit.

THE PENTECOST VIGIL

The church's life of worship has often continued the Jewish way of counting a day as beginning at sundown on the previous day, hence the custom of vigils. The Prayer Book invites congregations to prepare for Pentecost by a Vigil, as they do for Easter.

The Prayer Book (pp. 175, 227) outlines a rite for the Vigil of Pentecost which begins with the Service of Light (BCP, p. 109) and passes to readings from scripture. Seven readings are listed in the lectionary (BCP, pp. 896, 906, 917). Four of them are from the Jewish scriptures, and they are the same for all three lectionary years. *Three or more of the appointed Lessons are read before the Gospel, each followed by a Psalm, canticle, or hymn* (rubric, pp.175, 227). Since the Vigil is a part of the Day of Pentecost, it, like the Day itself, is a time appropriate for baptism. *Holy Baptism. . .follows the Sermon.* (When a bishop is present, Confirmation or the Renewal of Baptismal Vows may take place at this point in the rite.)

The readings for the Vigil are as follows.

The Tower of Babel: Genesis 11:1-9

Now the whole earth had one language and the same words. And as they migrated from the east, they came upon a plain in the land of Shinar and settled there. And they said to one another, "Come, let us make bricks, and burn them thoroughly." And they had brick for stone, and bitumen for mortar. Then they said, "Come, let us build ourselves a city, and a tower with its top in the heavens, and let us make a name for ourselves; otherwise we shall be scattered abroad upon the face of the whole earth." The LORD came down to see the city and the tower, which mortals had built. And the LORD said, "Look, they are one people, and they have all one language; and this is only the beginning of what they will do; nothing that they propose to do will now be impossible for them. Come, let us go down, and confuse their languages there, so that they will not understand one another's speech." So the LORD scattered them abroad from there over the face of all the earth, and they left off building the city. Therefore it was called Babel, because the LORD confused the language of all the earth; and from there the LORD scattered them abroad over the face of all the earth.

As the story of the Tower of Babel has it, the world's people originally had a single language. Having settled in one place, they determined to build a city and a high tower to the heavens to make a name for themselves. God saw their work and its arrogance, and, lest it succeed because of the unity of human language, God confused the languages of earth so that groups could not understand one another. The language communities were scattered, and the tower remained unfinished.

This story is not historical anthropology, but myth. It was originally no doubt etiological, intended to account for the variety of human languages. And it may have been suggested by the presence in the land of ancient and grand, but unfinished brick structures. But the ancient myth is profound and perennially relevant. As Reinhold Niebuhr said in the mid-thirties, "Every civilization and every culture is a tower of Babel."[23]

All human communities are communities of discourse, bound by words in significant relation. Each person constructs a self and a world by means of the shared language that surrounds one from birth. But the languages are not the same; people from different language communities can only understand one another with difficulty. To a great extent things said in one language can be translated into others, suggesting some sort of universality in the language-making capacity. Yet language separates groups from one another, just as it unites persons within a group. There is an inevitable human tendency to develop collective pride around one's own language community and to look down on those one cannot understand or to whom one cannot make oneself understood. This ancient biblical story sees the multiplicity of languages in moral terms, saying that the unity of the human community is broken, at the crucial point of verbal communication, as divine judgment on pride and ambition.

The placement of this story on the Vigil of Pentecost intends that we link it with the Day of Pentecost in Jerusalem, when persons of different languages could all understand the apostles' witness to *God's mighty deeds of power*. The account in Acts makes no explicit reference to the Tower of Babel, but it is hard to suppose that a link is not implied. The Spirit binds persons from *all tribes and peoples and languages* (Rev. 7:9) into a community of understanding. Redemption addresses the ruin and division brought about by sin and pride. Baptism is a sign of the new unity created in Christ and the Spirit.

With Psalm 33:12-22

(see pp. 50, 118)

Israel encamped before Mount Sinai: Exodus 19:1-9, 16-20a; 20:18-20

On the third new moon after the Israelites had gone out of the land of Egypt, on that very day, they came into the wilderness of Sinai. They had journeyed from Rephidim, entered the wilderness of Sinai, and camped in the wilderness; Israel camped there in front of the mountain. Then Moses went up to God; the LORD called to him from the mountain, saying, "Thus you shall say to the house of Jacob, and tell the Israelites: You have seen what I did to the Egyptians, and how I bore you on eagle's wings and brought you to myself. Now therefore if you obey my voice and keep my covenant, you shall be my treasured possession out of all the peoples. Indeed, the whole earth is mine, but you shall be for me a priestly kingdom and a holy nation. These are the words that you shall speak to the Israelites."

So Moses came, summoned the elders of the people, and set before them all these words that the LORD had commanded him. The people all answered as one: "Everything that the LORD has spoken we will do." Moses reported the words of the people to the LORD. Then the LORD said to Moses, "I am going to come to you in a dense cloud, in order that the people may hear when I speak with you and so trust you ever after."

On the morning of the third day there was thunder and lightning, as well as a thick cloud on the mountain, and a blast of a trumpet so loud that all the people who were in the camp trembled. Moses brought the people out of the camp to meet God. They took their stand at the foot of the mountain. Now Mount Sinai was wrapped in smoke, because the LORD had descended upon it in fire; the smoke went up like the smoke of a kiln, while the whole mountain shook violently. As the blast of the trumpet grew louder and louder, Moses would speak and God would answer him in thunder. When the LORD descended upon Mount Sinai, to the top of the mountain, the LORD summoned Moses to the top of the mountain, and Moses went up.

When all the people witnessed the thunder and lightning, the sound of the trumpet, and the mountain smoking, they were afraid and trembled and stood at a distance, and said to Moses, "You speak to us, and we will listen; but do not let God speak to us, or we will die." Moses said to the people, "Do not be afraid; for God has come only to test you and to put the fear of him upon you so that you do not sin."

Pentecost began as a Jewish agricultural festival, called the Feast of Weeks or Firstfruits. Over time (in a process that lasted into the Christian Era but which had begun long before) the feast was transformed into a celebration of the giving of the law at Mount Sinai—the reason for the appointment of this reading at the Vigil of Pentecost.

(Exodus 19:1 figured in the determination of the date of Pentecost. It was interpreted to mean that Israel came to Sinai fifty days after leaving Egypt, hence Firstfruits was observed fifty days after Passover.)

In the narrative of Exodus, the people of Israel, free from Egypt and after some journeying, are encamped before Mount Sinai, where they encounter God and enter into the covenant with God that forever marked their distinctive existence. Whatever memory of actual events is retained in the account, the story as it has been transmitted is deeply permeated by symbolic interpretive features: the mountain and Moses going up to God and returning to the people at its foot, the sound and sight of the violent storm, the voice of God calling from the mountain. No doubt, thanks to the prophets and later experience, more was understood about the exodus by the time the story was written than was understood at the time of the actual events, and the account is told in such a way as to imply its rich significance for Israel's relation to Yahweh.

When Moses goes up the mountain, God gives him a message for the people, reminding them of what has been done for them in rescuing them from Egypt and calling on them to obey. If they do, they will be God's *treasured possession out of all the peoples. . .a priestly kingdom and a holy nation* (vss. 3-6). Moses assembles the people and reports God's words. They pledge themselves unitedly to obey (vs. 7).

In this exchange, God reminds the people, *"You have seen what I did,"* and they respond, *"Everything that God has spoken we will do."* This initiative by God and the consent by the people is the constitutive covenanting act in the history of Israel. It remains an anchor point for later Jewish prophets who seek to recall the nation to its original bond with God.

The people keep a safe distance at the foot of the mountain as they witness a terrifying display of divine power—a crescendo trumpet blast, smoke, earthquake, and thunder. (The terms are those of a storm god; compare Ps. 18:7-15 and Ps. 29). Moses is called to the top of the mountain and is then sent back to warn the people severely against drawing too close. Then he is summoned again to the mountain, this time with Aaron; but the people must keep back, lest the Lord *break out against them* (vss. 16-25). The scene held before Israel—as it holds before Christians who seek a comfortable God—the sense of God's mystery and otherness.

[At this point in the text of Exodus, Moses goes down to the people and delivers the Ten Commandments (20:1-17). They seem more terrified by the smoke on the mountain than focused on the divine imperative; they ask that Moses, not God, speak to them (20:18-19). The liturgical reading for the Vigil gives the context, but omits the commandments themselves. The giving of the Ten Commandments, omitting the scene-setting, is the reading for Lent 3, Year B.]

When the people ask that Moses, rather than God, speak to them, Moses replies that God has set these forbidding conditions *so that you do not sin.*

This passage is the principal source of Israel's sense of itself as *a priestly kingdom and a holy nation*—a sense of corporate identity that the Christian community applied to itself (1 Pet. 2:5, 9; Rev. 1:6). This designation is echoed in the liturgy and hymns of baptism. When this passage is read at the Vigil of Pentecost, it reminds Christians of the "New Covenant" in Christ which is described in "An Outline of the Faith" (BCP, p. 850f), and is articulated in the "Baptismal Covenant" (BCP, p. 304f), and which we enter at baptism.

With Canticle 2 or 13

These two canticles are the same passage, Canticle 2 in traditional rhetoric and Canticle 13 in contemporary rhetoric. The source is the Song of the Three Young Men, an addition to the book of Daniel—a fictional addition to an already fictional story, told to encourage Jews to be faithful. The three young Jewish captives in the midst of the fiery furnace do an irrational thing; they sing a hymn of praise to God. These canticles make no reference to this setting, but are expressions of the blessedness/the glory of God.

The valley of dry bones: Ezekiel 37:1-14

Ezekiel's vision is also appointed for the Easter Vigil and was commented on above (pp. 58, 266). The gift of life by the breath of God's Spirit makes this reading especially appropriate to Pentecost.

With Psalm 130

This psalm is a deeply felt appeal for help, well matched with the reading from Ezekiel. Crying from the depths, the psalmist asks to be heard (BCP vs. 1; NRSV vss. 1-2); he anticipates forgiveness (BCP vss. 2-3; NRSV vss. 3-4) and expresses an attitude of devout waiting and hope (BCP vss.4-5; NRSV vss. 5-6). The psalmist turns to the people, calling on Israel to *wait for the LORD. . . .and he shall redeem Israel from all their sins.*

Joel 2:28-32

The lectionary appoints for the Pentecost Vigil the passage from Joel which Peter uses on the Day of Pentecost, verses which are also appointed as an alternative reading for Pentecost in Year C and which will be commented on below (p. 108).

With Canticle 9

This canticle from Isaiah 55 is also appointed as a reading for the Great Vigil of Easter (p. 53), where it carries the heading "Salvation offered freely to all."

Acts 2:1-11

At the Vigil, the account of the events in Jerusalem at Pentecost may be read. The passage is appointed for the eucharist of Pentecost, and comment on it will be made in connection with that day and its scriptures (p. 103.)

With Psalm 104:25-32

These psalm verses are one of the portions for the Day of Pentecost and are commented on below (p. 117).

Romans 8:14-17, 22-27

For all who are led by the Spirit of God are children of God. For you did not receive a spirit of slavery to fall back into fear, but you have received a spirit of adoption. When we cry "Abba! Father!" it is the Spirit bearing witness with our spirit that we are children of God, and if children, then heirs, heirs of God and joint heirs with Christ—if, in fact, we suffer with him so that we may be glorified with him. . . .

We know that the whole creation has been groaning in labor pains until now; and not only the creation, but we ourselves, who have the firstfruits of the Spirit, groan inwardly while we wait for adoption, the redemption of our bodies. For in hope we were saved. Now hope that is seen is not hope. For who hopes for what is seen? But if we hope for what we do not see, we wait for it with patience.

Likewise the Spirit helps us in our weakness; for we do not know how to pray as we ought, but that very Spirit intercedes with sighs too deep for words. And God, who searches the heart, knows what is the mind of the Spirit, because the Spirit intercedes for the saints according to the will of God.

Paul's thought in verses 14-17 is structured by a family image. The Spirit makes persons children of God. In Paul's theology, estrangement between God and humanity must be overcome; persons are not children of God by reason of their humanity, but are delivered from the fear and anxiety of slaves and adopted as the free children of God's family by grace.

The powerful image of adoption says that God's gracious initiative has brought us into the divine family with the status of sons and daughters. Adopted children are always wanted children. Our new situation touches us inwardly, for the Spirit gives testimony within us to our new condition. The personal engagement of God with human life is an engagement of Spirit with spirit, *the Spirit bearing witness with our spirit*. The Spirit not only makes us children of God, the Spirit works within to make us conscious of the new relation.

Describing the heart of the divine-human relation, Paul says that God reaches persons in grace. However, the divine outreach must elicit response. Then, going into the relation more deeply, Paul says that the human response is itself God-given. It is the work of the Spirit within. The same Spirit which bears witness to a believer of God's kindness is the power by which a believer replies.

The Spirit-prompted response takes the form of speech—confessional speech which is addressed to God before it is addressed to anyone else. The vocative case is primary. In our earliest emotional experience, before we have the category "mother" or "father" by which to speak *about* our parents, we say directly and spontaneously "Mommy" and "Daddy." We speak *to* them before we are able to speak *about* them. This second-person speech is an immediate witness to our relatedness. In the family and indeed in all intimate relations, our "you" precedes and determines any "she" or "he" we may come to say. (If we do come to know about a person before we meet him or her, when we say "you," all our prior third-person knowledge is suddenly up for revision in the light of personal encounter.) The Spirit, Paul says, prompts within a believer an immediate awareness of God and one's intimate bond as a child of God, and this Spirit-given awareness prompts a spontaneous cry, *"Abba! Father!"*

Paul's term *Abba* is an Aramaic word—a term of intimacy and endearment which Jesus himself used in speaking to God (Mk. 14:36). His followers seem to have recalled his very syllables. Greek-speaking Christians used Jesus' word, as though his own relation to God had been opened to them by the *adoption* of which Paul speaks (see also Gal. 4:6). When they spoke to the Father who had brought them into the family, the words they used were theirs, of course. But before they were their words, they were Jesus' words—his words, made over to Christians by the inner witness of the Spirit.

Today the term *Abba,* which was immediately accessible in Jesus' culture, is remote and must be explained. (But Paul's Greek-speaking readers would have had to learn it, just as we would.) We may take the apostle to be saying that a person who believes is drawn into a new personal, parent-child relationship, in which one speaks in awe-struck, yet intimate, recognition. He would certainly allow us to characterize God in the available heartfelt vocabulary. The *Good News Bible* translates *"Father! my Father!"*

This new relation with God gives much now, but it is also full of promise, for, unlike slaves, the children of the family are heirs. Since the membership in the family is conferred in Christ, who is himself God's child, those who are in him are heirs of God and *joint heirs with Christ*.

But Paul does not encourage unreality. The promise of eventual glory does not exempt one from suffering; however, both the suffering and the glory that lies beyond the suffering are with Christ.

In verses 22-27, Paul, who has spoken of the inward life of Christians, enlarges his thought to cosmic scale. (The two are not discrepant. In biblical thought, humanity and the physical world are regarded as linked in creation, fallenness, redemption, waiting, and destiny.) The whole creation waits (vs. 19f). The old age is in labor until the new comes to birth (vs. 22). Believers, for their part, have been given the Spirit, the first fruits of the glory to come (vs. 23a)—a token of the full harvest in the future. However, as Neville Clark has said, "The transformation begun in us in baptism is not yet completed; the body of sin and death, crucified in principle, remains a present though a dying reality; the body of Christ awaits completion."[24] Knowing what is, but is not yet, Christians *groan inwardly*, waiting for complete redemption, that is to say *the redemption of our bodies* (vs. 23b). Thus Christians wait in patient hope (vss. 24f).

In this strange mode of existence marked by possessing and yet not possessing, having and yet waiting, *the Spirit helps us in our weakness* (vs. 26a). The activity of a believer, in this in-between time that Paul mentions specifically, is prayer. *We do not know how to pray as we ought,* but the Spirit makes up for our inarticulateness, expressing in our behalf things that are *too deep for words.* God knows what the Spirit is saying as intercessor for us (vss. 26b-27). Paul touches here the deepest secret of prayer, saying that God not only receives human prayer, but God, by the Spirit, gives human prayer.

This passage has a triadic structure, describing a single act of divine redemption in which the Father (*Abba*), the Son, and the Spirit interact. Trinitarian doctrine is not based in speculation or formal theological reasoning, but in the faith community's profound experience of divine redemptive action.

Although in this passage Paul does not mention baptism expressly, he describes triumphantly the relation with God into which a Christian is brought by the Spirit—the Spirit by whom we are sealed in baptism and sustained after baptism. The themes of the Spirit of God as present possession and passionate intercessor, of Christians being made children of God, rather than slaves, and of the pledges of final glory, all speak of the reality which baptism signifies and conveys.

John 7:37-39a

> *On the last day of the festival, the great day, while Jesus was standing there, he cried out, "Let anyone who is thirsty come to me, and let the one who believes in me drink. As the scripture has said, 'Out of the believer's heart shall flow rivers of living water.'" Now he said this about the Spirit, which believers in him were to receive.*

At the Festival of Booths in Jerusalem, water was brought in a golden vessel with much ceremony from the Gihon spring to the temple and poured out at the altar. Jesus attended this festival, and at its conclusion he claimed the attention of the crowd, crying out *Let anyone who is thirsty come to me, and let the one who believes in me drink.* Quite audaciously this Johannine water-saying puts Jesus in God's role. His offer has the tone of the invitation of Isaiah 55, which says that Israel does not live by itself, from itself, but in and by its relation to God and his salvation. Jesus' saying also suggests Jeremiah 2:13, which compares Israel's dependence on God to a reliable source of water, and its turning from God to looking for refreshment from a dry wadi. Those who had understood through the prophets that they drew their life from their relation to God now hear that they live from and in relation to Jesus. This deeply christological saying builds on Jesus' previous offers of himself as water for life (4:14; 6:35). Jesus is the source, the giver; he does not tell thirsty people where water can be found; rather, they are invited to come and drink of him. "Drinking" is obviously a way of describing believing in him.

The thought continues with an unexpected twist. In verse 37 (as in chapter 4) water is taken in; one drinks to satisfy thirst. Then verse 38 speaks (as chapter 4 does not) of water flowing out from the heart. One receives this water of life from a transcendent source; it takes root within oneself, in the heart. But it does not stay there, as in a cistern; rather, the receiver becomes in turn a source. The *outflow* is more vividly described than the *inflow*. Jesus speaks of *rivers of living water,* indicating excess, abundance. Paradoxically, one gives more than one can receive. The words suggest the vision in Ezekiel 47:1-12 of the waters that flow abundantly from the temple, giving life wherever they pass. Zechariah 14 was read at the Feast of Booths, and verse 8 speaks of living water flowing out from Jerusalem. (These visions in Ezekiel and in Zechariah speak in exaggeration, as visions often do, for the actual Jerusalem temple stood on a waterless hill.) Jesus is saying that one who receives this water from this source in turn becomes a spring. (The image was anticipated when Wisdom was described as an inner fountain in Prov. 18:4, in Isa. 58:11, and most expressly in Sir. 24:30-34.) The one who takes life from Christ becomes, in Christ and like Christ, a source of life. The role of giver of life to the thirsty that Jesus claims for himself is reproduced in those who believe in him.

This inflow/outflow pattern appears later when, after the resurrection, Jesus' gift of the Spirit is closely linked with his missionary commission (20:21). What one receives from Christ is to be enjoyed, but it is not enjoyed unless and until it is shared.

After Jesus has spoken, the evangelist makes an explanatory comment (vs. 39). Jesus, he says, was speaking about *the Spirit, which believers in him were to receive; for as yet there was no Spirit, because Jesus was not yet glorified.* The Greek is abrupt, saying, in effect, "for as yet, no Spirit." The evangelist does not mean to deny the previous existence of the Spirit, who has already been spoken of at Jesus' baptism. Rather, he means that the Spirit has not yet been given in the specifically Christian sense, which depends on the completion of Jesus' work (16:7). He anticipates the giving of the Spirit by the risen Jesus in 20:22.

In speaking of life in Jesus and the Spirit, this reading for the Vigil of Pentecost speaks of the divine reality in which baptism is constituted and in which each baptized person lives.

[How do the ideas of 37b-38a go together?]

Jesus' words could read, *If anyone thirst, let him come to me and drink. He who believes in me, as the scripture has said, "Out of his* [i.e. the believer's] *heart shall flow. . . ."* According to this construction (which has been adopted here), the believer who drinks from Jesus becomes a source of life for others. Or the words could read, *If anyone thirst, let him come to me, and let him who believes in me drink. As the scripture has said, out of his* [i.e. Jesus'] *heart shall flow. . . ."* By this reading, Jesus is the sole source of life. Both ways of reading the words have support among scholars and in the tradition.

An interpreter who has the necessary skills should analyze the Greek text and consult the commentators and decide independently on this point. Otherwise, one must accept and follow one of the English translations, recognizing that any translator has had to close some questions.

Another difficulty in the passage is that there is no clear source for the words that are cited in verse 38 as scripture. This matter, however, does not affect the way the text is understood.]

Pentecost

We have noted the crucial place in the redemptive story that Pentecost fills in the time-scheme of Luke/Acts which governs the Church Year. At the conclusion of Luke's gospel, Jesus instructs his followers to wait in Jerusalem *until you have been clothed with power from on high* (Lk. 24:49). At the beginning of Acts, Luke says that the risen Jesus commanded his followers *not to leave Jerusalem, but to wait there for the promise of the Father. "This," he said, "is what you have heard from me; for John baptized with water, but you will be baptized with the Holy Spirit not many days from now"* (Acts 1:4f). In the first important event of Acts, on the Day of Pentecost, the waiting passes over to actuality. By this *power from on high,* Jesus' followers are transformed into confident witnesses.

The scriptures appointed for Pentecost are the same in all three lectionary years.

Acts 2:1-11

When the day of Pentecost had come, they were all together in one place. And suddenly from heaven there came a wind, and it filled the entire house where they were sitting. Divided tongues, as of fire, appeared among them. All of them were filled with the Holy Spirit and began to speak in other languages, as the Spirit gave them ability.

Now there were devout Jews from every nation under heaven living in Jerusalem. And at this sound the crowd gathered and was bewildered, because each one heard them speaking in the native language of each. Amazed and astonished, they asked, "Are not all these who are speaking Galileans? And how is it that we hear, each of us, in our own native language? Parthians, Medes, Elamites, and residents of Mesopotamia, Judea and Cappadocia, Pontus and Asia, Phrygia and Pamphylia, Egypt and the parts of Libya belonging to Cyrene, and visitors from Rome, both Jews and proselytes, Cretans and Arabs—in our own languages we hear them speaking about God's deeds of power."

In the opening scene of Acts (1:1-11, and see Lk. 24:49), the risen Jesus asks his disciples to remain in Jerusalem until, after not many days, they would be *baptized with the Holy Spirit.* That baptism *with the Holy Spirit* took place at Pentecost—a Jewish feast with biblical origins that continues today in Judaism as well as in the church. In the Jewish scriptures it is referred to as the Feast of Weeks, which was originally dated by harvest time and was celebrated by the cessation of work and the offering of animals and grain (Ex. 23:16; 34:22; Lev. 23:15-21). In time, the meaning of the feast shifted away from agriculture and toward an observance of events rooted in the history of Israel. Later, the feast became associated specifically with the giving of the covenant on Mount Sinai. (It is not certain that this meaning was well established at the time of Jesus and the apostles.) The date was set at fifty days after Passover. (The word "Pentecost" is from the Greek "fiftieth.") Jesus' death and resurrection took place at Passover, and the event narrated in Acts was seven weeks later.

This first reading for Pentecost tells of the *baptism with the Spirit* which Jesus had promised and for which the disciples had waited. As Acts tells it, on the day of Pentecost the disciples were *together in one place* when a sound like a wind came from heaven and tongues of fire rested on them. The disciples and others who were with them were *filled with the Holy Spirit and began to speak in other languages, as the Spirit gave them ability.* The pilgrims who were gathered in Jerusalem from many countries were attracted, and they were astonished that they all could hear these Galileans speaking of God's deeds of power in the languages each of them understood.

[This phenomenon of persons speaking and hearing in a variety of known languages is different from the phenomenon of *tongues* which Paul identifies as one of the gifts of Spirit. In the Pauline churches, *tongues* seems to have meant ecstatic utterance which was unintelligible and could not benefit the community unless it was interpreted by someone with the companion gift of *interpretation of tongues* (1 Cor. 12:10; 14:1-19).]

In Luke's first volume, a new work of God—the mission of the Messiah—was signified by the Holy Spirit anointing and leading Jesus (Lk. 1:35, 41f, 67; 2:26; 3:16, 21f; 4:1, 14, 18). In his second volume, Luke establishes that the Spirit who validated Jesus at his baptism (Lk. 3:21f, and see 4:1, 14, 18) now validates the church at its beginning by a baptism *with the Holy Spirit* (Acts 1:5). The community of Christ does not put itself before the world as a vigorous and promising movement with a new doctrine and way of life. Rather, the transcendent Spirit has the initiative, vitalizing the community, giving it its power and authority.

Since the narrative emphasizes that Jerusalem was full of people from many nations and languages, all of whom heard the apostles' message in their native speech, it seems likely that this story is meant to be read as a reversal of the Genesis myth of the Tower of Babel, where, as a consequence of human pride, the race was shattered into language communities which could not understand one another. Here, communication that leaps over language differences is a sign of a reconstituted human community. However, in the account itself no allusion is made to the Tower of Babel story, only to Joel's prophecy of the outpouring of the Spirit. Moreover, there is no outreach here to the Gentile world; all the persons who hear are Jews, either by birth or by conversion, and they all could probably understand speech in *koine* Greek.

[This passage, which is appointed for the day in all three lectionary years, tells the story of Pentecost only as far as the question asked by the puzzled crowd. The next section of the story, which is an account of Peter's sermon, followed by the response of the hearers, is one of the readings for Easter Day.]

With Psalm 104:25-37

(to be used also if the following alternative reading is chosen; see p. 117.)

Ezekiel 11:17-20 (an alternative for Year A)

Therefore say: Thus says the Lord GOD: I will gather you from the peoples, and assemble you out of the countries where you have been scattered, and I will give you the land of Israel. When they come there, they will remove from it all its detestable things and all its abominations. I will give them one heart, and put a new spirit within them; I will remove the heart of stone from their flesh and give them a heart of flesh, so that they may follow my statutes and keep my ordinances and obey them. Then they shall be my people, and I will be their God.

This oracle is spoken to exiles and spoken in the voice of God: *I will gather you,. . .assemble you,. . .give you,. . .give,. . .remove,. . .I will be.* God promises that the people will be gathered from the nations where they have been scattered and restored to their own land. When they occupy it again, they will remove all the signs of idolatry and the cults of the nations. This purification of the land will evidence a new character. The people cannot obey God without an interior renewal, but they will be given a new, responsive heart.

God sums up the promise with a pledge: *Then they shall be my people, and I will be their God.* The words appear elsewhere in Ezekiel and echo the foundational event of Jewish history, the covenant between God and Israel which was entered into at Sinai (Ex. 19, one of the readings for the Vigil, p. 94). That Israel should be in its own land is a part of its covenant with God.

The clause *I will put a new spirit within them* makes the passage appropriate for Pentecost. (The emphasis on the divine spirit is a prominent feature of Ezekiel as it is used in the lectionary.) What does "spirit" mean here? Observation would have made clear to the ancient Hebrews the connection between breath and life. While human beings (indeed, all animals) breathe, they live; when breath stops, life stops. Then in a bold piece of anthropomorphism, the living God is spoken of as having breath or spirit. Moreover, the divine spirit or life can be communicated to humanity. It was so at the creation (Gen. 2:7), and it may be so whenever human life has grown sterile and lifeless.

Isaiah 44:1-18 (an alternative for Year B)

> *But now hear, O Jacob my servant,*
>   *Israel whom I have chosen!*
> *Thus says the LORD who made you,*
>   *who formed you in the womb and will help you:*
> *Do not fear, O Jacob my servant,*
>   *Jeshurun whom I have chosen.*
> *For I will pour water on the thirsty land,*
>   *and streams on the dry ground;*
> *I will pour my spirit upon your descendants,*
>   *and my blessing on your offspring.*
> *They shall spring up like a green tamarisk,*
>   *like willows by flowing streams.*
> *This one will say, "I am the LORD's,"*
>   *another will be called by the name of Jacob,*
> *yet another will write on the hand, "The LORD's,"*
>   *and adopt the name of Israel.*
> *Thus says the LORD, the King of Israel,*
>   *and his Redeemer, the LORD of hosts:*
> *I am the first and I am the last;*
>   *besides me there is no god.*
> *Who is like me? Let them proclaim it,*
>   *let them declare and set it forth before me.*
> *Who has announced from of old the things to come?*
>   *Let them tell us what is yet to be.*
> *Do not fear, or be afraid;*
>   *have I not told you from of old and declared it?*
>   *You are my witnesses!*
> *Is there any god besides me?*
>   *There is no other rock; I know not one.*

All who make idols are nothing, and the things they delight in do no profit; their witnesses neither see nor know. And so they will be put to shame. Who would fashion a god or cast an image that would do no good? Look, all its devotees shall be put to shame; the artisans too are merely human. Let them all assemble, let them stand up; they shall be terrified, they shall be put to shame.

The ironsmith fashions [an ax] and works it over the coals, shaping it with hammers, and forging it with his strong arm; he becomes hungry and his strength fails, he drinks no water and is faint. The carpenter stretches a line, marks it out with a stylus, fashions it with planes, and marks it with a compass; he makes it in human form, with human beauty, to be set up in a shrine. He cuts down cedars or chooses a holm tree or an oak and lets it grow strong among the trees of the forest. He plants a cedar and the rain nourishes it. Then it can be used as fuel. Part of it he takes and warms himself; he kindles a fire and bakes bread. Then he makes a god and worships it, makes it a carved image and bows down before it. Half of it he burns in the fire; over this half he roasts meat, eats it and is satisfied. He also warms himself and says, "Ah, I am warm, I can feel the fire!" The rest of it he makes into a god, his idol, bows down to it and worships it; he prays to it and says, "Save me, for you are my god!"

They do not know, nor do they comprehend; for their eyes are shut, so that they cannot see, and their minds as well, so that they cannot understand. No one considers, nor is there knowledge or discernment to say, "Half of it I burned in the fire; I also baked bread on its coals, I roasted meat and have eaten. Now shall I make the rest of it an abomination? Shall I fall down before a block of wood?" He feeds on ashes; a deluded mind has led him astray, and he cannot save himself or say, "Is not this thing in my right hand a fraud?"

This passage, another of the Servant Songs, announces hope for Israel in exile. It opens as poetry (vss. 1-8). As in Isaiah 42:1-9, which was considered above, God addresses the Servant (vss. 1, 2), and again the Servant is Israel, God's chosen (vs. 2). God has formed his servant in the womb (vs. 2), indicating a deep-laid divine purpose for him. The purpose will be accomplished through God's spirit (that is, the divine breath, the divine vitality) which, like water on a dry ground, will bring rich new life where there seemed to be only death (vss. 3-4). Israel will joyfully recognize its relation with God (vss. 4-5). This renewal is entirely the work of God, Israel's Redeemer, the only God, who acts and calls his people to witness to his works (vss. 6-8).

At verse 9, with no transition, the prophet's style and tone change. Poetry shifts to prose, and the language of vision changes to a sarcastic exposé of the folly of idolatry. The prophet's principal thrust is that persons who worship idols are worshiping the lifeless product of their own skill. They take wood from the forest, part of which they use as fuel to warm their houses and bake their bread, and part of which they carve into an idol. When they have made their own gods, they worship them and implore their help. They should know that these gods are helpless, but the deluded makers *feed on ashes.*

The prophet spoke in a world in which craftsmen did make images out of wood and stone which were then made objects of worship. He spoke from the Jewish tradition which knew idolatry to be folly; for Israel's God, the true and living God, was beyond any human representation and should not be imaged lest the image be mistaken for reality. However, the message in this reading goes to the heart of prophetic religion and is pertinent in any culture. Humanity has an intrinsic need to worship, but this powerful impulse is undiscriminating. Noble and beautiful things have been worshiped, but so have debasing and ugly things. Things made by human hands have been worshiped, but so have things made by human minds. The prophets of Israel spoke against such self-made divinities and in behalf of the living, creating God who in sovereign freedom speaks and calls, disclosing the divine character and drawing men and women away from false and deluding gods and into a new, dignifying existence. The society in which the Christian church grew up was a pagan society; every city was full of shrines and temples to false gods. Those who were baptized were required to renounce the deities to which they had formerly given allegiance. They had to learn the peril of idolatry. Today's society has its false deities and its deceptive claims. Turning to Christ requires a deep turning away from Christ's rivals. The call to identify and renounce idolatry is as relevant now as it was when the prophet wrote or when the early Christians were baptized in Hellenistic society.

Joel 2:28-32 (an alternative for Year C)

Then afterward
I will pour out my spirit on all flesh;
your sons and your daughters shall prophesy,
your old men shall dream dreams,
and your young men shall see visions.

Even on the male and female slaves,
in those days, I will pour my spirit.

I will show portents in the heavens and on the earth, blood and fire
and columns of smoke. The sun shall be turned to darkness, and the moon
to blood, before the great and terrible day of the LORD comes. Then ev-
eryone who calls on the name of the LORD shall be saved; for in Mount
Zion and in Jerusalem there shall be those who escape, as the LORD has
said, and among the survivors shall be those whom the LORD calls.

This is the prophetic passage on which, on the Day of Pentecost, Peter draws as he seeks to give his astonished hearers some account of what they are witnessing. The disciples, he says, are not drunk, as some by-standers had thought. Rather, God is stirring; the final days are present; the anticipated age of the Spirit is dawning. The promises are being ful-filled, and what the prophet Joel spoke of long ago is coming to pass be-fore your very eyes and ears, as Peter shows by citing this extended pas-sage (Acts 2:17-21).

In the section of Joel which Peter quotes, God, through the prophet, promises that the divine spirit (God's own breath or life) will be poured out *on all flesh*, i.e. on everyone. In Jewish history, many persons had been gifted by the spirit to speak the word of God or to do feats of unusual skill or strength. But the special endowments had been for a few, and they were temporary—strangely given and strangely withdrawn. Thus it is a dramatic moment when the Spirit is poured out on all. Joel itemizes so as to suggest the whole range of the community, *your sons and your daughters, . . .your old men. . .and your young men.* The spirit will even be poured out *on the male and female slaves.* Distinctions of sex, age, and status will be obliter-ated; ecstasy, prophecy, visions, and dreams will be experienced by all. In the day of the Lord, all the Lord's people will be prophets (Num. 11:29).

At verse 30, with no transition, the prophet's tone changes. He drops his vision of the community in the Spirit and begins to speak in the style known as "apocalyptic." (*Apocalyptic* and the related word *apocalypse* come from Greek terms meaning "revelation" or "unveiling." Things that are hidden in the future are made known.) This Jewish thought-idiom grew up in the exile. The Jews were a proud people, carriers of a God-given des-tiny. Yet they were defeated, held captive, and nearly destroyed. In this time of bafflement and despair, the apocalyptic idiom spoke to the national hopelessness.

Apocalyptic literature had a general pattern. Visionaries looked be-yond the present, usually saying that things which were bad now were going to get worse. But just as they became unendurable, God would break in by actions which would bring about terrible conflict, often associated with cosmic disruptions. The few who were faithful would be preserved through it all. Finally, after a climactic struggle, God would overturn the present order of things, set the oppressed on thrones, and bring in an age of harmony and unopposed divine rule. This literature, which originated in times of extremity, seems to become relevant when such times recur in cultural history.

Only a few parts of the Jewish scriptures are written in this idiom—portions of Daniel, fragments of Ezekiel, Isaiah, and Amos, and this passage in Joel. But the literature of apocalyptic grew in the inter-testamental period, some of it becoming extreme and quite bizarre. In the Christian scriptures, apocalyptic provides the direct background for some of Jesus' sayings in the gospels (notably Mark 13), for parts of Paul's earliest letters (1 and 2 Thessalonians), and for the book of Revelation. Apocalyptic had an influence on the structure of the Christian message which cannot be traced simply by identifying a few visionary motifs or passages. The general sense that God was acting in history, that conflict was sharply drawn with Satan, and that a new age was suddenly appearing in the midst of an old and corrupt age, pervades much of the New Testament, even when apocalyptic vision has been tamed. When Jesus opens his ministry proclaiming, *"The time is fulfilled, and the kingdom of God has come near; repent and believe the good news"* (Mk. 1:15), he draws on a sense of history that had been sharpened and informed by the visions of the apocalyptists.

The passage from Joel speaks of nature thrown into chaos—*portents in the heavens and on the earth, blood and fire and columns of smoke. The sun shall be turned to darkness, and the moon to blood, before the great and terrible day of the Lord.* But in the midst of this horror, Joel says, that *everyone who calls on the name of the Lord shall be saved*—that is, saved from this terrible calamity in nature and society. The apocalyptic writers may have taken their imagery literally, anticipating that the stability of nature itself would be shaken. However, the Hebrews had no sense of self-existent nature; an upset in nature spoke of divine judgment and of an upset society and an upset mind. The final verse of Peter's long quotation of Joel in his Pentecost sermon (which is also the final verse of the liturgical reading) is used to make an appeal in a situation in which people were amazed—even though the heavens and the earth seem to have been behaving quite normally. In the midst of cosmic and political disruption, Joel says, *Then everyone* (i.e. every Jew) *who calls on the name of the* LORD *shall be saved.* (Of course, a Christian preacher is giving the prophet's word "saved" an evangelical sense and interpreting "the Lord" as Christ.) Paul cites Joel 2:32 in Romans 10:13 to make the point that grace is available to Jew and Gentile alike, for *everyone who calls on the name of the Lord shall be saved.* This short passage from Joel was evidently used by the early Christians to demonstrate from the Jewish scriptures that anyone might be saved by calling on the name (i.e. the very person) of Christ.

1 Corinthians 12:4-13

Now there are varieties of gifts,
but the same Spirit;
and there are varieties of services,
but the same Lord;
and there are varieties of activities,
but it is the same God who activates all of them in everyone.
To each is given the manifestation of the Spirit for the common good.
To one is given through the Spirit the utterance of wisdom,
and to another the utterance of knowledge
according to the same Spirit,
to another the working of miracles,
to another prophecy,
to another the discerning of spirits,
to another various kinds of tongues,
to another the interpretation of tongues.
All these are activated by one and the same Spirit,
who allots to each one individually just as the Spirit chooses.

For just as the body is one and has many members, and all the members of the body, though many, are one body, so it is with Christ. For in the one Spirit we were all baptized into one body—Jews or Greeks, slaves or free—and we were all made to drink of one Spirit.

When Paul writes of the body and the members, the one Spirit and the varied gifts, he seeks to hold together unity and diversity, commonality and individuality. Each Christian is gifted individually by the sovereign Spirit, but in Christ no one can be complete alone. There are many gifts and ministries, he says, but all of them—wisdom, knowledge, discernment, miracles, tongues, and interpretation—are given by the one Spirit for the well-being of the common life.

The presence of gifts in the church must have seemed to the early Christians a remarkable validation of their gospel. They were people who as society saw them were of little account. Yet in the new life of the Spirit in the church, some of them became trusted prophets, pastors, teachers, and "helps"—persons who showed responsibility and articulateness in ways that nothing in their prior record would have predicted. Something in their God-given potential that had been held down in the sin-structured social order of society was released by the sovereign Spirit acting in the new people of God.

The Spirit's gifts, Paul says, are to be exercised freely and thankfully. But the apostle is at the same time concerned for control. The gifts are from the Spirit and are to be used not for indulgent display, nor in ways that divide, but for the Spirit's purposes and for the building up of the one body—the body that is formed by baptism.

As Paul describes the varied, Spirit-endowed community, he only mentions baptism itself in the final sentence of this excerpt. Since Pentecost is one of the church's baptismal occasions, that sentence requires fuller attention here.

Present-day Christians are inclined to think of baptism in societal terms—as a sacramental act that incorporates one in a community of shared faith and life. This emphasis is true, and it draws on the New Testament idea of the church; one cannot be in Christ without being at the same time in Christ's people. But it is remarkable that the New Testament itself seldom speaks about being baptized into the collective, ecclesial life. 1 Corinthians 12:13 fills the general silence.

Paul's emphasis on "one" is unmistakable—*one body, one Spirit.* (He uses the word "one" three times in vs. 13 and five times if we go back to include vs. 12.) Writing to a community inclined to rivalry and division, the apostle cites the commonality that is demonstrated in baptism.

Although this text mixes metaphors, it is sufficiently clear. Christians are:

◆ *baptized* in the Spirit. A vigorous material image depicts a non-material action. "Baptized" has the idea of "plunged" or "washed," as though the Spirit were the element into which Christians were baptized, much as John's candidates were plunged into the river Jordan. To be baptized in the Spirit is not a higher experience reserved for some Christians; rather, it is constitutive of every believer's very identity as a Christian.

◆ *into one body*, into a single unified life. In Romans 6, Paul speaks of Christians being baptized into Christ's death and resurrection;

in 1 Corinthians 12:13 he speaks of them entering a collective life, which he describes in an organic metaphor, as a body. Since the church is in Christ, to be united with him is to be united with it.

The passage becomes specific, saying that this societal life brings together persons from former religious and social divisions, two of which it cites: Jew or Greek, slaves or free. The new communal life joined persons who had lived within the covenant with God, and persons who had been outside it. It linked persons who were free citizens and persons who were held as property. We shall come again upon this claim that baptism overcomes the deep divisions in Hellenistic (or in any) society. The Pauline Christians must have celebrated this unifying power of the new life as the reality of God demonstrated concretely in their life together. New Testament scholars sometimes speak of the words by which this power is described as "the baptismal reunification formula."

◆ *drink* of one Spirit. The Spirit which was described as the element into which one is baptized is now spoken of as received inwardly for life, refreshment.

The metaphor of drinking the Spirit—taking the Spirit internally—is unusual, for the baptismal water is not drunk, but is only used externally as it is put on candidates or as candidates are put in it. However, earlier in this letter, in 10:1-5, Paul had spoken of the Israelites who came out of Egypt as having been *baptized into Moses in the cloud and in the sea.* Then, thinking of the water from the rock in the story of Israel's exodus (Ex. 17:1-6), he says that the Israelites *all drank the same spiritual drink. For they drank from the spiritual rock that followed them, and the rock was Christ.* Paul's expression in 12:13, *drinking of one Spirit,* is not to be interpreted by baptismal custom, but by Paul's christological reading of Moses and the exodus. As the perishing Israelites drank water from the rock which was Christ, so the Christians drink of the Spirit of Christ. The incarnational mind of the biblical writers opens them to a range of bodily metaphors for speaking of the relation of the Christian with the Spirit.

With Psalm 33:12-15,18-22

(see pp. 50, 118)

John 20:19-23

> *When it was evening on that day, the first day of the week, and the doors of the house where the disciples had met were locked for fear of the Jews, Jesus came and stood among them and said, "Peace be with you." After he said this, he showed them his hands and his side. Then the disciples rejoiced when they saw the Lord. Jesus said to them again, "Peace be with you. As the Father sent me, so I send you." When he had said this, he breathed on them and said to them, "Receive the Holy Spirit. If you forgive the sins of any, they are forgiven them; if you retain the sins of any, they are retained."*

This narrative from John which reports Jesus' giving of the Holy Spirit—the Johannine Pentecost—expresses a different time sequence from that of Luke/Acts, and the different sequence is based in a different theology. Although the Lukan sequence, with the feast of Pentecost falling seven weeks after Easter, is familiar from the Church Year, the Johannine sequence should be set over against it.

When it was evening on that day, the first day of the week. The time is Easter Day itself—the evening of the same day in which Peter and the Beloved Disciple had seen the empty tomb and in which the risen Jesus had been met by Mary Magdalen (20:1-18). Luke's staged-out chronology gives us Easter, followed forty days later by Ascension and then Pentecost after ten more days. Perhaps the spacious rhythms of the Church Year can let worshipers focus on these three great spiritual realities one at a time without hermeneutical mischief. But it is also possible that in Christians' minds, reinforced by their liturgical behavior, the three events may become separated in idea as well as in time. A resurrection act is followed at some remove by an ascension act and still later by a Holy Spirit act. In the Johannine sequence, by contrast, Jesus' death is his passage to the Father; and it, the demonstration of the resurrection, and the giving of the Spirit all fall on the same day. Cross, resurrection, ascension, and the Holy Spirit are united, virtually a single act. This Johannine unity of the redemptive act must be allowed to stand over against the more familiar Lukan presentation of four acts in sequence, modifying and correcting any tendency there may be to fragment the work of Christ and the Spirit.

The story in this gospel reading tells of the first appearance of the risen Jesus to his disciples as a group. Although the doors are shut, Jesus appears in their midst and says *Peace be with you,* the common Jewish greeting. With no further word, he shows them the marks of his crucifixion. The risen Jesus is the crucified Jesus. William Temple says, "The wounds of Christ are his credentials to the suffering race of men."[25] Jesus repeats *Peace be with you*. His words are performative, a bestowal of the divine *shalom*, the right ordering of things under God. After the trauma of chapters 18-19, the *shalom* is here.

The peace is at once associated with a sending. Jesus' legacy to his people is a mission—their participation in his own mission from the Father: *As the Father sent me, so I send you*. Here we find the familiar Johannine proportion: As I am to the Father, so you are to me. In this place Jesus adds: As I have been to the world, so you are to be to the world.

Then Jesus *breathed on them and said to them, "Receive the Holy Spirit."* Sending is followed by the giving of the Spirit. The Spirit is given for mission; mission is rooted in the Spirit. The breathing is an echo of the creation story in which God breathes into Adam the breath of life (Gen. 2:7). The words are a transition from the age of Jesus to the presence and age of the Spirit. They are a way of saying: The promised Paraclete is now among and within you. You receive him from accredited hands.

The sent community is an actual, effective agent of forgiveness and judgment: *If you forgive the sins of any, they are forgiven them; if you retain the sins of any, they are retained*. John's gospel has not spoken of forgiveness until this point. It enters here as a gift of the risen Jesus. Forgiveness is based on Easter, on Jesus' glorification. The new age of the Spirit is an age of forgiveness. The mission is an offer of forgiveness—an absolution which is enacted in baptism.

John 14:8-17

> Philip said to him, "Lord, show us the Father, and we will be satisfied." Jesus said to him, "Have I been with you all this time, Philip, and you still do not know me? Whoever has seen me has seen the Father. How can you say, 'Show us the Father'? Do you not believe that I am in the Father and the Father is in me? The words that I say to you I do not speak on my own; but the Father who dwells in me does his works. Believe me that I am in the Father and the Father is in me; but if you do not, then believe me because of the works themselves. Very truly, I tell you, the one who believes in me will also do the works that I do and, in fact, will do greater works than these, because I go to the Father. I will do whatever you ask in my name, so that the Father may be glorified in the Son. If in my name you ask me for anything, I will do it.
>
> If you love me, you will keep my commandments. And I will ask the Father, and he will give you another Advocate, to be with you forever. This is the Spirit of truth, whom the world cannot receive, because it

neither sees him nor knows him. You know him, because he abides with you, and he will be in you.

The disciples are dismayed when Jesus says that he is about to leave them (13:33). Jesus, confident in the Father and in himself, seeks in a lengthy farewell (John 13-16) to quiet their troubled hearts and to prepare and instruct them.

Jesus has assured the disciples that they know and have seen the Father (vss. 6-7). Philip (probably speaking for all) says *show us the Father*. If the disciples have seen the Father, they do not know that they have seen the Father. Without more evidence than they have been given they cannot be *satisfied*. Jesus replies by speaking of himself. They have seen the Father because they have seen him; and the union between himself and the Father is so complete that whoever has seen him has seen the Father.

Jesus makes the point generally in terms of a reciprocal indwelling, *I am in the Father, and the Father is in me.* Then he repeats it more specifically, saying that his *words* are the Father's words and his *works* are done through the indwelling Father. Jesus, through the words and acts by which he engages the world, makes the Father visible and knowable insofar as the Father is visible and knowable. Less would be inadequate; more is impossible.

Having mentioned his own works, Jesus speaks reassuringly to his followers of their works. Those who believe in him, he says, will do *the works that he does*. The church will be in many ways continuator of his ministry—healing, teaching, judging, witnessing to the truth, forgiving sin, as he had. As he was in and to the world, so it will be. Then Jesus adds that because he is going to the Father the church will do *greater works* than he has done. Readers must conjecture about what the text has in mind, but very likely it refers to the geographical spread and the enlarged human inclusiveness of the community of faith. (Oscar Cullmann has proposed that the Christian sacraments are the "greater works," taking the place in the church of the miracles of Jesus' ministry.)[26] Jesus is emphasizing that his departure will not be a loss for his followers, but a gain. Things will be possible and will be understood when he has gone that have not been possible or comprehensible while he was present.

He adds that when he is gone, he will remain accessible through prayer—through an *asking* which may be spoken in his name. As askers, his people will act in dependence on him, as he acted in dependence on the Father.

This excerpt from Jesus' farewell is a Pentecost reading because of its final verses (15-17), in which Jesus promises the gift of the *Advocate*. The term translates *Paraclete*, a Greek word for which there is no adequate English equivalent. Translators have tried "Helper" or "Counselor." (The seventeenth-century Authorized Version of the Bible used "Comforter," which for Wycliff and Tyndale meant "strengthener" or "encourager," but the translation became misleading as the language changed.) The word came from law, where it referred to someone who stood with a party in court, one who took another's part. This *Paraclete* is only introduced in a few passages in Jesus' farewell; it is explained in 14:25 that the *Paraclete* is the one known elsewhere as the Holy Spirit. When Jesus says that the Advocate will be *"another Paraclete,"* he implies that he has himself been a *Paraclete* to his followers, and the Holy Spirit will be to them as he had been. The *Paraclete* will not so much be Jesus' successor as his *alter ego*— as though Jesus, who in one sense is leaving, is in another sense, by the Spirit, staying on.

The Paraclete is *the Spirit of truth,* a term that was in use in the Dead Sea Scrolls community. As Jesus is *the truth* (14:6), the *Paraclete* will minister in behalf of truth in a world which is so flawed as to give the truth a hostile reception. But what the world cannot know, the disciples will know. They will know by a participatory knowing, for the *Paraclete* will remain with them (unlike Jesus, whose ministry among them comes to an end) and will be in them.

Psalms for Pentecost:

[These psalms are appointed for all three lectionary years.]

Psalm 104:25-37 or 104:25-32

The appointed verses are the second half of a great psalm of creation. It opens by speaking of the sea. The Hebrews were not a seafaring people, and the psalms and prophets often speak of the sea as alien and menacing. But in verses 26-27 the psalmist takes delight in it as though God had tamed it and made it virtually a playground. Verses 28-31 speak of the creatures (of vs. 25) as sustained by God. The Hebrews had little interest in secondary causation; they would not have shown much interest in the great chain of life; and they knew nothing of a self-existent nature observing its own laws. Rather, they saw all natural things as directly supported by God. All creatures are fed by God, who *gives them their food in due season.*

When God's hand is open they are filled; when God turns away, they die and turn to dust.

The psalm is appropriate for Pentecost because of the emphasis in verse 31: *You send forth your Spirit, and they are created; and so you renew the face of the earth.* All things are sustained by the life-giving breath of God. Despite the upper case "S" in the Prayer Book Psalter, the term need not be Christianized. As Archbishop Michael Ramsey said: "'Spirit' in the writings of the Old Testament is not a person or a definable object or substance. It is a mode of describing how the holy God is active in the world which he created, and especially in persons in whom his purpose is fulfilled."[27] This psalm speaks of the God who is beyond the world as also in the world, imparting the divine life to the whole creation.

[The verse numbering in this psalm in the Prayer Book differs from that in most Bibles. The references in the above comments are to the Prayer Book Psalter.]

Psalm 33:12-15, 18-22

This psalm expresses the bond between God and his people, *Happy is the nation whose God is the* LORD*! happy the people he has chosen to be his own!* God *looks down from heaven and beholds all the people in the world,* an expression which "asserts both that God is utterly free of the world and yet is utterly attentive to it."[28] As the One who fashions human hearts and understands human works, it is God whose *eye. . . is upon those. . .who wait upon his love.* But he does not simply watch; he *plucks their lives from death* and *feeds them in time of famine.* Hence the psalm ends with a deep sense of trust in the Lord. This psalm can speak for those who at the time of baptism trust their lives to God.

CHAPTER 4

The Scriptures for the Christmas/Epiphany Complex

Christians in the West tend to think of the Christian Year in rather biographical or life-of-Jesus terms. However, the Year handles time freely and dramatistically, carrying the church in less than half a year from Jesus' birth to his death and resurrection, giving most emphasis to the final days of his historic life. Liturgical time compresses historical time, treating it almost playfully. In the Church Year, history meets eschatology. The Christmas-Epiphany cycle takes us, in a little more than two weeks, from Jesus' birth to his entry, as a young adult, on his public life, and the Temptation falls at the beginning of Lent rather than among the inaugural events of Jesus' mission.

In the earliest generations, Christians had no liturgical observance of Jesus' birth. Early in the fourth century, however, a feast of Jesus' "showing" or "appearing" (*epiphaneo*) grew up in the East, falling in early January. The origin of this observance is obscure; it may be a Christianization of a pagan festival or of the Jewish Feast of Booths.

The feast of Jesus' "showing" spoke of several things: It celebrated Jesus' birth, including the story of the visit of the Magi, and it observed Jesus' "manifestations" at his baptism and at the miracle at Cana (which is spoken of as revelatory in Jn. 2:11). This season of "showing forth" was suffused with themes of light and splendor.

In the more literal-minded West an observance which focused on Jesus' birth came to be held near the winter solstice in late December. To observe the day as the day of the nativity made the christological point that Jesus' "showing forth" was at his birth. He was who he was from his arrival on the human scene; he did not become incarnate divinity at some subsequent time.

Neither the Eastern nor the Western date had any connection with the time of Jesus' actual birth, which had long been forgotten. These Christian festivals challenged a time of the year that had been marked by pagan celebrations—the time when the sun grew weaker and lower in the sky, but when each year it reversed its decline and returned in strength, the "death and rebirth of the sun." In Christian hands, this time spoke of the coming of the world's true light.

Eventually the Western church observed a feast of Jesus' birth on December 25, while the Eastern festival on January 6 became, in the West, the Feast of the Epiphany, which was associated with the Matthean story of the visit of the Magi—the "showing" of Christ to the Gentiles. The two dates gave the West "the twelve days of Christmas."

The themes that gathered around Epiphany in the early centuries and that remain associated with the season—themes of light, manifestation, showing forth—are "Johannine" themes. (It oversimplifies to say it so, but the Western concentration of baptismal emphases at Easter and around the theme of death and resurrection might be thought "Pauline.") It is the Johannine writings that say: *God is light* (1 Jn. 1:5), and *I am the light of the world* (Jn. 9:5). These themes draw on the persistent, but vulnerable, character of light. It is the way of light to shine and spread, to enter wherever it is admitted. Yet it can be obstructed by anything opaque. In Epiphany the church thinks of boundaries—boundaries of space, of ethnicity, and of the mind—being pressed back by the advancing light. John puts forward the theme of the eternal light that goes on shining in the darkness and is not overcome by the darkness (1:5). The glory was made manifest in Jesus; it was generally refused, but the church (the evangelist's "we") is the community of those who *have seen his glory, glory as of a father's only son* (1:14).

The early church, as we have noted, spoke often of baptism as "illumination." Epiphany was sometimes called "the Feast of Lights." Epiphanytide sermons were developed on the theme of light—the most notable being Gregory of Nazianzus' fortieth Oration, preached in 381, at which he said of baptism:

> Illumination [i.e. baptism] is the greatest and most magnificent of the Gifts of God. For just as we speak of the Holy of Holies, and the Song of Songs, as more comprehensive and more excellent than

others, so is this called Illumination, as being more holy than any other illumination that we possess.[1]

As a celebration of light, Epiphany was a fitting time for the sacrament of enlightenment, and in much of the East, Epiphany was a time for baptism; and in parts of the early church Christian baptism was informed more by the model of Jesus' baptism in the Jordan than by his passion and resurrection.[2]

But the bishops of Rome generally rejected baptisms at times other than the Pascha or Pentecost. In 449, Leo the Great wrote to the bishops of Sicily noting that he had heard that there were in that region more baptisms at Epiphany than at Easter, a practice that he deplored, commending the appropriateness of the day on which Jesus rose from the dead over the day on which he was worshiped by the wise men. The actions of the church ought to suit the actions of the church's head.[3] However, in the course of putting the custom down, the letter of Pope Leo bears witness to the prevalence of the practice of baptism at Epiphany.

Over the centuries the gospel story of Jesus' baptism was generally read at Epiphany in the West (not, however in the readings of the Sarum system, which omitted the baptism account altogether). The 1928 Prayer Book modified the tradition of readings and appointed the story of the Magi on Epiphany, the account of the boy Jesus at the temple on the First Sunday after Epiphany, and Mark's narrative of Jesus' baptism on the Second Sunday after Epiphany. This Sunday was not especially commended as a time for baptism.

In the late-twentieth-century revisions of the Year and of the system of liturgical readings, the First Sunday after the Epiphany is observed in all three lectionary years as the Feast of the Baptism of Jesus, using for its gospel readings the synoptic accounts of the baptism. Following some early, but largely forgotten precedent, this Sunday and the Eve of the Baptism of Our Lord are appointed in the Episcopal Church as occasions for Christian baptism. Then the following Sunday sustains the Epiphany emphasis with three incidents from the early chapters of John's gospel, all of which contain an aspect of the "showing forth" of Christ: In Year A it is John's story of Jesus' baptism. Year B tells of the call of Philip and Nathanael. And in Year C the church hears of Jesus' sign at Cana.

It seems a historical certainty that Jesus was baptized. His coming to John's baptism, which was a baptism of repentance, raises so many problems for popular christology that the story would not have been invented by his followers. Yet there is an impenetrable mystery about the event. Modern readers would like psychological accounts—how did the baptism fit in with Jesus' sense of his distinctive vocation? How did it grow from his prior experience? What self-understanding came from it? But the gospels do not psychologize. We seek historical actuality. Who reported this event? If a journalist had been present, what would have been seen and heard? John's gospel says that some of Jesus' first disciples had been followers of John the Baptist, and they seem to have been present at the baptism (Jn. 1:35f). It may have been so. But the synoptic gospels do not connect the call of the first disciples with John the Baptist or with Jesus' baptism. It seems unlikely that any follower of Jesus was present or that the baptism narrative was written by an eyewitness. The gospel records (which are all that we have) give the event an overlay of symbolic, christological interpretation—the water, the dove, the voice from heaven and its declaration of sonship, the triadic presence, the allusions to Jewish scripture.

All the gospels, as well as the summary of Jesus' ministry in Acts 10:36-43, begin the account of Jesus' mission with the figure of John the Baptist and with Jesus' baptism by him. Although there were a number of baptizing movements in the land and time of Jesus, and while Jewish antecedents can be traced in proselyte baptism and in water rituals of the Dead Sea Scrolls community, the New Testament does not encourage us to look into such precedent sources. The roots of the Christian initiatory rite lie in the originality and the specific character of John's baptism and in Jesus' baptism by John.

The accounts of Jesus' baptism in the gospels were written by a baptizing community, and they have no doubt in some respects been assimilated to features of the church's rite, although it is hard to know how far this influence extended and whether or not it moved in both directions—Jesus' baptism influencing Christian practice, and Christian practice influencing the way in which Jesus' baptism was remembered and told. Several elements in the gospel story suggest acts and meanings that are found in early Christian initiatory rites and interpretations. In Jesus' baptism, as in many early Christian baptisms, a water act is associated with a Spirit act. The account in the synoptic gospels has a Christian "triadic" element, as it introduces Jesus, the Spirit, and the Father. The declaration of Jesus' sonship and the use of the term *the Beloved* (which will be used again by the voice at the Transfiguration, 9:7) suggests the way in which Christian baptism brings one into a spiritual family and relates one to a divine Father.

Christians may properly link Jesus' baptism with their own, recognizing always the priority of his baptism and the dependence of theirs. Jesus seems to have gone to John, associating himself with the eschatological expectancy and the moral seriousness of the Baptist's movement. He stood with the repentant and prepared group within Israel that had been shaped by John's summons. The incident, seen from the vantage of Christian experience, may be taken to say that this baptism, with which Jesus' redemptive mission began, united him with us in our sinfulness and need. Our baptism unites us with him in his righteousness, his life, and his mission for the world.

VIGIL FOR THE EVE OF THE BAPTISM OF OUR LORD

The Book of Occasional Services provides a Vigil for the Eve of the Baptism of Our Lord (pp. 51-52). This rite begins with the Service of Light (BCP, p.109) and continues with the Collect of the Day. At the service of the Word three or more lessons are read before the gospel, each followed by a period of silence and a psalm, canticle, or hymn. This Vigil, like the feast day which it anticipates, is commended as an occasion for baptism. The rubric provides that *Holy Baptism or Confirmation (beginning with the presentation of the Candidates), or the Renewal of Baptismal Vows, Prayer Book, page 292, follows the Sermon.*

Five scripture readings are provided for the Vigil, each of which is given a title, and at least three of which are to be used.

The story of the flood: Genesis (7:1-5, 11-18); 8:6-18; 9:8-13

This story of judgment and preservation is also used in the review of God's mighty acts at the Easter Vigil and is commented on above (p. 45).

With Psalm 25:3-9 or Psalm 46

The writer of Psalm 25 repeatedly asks *teach me, lead me, remember me*. He asks for help, direction and forgiveness, knowing that God is a God of truth, salvation, mercy, steadfast love, and goodness. The Lord *leads the humble in what is right, and teaches the humble his way.*

On Psalm 46, see p. 48.

The Lord who makes a way in the sea: Isaiah 43:15-19

I am the LORD, your Holy One,
*   the Creator of Israel, your King.*
Thus says the LORD,
*   who makes a way in the sea,*
*   a path in the mighty waters,*
who brings out chariot and horse,
*   army and warrior;*
they lie down, they cannot rise,
*   they are extinguished,*
*   quenched like a wick:*
Do not remember the former things,
*   or consider the things of old.*
I am about to do a new thing;
*   now it springs forth, do you not perceive it?*
I will make a way in the wilderness
*   and rivers in the desert.*

Israel is held captive in Babylon; but God, through the prophet, promises that the nation will return to its own land. The return from Babylon will be through an arid land. Yet the prophet describes it in terms drawn from the exodus from Egypt, saying that a way will be made *in the sea* and *in the wilderness* (vss. 16, 19b); chariots and horses will be overcome (vs. 17); God will provide water, making *rivers in the desert* (vs. 19b). However, the new exodus through the wilderness from Babylon to Palestine will be more glorious than the old. The nation is not to limit its expectation by the former experience or by comparing, for God is *about to do a new thing* (vss. 18-19b).

The passage is an instance of the prophetic use of typology—interpreting the new through the old. (The practice continues, as in Leon Uris' panoramic novel of the modern-day return of Jews to Israel, which is entitled, almost inevitably, *Exodus*.) Thus it is hardly surprising that Christians saw Christ, redemption, and baptism in exodus terms. In baptism, as in redemption which is signified in baptism, God is doing a new thing, but following familiar ways in bringing captives to freedom.

With Psalm 114

This psalm is also appointed for the eucharist of Easter Day (see p. 64).

The washing and anointing of Aaron: Leviticus 8:1-12

> *The LORD spoke to Moses, saying: Take Aaron and his sons with him, the vestments, the anointing oil, the bull of sin offering, the two rams, and the baskets of unleavened bread; and assemble the whole congregation at the entrance of the tent of meeting. And Moses did as the LORD commanded him. When the congregation was assembled at the entrance of the tent of meeting, Moses said to the congregation, "This is what the LORD commanded to be done."*
>
> *Then Moses brought Aaron and his sons forward, and washed them with water. He put the tunic on him, fastened the sash around him, clothed him with the robe, and put the ephod on him. He then put the decorated band of the ephod around him, tying the ephod to him with it. He placed the breastpiece on him, and in the breastpiece he placed the Urim and Thummim. And he set the turban on his head, and on the turban, in front, he set the golden ornament, the holy crown, as the LORD commanded Moses.*
>
> *Then Moses took the anointing oil and anointed the tabernacle and all that was in it, and consecrated them. He sprinkled some of it on the altar seven times, and anointed the altar and all its utensils, and the basin and its base, to consecrate them. He poured some of the anointing oil on Aaron's head and anointed him, to consecrate him.*

These verses are the directions for the initial washing, vesting, and anointing by which first Moses' brother Aaron and then Aaron's sons were set apart to be Israel's first high priest to begin Israel's priestly succession. The prosaic rubrics prescribing the right garments and the right gestures all but conceal an occasion that would have been filled with color and splendor. Priests are to represent the people, and their setting-apart is carried out before *the whole congregation at the entrance of the tent of meeting.* The actions such as washing, vesting, and anointing must be thought of as carried out by solemn, public gestures that could be seen by a large crowd, assembled in the open.

It is significant that the actions of consecrating the priests and launching the sacrificial system are all reported as carried out by Moses, who is not himself a priest. He gathers the materials (vs. 2); he assembles the people and makes an initial announcement (vss. 4f); he washes the priests (vs. 6). Moses garbs Aaron with his robes and the insignia of office (vss. 7-8) and crowns him (vs. 9). He anoints first the tabernacle and its furnishings (vss. 10f) and then Aaron's head (vs. 12). Even when the sacrifices are carried out (8:14—9:24), Moses is the principal actor. By virtue of his leadership and his status as a prophet, he holds primacy over the priests.

There is an initial washing (vs. 6), followed by a complex vesting (vss. 7-9), and an anointing of Aaron and of the priestly vessels (vs. 12). These actions from the cultic life of an ancient Near Eastern tribe are continued, in modified ways to be sure, in the actions and the images of Christian baptism. They have been altered outwardly and interpreted by the Christian message, but the Semitic background still provides basic terms and meanings. In Christian baptism a person is introduced into a priestly community and made a sharer in Christ's fundamental priesthood. These verses from Leviticus describe the ritual washing, the special garb, and the anointing that were part of the making of a priest. Both in ritual and in spiritual senses, these things or actions still are insignia of one's consecration to share in the fundamental priesthood of the baptized.

With Psalm 23 or Psalm 133

Psalms 23 and 133, both of which speak of anointing and are widely associated with baptism, are discussed on pp. 251 and 273.

The anointing of David: 1 Samuel 16:1-13

The LORD said to Samuel, "How long will you grieve over Saul? I have rejected him from being king over Israel. Fill your horn with oil and set out; I will send you to Jesse the Bethlehemite, for I have provided for myself a king among his sons. Samuel said, "How can I go? If Saul hears of it, he will kill me." And the LORD said, "Take a heifer with you, and say, 'I have come to sacrifice to the LORD.' Invite Jesse to the sacrifice and I will show you what you shall do; and you shall anoint for me the one whom I shall name to you." Samuel did what the LORD commanded, and came to Bethlehem. The elder of the city came to meet him trembling, and said, "Do you come peaceably?" He said, "Peaceably; I have come to sacrifice to the LORD; sanctify yourselves and come with me to the sacrifice." And he sanctified Jesse and his sons and invited them to the sacrifice.

When he came, he looked on Eliah and thought, "Surely the LORD's anointed is now before the LORD." But the LORD said to Samuel, "Do not look on his appearance or on the height of his stature, because I have rejected him; for the LORD does not see as mortals see; they look on the outward appearance, but the LORD looks on the heart." The Jesse called Abinadab, and made him pass before Samuel. He said, "Neither has the LORD chosen this one." Then Jesse made Shammah pass by. And he said, "Neither has the LORD chosen this one." Jesse made seven of his sons pass before Samuel, and Samuel said to Jesse, "The LORD has not chosen any of these." Samuel said to Jesse, "Are all your sons here?" And he said, "There remains yet the youngest, but he is keeping the sheep." And Samuel said to Jesse, "Send and bring him; for we will not sit down until he comes here." He sent and brought him in. Now he was ruddy, and had beautiful eyes, and was handsome. The LORD said, "Rise and anoint him; for this is the one." Then Samuel took the horn of oil and anointed him in the presence of his brothers; and the spirit of the LORD came mightily upon David from that day forward. Samuel then set out and went to Ramah.

Saul, Israel's first king, began with great promise. But when his personal flaws made him unable to reign well, God rejected him. This story tells of the divine choice of a new king—a choice which disregards the criteria set by ordinary human expectation. Samuel is sent to Jesse, one of whose sons he has been told is God's chosen. So Samuel, guided by Jesse's knowledge of the order of his sons' birth, goes through the young men of the family, beginning at the eldest. It is made clear to Samuel that none of them is God's choice.

Samuel will not conclude his mission until all Jesse's sons are considered. David, the youngest son, who is not at his father's house, but is tending the sheep, must be brought. This king will be chosen by divine designation, and, contrary to even his father's expectations, God's choice is David. It is a motif of the Bible that God's choice often falls on the unlikely person, the insignificant tribe, or the obscure place—the ones who in the usual way of things would be overlooked. *The LORD does not see as mortals see.* The youngest son is preferred over the eldest son.

When the choice is clear, Samuel is told, *"Rise and anoint him; for this is the one."* More must happen before David effectively becomes king, but the designation has been given in this anointing by Samuel.

This story, when it is read at the Vigil of Epiphany, connects many things: Anointing is a mark of divine choice, divine favor. It is a sign of kingship. David was anointed, and his posterity are to be known as heirs of David and sharers in God's love for David. The New Testament writers identify Jesus as being a descendant of David through Joseph (Mt. 1:1, 6,

20 et passim; Rom. 1:3; 2 Tim. 2:8; Rev. 22:16). Jesus is anointed (Lk. 4:18; Acts 10:38), and, as the Anointed One, by his death and resurrection, he has a life that is open to all and shared by many. The baptized are anointed in him and made sharers in his kingly life. Yet as they share in his kingship, they cannot presume, for his kingship was exercised through sacrifice, and it was cruelly repudiated at the cross: "Hail, king of the Jews."

With Psalm 2:1-8 or Psalm 110:1-5

Both Psalm 2 and Psalm 110 are royal psalms, perhaps actually used at coronations. In Psalm 2, the nations seek to overthrow the king, but God, who is greater than the nations, favors the king and declares him his son, *You are my son; today I have begotten you* (vs. 7)—a formula of adoption, which is the source of the words that are spoken from heaven at Jesus' baptism in the synoptic accounts.

In Psalm 110:1 the lord (i.e. the king) is set at the right hand of *the* LORD (i.e. God). The right hand is a position of honor, of executive authority, and of mediatorship. The king who is a strong conqueror (vss. 3, 5) is at the same time a priestly figure, suggesting the mysterious priest-king Melchizedek of Genesis 14:17-20. The New Testament writers (the author of Hebrews in particular) plunder this psalm for images of Christ.

The cleansing of Naaman in the Jordan: 2 Kings 5:1-14

Naaman, commander of the army of the king of Aram, was a great man and in high favor with his master, because by him the LORD *had given victory to Aram. The man, though a mighty warrior, suffered from leprosy. Now the Arameans on one of their raids had taken a young girl captive from the land of Israel, and she served Naaman's wife. She said to her mistress, "If only my lord were with the prophet who is in Samaria! He would cure him of his leprosy." So Naaman went and told his lord what the girl from the land of Israel had said. And the king of Aram said, "Go then, and I will send along a letter to the king of Israel."*

He went, taking with him ten talents of silver, six thousand shekels of gold, and ten sets of garments. He brought the letter to the king of Israel, which read, "When this letter reaches you, know that I have sent you my servant Naaman, that you may cure him of his leprosy." When the king of Israel read the letter, he tore his clothes and said, "Am I God, to give death or life, that this man sends word to me to cure a man of his leprosy? Just look and see how he is trying to pick a quarrel with me."

But when Elisha the man of God heard that the king of Israel had torn his clothes, he sent a message to the king, "Why have you torn your clothes? Let him come to me, that he may learn that there is a prophet in Israel." So Naaman came with his horses and chariots, and halted at the entrance to Elisha's house. Elisha sent a messenger to him, saying, "Go, wash in the Jordan seven times, and your flesh shall be restored and you shall be clean." But Naaman became angry and went away, saying, "I thought that for me he would surely have come out, and stand and call on the name of the LORD his God, and would wave his hand over the spot, and cure the leprosy! Are not Abana and Pharpar, the rivers of Damascus, better than all the waters of Israel? Could I not wash in them, and be clean?" He turned and went away in a rage. But his servant approached and said to him, "Father, if the prophet had commanded you to do something difficult, would you not have done it? How much more, when all he said to you was, 'Wash, and be clean'?" So he went down and immersed himself seven times in the Jordan, according to the word of the man of God; his flesh was restored like the flesh of a young boy, and he was clean.

Naaman, a highly placed pagan military officer, is reduced by an affliction from which his position cannot protect him. ("Leprosy," as a biblical term, refers to a variety of conditions and not specifically to Hansen's disease.) A Jewish slave girl suggests that he seek help from "the man of God" in Israel. When the suggestion reaches Naaman, he is willing to try anything, so he travels to Israel to ask for help from the king, who must be "the man of God." The king is distraught at this request for healing. The prophet Elisha hears of the king's distress and asks that Naaman be sent to him. When he comes, Elisha sends a servant out to him with counsel he cannot accept. *"Go, wash in the Jordan seven times, and your flesh shall be restored and you shall be clean."* The healing that Naaman seeks he must have on his own terms. He wants a reception and a grand gesture befitting his position. If there is to be a washing, there are perfectly good rivers in his own land, but he is asked to go to the river of an inconsequential people—as though his disease were not humiliation enough!

A servant of his party (again sound advice comes from a servant) suggests that he put aside his petulance and his chauvinism and wash in the Jordan. When he does so, he is healed at once.

Ambrose of Milan was preaching after Easter in about 391 CE. When in his account of the baptismal rite he got to the water, he told the story of Naaman. He conjectures that Naaman, when he was told what he must do, said to himself, "Is that all? I come from Syria to the land of the Jews and someone says to me: 'Go to the Jordan, bathe there and you will be cured.'" [4] Several of the church fathers emphasize that in the Christian sacraments mighty results come from insignificant means, as though one must be humble enough to accept grace on its own modest terms.

Ambrose goes on to emphasize that the waters of baptism heal, just as the water of the Jordan healed Naaman. The story in 2 Kings 5 tells of a divine miracle. Yet, like much of the biblical presentation of the miraculous—and like the Christian sacraments—the act draws on and heightens deep natural associations. Mineral springs, warm springs, or sacred wells are and have long been places of healing. The Victorians coined the word "hydropathy" for treatment at the medicinal "watering places" in which many of them put much trust. Doctors and nurses require clean water for their work.

The New Testament imagery of baptism makes surprisingly little use of sin as sickness and water as healing, and the baptismal tradition has made only modest use of the Naaman story. Yet sickness suggests sin—a condition of limitedness, flawedness, anxiety, threat, and sometimes pain, that cannot be remedied by an act of will. Water, too, carries deep suggestion. We bring our tired, pain-filled, diseased bodies and minds to water, and wholeness begins to return. In nature and in sacrament, the healing through water is a gift of God.

This story as it was used in the church (although the point was probably not intended in the Jewish scriptures) may also suggest that in baptism, cleansing and salvation are offered to Gentiles as well as to Jews.

With Psalm 51:8-13

These verses from an intense psalm of penitence ask God, *Restore to me the joy of your salvation* (vss. 8, 12). Divine restoration is spoken of, as it often is, as cleansing: *Create in me a clean heart, O God* (vs. 10). The penitent asks for God's sustaining power: *Do not take your holy spirit from me* (vss. 11f).

Salvation offered freely to all: Isaiah 55:1-11

This passage is read at the Great Vigil of Easter. Comments are found on p. 53 above.

With Canticle 9 (The First Song of Isaiah)

See comments on pp. 55, 216.

A new Heart and a new Spirit: Ezekiel 36:24-28

This passage is read at the Great Vigil of Easter. Comments are found on p. 55.

With Psalm 42

This psalm, which occurs several times in the baptismal scriptures, is discussed on p. 244, below.

The spirit of the Lord is upon me: Isaiah 61:1-9

The spirit of the Lord GOD is upon me,
    because the LORD has anointed me;
he has sent me to bring good news to the oppressed,
    to bind up the brokenhearted,
to proclaim liberty to the captives,
    and release to the prisoners;
to proclaim the year of the LORD's favor,
    and the day of vengeance of our God;
    to comfort all who mourn;
to provide for those who mourn in Zion—
    to give them a garland instead of ashes,
the oil of gladness instead of mourning,
    the mantle of praise instead of a faint spirit.
They will be called oaks of righteousness,
    the planting of the LORD, to display his glory.
They shall build up the ancient ruins,
    they shall raise up the former devastations;
they shall repair the ruined cities,
    the devastations of many generations.
Strangers shall stand and feed your flocks,
    foreigners shall till your land and dress your vines;
but you shall be called priests of the LORD,
    you shall be named ministers of our God;
you shall enjoy the wealth of the nations,
    and in their riches you shall glory.
Because their shame was double,
    and dishonor was proclaimed their lot,
therefore they shall possess a double portion;
    everlasting joy shall be theirs.
For I the LORD love justice,
    I hate robbery and wrongdoing;
I will faithfully give them their recompense,
    and I will make an everlasting covenant with them.
Their descendants shall be known among the nations,
    and their offspring among the peoples;
all who see them shall acknowledge
    that they are a people whom the LORD has blessed.

In the last chapters of Isaiah, Israel is back in its own land, but conditions are harsh. In the midst of the disappointment and general despair, the Servant is anointed by the spirit of the Lord *to bring good news to the oppressed, to bind up the brokenhearted, to proclaim liberty to the captives.* The phrase *to proclaim the year of the LORD's favor* (vs. 2a) uses metaphorically the Jewish institutions of the Sabbatical Year, which came every seventh year (Ex. 21:2-6; Deut. 15:1-6, 12-18), and the Year of Jubilee, which came every fiftieth year (Lev. 25:8-17, 23-55; 27:16-25). On these occasions, debts were canceled and Israelite slaves set free. In effect, the unjust and unequal patterns of economic and social life which inevitably grow up, and which time only seems to make worse, were set aside, and the covenant people was to make a fresh beginning. It is not clear how often this remarkable legal provision was put into effect, but lodged in the Torah as it was, it must have occupied an important place in the imagination of the people. The prophet uses it as a picture of the age that is coming.

Verses 3ff speak in contrasts: *a garland instead of ashes.* The ruined cities will be rebuilt, while foreigners tend the flocks and lands. The nation will be priests, as declared in Exodus 19:6. The people which underwent double shame will receive double joy (vs. 7). Setting these things right is an act rooted in the character of God (vs. 8), who will reestablish the covenant and give the nation recognition as divinely blessed (vs. 9).

Luke 4:16-21 tells of Jesus' appearance in the synagogue at Nazareth, his native town, where he read the beginning of this passage, Isaiah 61:1-2a, and said, *"Today this scripture has been fulfilled in your hearing."* He was the one anointed by the Spirit to inaugurate the long-awaited Year of Jubilee. Wherever he went in Israel, bodies were healed, tormented minds were eased, ill-gotten gains were returned, and sins were forgiven.

The Isaiah passage suits a sacramental occasion in which a Christian is anointed, in the Anointed One, to receive his redemptive gift and then to share in his redemptive mission.

An alternative reading, *Behold my Servant: Isaiah 42:1-9,* is also appointed for the day itself and is commented on below.

With Psalm 89:20-29

These verses speak of God's anointing of David and his posterity to rule Israel. Their special emphasis is that the divine anointing pledges God's support for David, *My hand shall always remain with him.* (See also p. 144.)

When God's patience waited in the days of Noah: 1 Peter 3:15b-22

Always be ready to make your defense to anyone who demands from you an accounting for the hope that is in you; yet do it with gentleness and reverence. Keep your conscience clear, so that, when you are maligned, those who abuse you for your good conduct in Christ may be put to shame. For it is better to suffer for doing good, if suffering should be God's will, than to suffer for doing evil. For Christ also suffered for sins once for all, the righteous for the unrighteous, in order to bring you to God. He was put to death in the flesh, but made alive in the spirit, in which also he went and made a proclamation to the spirits in prison, who in former times did not obey, when God waited patiently in the days of Noah, during the building of the ark, in which a few, that is, eight persons, were saved through water. And baptism, which this prefigured, now saves you— not as a removal of dirt from the body, but as an appeal to God for a good conscience, through the resurrection of Jesus Christ, who has gone into heaven and is at the right hand of God, with angels, authorities, and powers made subject to him.

This passage holds many puzzles, yet its general thrust is clear enough. Christians threatened with persecution should be able to give an account of themselves to their opponents—taking care not to do so in a contentious manner (vs. 15b). The gospel which they have accepted has set their lives in a context of meaning, and they should be prepared to declare that meaning with courage. The homilist credits the pagan society with an ability to recognize the integrity of Christians (vs. 16). Believers, if they suffer, must suffer for doing good, not evil (vs. 17).

The homilist's mind works by associations, rather than by linear argument. The possibility that Christians may suffer makes him think of Christ's suffering. That thought leads him into a lengthy, creed-like reference to the work of Christ (vss. 18-22).

When, in his christological affirmations, the homilist speaks of Christ's resurrection, he passes to the difficult saying that Christ made *a proclamation to the spirits in prison*. The homilist probably refers to a tradition based in Genesis 6 and in 1 Enoch about angels who corrupted human life and brought on the judgment of the flood—the worst imaginable sinners (vs. 20a). Jesus in his death *proclaimed* to them. (Was it judgment or mercy that he proclaimed?) The homilist uses this reference to say that his hearers should bear witness in their difficult situation. "Christ's preaching to the spirits in prison is the prototype of the preaching of Christian messengers."[5]

The reference to these "spirits" makes the homilist think of Noah, of judgment, and of salvation. In the destruction that fell on the world in the flood, *eight persons were saved through water* (vs. 20b). The homilist implies that the church is the ark, the place where persons are preserved from judgment. The reference to *eight persons* may be not mean that only a few are saved, but rather, since eight can be a number of wholeness, to the totality of the redeemed. In the homilist's mind, the reference to salvation through water suggests baptism, which *now saves you* (vs. 21a). (The "now" may have referred to a baptism that had just been performed.)

The homilist, having ended his Noah/baptism digression, returns to his christological construction, concluding it with the ascended Christ at God's right hand (vs. 22).

Although we have been treating 1 Peter as a work composed for a baptismal occasion and as possibly a baptismal homily, 3:21 is the only place in which it expressly mentions baptism: *baptism. . .now saves you.* Baptism is taken to be an effective act. It is not simply declaratory; it saves. It does not save automatically, however, but is in the service of a saving good news and of a deeply amended and believing life.

The homilist seeks to be encouraging and at the same time realistic. In the first century—and at many times and places since—it was an act of courage to present oneself for baptism. To declare oneself for Christ opened one to misunderstanding, ostracism, and possibly to outright danger. Yet the homilist, with his Noah analogy in mind, is saying that the society stands under judgment, while believers are within the divine saving purpose.

[This passage is also read on Lent 1 in Year B, where it stands with the Noah story itself. But it was only noted briefly in the remarks on the Lenten readings, fuller comment having been reserved for this place.]

The alternative reading, *God anointed Jesus with the Holy Spirit: Acts 10:34-38,* is also appointed for the Baptism of Our Lord itself, as are four readings from the gospels. These passages are commented on below.

THE BAPTISM OF OUR LORD (EPIPHANY 1)

The liturgical observance of the baptism of Jesus on the First Sunday after Epiphany carries a rich selection of scripture passages.

Isaiah 42:1-9 [The first reading for Epiphany 1 in all three years.]

Here is my servant, whom I uphold,
my chosen, in whom my soul delights;
I have put my spirit upon him;
he will bring forth justice to the nations.
He will not cry or lift up his voice,
or make it heard in the street;
a bruised reed he will not break,
and a dimly burning wick he will not quench;
he will faithfully bring forth justice.
He will not grow faint or be crushed
until he has established justice in the earth;
and the coastlands wait for his teaching.

Thus says God, the LORD,
who created the heavens and stretched them out,
who spread out the earth and what comes from it,
who gives breath to the people upon it
and spirit to those who walk in it:
I am the LORD, I have called you in righteousness,
I have taken you by the hand and kept you;
I have given you as a covenant to the people,
a light to the nations,
to open the eyes of the blind,
to bring out the prisoners from the dungeon,
from the prison those who sit in darkness.
I am the LORD, that is my name;
my glory I give to no other,
nor my praise to idols.
See, the former things have come to pass,
and new things I now declare;
before they spring forth,
I tell you of them.

Here is my servant. The voice of God presents or commends the mysterious, powerful yet gentle figure "the Servant of God," who appears in several other passages in Second Isaiah. The Servant is described in quite personalized terms, as though he were an individual; but some related texts speak of the Servant as corporate, implying that the Servant is Israel (49:3). Probably the prophet thinks of the Servant as something like an idealized depiction of the nation in its chosenness and its unique mission.

The Servant is upheld by God, chosen by God, and is one in whom God delights and upon whom God's spirit has been put (vs. 1). God has taken him by the hand and kept him (vs. 6). Thus the large public tasks which are committed to him—to *bring forth justice to the nations*—are rooted in a unique, sustained, fulfilling interior relation in which he is affirmed, supported, and commissioned by God and anointed with divine power.

Through the figure of the Servant, the prophet seems to be calling Israel to rid itself of its provincialism and address its divinely given vocation to *establish justice in the earth* (vss. 3b-4), to be *a light to the nations* (vs. 6b), to open blind eyes and bring prisoners out of their dungeons (vs. 7).

In the character of the Servant there is a mixture of strength and gentleness. Although the quest for justice has often seemed incompatible with the ways of quiet persuasion, the Servant works patiently and gently, speaking in a soft voice and appreciating and cherishing life where he finds it—even if it is as weak as a bent blade of grass or an oil lamp which is about to go out (vss. 2-3a).

On the Feast of the Baptism of Our Lord we observe in this passage the divine voice saying *I have put my spirit upon him*—suggesting the descent of the Spirit on Jesus. We note, too, that the opening words of this Servant Song, *my chosen in whom my soul delights,* are the source of the divine attestation *in whom I am well pleased* that is repeated in all the synoptic baptism stories (Mt. 4:17; Mk. 1:11; Lk. 3:22). Do the evangelists, when they make these allusions in telling the story of Jesus' baptism, mean for their biblically literate readers to overhear the larger context of this Servant Song as a whole? If so, they are saying that Jesus is the Servant—and since Israel is the Servant, Jesus is Israel. This song suggests Jesus' chosenness and calling in righteousness, his unobtrusiveness, his ministry of justice and liberation. (Isa. 42:1-4, a lengthy passage, is cited in Mt. 12:18-21 as fulfilled in Jesus.)

The passage closes emphasizing that the Lord who commissions the Servant is the only God, and the mission of the Servant is for the glory and praise of God: *I am the LORD, that is my name; my glory I give to no other, nor my praise to idols.*

Acts 10:34-38 [Second reading for Epiphany 1, all three years.]

Then Peter began to speak to them: "I truly understand that God shows no partiality, but in every nation anyone who fears him and does what is right is acceptable to him. You know the message he sent to the people of Israel, preaching peace by Jesus Christ—he is Lord of all. That message spread throughout Judea, beginning in Galilee after the baptism that John announced: how God anointed Jesus of Nazareth with the Holy Spirit and with power; how he went about doing good and healing all who were oppressed by the devil, for God was with him.

Peter is in the house of Cornelius, a Gentile who knows and respects the traditions of the Jews. There is surprise, even shock, all around that Peter should be there. But as Peter (vss. 28-29) and Cornelius (vss. 30-33a) review the events that brought them together, they are convinced that their course has been divinely led.

When Peter is invited to speak (vs. 33b) he begins with what his visit has shown him, almost against his will. He *truly understands,* or he perceives for himself, that God's interest is not confined to any one group of persons, but rather that God responds to those from any nation who truly fear him and do what is right.

While these remarks by Peter imply a universal interest and care on the part of God and a universal access to God for all, they should not be misunderstood. They are said by a missionary who has come to tell a specific story and to make a particular appeal. Peter's point is that he respects what has happened before his arrival; God had been at work long before Peter came to Cornelius' door, Peter's coming completes all that had gone before.

Peter begins with a précis of the ministry of Jesus, speaking as though all or some of it is already known to his hearers. His account is more circumstantial than any other New Testament reference to the ministry of Jesus outside the gospels. This summary begins with John the Baptist and Jesus' baptism. In all the gospels, Jesus' baptism fills a structural place as the inaugural event of his ministry. One cannot tell his story adequately and leave this incident out. Thus it is remarkable how few references there are to Jesus' baptism outside the gospels. In addition to the present one, see Acts 1:21f., which describes the span of Jesus' ministry as . . .*all the time that the Lord Jesus went in and out among us from the baptism of John until the day when he was taken up from us.*

Peter speaks of Jesus' baptism as the moment when God anointed him *with the Holy Spirit and with power.* (Jesus is spoken of as anointed by God in Lk. 4:18, and in a prayer in Acts 4:27, and in a quotation in Heb. 1:9; but only in Acts 10:38 is Jesus' anointing expressly connected with his baptism.) The symbol of divine anointing is christological. The Greek word "the Christ" is the equivalent of the Hebrew "the Messiah," and both mean "the Anointed," the "en-Christed." "Messiah" is a term which gathers up the Jewish saga of history and promise, relating Jesus to the hope, disappointment and yearning of Israel. Jesus' baptism (i.e. his anointing) identified him as one on whom that long expectation came to rest. His anointing set him in a representative role; he was designated for a saving task. But the image which is christological is also ecclesiological, for in him a people is anointed (1 Jn. 2:20). Thus the divine anointing is a motif both of Jesus' baptism and of ours.

In the rite of Holy Baptism, the Thanksgiving over the Water (BCP, p. 306) refers to this circle of ideas. The celebrant, speaking of Christ and his people, gives thanks *for the gift of water. . .In it your Son Jesus received the baptism of John and was anointed by the Holy Spirit as the Messiah, the Christ, to lead us, through his death and resurrection, from the bondage of sin into everlasting life.*

[This reading for the Baptism of Christ only includes the first part of what Peter says and does not continue with his account of the death and resurrection of Jesus or with the dramatic events that interrupted his address. Other parts of the story of Peter at Cornelius' house are used elsewhere. See the index of scripture passages.]

Matthew 3:13-17 [Epiphany 1, Year A]

Then Jesus came from Galilee to John at the Jordan, to be baptized by him. John would have prevented him, saying, "I need to be baptized by you, and do you come to me?" But Jesus answered him, "Let it be so now; for it is proper for us in this way to fulfill all righteousness." Then he consented. And when Jesus had been baptized, just as he came up from the water, suddenly the heavens were opened to him and he saw the Spirit of God descending like a dove and alighting on him. And a voice from heaven said, "This is my Son, the Beloved, with whom I am well pleased."

John preaches in the wilderness near the Jordan, where he baptizes those who repent of their sins (3:1f, 5). His mission is radical. Convinced that judgment is imminent, and speaking in his undiplomatic way, he compares the Pharisees and Sadducees who come to hear him to snakes scurrying before a wildfire. *"You brood of vipers! Who warned you to flee from the wrath to come?"* (3:7). He urges that to be a Jew by birth is not enough (3:9). The ax is even now at the root of the trees (3:10). Baptism by John signifies a break with the compromised, unprepared nation. But John's baptism was anticipatory. A greater one is soon to come who will separate the wheat from the chaff and who will baptize with the Holy Spirit and with fire (3:11f).

By coming to John, Jesus indicates that he is moving in the same circle of eschatological urgency as John; a new age is imminent, and he identifies himself with the sense of crisis. He stands with the children of Abraham who want to break with the disobedience and unfaithfulness that had brought destruction and held back the kingdom. He associates with the prepared community.

Matthew's account contains an exchange between John and Jesus. (It is only in Matthew that Jesus says anything at his baptism.) The evangelist has given no indication that John knew Jesus, but when Jesus comes to John to be baptized, John objects: *I need to be baptized by you, and do you come to me?* Very likely the question that the evangelist assigns to John was the early church's question: Why should the greater figure consent to be baptized by the lesser figure? Why should the sinless one come to a baptism of repentance?

The inevitable question as to why the sinless Jesus went to a baptism of repentance is a poor question insofar as it considers Jesus as an isolated individual. But Jesus' words identify him as the Servant, i.e. as Israel. His calling *to fulfill all righteousness* is carried out as a representative. He goes to John's baptism because his mission must take him among sinners. The New Testament scholar Heinrich Schlier has written:

> He the obedient, places himself with sinners, he who comes from God and abides with God, with those who must turn to God. Now at the beginning of his way, on which time and time again he will stand "with" sinners, in order to grant them the righteousness of his presence, he joins them in the baptism which he asks of the Baptist. From then on, he who always comes to them as one who already stands with them, becomes more and more profoundly involved in such standing with them until it is manifest on the Cross as his dying for them. And so this baptism in water by John becomes the anticipatory sign of that baptism which is his death on the Cross.[6]

The words that the evangelist offers in explanation are not easy to interpret. Jesus' words, *"Let it be so now; for it is proper for us in this way to fulfill all righteousness,"* suggest the words, *I am the LORD, I have called you in righteousness* from the Servant Song of Isaiah which is the first reading (Isa. 42:8). Jesus is the Servant, called to fill his crucial place in God's righteous purpose. He is thinking of John's baptism in terms of the call for righteousness that lay behind John's appeal to repent. When Jesus comes to John, he identifies with a righteous purpose which he will henceforth serve faithfully and self-givingly. There may also be an allusion to the Servant of Isaiah 53:11, *The righteous one, my servant, shall make many righteous, and he shall bear their iniquities.* Jesus, at the Jordan, stands with the repentant, numbering himself with the transgressors so that he might bear the sin of many (vs. 12b).

There may be some further illumination of Jesus' words in Schuerer's report that some rabbis had calculated that the time for the Messiah's coming had already arrived, but he could not come until the people repented and perfectly fulfilled the law. "If all Israel would together repent for a whole day, the redemption by Messiah would ensue." "If Israel would only keep two Sabbaths properly, we should immediately be redeemed."[7] Jesus is *fulfilling all righteousness.* He is acting as Israel, standing with it, being righteous in it and for it.

In Matthew's account, the attestation of Jesus' sonship is public, spoken for all who would hear. (In Mark it is private, for Jesus himself.) The open heavens and the voice declaring that Jesus is God's son make the narrative of Jesus' baptism appropriate for the season of "epiphany," or "manifestation."

Mark 1:7-11 [Epiphany 1, Year B]

> John proclaimed, *"The one who is more powerful than I is coming after me; I am not worthy to stoop down and untie the thong of his sandals, I have baptized you with water; but he will baptize you with the Holy Spirit.*
>
> *In those days Jesus came from Nazareth of Galilee and was baptized by John in the Jordan. And just as he was coming out of the water, he saw the heavens torn apart and the Spirit descending like a dove on him. And a voice came from heaven, "You are my Son, the Beloved; with you I am well pleased."*

Mark's account of Jesus' baptism by John the Baptist is the earliest and simplest. It moves with almost breathless speed. Yet the brief narrative is full of ideas and images telling of a significant moment in the redemptive story.

John was an isolated, austere figure who called Israel to repentance (1.4-6). He did not preach in a population center, but in the wilderness near the Jordan river. His remote location and his rough garb identify him with

Elijah, who was expected to return as a harbinger of the day of the Lord (Mal. 3:1-2; 4:5f; Mk. 6:15; 9:11-13). People came to John in large numbers, and he baptized those who heeded his message and confessed their sins. Several Jewish groups of the time observed ritual baptisms, but in them the candidates baptized themselves before witnesses. The name, "John the Baptizer," indicates that John actively (and perhaps none too gently) baptized those who came to him. Even though he was a strong personality, he regarded his mission as anticipatory, heralding one who was coming after him who would offer a greater baptism (1:7-8).

As Jesus begins to entertain questions about himself and his work, he is drawn to where the deepest spiritual initiative is stirring in Israel; he identifies with John and with the repentant, prepared people that were stirred into life by his preaching.

This account gives no description of Jesus' actual baptism. The story hurries to the confirmation that was given to Jesus from the divine side as he *was coming out of the water*. Modern readers may ask insistently, "What really happened? If a reporter or a news photographer had been there, what would have been seen or heard?" But the New Testament account has little interest in such a question. The evangelist, writing some years after the event (an event at which no follower of Jesus was present), uses material that has come to him through Christian tradition; his language is full of suggestion and overtones; he is less a reporter than an interpreter. He cites visual and audible witnesses which provide a theological meaning for the baptism.

What happens in the story happens for Jesus—what he saw and heard. The heavens are torn, signifying direct contact with the divine realm (Isa. 64:1; Ezek. 1:1; Jn. 1:51; Acts 7:56; Rev. 4:1; 11:19; 19:11). The really real, which is ordinarily veiled, suddenly stands open; and a voice from the other side speaks to Jesus.

The Spirit descends on Jesus. In Jewish thought of the time it was understood that although prophecy was silent and the Spirit was stilled, the age of the Messiah would be an age of the Spirit—an age which, Mark's account implies, had begun to dawn.

Several interpretations have been offered for the Spirit descending *like a dove*.[8] The image may suggest the "brooding" or stirring of the Spirit over the waters in the creation story (Gen. 1:1f), which some rabbinic thought compared to a dove hovering over her young. A connection with Genesis would suggest that in Jesus and his mission God was moving freshly, as at the primal creation. But the dove may derive from the flood story, in which Noah sends out a dove which returns with an olive branch (Gen. 8:6-12) suggesting peace and restoration. Or it may allude to the voice of the dove in Song of Solomon 2:12, which was spoken of in rabbinic tradition as "the voice of the Holy Spirit of salvation." This uncertain but suggestive image speaks of the Spirit, God's very "breath," anointing Jesus for his mission.

A voice from heaven (the *bath qol*, "the daughter of the voice," a rabbinic convention) speaks directly to Jesus; the voice was for him, not for any overhearers. *You are my son, my Beloved, in you I am well pleased.* These words of divine approval or designation contain a compound allusion to Jewish scriptures:

The words *You are my son* are from Psalm 2:7, a royal psalm in which, in an enthronement declaration, God says to the king: *"You are my son; today I have begotten you."* Throughout Mark's story there is much evasiveness about who Jesus is. People ask him, "Are you who we think you may be?" But when anyone gets close to the truth of the matter, Jesus tells them to keep silent (8:29f). But Mark lets his readers in on the secret. Early, at the baptism (1:1, 11); then in the middle, at the transfiguration (9:7), through a heavenly voice; and finally late, through a Roman centurion at the crucifixion (15:39), he tells his readers that Jesus is the Son of God.

The words *with you I am well pleased,* cite a prophetic passage about a Servant of God who is anointed for a redemptive mission, *"Here is my servant. . ., my chosen, in whom my soul delights; I have put my spirit upon him,"* (Isa. 42:1). One interpreter describes these words in the baptism account as "a Christian hymnic translation" of Isaiah 42:1.[9] (The Isaiah passage which lies behind the words *with you I am well pleased* is the first reading for the day and was considered above.)

These sources, Psalm 2:1 and Isaiah 42:1, are combined. The Messiah's royal vocation will be worked out through the role of the Servant of God.

Jesus' baptism, which is clearly seen as an anointing or setting-apart, has a striking anticipation in a pre-Christian Jewish writing, *The Testament of Levi,* which says about a new priest whom God will raise up:

The heavens will be opened,
and from the temple of glory sanctification will come upon him,
with a fatherly voice, as from Abraham to Isaac.
And the glory of the Most High shall burst forth upon him.
And the spirit of understanding and sanctification
shall rest upon him [in the water].[10]

Luke 3:15-16, 21-22 [Epiphany 1, Year C]

As the people were filled with expectation, and all were questioning in their hearts concerning John, whether he might be the Messiah, John answered all of them by saying, "I baptize you with water; but one who is more powerful than I is coming; I am not worthy to untie the thong of his sandals. He will baptize you with the Holy Spirit and fire. . . .Now when all the people were baptized, and when Jesus also had been baptized and was praying, the heaven was opened, and the Holy Spirit descended upon him in bodily form like a dove. And a voice came from heaven, "You are my Son, the Beloved; with you I am well pleased."

Luke's story is modeled on Mark, but with some differences. His narrative is set against a background of popular expectation and questioning whether or not John might be the Messiah. John says he is not, and at once he turns attention from himself and to the one who is coming, who is superior to himself and brings a greater baptism. The two men and the two missions flow from one to the other. Luke is even more brief and incidental than were either Mark or Matthew in telling of Jesus' actual baptism, using only an adverbial phrase, *and when Jesus also had been baptized.*

When Luke says *when Jesus also had been baptized and was praying, the heaven was opened,* it sounds as though the heaven opened because Jesus was praying. The prayer of Jesus is mentioned often in Luke (5:16; 6:12; 9:18, 28, 29; 11:1), and the epiphany at his baptism is linked with the epiphany at the transfiguration, which also takes place when Jesus was praying (9:28f).

In the synoptic accounts, the divine voice uses the term *Beloved—* *"You are my Son, the Beloved."* The address traces to the divine description of the Servant in Isaiah 42:1, *"my chosen, in whom my soul delights."* (This "servant song" is also quoted more extensively in Mt. 12:18-21 as fulfilled in Jesus.) The term may have been prompted also by Isaiah 5:1, in which God says, *Let me sing for my beloved* [i.e. my beloved Israel] *my love-song concerning his vineyard.* Almost certainly it carries echoes from Abraham's relation to Isaac, *"Your son, your only son Isaac, whom you love"* (Gen. 22:2, 12). In the Fourth Gospel it is a basic christological theme that Jesus is an only Son who is loved by the Father (3:35; 5:20; 10:17; 15:9; 17:23f, 26). Clearly the expression speaks of a deep, unique intimacy between the Father and the Son. The one who loved others and brought divine love to them and taught them to love was himself first the object of love. In Ephesians 1:6 the term has become a christological title; God has bestowed grace on us *in the Beloved.* This name of Jesus, this verse suggests, may well relate to Christians who by baptism are a people beloved in the Beloved One.

Psalm 40:1-10 [Epiphany 1, Year A]

This psalm glows with joy and gratitude. God has done something wonderful for the psalmist—something for which he had waited patiently. When he speaks of it to others, he describes it vividly, but uncircumstantially: *He lifted me out of the desolate pit, out of the mire and clay; he set my feet on a high cliff and made my footing sure.* God has given the psalmist a new song. Verse 4 is a general exclamation, a "beatitude." *Happy are they who trust in the LORD!*

At verse 5 the psalmist begins to address God directly: *Great things are they that you have done, O LORD my God!* Your goodness is too great to be given adequate expression; your kindnesses *are more than I can count.* The first expression to come from a grateful person might well be sacrifice, but the psalmist pledges instead to listen to God and to obey God: *I love to do your will, O my God; your law is deep in my heart.* The gratitude and self-dedication of this psalm may give voice to persons who are being baptized or to persons who are remembering their baptism.

Psalm 89:1-29 or 89:20-29 [Epiphany 1, Years B and C]

This psalm passage (whether it is read in the short or the long form) is very full. It speaks of the faithfulness of God which is witnessed in the reliability of the heavens (vss. 2, 5) and in the trustworthiness of God's covenant (vss. 3f). God is supreme in the council of the holy ones (vss. 6-8) and rules in the natural world (vss. 9-12). God's power is rooted in righteousness and justice (vs. 14). Thus the people who know such a god are happy (vss. 15-18).

Verses 20-29 of the psalm are spoken in the voice of God, as though God were telling what had been said in promise to David. *Forever I will keep my steadfast love for him, and my covenant with him will stand firm.*

The Second Sunday after Epiphany

We have noted that in the early centuries, and still in the East, Epiphany was and is a feast of the incarnation which holds together the "showing forth" of Jesus at his birth (including the coming of the Magi), at his baptism, and at the wedding at Cana. The dominant Western emphasis at Epiphany on the story of the visit of the Magi ("the manifestation to the

Gentiles") has narrowed this meaning. The Prayer Book lectionary, drawing on older and Eastern emphases, enriches the season, adding further Johannine "showings" of Jesus.

John 1:29-34 [Epiphany 2, Year A]

The next day John saw Jesus coming toward him and declared, "Here is the Lamb of God who takes away the sin of the world! This is he of whom I said, 'After me comes a man who ranks ahead of me because he was before me.' I myself did not know him; but I came baptizing with water for this reason, that he might be revealed to Israel." And John testified, "I saw the Spirit descending from heaven like a dove, and it remained on him. I myself did not know him, but the one who sent me to baptize with water said to me, 'He on whom you see the Spirit descend and remain is the one who baptizes with the Holy Spirit.' And I myself have seen and have testified that this is the Son of God."

Many features of this Johannine account set it apart from the baptism narratives in the synoptic gospels and bring it within the distinctive point of view of the Fourth Gospel. One may notice that this text does not actually say that Jesus was baptized. (Similarly, the Gospel of John contains no account of the institution of the Lord's Supper.) What the Fourth Gospel does say about the sacraments is contained in the long discourses which mark the text. Being *born again* or *born from above* is the subject of chapter 3, the *water of life* is developed in chapter 4 and in 7:37-39, and *the bread from heaven* is developed in the discourse of chapter 6. Needless to say, interpreters ask why the evangelist tells his story in a way that seems almost evasive. Perhaps he was correcting mistaken emphases by throwing attention away from the sacraments themselves and to the realities in and behind the sacraments.

John (who is not called "the Baptist" in this gospel) was baptizing at the Jordan (1:28). Even though he did not know Jesus (vss. 31f), when he saw Jesus coming to him he identified him as the one who was to come, declaring him to be *the Lamb of God who takes away the sin of the world* (1:29f). John reports that he saw the Spirit descend on Jesus as a dove (vs. 32), a sign from God (vs. 33). (It is not expressly said that John's vision of the descending Spirit came after Jesus' baptism, though doubtless we are to understand it so.) John (and not a voice from heaven) bears witness that Jesus is the Son of God (vs. 34). John says that this announcement of the God-designated Son was the central purpose of his ministry (vss. 31, 33f). The pronouncement of verse 29, *"Here is the Lamb of God who takes away the sin of the world!"* may be understood to be the result of the disclosure of verses 32f, although for literary reasons it is set at the head of the passage.

Despite the puzzles of the passage and its intention, two emphases are clear:

(1) The author mentions twice that the Spirit *descended and remained* on Jesus (vss. 32, 33). ("Remain" or "abide" is a favorite word of the evangelist.) In the experience of Israel, the divine Spirit seems somewhat occasional—a divine power given for special tasks, but withdrawn after a task is completed. But the Spirit descends on Jesus and remains—not staying briefly nor coming and going intermittently, but in a sustained relationship. (Later, in Jesus' farewell, he will tell his followers that the Spirit will be with them forever, 14:16f.)

(2) The Fourth Gospel tells the story of Jesus' baptism entirely from the point of view of John—what he saw, heard, understood, and said. There is no exchange between Jesus and John and no voice from heaven. The narrative gives no indication that the event held any critical importance for Jesus himself. The evangelist's emphasis is on witness. His account begins, *This is the testimony given by John* (1:19). When John begins to speak, he points away from himself, saying, *"I am not the Messiah"* (1:20), and points to Jesus. He describes his purpose, saying: *"I came baptizing with water for this reason, that he might be revealed to Israel"* (1:31). The baptism, as it is understood in the Fourth Gospel, does not make something become true for Jesus; rather, it makes known openly something that is true. We may note the vocabulary: *testimony* (1:19), *confessed, and did not deny but confessed* (1:20), *declared* (1:29), *"that he might be revealed to Israel"* (1:31), *testified* (1:32). John concludes, saying *"I myself have seen and have testified that this is the Son of God"* (1:34). In the Fourth Gospel, this incident is a revealing, a publicizing, a declaration, a witness, a showing forth, an epiphany.

The first reading on the Sunday is *Isaiah 49:1-7,* which describes the Servant as secretly fashioned by God to be the one in whom God will be glorified. Despite opposition and frustrations, this servant is to be *a light to the nations*, through whom God's salvation reaches *to the end of the earth. Psalm 40:1-10* is a grateful song of deliverance; thanksgiving is sealed by obedience, which is better than sacrifice (vss. 6-8). The epistle is

1 Corinthians 1:1-9, in which Paul speaks of the grace that has been given to his readers, enriching them with gifts for their present witness and holding them blameless to the end.

John 1:43-51 [Epiphany 2, Year B]

> *The next day Jesus decided to go to Galilee. He found Philip and said to him, "Follow me." Now Philip was from Bethsaida, the city of Andrew and Peter. Philip found Nathanael and said to him, "We have found him about whom Moses in the law and also the prophets wrote, Jesus son of Joseph from Nazareth." Nathanael said to him, "Can anything good come out of Nazareth?" Philip said to him, "Come and see." When Jesus saw Nathanael coming toward him, he said of him, "Here is truly an Israelite in whom there is no deceit!" Nathanael asked him, "Where did you get to know me?" Jesus answered, "I saw you under the fig tree before Philip called you." Nathanael replied, "Rabbi, you are the Son of God! You are the King of Israel!" Jesus answered, "Do you believe because I have told you that I saw you under the fig tree? You will see greater things than these." And he said to him, "Very truly, I tell you, you will see heaven opened and the angels of God ascending and descending upon the Son of Man."*

In John, as in the other gospels, Jesus begins his ministry by gathering some followers. Whereas in the synoptics, the first disciples are fishermen, in the Fourth Gospel they are disciples of John the Baptist.

Jesus himself finds Philip, who in turn finds Nathanael and says to him, *"We have found him about whom Moses in the law and also the prophets wrote, Jesus son of Joseph from Nazareth"*—that is to say, "We have found the Messiah." When Nathanael expresses some hesitation (with vs. 46, compare 7:52), Philip does not argue, but urges Nathanael to try, to test, to look into the matter, *"Come and see."* When Jesus sees Nathanael coming to him, he seems to know him and describes him as *"Truly an Israelite in whom there is no deceit."* Jesus' description is a play on words, since *Israelite* means "descendant of Jacob," and while Jacob was a deceitful person, Nathanael is not. Nathanael does not modestly turn aside the description, but accepts it, and, impressed that Jesus knows his character, says to him, *"Rabbi, you are the Son of God! You are the King of Israel!"* (Israel's king was often spoken of as "the son of God.") The affirmation is one of several direct characterizations of Jesus by others in the Fourth Gospel; Jesus several times says, *I am,* but others say several times of him, *You are.*

Because of his affirmation, Jesus says that Nathanael has believed—the first-person in the story to do so. Jesus adds that although Nathanael may be impressed by what he has seen, if he follows Jesus, he will *see greater things than these*. He will, Jesus says, *"see heaven opened and the angels of God ascending and descending upon the Son of Man."* Jesus refers to Genesis 28:12, where Jacob sees a vision of a ladder reaching to heaven with angels ascending and descending on it. Jesus is saying to Nathanael, an Israelite, "You will see what your father saw." The christology of the remark is that in seeing Jesus with the eyes of faith, one sees the reality of earth engaged with heaven and the reality of heaven brought into engagement with earth. (See Eph. 1:10 and Col. 1:20 for another idiom which says that heaven and earth are united in Christ.)

What does this promise mean? Will Nathanael, if he follows, see these *greater things* in the course of Jesus' ministry? Or will he see them after Jesus' departure, in the life of the church under the Spirit? Or does the evangelist mean for us to understand both?

Jacob, at the close of the story of his dream, in a striking recognition, said, "How awesome is this place! This is none other than the house of God, and this is the gate of heaven" (Gen. 28:17). This verse in John, by its clear allusion, seems to say that where Christ is, where people meet in his name, where he is known, called upon, and served—there is none other than the house of God; there is the gate of heaven. Heaven and earth meet in a place of mystery and awe.

The christological affirmations of the incident (vss. 45 and 49, culminating in vs. 51) are clearly the heart of the story and the reason for its inclusion as a reading for Epiphany, with its emphasis on divine disclosure or showing forth. (One notes in this passage the terms of *finding, knowing,* and *seeing*.) Epiphany is a season of the disclosure of the really real. Baptism is a rite that admits one to the house of God and the gate of heaven.

The first reading is *1 Samuel 3:1-10 (11-20)*, the very human story of the call of the boy Samuel. *Psalm 63:1-8* is a prayer for divine help by one who has come into the sanctuary. The psalmist seeks God *because your steadfast love is better than life*. In *1 Corinthians 6:11b-20*, Paul rebukes the divisions at Corinth which subvert the message of the cross.

John 2:1-11 [Epiphany 2, Year C]

On the third day there was a wedding in Cana of Galilee, and the mother of Jesus was there. Jesus and his disciples had also been invited to the wedding. When the wine gave out, the mother of Jesus said to him, "They have no wine." And Jesus said to her, "Woman, what concern is that to you and to me? My hour has not yet come." His mother said to the servants, "Do whatever he tells you." Now standing there were six stone water jars for the Jewish rites of purification, each holding twenty or thirty gallons. Jesus said to them, "Fill the jars with water." And they filled them up to the brim. He said to them, "Now draw some out, and take it to the chief steward." So they took it. When the steward tasted the water that had become wine, and did not know where it came from (though the servants who had drawn the water knew), the steward called the bridegroom and said to him, "Everyone serves the good wine first, and then the inferior wine after the guests have become drunk. But you have kept the good wine until now." Jesus did this, the first of his signs, in Cana of Galilee, and revealed his glory; and his disciples believed in him.

This story (which was appointed for Epiphany 3 in the 1928 Prayer Book) suits the Epiphany theme because in the sign at Cana Jesus *revealed his glory*. But what is revealed?

The Jesus of the gospels is not abstemious, but rather, unlike John the Baptist, he "comes eating and drinking." In this story, he is at a village wedding, an occasion in which a happy couple is surrounded by well-wishers. This time of festivity carries the community beyond the means-and-ends-dominated work week. Here people, through sharing in food, share in life.

But the occasion is marred. The wine runs out. Embarrassment all around! The neighbors will talk for years! Even our festive occasions have their anxieties: Will there be enough? What can we serve that everyone will eat? Will the guests like it? We hope people will drink, but will some of them drink too much? Will people think we are too cheap? Too extravagant?

The story portrays Jesus present among ordinary people doing ordinary things. But he is not simply someone who came along (bringing his friends) because the family knew his mother. Rather, before the meal is over this guest has become the genial host, the Lord of the Dance, the preparer of Babette's Feast, the invited friend who saves the occasion.

This story contains hints of lurking meanings beyond the obvious—Jesus' mention of his *hour*, the *six* water pots of Jewish purification, the designation of Jesus' act as a *sign* which manifested his glory. Interpreters who look for subsurface meanings will find them. But at an obvious level the story speaks of Jesus as one who offers joy which is to all other joys as wine is to water. His gospel is not given to carry us out of ordinary life, but to let us live it fully and truly. The Gospel of John will say many other things before it is through. Its story will come to a bitter cross. But in this "frontispiece," Jesus' first sign at Cana of Galilee, it opens the possibility that those who are associated with Christ are enabled to say a wholehearted "yes" to life. They can live in God's world on God's terms, and find it good.

On the Sunday on which this gospel is read, the first lesson is *Isaiah 62:1-5:* God will vindicate and bless Israel. *Psalm 96* is a call to praise the God who made and rules all things. The epistle reading is *1 Corinthians 12:1-11.* The one Spirit of God distributes to Christians varieties of gifts, all intended for the common good.

CHAPTER 5

The Scriptures for the Vigil of All Saints and All Saints' Day

In its New Testament sense, the word *saint* does not refer to persons of sterling character who have made significant spiritual achievements. Rather, to be a Christian is to be a "saint." The English word *saint* comes from the Latin *sanctus,* which means "holy," and all the baptized make up a "holy people"—holy in the Holy One (see 1 Pet. 2:9, which draws on Ex. 19:6). All believing people are sinful, and many of them have grave weaknesses. Yet they are made saints, not by their worthiness or their effort, but by grace, by divine acceptance. This idea of "holiness" had its roots in Jewish cultic life, where it spoke of things (such as the altar) or times (such as the sabbath) or persons (such as the priests and Levites) which were "holy" because they were set apart for God. It was an important part of Israel's self-awareness that the entire people was a holy people, consecrated to God by God's own call and the people's consent, *You shall be for me a priestly kingdom and a holy nation* (Ex. 19:6). This collective identification of Israel as a people special to God has been claimed by Christians, all of whom are, by faith in Christ—a faith signified in baptism—made special, set apart by God for the service of God: *You are a chosen race, a royal priesthood, a holy nation, God's own people* (1 Pet. 2:9).

Yet, while holiness, in this biblical sense, is not primarily ethical, it carries moral demands. Holiness, individual and collective, requires justice and faithfulness, for, as the law and the prophets urged, covenant brings persons into relation with a righteous God, and as God is, so God's people should be. In the community that is called to holiness, some persons hear and follow that summons more faithfully than others. The leading and discipline of the divine call shapes certain persons deeply, making them to a new image. Even persons who show manifest flaws and one-sidedness may exemplify some aspect of what Christians aspire to be. Christians need to hold before themselves persons from the past or the present who are close-at-hand and very human and who are at the same time signs of the transcendent. Most of life, including life in faith, is quite ordinary. Yet ordinary people can find their lives lifted out of ordinariness by models—by persons who focus and concretize some aspect of a call that is hard to respond to when it is described in general terms. In the mysterious exchanges of life in the community formed by grace, exemplary persons can point beyond themselves and mediate Christ. Paul puts himself in such a role when he counsels his readers, *Be imitators of me, as I am of Christ* (1 Cor. 11:1).

The honoring of paradigmatic Christian persons began very early in the church's life, centering at first on the martyrs. The word *martyr* (Greek *martyria*) means "witness," and before many years had passed, a growing number of people had given witness to their faith, even to death. By the second century, Christians held commemorations of locally known martyrs, often at their graves and on the anniversary of their death—which was regarded as their true "birthday in heaven."[1]

It took no leap of the imagination to connect martyrdom with baptism and birth with death. Both are moments when, in the midst of proximate things, we touch ultimate things. Martyrdom is a witness, but baptism is also an act of witness. While baptism is a dying, it pledges eternal life; while it is a birth, it speaks to a Christian's death.

In the early church, it was not a casual matter to be enrolled as a catechumen and to be baptized into Christ's people. To commit oneself to Christ in baptism might carry fearful consequences. Boone Porter said memorably: "For the ordinary early Christian as for St. Paul, to die with Christ was neither a far-fetched metaphor nor a mere act of ceremonial. It was an intensely real and intensely painful experience of sacrificing all the things on which one's security and self-respect had been based."[2] There is a somewhat unexpected bit of realism in Hippolytus, who, writing in the early third century, said that catechumens should not be concerned if they were martyred for their faith before they were baptized, for if that happened, they were *baptized in their own blood.*[3] The realities of baptism and martyrdom lay close together in the mind of the early church.

During the centuries of persecution, so many Christians had been killed for their faith that there were more martyrs than there were days in the year and more martyrs than any one part of the church could identify with. As early as the fourth century, some writers spoke of a day for the collective commemoration of all the martyrs.

Words mean what usage makes them mean, and in time, when Christianity had spread throughout much of ancient society, East and West, and virtually all members of the society were Christians—i.e. "saints" in the New Testament sense—the term "saint" came to stand for persons who exemplified some aspect of the life to which all were called. In time, persons who were not martyrs but who were recognized as ideals, models, or exemplars of faith, self-sacrifice, or spiritual attainment came to be recognized as saints. All Saints' Day, November 1 in the West, became, particularly in England, a popular festival celebrating these persons of varied achievement.

The Church of England at the Reformation dropped the process of canonization, the theology of merits, and the popular cult of saints. However, the Prayer Book continued to designate days to commemorate the apostles and some other persons who are mentioned in the New Testament. It also kept the observance on November 1 of All Saints, but the day was evidently intended to follow the biblical sense by referring to the whole company of the faithful rather than to a select group. (In later English Prayer Books, traditional days were designated for a list of non-biblical persons, but no liturgical material was provided for their observance, and these "Black Letter Days," had little impact on popular devotion. Since they were quite English, they were not continued in the Prayer Book of the American church.) This inclusive biblical way of using the term "saint" and of understanding All Saints' Day continued officially in the Anglican liturgical tradition through the 1928 Prayer Book. Nevertheless, many Episcopalians—influenced by popular piety, by the names of churches and guilds and by the words of many hymns—used the term saint, at least some of the time, in its popular, more restricted sense. Many church members no doubt thought that All Saints' Day was intended to celebrate heroic or notable persons from the church's past.

The 1979 Prayer Book has to some extent accepted this dual usage and has divided the meaning of the liturgical observance. The Christian imagination seems to need heroes of the faith. Yet at the same time, it needs a witness to the inclusion of all—including the many ordinary, unheroic, and largely unremembered Christians—in the community of grace. Many Christian believers lead lives of quiet faithfulness and courage. By baptism, they are under the sign of the cross. While the Prayer Book has set All Saints' Day on November 1, letting us remember the notable persons of faith who have gone before us, the day is followed at once on November 2 by "The Commemoration of All Faithful Departed," which is the liturgical recognition of the company of all believers. This Prayer Book provision is new and not well defined, and congregations are using it in varying ways and with varying understandings.

While All Saints is one of the days designated by rubric for baptism, there is no history for All Saints being a baptismal day (although saints' days were sometimes baptismal occasions in the early church). It is an innovation of the 1979 Prayer Book. But it is a valuable innovation, emphasizing that baptism is one's incorporation into the common life in Christ. In a sense, baptism is always particular and local. It always takes place in a specific congregation where one is baptized by one's own individual name and is surrounded by family, friends, and a local Christian community—persons who pledge themselves to support one another in the life in Christ. But the emphasis on particularity, on its own, risks making baptism sectarian, provincial, or sentimental. Baptism at All Saints' Day reminds that one is not baptized into a congregation or a denomination, but into the Great Church—Christ and all his people. One is united with persons *from every nation, from all tribes and peoples and languages* into a community which binds each one into the life that is shared in Christ among the dead, the living and the yet unborn.

[All Saints falls on a calendar day, November 1. Its emphasis on the faithful departed and its great hymns and scriptures make it a much-loved liturgical event. Yet many persons find it difficult to attend weekday services. The rubrics (BCP, p. 15) allow All Saints' Day to be observed *on the Sunday following November 1 in addition to its observance on the fixed date.* That Sunday being a congregation's All Saints' Day, it is a day for baptism.]

THE VIGIL OF ALL SAINTS OR OF THE SUNDAY AFTER ALL SAINTS

The *Book of Occasional Services* provides a Vigil which may be observed before All Saints or before the Sunday which follows (pp. 106f). The rite begins with The Service of Light (BCP, pp. 108-14). The text of the Vigil provides eight lessons, the last two of which are also the propers for the eucharist of All Saints' Day (and the last has three alternates from which to choose). Three or more of these lessons are to be read, each followed by a period of silence, and a psalm, canticle, or hymn. This Vigil, as a part of All Saints, is among the commended baptismal occasions; a rubric provides that *Holy Baptism or Confirmation (beginning with the Presentation of the Candidates), or the Renewal of Baptismal Vows, Prayer Book, page 292, follows the Sermon.*

The scriptures for the Vigil are:

The Call of Abraham: Genesis 12:1-8

Now the LORD said to Abram, "Go from your country and your kindred and from your father's house to the land that I will show you. I will make of you a great nation, and I will bless you, and make your name great, so that you will be a blessing. I will bless those who bless you, and the one who curses you I will curse; and in you all the families of the earth shall be blessed.

So Abram went, as the LORD had told him; and Lot went with him. Abram was seventy-five years old when he departed from Haran. Abram took his wife Sarai and his brother's son Lot, and all the possession that they had gathered, and the persons whom they had acquired in Haran; and they set forth to go to the land of Canaan. When they had come to the land of Canaan, Abram passed through the land to the place of Shechem, to the oaks of Moreh. At that time the Canaanites were in the land. Then the LORD appeared to Abram, and said, "To your offspring I will give this land." So he built there an altar to the LORD, who had appeared to him. From there he moved on to the hill country on the east of Bethel, and pitched his tent, with Bethel on the west and Ai on the east; and there he built an altar to the LORD and invoked the name of the LORD.

Abraham has been mentioned in Genesis before this incident, but he is totally embedded in his family—his ancestors, his wife, and her ancestors—and his location (11:27-32). Then out of nowhere comes an imperious voice. God summons Abraham to leave family and place and go to an unspecified destination. *"Go from your country and your kindred and from your father's house."* Even though a great inheritance is promised to him, Abraham's obedience is entirely a matter of trust. The validation, if it comes at all, will come after Abraham follows, not before.

Later in the story, when God has extended a seemingly impossible promise to Abraham, the narrative says that Abraham *believed the LORD; and the LORD reckoned it to him as righteousness* (Gen. 15:6). This trust is the determining feature of Abraham's relation to God. This significant passage is recalled in 1 Maccabees 2:52 to encourage faithfulness. Paul cites it in Galatians 3:6 in support of justification through faith, and in Romans 4:11, it is the trait that constitutes Abraham *the ancestor of all who believe.*

This story of Abraham's call may be read at baptism, where a struggling member of twentieth-century society gives an answer to a divine call—usually a call not well understood at the time. This call can later grow to be deeply heard, shaking one loose from ordinary ties and small views of one's purpose, and setting one on a journey whose destination is not known. *Do you renounce? Do you promise to follow?* Like Abraham, one follows in faith.

With Psalm 113

The name of the Lord merits constant praise (vss. 1-4). God, who *is seated on high,* yet looks far down on earth (vss. 5-6). His looking is an involvement, an action. He raises the poor and the needy (vs. 7) and sets them with princes (vs. 8). He makes the barren woman to be *the joyous mother of children.* This psalm, like 1 Samuel 2:4-8 and like the *Magnificat,* Luke 1:46-55, says that God turns social orders on their end. In the liturgy, it refers to Sarah when it says that God makes the barren woman bring forth children. It refers further to the baptized, who are called out of ordinary lives defined by circumstance and set upon a journey whose goal they do not know, but they trust the one who has called them.

Daniel delivered from the lions' den: Daniel 6: (1-15) 16-23

> *Then the king gave the command, and Daniel was brought and thrown into the den of lions. The king said to Daniel, "May your God, whom you faithfully serve, deliver you!" A stone was brought and laid on the mouth of the den, and the king sealed it with his own signet and with the signet of his lords, so that nothing might be changed concerning Daniel. Then the king went to his palace and spent the night fasting; so no food was brought to him, and sleep fled from him.*
>
> *Then, at break of day, the king got up and hurried to the den of lions. When he came near the den where Daniel was, he cried out anxiously, "O Daniel, servant of the living God, has your God whom you faithfully serve been able to deliver you from the lions?" Daniel then said to the king, "O king, live forever! My God sent his angel and shut the lions' mouths so that they would not hurt me, because I was found blameless before him; and also before you, O king, I have done no wrong." Then the king was exceedingly glad and commanded that Daniel be taken up*

out of the den. So Daniel was taken up out of the den, and no kind of harm was found on him, because he had trust in his God.

As the story has it, Daniel is a Jew living in exile who has gained a high place in the service of the king of Babylon. His loyalty to God has made him disobey the Babylonian king, and he is put in a den of lions. But not only does God deliver him, but Daniel's witness impresses the king. This story is a moral allegory—a part of an unusual Jewish writing from the third century BCE which mixes incident with apocalyptic vision. The nation is facing persecution, and the stories of Daniel and the other Jewish prisoners are told to encourage Jews at the time of writing to be faithful even though they live under alien domination. Persons who must show courage can be helped by stories of courage.

When the passage is read at the Vigil of All Saints it is a reminder that Christians always live in an alien land. The story of Daniel may encourage believers in any age to remain faithful, for no matter what the cost may be, God is always with them. The story of Daniel is the story of the saints and martyrs; it is a story for All Saints' Day; and it is encouragement for those who are being baptized and whose new life under a new loyalty may set them in opposition to the ways that surround them.

With Canticle 2 or 13

These canticles are appointed for an alternative reading at the Vigil of Pentecost (see p. 97).

The testament and death of Mattathias: 1 Maccabees 2:49-64

Now the days drew near for Mattathias to die, and he said to his sons: "Arrogance and scorn have now become strong; it is a time of ruin and furious anger. Now, my children, show zeal for the law, and give your lives for the covenant of our ancestors.

"Remember the deeds of the ancestors, which they did in their generations; and you will receive great honor and an everlasting name. Was not Abraham found faithful when tested, and it was reckoned to him as righteousness? Joseph in the time of his distress kept the commandment, and became lord of Egypt. Phineas our ancestor, because he was deeply zealous, received the covenant of everlasting priesthood. Joshua, because he fulfilled the command, became a judge in Israel. Caleb, because he testified to the assembly, received an inheritance in the land. David because he was merciful, inherited the throne of the kingdom forever. Elijah, because of great zeal for the law, was taken up into heaven. Hananiah,

Azariah, and Mishael believed and were saved from the flame. Daniel, because of his innocence, was delivered from the mouth of the lions.

And so observe, from generation to generation, that none of those who put their trust in him will lack strength. Do not fear the words of sinners, for their splendor will turn into dung and worms. Today they will be exalted, but tomorrow they will not be found, because they will have returned to the dust, and their plans will have perished. My children, be courageous and grow strong in the law, for by it you will gain honor.

The revered Mattathias is dying, and like Jacob and Moses and Samuel, he leaves his parting counsel with those who will succeed him. His children, in situations that require courage and steadfastness, must *remember the deeds of the ancestors.* Mattathias recalls the faithfulness of Abraham, the integrity of Joseph, the zeal of Phineas, the obedience of Joshua, the witness of Caleb, the mercy of David, the passion of Elijah, the trust of the three young men in the fiery furnace, and the innocence of Daniel. All these persons were true to God in difficult circumstances, and they were all vindicated.

This passage expresses a view that a reliable moral order lies at the heart of things, and goodness is rewarded, while sin brings ruin. This doctrine of providence (sometimes called the "Deuteronomic" view) is found fairly widely in the Bible: God delivers those in peril and brings the wicked to account. Persons of good will need to be confident that there is a moral order in and behind human existence, and that rectitude is not futile.

While this moral vision has supported many persons, and while wonderful deliverances are reported with awe and gratitude, on its own the Deuteronomic view is inadequate. The expectation that providence will bring about within history an equivalency between virtue and reward is not borne out in experience. (Many devout persons, baffled by adversity, have been led by their trust in this doctrine to ask tormented questions about themselves: What did I do?) Moreover, this Deuteronomic view is not the only or even the predominant biblical view of the ways of God. The Bible, at its most profound, takes account of the terrible negative evidence and asks why the wicked prosper and the righteous so often suffer. Much faithfulness is, as far as one can see, unrewarded. Pleas are made, and the heavens are silent. The Christian message centers on a crucified Messiah who, as far as history knows him, dies forsaken by God.

The contradictions of human life in history cannot be put under any simple doctrine. The somewhat naive view that is expressed in this passage might be held up against other biblical ways of thinking about providence. In 1 Peter, which we have taken to be a piece of spoken counsel for the newly baptized, the homilist, in 3:10-12, urges his hearers to remain faithful, but he cites not virtue and reward, but the innocent suffering of Jesus. He encourages them, quoting scriptural assurance that God is a watcher and a listener. If the view of providence in this passage appointed for the Vigil of All Saints seems to say that God always carries the devout through adversity and delivers them from peril, and while such deliverance does happen, yet, at its deepest, the Bible tells believers not to presume—but also not to despair, for in every extremity God is present in and with those who trust. God is afflicted in their affliction, and God is powerful and faithful through and beyond the worst that can befall one in this life.

With Psalm 1

This psalm is a "beatitude," describing the stability and delight that is found in following the law of the Lord and contrasting it with the insubstantial way of the wicked.

The martyrdom of the seven brothers: 2 Maccabees 6:1-2; 7:1-23

Not long after this, the king sent an Athenian senator to compel the Jews to forsake the laws of their ancestors and no longer to live by the law of God; also to pollute the temple in Jerusalem and to call it the temple of Olympian Zeus, and to call the one in Gerizim the temple of Zeus-the-Friend-of-Strangers, as did the people who lived in that place.

It happened also that seven brothers and their mother were arrested and were being compelled by the king, under torture with whips and thongs, to partake of unlawful swine's flesh. One of them, acting as their spokesman, said, "What do you intend to ask and learn from us? For we are ready to die rather than transgress the laws of our ancestors."

The king fell into a rage, and gave orders to have pans and caldrons heated. These were heated immediately, and he commanded that the tongue of their spokesman be cut out and that they scalp him and cut off his hands and feet, while the rest of the brothers and the mother looked on. When he was utterly helpless, the king ordered them to take him to the fire, still breathing, and to fry him in a pan. The smoke from the pan spread widely, but the brothers and their mother encouraged one another to die nobly, saying, "The Lord God is watching over us and in truth has compassion on us, as Moses declared in his song that bore witness against the people to their faces, when he said, 'And he will have compassion on his servants.'"

After the first brother had died in this way, they brought forward the second for their sport. They tore off the skin of his head with the hair, and asked him, "Will you eat rather than have your body punished limb by limb?" He replied in the language of his ancestors and said to them, "No." Therefore he in turn underwent tortures as the first brother had done. And when he was at his last breath, he said, "You accursed wretch, you dismiss us from this present life, but the King of the universe will raise us up to an everlasting renewal of life, because we have died for his laws."

After him, the third was the victim of their sport. When it was demanded, he quickly put out his tongue and courageously stretched forth his hands, and said nobly, "I got these from Heaven, and because of his laws I disdain them, and from him I hope to get them back again." As a result the king himself and those with him were astonished at the young man's spirit, for he regarded his sufferings as nothing.

After he too had died, they maltreated and tortured the fourth in the same way. When he was near death, he said, "One cannot but choose to die at the hands of mortals and to cherish the hope God gives of being raised again by him. But for you there will be no resurrection to life!"

Next they brought forward the fifth and maltreated him. But he looked at the king, and said, "Because you have authority among mortals, though you also are mortal, you do what you please. But do not think that God has forsaken our people. Keep on, and see how his mighty power will torture you and your descendants!"

After him they brought forward the sixth. And when he was about to die, he said, "Do not deceive yourself in vain. For we are suffering these things on our own account, because of our sins against our own God. Therefore astounding things have happened. But do not think that you will go unpunished for having tried to fight against God!"

The mother was especially admirable and worthy of honorable memory. Although she saw her seven sons perish within a single day, she bore it with good courage because of her hope in the Lord. She encouraged each of them in the language of their ancestors. Filled with a noble spirit, she reinforced her woman's reasoning with a man's courage, and said to them, "I do not know how you came into being in my womb. It was not I who gave you life and breath, nor I who set in order the elements within each of you. Therefore the Creator of the world, who shaped the beginning of humankind and devised the origin of all things, will in his mercy give life and breath back to you again, since you now forget yourselves for the sake of his laws."

At the All Saints' Vigil the rite allows choices of readings, and this lesson, which is long and at times may seem almost garish, may not often be chosen, yet it should not be dismissed. The baptized stand in a tradition of sacrifice. Two things may be observed about the material of this passage:

(1) Martyrologists do not spare details. It goes with the task. The cruelty of oppressors must be shown in detail, and the oppressed must exemplify heroic courage. Over the generations, written texts have been supplemented by book illuminations, stained glass, and woodcuts, and readers have been held spellbound. Yet chroniclers do not need to exaggerate. The cruelty and sadism of persecutors seems to feed on itself, and the calm dignity of persons of faith draws on unguessable interior resource. Instances of multiple martyrdoms within a single family, such as the one recorded in this passage, are not unknown in the twentieth century. Stories of martyrs appeal to the imagination and have inspired persons in faith traditions in all periods of history, ancient, medieval, and modern. The phenomenon of martyrdom is not lodged safely in the past, and the twentieth century seems likely to become known as "the century of martyrs." This liturgical reading is not remote or somewhat bizarre, but is part of the tradition in which all the baptized stand.

(2) Early Christians drew inspiration from the courage of these Jewish martyrs. When the New Testament Letter to the Hebrews was written, there were only a few Christian martyrs. (In time there came to be a great many.) Its author, seeking to encourage Christians who were being sorely tested, drew up (in his eleventh chapter) a list of heroes of faith: Abel, Noah, Abraham, and others. Toward the end of his list, he cites groups (Heb. 11:32-38). But at the time he wrote, few Christians had been cruelly tortured, stoned to death, sawn in two, or killed by the sword. Few Christian women had *received their dead by resurrection*. To make his point, the author cited heroes of faith that were known and admired by Christians—the Maccabean martyrs, who *were tortured, refusing to accept release, in order to obtain a better resurrection* (Heb. 11:35). The Christians acknowledged their admiration for, their continuity with and their debt to a succession of Jewish heroes of faith.

With Psalm 111

This psalm praises God's gracious, just and righteous works. *The works of his hands are faithful and just; all his precepts are trustworthy.*

The eulogy of the ancestors:
Ecclesiasticus (NRSV Sirach) 44:1-10, 13-14

This reading is also appointed for All Saints' Day and is commented on below.

When this passage is read at the Vigil (but not when it is read on All Saints' Day) it is matched with *Psalm 116,* in which the psalmist thanks God because he has been heard in a time of distress. On the Eve of All Saints, emphasis might well be on verse 13 (NRSV vs. 15), *Precious in the sight of the LORD is the death of his servants.*

Surrounded by a great cloud of witnesses:
Hebrews 11:32 (33-38) 39—12:2

And what more should I say? For time would fail me to tell of Gideon, Barak, Samson, Jephthah, of David and Samuel and the prophets—who through faith conquered kingdoms, administered justice, obtained promises, shut the mouths of lions, quenched raging fire, escaped the edge of the sword, won strength out of weakness, became mighty in war, put foreign armies to flight. Women received their dead by resurrection. Others were tortured, refusing to accept release, in order to obtain a better resurrection. Others suffered mocking and flogging, and even chains and imprisonment. They were stoned to death, they were sawn in two, they were killed with the sword; they went about in skins of sheep and goats, destitute, persecuted, tormented—of whom the world was not worthy. They wandered in deserts and mountains, and in caves and holes in the ground.

Yet all these, though they were commended for their faith, did not receive what was promised, since God had provided something better so that they would not, apart from us, be made perfect.

Therefore, since we are surrounded by so great a cloud of witnesses, let us also lay aside every weight and the sin that clings so closely, and let us run with perseverance the race that is set before us, looking to Jesus the pioneer and perfecter of our faith, who for the sake of the joy that was set before him endured the cross, disregarding its shame, and has taken his seat at the right hand of the throne of God.

The Letter to the Hebrews is written for persons of Jewish background who have committed themselves to Christ but who have come under strong pressures to go back. After several chapters of argument and encouragement, the author turns to a lengthy catalog of examples of faith, vision, and steadfastness (11:1—12:2). The heroes of faith in this catalog are, of course, all Jewish heroes, but they are cited with honor by a Christian writing for other Christians. After moving somewhat slowly through chapter 11 and

speaking circumstantially of Abel, Noah, Moses, and other faithful individuals, in this concluding portion of the passage the writing gathers speed.
After verse 33, names are not mentioned, only groups. A reader can make
good guesses at the identities of many of the persons referred to. Some are
persons from the canonical histories, and some seem to be heroes of the
Maccabean revolt. Those who *were tortured* (vs. 35) may be the youths of
2 Maccabees 7, the incident that is narrated in the previous reading. The
author who begins with persons from scripture broadens to include recent
Jewish history and legend. In verse 40 he says that the great tradition of
faith requires that, while Christians look to paradigmatic Jewish heroes, it
is also the case that *they would not, apart from us, be made perfect.* In the
interdependence of the divine purpose, the author says that Jews and Christians need each other.

At the close of the passage (12:1-2), the author pictures the Christians
who are living under great stress as runners in an amphitheater surrounded
by a supporting *cloud of witnesses,* i.e. the faithful who have gone before.
They are to lay aside every sinful compromise that would hold them back,
and *run with perseverance.* Above all, they look to Jesus, who pioneered
the way, through suffering and shame, for those who would follow, to the
throne of God. Racers run, despite their exhaustion, for a goal. Earlier in
the chapter the writer has said that some of the heroes persevered in the
race because they envisioned what lay ahead and had been promised (11:10,
16) or because they saw the invisible (11:27). So Jesus ran his appointed
race *for the joy that was set before him* (12:2). Christians, too, should run
determinedly, looking beyond what can be seen.

When this passage is read at baptism, it says that Christians are setting
upon a journey of faith, which requires constancy. It is not easy, but it has
a deep history, a large body of encouraging spectators, an admirable model,
and a promised future.

The psalm for this lesson, *Psalm 149,* along with the two lessons that
are listed next, *Revelation 7:2-4, 9-17* and *Matthew 5:1-12,* are also the
proper readings for All Saints and are discussed below. However, the All
Saints' Vigil contains two further readings that are, at the Vigil, alternatives to the day's gospel:

or "I will give you rest": Matthew 11:27-30

*"All things have been handed over to me by my Father; and no one knows
the Son except the Father, and no one knows the Father except the Son
and anyone to whom the Son chooses to reveal him.*

*"Come to me, all you that are weary and are carrying heavy bur-
dens, and I will give you rest. Take my yoke upon you, and learn from me,
for I am gentle and humble in heart, and you will find rest for your souls.
For my yoke is easy, and my burden is light."*

This reading is in two parts. Verse 27 speaks of the mutual knowing
that persists between the Father and the Son. This theme, plus the reference to simply *the Father* and *the Son,* gives the verse an unmistakably
"Johannine" sound, as though it belonged to a late-first-century stage of
christological development (cf. Jn. 3:35; 7:29). However, this passage has
a parallel in Luke 10:21-22, placing it in the early synoptic tradition. The
text claims that Jesus is uniquely known by the Father and has unique
knowledge of the Father. No one else is to the Father as he is, and the
Father is to him as the father is to no one else. Yet it also claims that Jesus
opens his knowledge of the Father to others he chooses. The relationship in
which he stands is his to share.

In verses 28-30 Jesus speaks in invitation, calling the weary and burdened to come to him and find rest. (His words echo personified Wisdom;
see Sir. 24:19; 51:23.) Jesus' expression *Take my yoke upon you* uses the
Jewish metaphor of the glad burden of obedience to the Torah. According
to the Talmud, to say the *shema* (Israel's declaration of belief; see Deut.
6:4-9) is "the acceptance of the yoke of the kingship of God." Jesus pledges
that his yoke is easy and leads to rest.

When the passage is read at baptism, the previous verses might be kept
in mind, in which Jesus speaks of hidden things which are made known to
infants (vs. 25). In baptism Christ admits one to the profound knowing
(which means sharing) that persists between himself and the Father. And
in baptism he says, *Come*, and he offers *rest for your souls.*

or The resurrection and the Great Commission: Matthew 28:1-10, 16-20

Matthew 28:1-10 narrates the first resurrection encounter in Matthew's
gospel. It is read on Easter Day, Year A, and is noted above (pp. 65, 67).

Matthew 28:16-20, Jesus' final appearance to his disciples later that
same day, appears only here in the lectionary; it is to be used only when the
Vigil falls on a Saturday evening.

*Now the eleven disciples went to Galilee, to the mountain to which
Jesus had directed them. When they saw him, they worshiped him;
but some doubted. And Jesus came and said to them, "All authority*

in heaven and on earth has been given to me. Go therefore and make disciples of all nations, baptizing them in the name of the Father and of the Son and of the Holy Spirit, and teaching them to obey everything that I have commanded you. And remember, I am with you always, to the end of the age."

This passage is Matthew's account of the risen Jesus' parting words, his "Great Commission." When he meets his eleven disciples at a mountain in Galilee, they react with a mixture of reverence and doubt. Jesus provides reassurance (vss. 18, 20b), but at the same time a commission to evangelize, baptize, and teach (vss. 19-20a).

The early church was from the beginning a missionary community, a baptizing community, and a teaching community. The gospel was bound up with a collective life and with baptism, the sign-act which formed it. But what rootage did this sign of the church have in the life and ministry of Jesus? Most Christians over the centuries would have answered the question by pointing to this passage as an act of "institution" which rooted both mission and baptism in an express command of Christ. Yet even when we read the resurrection stories fairly literally, there are reasons for thinking that this passage, rather than being a directive from the risen Jesus, carries the marks of the first-century church's understanding of itself and its purpose.

One reason is the slowness, documented in the book of Acts, of Jesus' followers to set about a widespread mission. The lead in envisioning and pioneering a worldwide mission was taken by Paul, who had not associated with Jesus. Even when some of the disciples began to engage in missionary activity, many of them stayed close to Jerusalem. Is it likely that Jesus' followers would have been so reluctant to undertake this sort of mission if they had had a direct command from the risen Jesus to *go and make disciples of all nations?*

A second question arises from the use of the triadic formula in Jesus' command to baptize. He directs his followers to baptize *in the name of the Father and of the Son and of the Holy Spirit.* Yet the baptisms that are described in Acts and in the epistles (as we shall see in more detail in a later section) are all in the name of Jesus, and the first baptisms that mention the triadic formula are sub-apostolic in date. Again, would persons who had received an express direction from Jesus have so clearly failed to follow it?

The triadic formula given in Matthew 28:19 names the fullness of God. The wording in Matthew 28:19 should not be described as "trinitarian," for the term *trinity* does not enter the Christian vocabulary until the late second century, and its definition developed after the term came into use. Neither should these words be taken to mean that the church from and for which Matthew's gospel was written used the triune name at baptism in the way in which we use it now. The evangelist's words do not tell what was said at baptism, but rather they mean that persons were (as they still are) baptized into the divine reality as it had been made known in Jesus Christ.

Yet the church's mandate to baptize does trace to Jesus. The church makes disciples, teaches, and baptizes on the basis of the risen Christ to whom plenary authority has been given (vs. 18). However, the church's witnessing and baptizing work at its frontier with the world derives its authority not so much from a particular dominical command as from the whole work of Christ, his life and death and vindication—a work which was for the world's sake. The mission of the church is always under the triumphant Jesus and is supported by his everlasting presence (vss. 18, 20b).

Jesus' commission to evangelize is bound up with the commission to baptize. As a recent writer says, "A missionary community will necessarily have a rite of initiation."[4] Jesus' commission to "make disciples" means more than bringing persons to a moment of decision. The expression "disciples" speaks of whole, dedicated, loyal followers, and making disciples involves baptizing, teaching, and formation. Jesus' gospel is not a message let loose in the world to make its way as best it can; it is linked with an initiatory act which shapes a space-time-specific community, its faith and disciplines. Making disciples and baptizing are linked with teaching. The Christian message has a content, a sharable substance, which comes through Jesus Christ—but through him in the heritage of Judaism and the context of the Christian church and its tradition of faith and life. A grasp of a basic account of reality is required for stable, responsible life in the church. A body of shared lore must be imparted for the sake of the member and for the continued integrity of the collective life.

Not literally, but in some of the broader senses that have been suggested here, Matthew 28:18-20 does provide a New Testament mandate for the baptizing church. Reading it on the Eve of All Saints is a reminder that the church is by necessity a missionary church. The sacramental act of gathering in is a consequence of an earlier sending out, and from it arises a further mission. One of the promises at baptism asks the candidate: *Will you proclaim by word and example the Good News of God in Christ?* (BCP, p. 305).

ALL SAINTS' DAY

The scriptures for the Feast of All Saints itself are:

Ecclesiasticus (NRSV Sirach) 44:1-10, 13-14

Let us now sing the praises of famous men,
our ancestors in their generations.
The Lord apportioned to them great glory,
his majesty from the beginning.
There were those who ruled in their kingdoms,
and made a name for themselves by their valor;
those who gave counsel because they were intelligent;
those who spoke in prophetic oracles;
those who led the people by their counsels
and by their knowledge of the people's lore;
they were wise in their words of instruction;
those who composed musical tunes,
or put verses in writing;
rich men endowed with resources,
living peacefully in their homes—
all these were honored in their generations,
and were the pride of their times.
Some of them have left behind a name,
so that others declare their praise.
But of others there is no memory;
they have perished as though they had never existed;
they have become as though they had never been born,
they and their children after them.
But these also were godly men,
whose righteous deeds have not been forgotten. . .
Their offspring will continue forever,
and their glory will never be blotted out.
Their bodies are buried in peace,
but their name lives on generation after generation.

This familiar reading, from a long wisdom text, is a call to celebrate persons who have gone before, many of whom go largely unremembered. The passage begins a lengthy section (chapters 44-49) which speaks of a number of notable ancestors and then culminates in chapter 50 with a vivid depiction of Simon, the then living high priest. (The author of Ecclesiasticus,

Ben Sira of Jerusalem, supports the temple system, and Simon seems to have been his hero.)

Before specific leaders are mentioned (chapters 45-49), there is a general recalling (in chapter 44) of the persons on whom the stability and continuity of the community has depended. Since the mind-set that lay behind Ecclesiasticus was patrilineal, when this passage speaks of "ancestors," it is the NRSV rendering of the "famous men" and "our fathers" of the original. Ben Sira's vision of the national past in terms of masculine achievement creates problems for the use of this reading in the liturgy of a twentieth-century church. Some persons have tried recasting the ideas to make them more inclusive, sometimes with considerable success. Other persons think that the passage, if it is to be used with integrity, must be used pretty much as it stands.

It may be noted that the gifts which are celebrated in this general passage are civic virtues and public, cultural contributions—counsel, wisdom, music, poetry, mercy—gifts that are at least as widely distributed among women as among men. The passage expresses the Jewish sense that the characteristics which are required for a sound community, no less than what might be thought of as the more specifically religious endowments, are all from God. It also witnesses to the Jewish sense of obligation of the living to remember the dead—to remember those who without us would go unremembered.

Revelation 7:2-4, 9-17

I saw another angel ascending from the rising of the sun, having the seal of the living God, and he called with a loud voice to the four angels who had been given power to damage earth and seas, saying, "Do not damage the earth or the sea or the trees, until we have marked the servants of our God with a seal on their foreheads."

And I heard the number of those who were sealed, one hundred forty-four thousand, sealed out of every tribe of the people of Israel. After this I looked, and there was a great multitude that no one could count, from every nation, from all tribes and peoples and languages, standing before the throne and before the Lamb, robed in white, with palm branches in their hands. They cried out in a loud voice, saying,

> *"Salvation belongs to our God*
> *who is seated on the throne,*
> *and to the Lamb!"*

And all the angels stood around the throne and around the elders and the four living creatures, and they fell on their faces before the throne and worshiped God, singing,

> *"Amen! Blessing and glory and wisdom*
> *and thanksgiving and honor*
> *and power and might*
> *be to our God forever and ever! Amen"*

Then one of the elders addressed me, saying, "Who are these, robed in white, and where have they come from?" I said to him, "Sir, you are the one that knows." Then he said to me, "These are they who have come out of the great ordeal; they have washed their robes and made them white in the blood of the Lamb."

> *For this reason they are before the throne of God,*
> *and worship him day and night within his temple,*
> > *and the one who is seated on the throne will shelter them.*
> *They will hunger no more, and thirst no more;*
> > *the sun will not strike them,*
> > *nor any scorching heat;*
> *for the Lamb at the center of the throne will be their shepherd,*
> > *and he will guide them to springs of the water of life,*
> > *and God will wipe away every tear from their eyes.*

The book of Revelation is a visionary, dramatic work which, despite its puzzles, communicates an overwhelming sense of the ultimate triumph of God. The passage that precedes this reading has spoken of terrible natural and political upheaval and destruction. The seer then turns to describe those servants of God who will be delivered by divine power from the almost unimaginable horrors he has strained language to describe.

Four angels who could do immense havoc withhold their powers and produce a great stillness (vss. 1f). Then another angel tells the first four to damage nothing until the servants of God have been marked on their foreheads (vss. 2f). Then one hundred forty-four thousand persons are sealed, twelve thousand from each of the tribes of Israel (vss. 4-8). The seer thinks of the church as spiritual Israel, and the number (12 x 12,000) is not meant to indicate a census figure, but the completeness of the faithful people.

The divine seal is something like a brand which declares ownership and gives protection. In some of the earliest baptismal customs of which we have record, the newly baptized are signed on the forehead in a gesture that was often called a "seal." Was such a custom in use at baptism in the church from which the book of Revelation came? Or did the poetic image of Revelation (based on Ezek. 9:4-6), suggest the ritual act which came later? The people who carry the divine seal may not be touched, like the children of Israel who were delivered from the plagues which attacked their Egyptian neighbors (Ex. 8:22; 9:4-7, 26; 10:23).

In verses 9-17 a vast group from every nation and people stands before God, robed in the white of heavenly purity and holding the palms of victory (vs. 9). They cry out in praise to the God who is seated on the throne and to the Lamb (vs. 10). Their praise is joined by angels and other creatures who fall on their faces (vss. 11f).

The scene is explained by one of the elders (vss. 13-17). These honored persons have come through a climactic time of testing—*the great ordeal.* They have been faithful under persecution, some of them even to death. In language that is offensive to some modern readers, and which must always have been considered paradoxical, their robes have been made white by being washed in the blood of the Lamb (vss. 13f). It is almost impossible to restore the whiteness of cloth which has been stained with blood. But in this vision, things that are soiled are made white by being washed in blood—the blood of one who had been slain (cf. 1:18; 5:6ff). This is a vivid way of speaking of forgiveness through the atoning death of Christ. Those whose clothing was bloodied by their faithfulness to Christ will have it made white by his blood.

In the imagination of this early Christian visionary, martyrdom and baptism were never far apart. The image of washing one's robes white (vs. 14) may allude to baptism, one's dying with Christ. The sealing (vss. 2f), the white garments and the palms of victory (vs. 9) all came to have unmistakable baptismal associations. Is it certain that they have none in the seer's vision? The hymn that ends the vision in a tone of quiet triumph (vss. 15-17) says that the multitude is before God's throne, worshiping him day and night. They are sheltered, fed, and protected from the heat. The *Lamb* (the royal one, the sacrificed one) will be their *shepherd* who will guide them to springs of the water of life and will banish sorrow. Massey H. Shepherd, Jr., pointed out that this heavenly hymn draws on Psalms 23, 42, and 121, the first two of which were associated with baptism from a very early time.[5]

This passage speaks not to a remote past, but to today. It has been said that in some parts of the world today, to be marked with the sign of the cross is to be a marked person. This text about martyrdom, read on one of the baptismal days, suggests the connection between our birth and our death in Christ. In our baptismal birth, we die; and in our baptismal death, we are born to a life that knows no dying.

Matthew 5:1-12

When Jesus saw the crowds, he went up the mountain; and after he sat down, his disciples came to him. Then he began to speak, and taught them saying:

> *"Blessed are the poor in spirit, for theirs is the kingdom of heaven.*
> *"Blessed are those who mourn, for they will be comforted.*
> *"Blessed are the meek, for they will inherit the earth.*
> *"Blessed are those who hunger and thirst for righteousness, for they will be filled.*
> *"Blessed are the merciful, for they will receive mercy.*
> *"Blessed are the pure in heart, for they will see God.*
> *"Blessed are the peacemakers, for they will be called children of God.*
> *"Blessed are those who are persecuted for righteousness sake, for theirs is the kingdom of heaven.*

"Blessed are you when people revile you and persecute you and utter all kinds of evil against you falsely on my account. Rejoice and be glad, for your reward is great in heaven, for in the same way they persecuted the prophets who were before you."

This rhythmic series of nine pronouncements is known as "the Beatitudes"—from the Latin *beati*, "blessed." Since the word *blessed* can seem remote and religious, some translators, seeking a common English equivalent, have used "happy are. . . ." However, *happy* seems to trivialize this gospel text, connoting as it does a sense of good feeling, often conferred by circumstance.

In the deep biblical sense, "blessedness" comes from the overflowing goodness and mercy of God, the Original Blesser (Gen. 1:22, 28; 2:3). While blessedness may lead to a sense of joy and well-being, it is not a feeling, or an experience, or one's estimate of oneself, but it is, first of all, a gift. The blessedness given in the primal creation has been lost. But by divine goodness, one who is blessed is set in a new, whole relation with God and with all things. Blessedness may have little to do with favorable circumstances, for it is known by those who mourn and those who are persecuted (5:4, 10, 11). It is so unlike what we ordinarily think of as "happiness" that the older, more distanced and special word "blessedness" may be the preferred translation.

The Beatitudes are not a set of general moral maxims, but are the ways of the kingdom which Jesus announces and inaugurates. Matthew gives Jesus' Sermon on the Mount a Messianic setting by citing a passage from Isaiah which he says is fulfilled: *The people who sat in darkness have seen a great light* (4:13-16). As his narrative opens, the dawning light takes the form of an announcement: *Jesus began to proclaim, "Repent, for the kingdom of heaven has come near."* (4:17) Then he calls his first disciples and begins to teach and heal in the synagogues. It is only after this initial announcement of the stir of God and the beginning of the gathering of a community of response that Jesus begins a lengthy speech, the "Sermon on the Mount," which by being delivered from a mountain suggests a new Moses giving a new law, and which serves as something of a manifesto of the kingdom.

Jesus addresses persons who, having heard the Good News of the reign of God, associate themselves with him. He is not telling people what they should do in order to receive God's favor. Rather, he speaks to those who have taken the first, radical step into the realm of divine favor and who may well wonder what they will discover and what will be required of them in their new situation of grace.

Jesus' description of blessedness is revolutionary, for it goes against expectations and shapes what might be called a counter-kingdom. This Messiah identifies not with the powerful, but with the modest, devout folk who have little and expect little. It is *the poor in spirit* and *those who mourn*—the humble and powerless, rather than the aggressive—who will inherit the land; and it is those who seek righteousness, rather than those who seek plenty, who will be filled. Those who are pure at the personal center, from which thought and action flow, will see God. Jesus' pronouncement of true blessedness presents a sharp alternative to the competitive, driven, image-conscious, materialistic, grasping, glamour-worshiping standards of sin-structured society.

The Beatitudes appear both in Matthew and in Luke, but in somewhat different wordings. (The Lukan version is appointed in the alternative propers for the day; see p. 176.) Matthew tends to "spiritualize" Jesus' sayings. Whereas in Luke Jesus speaks bluntly to the socially disinherited, saying: *Blessed are you who are poor. . .* and *who are hungry now*, in Matthew's version he speaks of *the poor in spirit* and those who *hunger and thirst after righteousness*.

Several of the Beatitudes contain biblical echoes. Isaiah 61:1f speaks of the brokenhearted and a garland of gladness for those who mourn. Psalm 37:11 says that *the meek shall inherit the land, and delight themselves in abundant prosperity* (NRSV). Deuteronomy 4:1 promises that those who heed God's statutes will enter the land. Psalm 24:3f says that those who have clean hands and pure hearts will stand in God's holy place. Thus this passage is thoroughly Jewish in character and gathers up the piety of the people of the land. It is spoken fittingly by one who says, "I have come to fulfill the law and the prophets" (cf. Mt. 5:17). Yet the words are not a pastiche of scriptural references, but belong to Jesus' proclamation as an original depiction of the members of the reign of God. They speak indirectly of him as the one who comforts those who mourn and fills those who hunger for righteousness. Yet at the same time, the words attach to promises; they point to the future, repeatedly saying *will*. In a coming reversal, the needy will be satisfied.

The gift, demand, and promise of the Beatitudes give some definition to the life into which one is called in baptism.

So that congregations which have a celebration on November 1 and another on the Sunday that follows will not have to use the same scripture passages at both, the lectionary provides an alternative set of propers for All Saints:

Ecclesiasticus (NRSV **Sirach) 2: (1-6) 7-11**

My child, when you come to serve the Lord,
prepare yourself for testing.
Set your heart right and be steadfast,
and do not be impetuous in time of calamity.
Cling to him and do not depart,
so that your last days may be prosperous.
Accept whatever befalls you,
and in times of humiliation be patient.
For gold is tested in the fire,
and those found acceptable in the furnace of humiliation.
Trust in him, and he will help you;
make your ways straight, and hope in him.

You who fear the Lord, wait for his mercy;
do not stray, or else you may fall.
You who fear the Lord, trust in him,
and your reward will not be lost.

You who fear the Lord, hope for good things,
for lasting joy and mercy.
Consider the generations of old and see:
has anyone trusted in the Lord and been disappointed?
Or has anyone persevered in the fear of the Lord and been forsaken?
Or has anyone called upon him and been neglected?
For the Lord is compassionate and merciful;
he forgives sins and saves in time of distress.

This poem of counsel says that one who serves the Lord can expect testing—a valuable theme for All Saints' Day and for Christian baptism. Anyone who expects a life of faith and obedience to be a life without adversity and conflict does so against the witness of the Bible, which is a very realistic book. The sage, Ben Sira, writes in the tone of the Wisdom literature, addressing a learner—*my child*—and using a series of imperative verbs: *prepare yourself. . .set your heart right and be steadfast. . .cling to him and do not depart. . .accept whatever befalls you. . . .* More than a dozen such directive verbs mark these eleven verses.

The virtues that are upheld in this passage—patience, acceptance, trusting, waiting, persevering—are rather unheroic, perhaps somewhat passive. At some times and among some people, more than passivity is possible and is wanted. The world needs persons who in godly impatience will not accept what is, but resolve to change it. But for most people most of the time, it calls for quiet courage just to endure. And when enduring the things that cannot be changed is all that one can do, it is important to do it.

The counsel of Ben Sira, however, is not just resignation. It is spoken in a deeply devout spirit and expresses repeatedly a trust in God and a determination to *cling to him, hope in him.* The sage affirms repeatedly the dependability of God. Before one is faithful to God, one is aware of God's faithfulness—as witnessed by *the generations of old* (vs. 10). Over the struggle to find the inner strength to remain true in times of testing, and over the mixed success which is all that most of us can report, the writer sets the affirmation: *The Lord is compassionate and merciful; he forgives sins and saves in time of distress.*

Ephesians 1: (11-14) 15-23

In Christ we also have obtained an inheritance, having been destined according to the purpose of him who accomplishes all things according to his counsel and will, so that we, who were the first to set our hope on Christ, might live for the praise of his glory. In him you also, when you

*had heard the word of truth, the gospel of your salvation, and had be-
lieved in him, were marked with the seal of the promised Holy Spirit; this
is the pledge of our inheritance toward redemption as God's own people,
to the praise of his glory.*

*I have heard of your faith in the Lord Jesus and your love toward all
the saints, and for this reason I do not cease to give thanks for you as I
remember you in my prayers. I pray that the God of our Lord Jesus Christ,
the Father of glory, may give you a spirit of wisdom and revelation as
you come to know him, so that, with the eyes of your heart enlightened,
you may know what is the hope to which he has called you, what are the
riches of his glorious inheritance among the saints, and what is the immeasurable greatness of his power for us who believe, according to the
working of his great power. God put his power to work in Christ when he
raised him from the dead and seated him at his right hand in the heavenly
places, far above all rule and authority and power and dominion, and
above every name that is named, not only in this age but also in the age to
come. And he has put all things under his feet and has made him the head
over all things for the church, which is his body, the fullness of him who
fills all in all.*

The writer of Ephesians uses long grammatical units, piling rich, complex expressions one on another. His ideas invite careful examination, but
for this place a rapid summary must do.

Verses 11-14 are part of a passage developing the spiritual blessings
that have been made accessible in Christ. The author's theme is the unity
of all things through God's purpose in Christ (vss. 9-10). Writing as a Jew
to a Gentile readership, he seeks to recognize the distinctness of each group
and yet at the same time to identify the unity between them. In verses 11-
12, the *we* is a Jewish *we*. By God's appointment, the Jewish Christians
were the first to claim the inheritance of faith. In verse 13, the *you* is the
you of Gentile Christians who, in their turn, when they heard the gospel
also believed. The *our* of verse 14 is inclusive; in the new life in Christ
both Jews and Gentiles are heirs of the same promise. What they have now
in grace is a pledge or "down payment" securing final redemption. Both
sections of this paragraph end with *to/for the praise of his glory*—one of
the many liturgical-sounding expressions in this letter.

Verses 15-23 are the author's prayer for his readers. It is a very theological prayer. The text gives no indication of the readers' circumstances or their
external needs. In saying what he seeks for them the writer introduces a rich
statement of his gospel. He speaks in splendid excess: *glory, riches, glorious,
immeasurable greatness, great power, every, all* (used five times).

Always thankful for what he has heard of his readers (vss. 15-16), he prays that they may be given wisdom and knowledge. He wants their minds to be stretched to grasp the greatness of the grace and power which has grasped them—*so that, with the eyes of your heart enlightened, you may know what is the hope to which he has called you* (vs. 18a). Compounding superlatives, he prays that they may come to know the rich inheritance that is theirs and the great power that has been shown in God's work for them (vss. 18b-19).

Having mentioned God's power, he must say more. The power of God was demonstrated when he raised Christ from the dead and set him in a place of utter cosmic supremacy. (This christological statement begins with the resurrection, making no mention of the cross.) The supremacy of the place accorded to Christ is emphasized by filling in some of what it exceeds—*far above all rule and authority and power and dominion, and above every name that is named, not only in this age but also in the age to come* (vs. 21). The author presses language of height to speak of a place that transcends all.

Having located Christ above all, the writer turns the figure around to say that everything else is below Christ. God *has put all things under his feet* (vs. 22). (Both this expression and the image in vs. 20 of Christ seated at God's right hand in heaven evidence the early church's christological reading of Pss. 8:6; 110:1.)

The emphasis has been exclusively on God's power demonstrated in Christ, but what was done in one person was for a universal end, and as the prayer closes, it brings in the church and the head and body image. The one, universal church is the correlative of the one, universal Christ. The final words about the church, *the fullness of him who fills all in all,* are difficult, but it is defensible to construe them as saying that while Christ fills all, the church fills Christ!

Baptisms on All Saints' Day can focus on the great community to which one is joined. This sweeping, wide-ranging passage from Ephesians gives dimension both to the day and to the sacrament. It gives rich expression to the great redemptive purpose which has been accomplished in Christ and is exhibited in the church and into which one is caught up in Holy Baptism.

Luke 6:20-26 (27-36)

[The following text and comments include only verses 20-26.]

> *Then Jesus looked up at his disciples and said:*
> *"Blessed are you who are poor,*
> *for yours is the kingdom of God.*

"Blessed are you who are hungry now,
for you will be filled.
"Blessed are you who weep now,
for you will laugh.
"Blessed are you when people hate you, and when they exclude you,
revile you, and defame you on account of the Son of Man. Rejoice in that
day and leap for joy, for surely your reward is great in heaven; for that is
what their ancestors did to the prophets.

"But woe to you who are rich,
for you have received your consolation.
"Woe to you who are full now,
for you will be hungry.
"Woe to you who are laughing now,
for you will mourn and weep.
"Woe to you when all speak well of you, for that is what their ances-
tors did to the false prophets."

Luke's version of the Beatitudes, which is appointed in the alternative propers for All Saints' Day, is less familiar than Matthew's and has its own characteristics. Here, unlike the third-person speech of Matthew, Jesus speaks directly to his hearers, *Blessed are you. . . . Woe to you.* Luke's version shows no tendency to spiritualize—Jesus does not say, *Blessed are the poor in spirit,* but, *Blessed are you poor.* Luke, unlike Matthew, pairs Jesus' pronouncement of blessedness to the poor and sorrowing (vss. 20b-21) with his pronouncement of "woes" to the rich and contented (vss. 24-25).

These words express a shocking reversal of ordinary expectations. Jesus says that those are blessed—are heirs of the real order of things—who are poor, hungry, suffering, and excluded. We usually think otherwise. Those who are happy, who "lead the good life," are the well-to-do, the well-fed, those who have frequent occasions for laughter and who are liked and accepted. We define ourselves and we define others by place, power, influence, and goods, and we spend an immense amount of energy seeking comfort and status for ourselves. This quest exacts a terrible cost in anxiety, competitiveness, and insecurity. Yet we find it difficult to entertain any other basis for self-definition.

Jesus turns our common values upside down, declaring that the wretched, the oppressed, the victims, the "unhappy" ones will be blessed and secure and will know well-being; while the "happy" ones—those who are complacent and self-satisfied in their hollow achievements—are in peril of judgment.

Jesus is speaking in and to his social order, but he is not delivering a social program. He is neither commending the overthrow of wealth and privilege nor suggesting that the poor be content with their present station in life. The thought of Jesus' proclamation of the reign of God belongs to a different order. He is anticipating the final kingdom, the "Great Reversal," the mighty reordering of things by God. In this divine act in which things are set right, the sinful, exploitive, power-dominated order will be humbled, and the meek will inherit the earth, and a little child will lead them.

Yet these words of Jesus have deep implications for the present—as powerful visions of the future always do. He speaks in the tradition of the Hebrew prophets who were shocked that there should be such a wide gap between the rich and the poor. Something had gone terribly wrong in the mutuality that should prevail among members of a covenant people. The prophets assumed that the rich have been made so in considerable measure by taking advantage of others. They spoke of a God of justice and compassion who favors the oppressed poor who trust in God. The Great Reversal is not just a promise for the end, but it is a factor that stirs in history in which—often through disregarded persons and in unexpected ways—God casts down and raises up.

To a greater extent than in the Matthean version, the Lukan Beatitudes show Jesus as a social critic in the spirit of Amos.

Psalm 149

[appointed for both sets of Propers]

In what sounds like a celebration of final victory, this psalm exhorts Israel to praise God. The people should sing "a new song," for new mercies invite new praises (vs. 1). Israel, glad in its Maker, dances and sings (vss. 2f). In a wonderful affirmation, the psalmist says that if the people enjoy their God, God *takes pleasure in his people* (vs. 4). The nation, with praise on its lips and a sword in its hand, undertakes battle against the nations who oppose God (vss. 5-9). Christians who find this final passage too vengeful and warlike can adopt the tradition of "spiritualizing" the biblical images of conflict so that enemies are spiritual adversaries or God's enemies. In the life of the baptized, obstacles are certain. But, read at baptism, this psalm and its tone of conquest may speak of a time when the conflicts of the life of faith come to an end and all things are subjected to God, *so that God may be all in all* (1 Cor. 15:28).

CHAPTER 6

Sunday as a Baptismal Day

An opening rubric gives Holy Baptism a setting on a festal day and in a celebrational ritual event—*within the Eucharist as the chief service on a Sunday or other feast* (BCP, p. 298). Although a later rubric (BCP, p. 312) identifies five occasions—four major feast days plus the visit of a bishop—at which *Holy Baptism is especially appropriate*, the first rubric of the rite opens any Sunday of the year as an occasion for baptism.

This Prayer Book direction brings together three things which have not inevitably been united in thought and practice. *Baptism* should fall (when the time can be controlled) on a *Sunday or other feast day* and be observed *within the Eucharist*. Sunday is always a celebration of Jesus' resurrection and of new life in him; every baptism brings a new person into Christ and the life he opens; and every eucharist is a restatement of the new life in Christ into which one is brought by baptism. Thus this one day and these two actions—Sunday, baptism, and eucharist—have deep, intrinsic affinities. In their distinct but complementary ways they give expression to the one redemptive reality. Together they make up a powerful enactment of the gospel. The day interprets the sacraments, and the sacramental actions declare the meaning of the day.

To look briefly at these three things and their connectedness:

Sunday and eucharist.   Sunday has its basis in the seven-day week and the sabbath of Judaism. The sabbath, an institution lodged deep in the Jewish ethos, is a part of the expressive shaping of time—the "architecture of time"—that Rabbi Heschel describes as the genius of Jewish worship. "The Sabbaths," he says, "are our great cathedrals. . .that neither the Romans nor the Germans were able to burn."[1]

The sabbath says something important about humanity. As a day of rest, it says that there is more to being human than can be expressed through work—just as the sabbath rest of the Creator says that God is more than the created world. Human beings meet and serve God in the working days: *Six days you shall labor and do all your work.* (Ex. 20.9). But in the sabbath, human beings, in a day beyond the workweek, also meet God in the divine rest.

In the Jewish scriptures, the sabbath is largely observed by cessation from work. However, after the synagogue arose at the time of the exile, it had become, by the time of Jesus, the day for the calling together of the community for praise, scripture, and prayer.

Virtually all the earliest Christians were practicing Jews, and their new forms of cultic life were adapted from the patterns they had known in the synagogue. Yet it seems that from the earliest years the Christians changed their principal time of assembly from the seventh day to the early morning of the first day of the week—the time when the Jewish sabbath ended. Apparently some Jewish Christians were able to maintain a dual practice, adding their Christian observance to the Jewish sabbath for a time.

The Christians' day, however, was not defined by divine rest, but by Jesus' resurrection. And they observed it by gathering for praise, scripture, prayer, alms, and the eucharistic meal. (The somewhat fragmentary evidence can be sampled in Acts 2:42; 20:7-12; 1 Cor. 14:26; 16:2; Heb. 10:25; 13:15.)

Indications that Christians gathered on Sunday for the eucharistic assembly begins very early, although some of it is indirect. The New Testament gospels, while there is as yet no Christian eucharist, do show symbolic ties between the Lord's Supper and the Lord's Day. Both in Jesus parables and in his acts of feeding, meals are signs of the kingdom. The stories of Jesus' resurrection are highly interpreted and full of symbols and suggestions. It seems significant that all the resurrection appearances which have a time reference fall on a Sunday—*After the sabbath, as the first day of the week was dawning* (Mt. 28:1); *Very early on the first day of the week* (Mk. 16:1); *On the first day of the week, at early dawn* (Lk. 24:1); *On that same day. . .*(Lk. 24:13); *Early on the first day of the week* (Jn. 20:1); *Evening on the first day of the week* (Jn. 20:19); *a week later* (Jn. 20:26). Several of these resurrection appearances carry eucharistic overtones, since they refer to Jesus eating and drinking with his followers (see especially Lk. 24:13-35; Jn. 21:4-14; see also references in Acts 1:4, margin; Acts 10:40f; Rev. 3:20). It is as though the New Testament describes Jesus' encounters with his community is such a way as to say that if one wants to meet the risen Christ, he will be found in the Christian eucharistic assembly early in the morning on the first day of the week.

Acts tells that before Paul's departure from Ephesus, the community met "on the first day of the week," which, reckoning the day in the Jewish way, would have meant after sundown on Saturday. There was a (quite eventful) all-night vigil, following which the community broke bread (Acts 20:7-12). There is some scholarly disagreement about this passage, but the surface meaning indicates that the Christians held their communal meal after the sabbath and before dawn on Sunday.

Early in the second century Ignatius remarks the change that Christians had made in the day of worship: "Those, then, who lived by ancient practices arrived at a new hope. They ceased to keep the sabbath and lived by the Lord's Day, on which our life as well as theirs shone forth, thanks to Him and his death." (*Letter to the Magnesians* 9:1). This change expressed a seismic shift in cultic life—something formative had happened on the first day in the week.

This early evidence is drawn together when the late-first- or early-second-century church order, the *Didache,* clearly designates Sunday as the eucharist-day: "On every Lord's Day—his special day—come together and break bread and give thanks" (*Didache* 14:1). Other writings make the same connection, Justin Martyr, for example, writing about 150 CE, says "On the day called Sunday there is a meeting in one place"—a meeting for word and sacrament (Justin's *Apology,* section 67).

Few things lie more deep in the *ordo* of Christian worship than Sunday as the day for the eucharistic assembly—meeting for word, praise, and prayer, and for the communal meal in which thanksgiving is voiced by the presider and the people partake of bread and wine. The Lord's Day is normatively observed by the Lord's Supper. Yet over the tortured centuries, Christian practice disregarded this elemental order. To identify the most obvious deformations: Some churches have minimized the Word, while others have observed Sunday by a non-eucharistic service entirely centered on the Word. Still other churches have held a eucharistic rite at which most baptized Christians, although they were present and in good standing, did not receive communion. Although liturgical reformers over the centuries have sought to restore Sunday as the day for the Christian gathering for Word and Sacrament, few of them have been more than partially successful. In the liturgical stir of the twentieth century, many churches are trying in their different ways to break out of old habits. It is this matter which the very first rubric of the Prayer Book (p.13) seeks to address when it speaks of *the Holy Eucharist, the principal act of Christian worship on the Lord's Day and other major Feasts.*

Baptism and eucharist. The Prayer Book rubric calls for the two great sacraments of the gospel to be observed together. *Holy Baptism is appropriately administered within the Eucharist* (p. 298). In their basic imagery, baptism and communion have a mutuality and complementarity. Baptism is a sign of birth, while the eucharist is a sign of feeding; and persons who are brought into life must be nourished from the start. What is begun in baptism is continued in the eucharist, and the eucharist is a frequent re-actualization of what is declared initially in the unrepeated act of baptism.

An early, albeit indirect suggestion of the relation between the two great gospel sacraments is the link between birth imagery and eating imagery in 1 Peter 2:2, *Like newborn infants, long for the pure, spiritual milk, so that by it you may grow.* The *Didache* says, "You must not let anyone eat or drink of your Eucharist except those baptized in the Lord's name" (*Didache* 9:4). Offering no rationale for its directive, this church manual says that baptism is the way of admission to the eucharist and that the eucharist is for the baptized.

In our earliest liturgical sources, baptism is never described alone, because it was never experienced alone. The unit in these sources is the plenary liturgical event of the Easter baptismal eucharist in which baptism is followed at once by admission to communion, as it still is in the East. Western medieval liturgical documents indicate that persons, including infants, were communicated at their baptism. Canon J. D. C. Fisher summarizes, "All churches in the West admitted infants to communicate until the twelfth century."[2] Even after that, the practice did not altogether die out.

Yet by the Late Middle Ages in the West, the intrinsic connectedness of these sacramental actions had become obscured. While baptism and eucharist continued to be observed faithfully, they had no visible connection with one another.

Anglican practice to a great extent followed this medieval pattern; baptism was often observed either in an essentially private ceremony, or else at morning or evening prayer—non-eucharistic occasions. Moreover, baptism was considered incomplete without episcopal confirmation. This understanding of baptism was expressed in the 1928 Prayer Book in the last promise by a child's sponsors (p. 277), in the rubric following the blessing (p. 281), and in the "confirmation rubric" (p. 299). Since one was admitted to communion by baptism plus confirmation, most Christians only began receiving communion several years after they had been baptized.

In the present Prayer Book, the confirmation rubric (which implied that baptism is less than full Christian initiation) has been dropped, and the opening rubric of the baptismal rite says that Holy Baptism is *full initiation by water and the Holy Spirit into Christ's Body the Church* (1979 BCP, p. 298). Persons are eligible to receive communion because they are baptized Christians, not because they have received an initiatory act beyond baptism.

Moreover, the inherent connectedness of baptism and eucharist in the economy of sacramental initiation is exhibited in the structure and flow of the rites on the Prayer Book pages. The Great Vigil passes the liturgical action to Holy Baptism (p. 292). After the baptismal rite ends with The Peace, the action *then continues with the Prayers of the People or the Offertory of the Eucharist* (BCP, p. 310). The initiatory rite which begins with the Word and the water culminates in the bread and wine. After one is baptized, one receives communion often; it ministers the same redemptive life into which one was initially brought by baptism and in which one always needs to be sustained.[3]

Sunday and baptism. If baptism and eucharist stand in the closest association with one another, it should follow that Sunday, the eucharist day, is a fitting time for baptism.

But evidence for Sunday as a baptismal day does not emerge at once. The first Christians apparently did not baptize at any special time, and only a few hints connect baptism with the eucharist. The *Didache*, we have noted, sets Sunday as the eucharist day and would admit only the baptized to the eucharistic meal. But it does not connect baptism with Sunday.

However, as the church began to explore the intrinsic order of sacramental life, structures and connections emerged. The *Apology* (c. 150 CE) by Justin Martyr, which contains the first circumstantial account of Christian worship, tells of baptism (sections 61-65), saying that candidates are taken to water and baptized. The newly baptized are then led to the assembly, where they join in the common prayers, in the kiss of peace, and in the eucharistic meal. Baptism culminates in communion. Then in a later section (67) Justin describes the Christian Sunday assembly for word and sacrament: "On the day called Sunday there is a meeting in one place." When the community is gathered, the scriptures are read and explained. Then follows the kiss of peace and the eucharistic meal. Justin's two accounts merge; the Sunday eucharist, after the readings and preaching, duplicates the sequence of the baptismal eucharist after the newly baptized have joined the community in the eucharistic room. Apparently when there was a baptism, it took the place of the service of the word, at least for the candidate(s) and attending ministers. Then, the newly baptized joined the Sunday assembly for the prayers, the peace, and the sacramental meal. Evidently by the second century at Rome, when there were baptisms, they were held on Sunday, and they led into the eucharist, the two actions joining at the communal prayers and the kiss of peace.

The *Apostolic Tradition* of Hippolytus of Rome (c. 215 CE), our most revealing early liturgical source, gives quite full directions for preparing candidates for baptism, baptizing them, and then leading them to their first communion. As Hippolytus describes the days immediately before baptism, he identifies days of the week. A preparatory washing takes place on Thursday; the candidates fast on Friday; there is a final exorcism by the bishop on Saturday; and baptism is clearly on Sunday.[4] Commentators usually assume that Hippolytus is speaking of Easter Sunday and the Thursday, Friday, and Saturday preceding. That may, of course, be the case. (Tertullian, Hippolytus' contemporary, speaks, as we have seen, of Passover as the time for baptism. And Hippolytus may speak of Easter baptism elsewhere in his writings.) But in the *Apostolic Tradition* he does not specify Easter; he simply speaks of Thursday, Friday, and Saturday, and he implies Sunday.

Baptism at the Paschal season soon came to prevail in the West (while baptism at Epiphany continued in parts of the East). As Easter baptism gained authority, writers had little to say about Sunday as a baptismal day. Yet the weekly Sunday was a baptismal day before the yearly Easter festival established itself as the preferred, and in the West virtually the only, time for baptism. (Pentecost, as we have seen, was regarded as a part of Easter.) In *The Origins of the Liturgical Year*, Thomas J. Talley has said that before the developed catechumenate limited baptisms to a few times in the year, baptisms had taken place on Sundays, although not on all Sundays. "It should not be at all surprising that Pascha became the principal occasion [for baptism] in much of the Church during the third century. It would be somewhat more surprising to learn that it had been so universally from the end of the apostolic age."[5]

In his valuable small study *The Day of Light: The Biblical and Liturgical Meaning of Sunday*, H. Boone Porter gives a glimpse into a later period, citing a decision about times for baptism by an eighth-century German council. The bishops recognized that Easter and Pentecost are the two legitimate times for baptism; yet when circumstances made these days difficult or impossible, they recognized also that the realities of the resurrection and the Holy Spirit, of which Easter and Pentecost speak, are present in the Lord's Day; hence baptism might be observed on Sunday, but, except in emergency circumstances, not on any other day.[6]

In time, whatever tradition there had been of baptism on Sunday with a congregation present largely lapsed, and customs that the early church would have thought suitable at best for emergency conditions became common practice throughout the West.

We noted earlier that the first English Prayer Book of 1549 sought change. In the first rubric of the baptism rite, arguing on historical and pastoral grounds, it supported Sunday as a baptismal occasion, directing, *It is most convenient that baptism should not be administered but upon Sundays and other holy days, when the most number of people may come together.* This rubric remained in subsequent English Prayer Books.

Evidently for a time some vicars sought to carry out the intention of this rubric. In the early seventeenth century, the Anglican poet and priest George Herbert set out his ideal of the country parson in his small classic, *A Priest to the Temple* (1632). Speaking of "The Parson in Sacraments," he said, "At Baptism, being himself in white, he requires the presence of all, and Baptizeth not willingly, but on Sundays, or great days."[7]

The rubric specifies morning and evening prayer on these days as the time for baptism, but in later generations, although Sunday appears to have been the preferred day for baptisms, they were usually performed at a time when no congregation was present and only family, sponsors, and friends attended.

Beginning in the nineteen-fifties, before Prayer Book revision had really engaged the church, many congregations, seeking to demonstrate the corporateness of the church and the reality of baptism as entry into the redeemed and redemptive community, found ways of holding baptisms at the main Sunday morning service, in full sight of everyone, and involving the congregation. So general a change in significant ritual conduct has rarely been brought about so rapidly without authority from rubrics or canons.

Even though rubrics have now addressed the matter, the recognition of a bond between baptism and Sunday does not turn on early models or on directions in early authorities or even on the regulations of the authorized Prayer Book so much as on affinities of themes.

Sunday carried, as it still carries, multiple significances. Justin Martyr placed the day in two circles of meaning. Referring to the primal creation story, he said to his reader, the Emperor, "We [Christians] hold this common gathering on Sunday, since it is the first day, on which God transforming darkness and matter made the universe" (*Apology,* section 67). It was the day when, speaking into the dark chaos, God said, "Let there be light." As the day of light, Sunday was the fitting day for baptism, the sacrament of illumination. Then, referring to the gospel histories, Justin said, "Jesus Christ our Saviour rose from the dead on the same day" (ibid.). Sunday was also the day of re-creation, of the banishing of darkness and the dawning of light, for it was the day of Jesus' resurrection.

Sunday, as the resurrection day, is the day on which the new life, the life beyond death, burst into the realm of death. Thus, Sunday is "the Lord's Day," Christ's day, the day to which by his rising he had laid claim. In Revelation 1:10 the seer says that he was *in the spirit on the Lord's day,* caught up ecstatically into a scene of heavenly worship. Did his vision of heaven as a liturgical community of unimaginable splendor take its materials from a Sunday eucharistic gathering of Christians? The *Didache* uses an intensive expression to speak of the day, saying literally "the Lord's Day of the Lord" which C. C. Richardson translates as "every Lord's Day— his special day." Ignatius says that Christians no longer observed the sabbath, but "lived by the Lord's Day" (*Magnesians* 9:1). Probably the expression "the Lord's Day" referred to the resurrection event but at the same time spoke beyond it to the presence of the living Christ in and to his assembled people. It was his day because on it he had risen and because on it he set his table for his followers.

The early Christians spoke of Sunday not only as "the first day," but also as "the eighth day." When Christians observed the Jewish week, including the sabbath, and followed it at once by their distinctive community meal in the early hours of Sunday, it would have been easy for them to think of the Jewish week of seven days, with their own plus—the eighth day. But the expression carried profound claims. Taking the Jewish week of seven days to be complete, they thought of Sunday not only as the first day of the week following, but also as a sign of a new, transcendent aeon which had broken upon the old. In the midst of cyclic time there had appeared the beginning of that which does not end, and the eighth day was its sign—a day that was part of our time and yet not confined to our time—"the perpetual First Day of a new age."[8] As Gordon Lathrop put it, "It is as if the [Christian] meeting were after the week, beyond the week, free of the week, an opening to a thing the week cannot contain."[9]

The Lord's Day, the eighth day, was the day for baptism. One scholar has said that "The title 'the eighth day' is principally to be explained by the practice of baptism on Sunday."[10] This theme may have been influenced by the Jewish custom of circumcising on the eighth day after birth (Lev. 12:3; Phil. 3:5), and the earliest Christians connected baptism with circumcision. The baptismal significance of the number eight was exhibited in the many early Christian baptismal pools which were built in octagonal shape, as were many of the baptistery buildings in which they were located. The fourth-century baptistery at Milan, quite certainly the one in which Ambrose baptized Augustine, carried an inscription whose first lines interpret the octagonal shape:

> This temple of eight niches was built for holy use;
> > an octagonal font is worthy of this gift.
> It was fitting that on this number
> > the hall of holy baptism
> > was built, by which true salvation has returned to the people
> > in the light of Christ rising again.
> For he who was freed from the prison
> > of death frees the dead from their tombs,
> > frees from every stain of guilt those who confess their sins,
> > and washes them in the stream of the purifying font.[11]

To summarize, the simple words of the second Prayer Book rubric on p. 298 seek to bring into significant relation three things—Sunday, baptism, and eucharist—three things that belong together but that had become separated. And in their separateness, they had become weakened and to a considerable extent unintelligible.

Behind the rubric is the conviction that each Christian Sunday is an Easter, and the themes of Sunday—light from darkness, resurrection, new creation—are also the themes of baptism, and the themes of baptism are the themes of the baptismal life that flows from baptism and is sustained by the eucharist.

CHAPTER 7

How the Earliest
Christians Baptized: Acts

The gospels describe Jesus' baptism, and the epistles tell us what baptism meant in the church's earliest years—indeed, what it means in any age. However, these descriptions and these accounts of meanings tell us almost nothing about the "externalities" of first century baptism. What was done? Who did it? What did they say? What water was used? (If we had only Paul's writings, we could only guess that baptism used water.) To see and hear the early Christians baptizing we must look beyond the baptismal passages that are offered in the lectionary and consider the book of Acts and what it can tell us of the practice of the first Christians.

Acts portrays the new community of belief in Jesus engaged in a radical divine aggression—a pageant of restless travel, courageous speech, healings, ecstasy, visions, struggle for doctrinal clarity, internal conflict and defection, confrontation with hostile officialdom, imprisonment, earthquake, shipwreck, floggings, and small riots. Of course, the record has its gentle moments as well: Rhoda's joy at hearing Peter's voice, Dorcas' life of good works, the meeting of Peter and Cornelius, Ananias to his surprise saying "brother Saul," Barnabas introducing Paul to the Christian community, Priscilla and Aquila explaining the Way of God more accurately to the gifted Apollos, Lydia's quiet conversion. But through it all, the unexpected is constantly overtaking people, and at each new movement of the community by the Spirit into the world, persons are baptized.

Acts comes from close to the events it narrates (although some parts of the book are closer than others). Its narratives remain basic to understanding the earliest Christian past, and they influence what we do today. Every incident in this earliest record is significant, and we can be frustrated when the narrator does not answer the pastoral or sacramental questions we put. But we must not suppose that the accounts in Acts were written to answer our questions.

In his first volume, the Gospel of Luke, the author has told the story of God's redemptive actions in the Spirit-filled mission of Jesus. Now, in his second volume, he continues with the story of God's redemptive actions through the Spirit-filled mission of Jesus' people. The young church is constantly innovating, sometimes pausing, but then advancing courageously. Conflicts and opposition always appear, but they do not stop the gospel. The church is a people gathered by the gospel of Christ and informed by the immediate presence of the Spirit—a people in and through which God is carrying out a long-laid purpose to save. The advance and deepening of the community is shaped by the interwoven forces of the divine initiative and the believing, obedient human response.

From the beginning, the church baptizes. Nothing suggests that baptism was introduced, after some discussion, when the church had been well launched. Although the church develops in different regions under different leaders, all parts of it baptize, and they all evidently recognize each other's baptisms. As the community of faith in Christ moves into new areas and new populations, it moves by preaching and by baptism.

Although the references to baptism in Acts are more numerous than in any other New Testament book, Acts still gives us no real descriptions. The author has no interest in scene-setting. He had no need to describe what everyone knew. Yet by statement and suggestion, Acts tells us a great deal about early Christian baptism.

OCCASIONS

We identify here the occasions of baptism in the book of Acts, summarizing each of them briefly. Then we shall examine the group as a whole thematically.

Pentecost. Acts 2:1-42

Unexpected events—the sound of wind, the tongues of fire and the disciples speaking in other languages—call the people in Jerusalem together (2:1-5). They propose an explanation—the disciples have had too much to drink (2:6-15). Peter, drawing on the prophet Joel, explains that what is seen and heard gives evidence that the new age of the Spirit has dawned (2:15-28). He tells briefly the story of Jesus (2:29-37). Many welcome his message and ask *"what should we do?"* Peter tells them: *"Repent, and be baptized every one of you in the name of Jesus Christ so that your sins may be forgiven; and you will receive the gift of the Holy Spirit"* (2:38).

The manifestations of the Spirit seem to have come only upon the apostles and the persons who were with them, not on those who were converted and baptized. The apostles themselves were not baptized with water in the name of Jesus. This Pentecost event, the promised *baptism with the Holy Spirit* (1:5), brought them decisively and dramatically into the new age of the Spirit.

In this event, the Spirit clearly takes the initiative, moving in divine freedom. Baptism is the visible, enacted response on the part of those who consent to the gospel.

[The opening events of the story (2:1-11) are read on Pentecost in all three lectionary years (BCP, pp. 896, 906, 916), and were commented on above. A central part of Peter's sermon (2:14, 22-32) is read on Monday in Easter Week. The part that includes the end of the Pentecost sermon and the hearers' response (2:36-41) is read on Tuesday in Easter Week in all three years (BCP, pp. 894, 905, 915).]

Philip at Samaria. Acts 8:4-17

Philip (who had been set apart as a "deacon," 6:1-6) left Jerusalem because of persecution there and went to Samaria, where he proclaimed Christ. His words were accompanied by healing, and he was listened to attentively (8:4-8). Soon many persons *believed Philip, who was proclaiming the good news about the kingdom of God and the name of Jesus,* and those who believed were baptized. Philip's mission challenged a local magician named Simon. Eventually, however, even Simon believed, was baptized, and stayed close to Philip (8:9-13). (Later events indicated that Simon's conversion was superficial, as though he had been dazzled by what seemed to him a superior magic.)

When the apostles in Jerusalem heard of this community of believers in Samaria, they sent Peter and John to them (8:14). The Samaritans who had believed and been baptized in the name of the Lord Jesus had not yet received the Holy Spirit. So Peter and John prayed for the Samaritan Christians and laid their hands on them, *and they received the Holy Spirit* (8:15-17). (There is no mention of specific signs of the Spirit such as tongues or prophecy. Should they be surmised?)

[This striking story is omitted from the Sunday lectionary. Perhaps the lectionary-makers thought that it raised questions that required interpretation—questions at which we will look a little later.]

Philip and the Ethiopian eunuch. Acts 8:26-40

Philip was on a road leading south from Jerusalem when an Ethiopian court official passed and invited him into his chariot. The official was a god-fearing Gentile who had come to Jerusalem to worship, and as he rode back to his home he was reading (probably aloud) the prophet Isaiah (Acts 8:26-33). The official was a eunuch, which meant that by Jewish law he could not receive proselyte baptism and circumcision. He had been drawn to the Hebrew faith "only to discover that his sexual status prevented him forever from identifying himself with the people of God."[1]

The eunuch asked Philip to explain to him what he was reading. Philip interpreted the passage in Isaiah 53 in terms of *the good news about Jesus*. They passed some water, and the eunuch said, *"Look, here is water! What is to prevent me from being baptized?"* It is not said in so many words that he believed, but his eagerness bespoke his faith. He had the chariot stopped; the two men went down into the water where Philip baptized the eunuch. Then *the Spirit of the Lord snatched Philip away; the eunuch saw him no more,* and went on his way rejoicing (8:34-39).

[The story is read on the Fifth Sunday of Easter in Year B.]

Paul's baptism. Acts 9:10-19a, also 22:12-16

Paul (who is still known here as Saul, his name in its Hebrew form) was on his way to Damascus, *breathing threats and murder,* to apprehend the Christians there (9:1-3); on his way he saw a dazzling light and was struck to the ground and blinded. He heard a voice from heaven, which was identified as Jesus, and his life was forever changed. At first he simply went into Damascus, as the voice had told him, where, still blind, he stayed for three days (9:4-9).

A Christian named Ananias, who lived in the city, was led, after understandable hesitancy, to go to Paul, assured that God had a great purpose for him. *"He is an instrument whom I have chosen to bring my name before Gentiles and kings and before the people of Israel."* Ananias obeyed and laid his hands on Paul and spoke to him, addressing him *"Brother Saul,"* saying that God had sent him that Paul might regain his sight and be filled with the Holy Spirit. Paul's sight was restored; he was baptized and took food and began to regain his strength (9:10-19a).

Paul became involved in the Christian community at once (vs. 19b), but it was only later that he began to take a leading role. The story of Paul's conversion is told three times in Acts (9:1-22; 22:1-21; 26:2-23), always with a sense of its mystery. Its unexpectedness witnessed that the initiative of God lay in and behind it. Somewhat surprisingly, it is not recounted in any of Paul's own letters.

When Paul speaks of his baptism, long after the event, he recalls Ananias saying, *"Get up, be baptized, and have your sins washed away, calling on his name"* (22:16). (Paul does not mention his baptism in the similar autobiographical account in chapter 26.) The expression *calling on his name* may be almost exorcistic—referring to the words that accompanied his vision: *I am Jesus of Nazareth whom you are persecuting* (22.8).

Although the account of Paul's conversion is dramatic and very human, it does not psychologize; it speaks in terms of Paul's actions and visions and of a divine voice, but not of motives or feelings.

[The account of this important incident is read on Easter 3, in Year C.]

Peter and Cornelius. Acts 10:1-48

In this strategically important incident in Acts, Cornelius, a godfearing Gentile military officer is told in a vision to send for Peter (10:1-8). At that same time, Peter had a vision in which levitically clean and unclean animals were shown him, and he was told to eat (10:9-16). While Peter is still wondering what his vision meant, messengers arrive and he is led to Cornelius' house where he is invited to speak (10:17-33). As he begins (10:34-43), Peter says, *I truly understand that God shows no partiality.* The events that had prepared for this meeting between a Jewish apostle and a Gentile seeker were divinely led. Then Peter tells the story of Jesus' ministry, death and resurrection. The response is described quite briefly. *While Peter was still speaking, the Holy Spirit fell on all who heard the word,* as evidenced by unmistakable signs, *speaking in tongues and extolling God.* Peter asks, *Can anyone withhold water for baptizing these people who have received the Holy Spirit just as we have?* The hearers were baptized at once, and Peter remained in the house for several days (10:44-48).

The Spirit has taken the initiative, as at Pentecost, and the believing community, led in directions it could not have anticipated, must respond by acknowledging, with baptism, the reality of the faith of the house of Cornelius.

[Only parts of this long story appear in the liturgical lectionary. Verses 34-43, in which Peter tells the story of Jesus, emphasizing the resurrection, are an alternative reading for Easter in Years A, B, and C. Verses 34-38, which speak of Jesus' anointing with the Holy Spirit and power, are read on the Feast of the Baptism of Our Lord, Epiphany 1, in all three years. These sections of Acts 10 were discussed above. These lectionary readings concentrate on Peter's speech and do not tell how he happened to be speaking in Cornelius' house, and they do not describe the response to his message. This story needs to be heard in its completeness.]

Lydia. Acts 16:11-15

Paul and Silas (perhaps joined by others who make up the "we" of vs. 11) are on a missionary journey which has taken them to the important city of Philippi. They go on the sabbath to a place outside the gate by the river where some women come to pray. There they meet a well-to-do woman named Lydia, who was evidently a god-fearer. She listens eagerly to what Paul says. Then she and her household are baptized, and she opens her home to the evangelists.

[This quiet, attractive incident does not appear in the eucharistic lectionary.]

The Philippian jailer. Acts 16:25-34

Paul and Silas are in prison; as they sing and pray during the night, there is an earthquake (16:25-26). In the ensuing chaos some of the prisoners' chains come loose, the shattered jailer, thinking that his prisoners Paul and Silas must have something to do with the disturbance, comes to them in panic asking what he can do to be "saved"—probably meaning saving his own position, or possibly his life (16:27-30). They accept his naive term and tell him about a salvation that goes beyond his conceiving. The household believes, *and at the same hour of the night. . .he and his entire family were baptized without delay,* (16:31-34).

[This vivid story is read on Easter 7, Year C.]

Crispus and others at Corinth. Acts 18:8

Crispus, a ruler of the synagogue at Corinth, *became a believer in the Lord, together with all his household; and many of the Corinthians who heard Paul became believers and were baptized.*

Apollos and Paul at Ephesus. Acts 18:24—19:7

These verses in Acts juxtapose two incidents which are separate, except that they both deal with persons who knew the baptism of John—indicating that the influence of John the Baptist persisted after his death and suggesting that there were awkward transitions for some persons. Both incidents contain enough puzzles to make a reader wonder what sources the writer was following.

In the first incident (18:24-28) Apollos, an eloquent Jew who was conversant with *the Way of the Lord,* came to Ephesus where *he taught accurately the things concerning Jesus,* even though he knew only the baptism of John. (It seems strange that he is described as *teaching accurately* about Jesus while he himself had not received Christian baptism.) Priscilla and Aquila, who were well-informed believers, heard him and supplied the understanding he lacked. (It is not said that Apollos was then baptized.)

In the second incident (19:1-7), while Apollos was away in Corinth, Paul came to Ephesus where he found *some disciples.* When he asked them whether or not they had received the Holy Spirit when they believed, they said that they had not so much as heard of the Holy Spirit. (This passage, again strangely, speaks of persons who believe and are called disciples, but who have neither received the Holy Spirit nor been baptized.) When Paul discovered that they had, through Apollos, known only John's baptism (which was an anticipatory rite), he told them the Christian message more fully; and they were baptized *in the name of the Lord Jesus.* Paul laid his hands on them, and *the Holy Spirit came upon them and they spoke in tongues and prophesied.* Here the Holy Spirit comes through a laying on of hands immediately after baptism, and it is witnessed by tongues and prophecy.

[These incidents at Ephesus are not included in the eucharistic lectionary. Perhaps it was thought that they contain so many complexities that if they were simply read out in the liturgy without informed interpretation, they could suggest some indefensible ideas.]

THEMES IN THE BAPTISMAL ACCOUNTS IN ACTS

Having identified the principal references to baptism in the book of Acts, we may trace in them a number of characteristic themes:

(1) Baptism is a response to the Word, the gospel; and it is an expression of faith.

The church from its beginning is a *preaching* church and a *baptizing* church. The word and the act are closely linked. As a missionary body, the church moves ahead, first by announcing what God has done in Jesus Christ for alienated humanity; then when hearers consent in faith to the gospel, they are baptized:

When they <u>heard</u> this, i.e. Peter's sermon, followed by the call to baptism (2:37-38), *those who <u>welcomed his message</u> were baptized* (2:41).

When they <u>believed</u> Philip's preaching of the good news, *they were baptized* (8:12). *Simon himself <u>believed</u> and was baptized.* (8:13).

Philip <u>proclaimed the good news about Jesus,</u> and the eunuch asks to be baptized (8:35f).

Lydia. . .<u>was listening to us</u>. . .The Lord <u>opened her heart</u> to listen to what was said by Paul. When she and her household were baptized. . .(16:14f).

They <u>spoke the word of the Lord</u> to him [the Philippian jailer]. . .*and he and his entire family were baptized* (16:32f)

Many of the Corinthians who <u>heard</u> Paul became <u>believers</u> and were baptized (18:8).

On <u>hearing this</u>, they were baptized in the name of the Lord Jesus (19:5).

Preaching the good news of Jesus and baptizing in his name were closely bonded as actions of the evangelizing church. W. F. Flemington called baptism "an embodiment of the *kerygma*."[2] Primacy belongs to the Word. The new reality which had been brought in Christ was first proclaimed in Christian preaching and heard in faith. Then faith came to expression in baptism and membership in the people of faith—the sign-community of the new reality. Baptism without the Word would be empty, virtually magic; but the Word without baptism would be a discarnate message, unrelated to a community of place and time which could express its common consent and order its life under the gospel. Thus *faith* and *baptism* were parts of a single response to the Good News. The baptismal act arose from the interior faith; the faith was demonstrated by the outward act.

(2) The baptisms in Acts took place as soon as there was an expression of faith.

The accounts in Acts report no pre-baptismal period of waiting, teaching, or probation such as we find in the more cautious next generations of the church. An expression of faith was followed without delay by the sign of faith.

In 8:26-40, the Ethiopian eunuch, a Gentile God-fearer, hears Philip explain that the passage from Isaiah he was reading, about the Servant, referred to Christ. He must have believed, although the account only implies it. No persuasion or appeal was required. The account does not tell how he might have known that faith led to baptism, but he said: *"Look, here is water! What is to prevent me from being baptized?"* He was baptized at once and continued on his way.

Other accounts similarly say that faith led at once to baptism: As soon as there are clear signs of the Spirit, the house of Cornelius is baptized (10:44-48). When Lydia opens her heart to what Paul said, she and her household are baptized (16:14b-15a). In the story of the Philippian jailer (16:25-35), after the earthquake the frightened jailer asks what he can do to be saved and Paul and Silas tell him the gospel of Christ, he believes, and *at the same hour of the night. . .he and his entire family were baptized without delay.*

This immediacy probably traces to two factors:

◆ There was a trust in the Spirit. An indication of faith meant without question that the new age had dawned, and its sign need not be delayed. Paul was convinced that no one could say the effecting words "Jesus is Lord [*Kyrios*]" except by the Spirit (1 Cor. 12:3). But where the Spirit acted, counterfeit spirits gathered. The case of Simon (8:9-24) suggests that even in the first century there could be mixed motives on the part of persons who sought baptism and misplaced trust on the part of those who administered it. But no one hesitated to baptize because of that uncertainty.

◆ At first most converts were either Jews or God-fearing Gentiles. As long as that was so, Christian evangelists could take for granted a certain amount of what is sometimes called today "pre-evangelism" which had come to their converts through prior Jewish teaching and ethics. It was sufficient if persons with Jewish experience confessed Jesus as the Messiah. Faith could be followed at once by the sign of faith, and baptism could be followed by teaching. (While this observation generally holds, the Gentile jailer at Philippi is an exception.)

The first-century church had teachers, some of whom may have been compensated for their work (Gal. 6:6). But as far as the evidence of Acts and Paul's letters carry us, they were teachers of the baptized. To be sure, conversion took place in a context of meaning. Converts were responding to preaching. Moreover, the hearers witnessed to their faith by an intelligible expression, carrying cognitive content. A reader cannot miss the presence of an intelligent heart in the story of Lydia: *The Lord opened her heart to listen eagerly to what was said by Paul.* And after her baptism, she said, *"If you have judged me to be faithful to the Lord, come and stay at my home."* (See also the rudimentary statements of belief in 9:20 and 11:7.) But baptism did not depend on instruction leading to a confession of faith.

By the early second century, a period of teaching and probation was required before baptism, and it soon became quite long and demanding. In time, a catechumenal period, perhaps lasting several years, preceded baptism, and the baptismal action included an avowal of faith. But the incidents recorded in Acts give no evidence that baptism was held until after some necessary learning had taken place.

Some present-day readers attribute the church's growing caution to a loss of self-confidence. But a more likely factor is that the Christian community was moving away from its Jewish base and into Gentile populations, and the conditions which had supported the practice of the prior generation no longer prevailed. Persons who came to Christ and the church from pagan religions and Hellenistic philosophies had a great deal to learn and to un-learn.

Several germinal credal forms can be found embedded in the New Testament epistles. They are brief, and they center on Jesus. However, they are hymns or acts of praise, and nothing associates them with baptism. A spurious text, Acts 8:37, gives an interesting early hint of a baptismal affirmation of belief. In the story of Philip and the Ethiopian eunuch, after the eunuch asks, *What is to prevent me from being baptized?* some early manuscripts contain, in varying forms, *And Philip said, "If you believe with all your heart, you may." And he replied "I believe that Jesus Christ is the Son of God."* Quite certainly this verse was not part of the book as originally written, and modern editions, if they include it at all, print it as a marginal note. The words were evidently inserted by an early copyist who knew the custom of requiring a baptismal confession of faith. One commentator remarks, "Clearly the interpolator thought that the eunuch could not have been baptized without repeating some sort of creed."[3]

(3)   The baptisms in the book of Acts are in the name of Jesus.

The evidence of the book of Acts is consistent:

◆ On the Day of Pentecost, the first mention of Christian baptism, Peter says, *"Repent and be baptized every one of you in the name of Jesus Christ"* (2:38).

◆ Acts 8:16 speaks of the Samaritans as having *been baptized in the name of the Lord Jesus*.

◆ In 10:48, Peter orders the household of Cornelius *to be baptized in the name of Jesus Christ.*

◆ And in 19:5, the persons in Ephesus who had previously only received John's baptism *were baptized in the name of the Lord Jesus*.

Acts is supported in this matter by Paul's letters in which he asks, *Were you baptized in the name of Paul?* (1 Cor. 1:13), implying that true baptism is in the name of Jesus and no one else. In 1 Corinthians 6:11, Paul speaks of baptism saying, *You were washed. . .in the name of the Lord Jesus Christ.*

The efficacy of the name appears in other connections. The apostles heal in the name of Jesus Christ of Nazareth (3:6; see also 3:16; 4:7, 10, 12); they claim that salvation is in the name (4:12); the apostles speak and teach in this name (4:17, 18); and they proclaim the good news about the Kingdom of God and the name of Jesus Christ (8:12).

What does it mean to baptize in(to) a name? In biblical idiom, one's name is as oneself; to honor or to slight one's name is to honor or to slight the person. One who acts in another person's name, is as that person. To be baptized in the name of another means to belong to that other. Rudolf Schnackenburg says, "The naming of a person had the meaning of attaching the baptized to this person so that the baptized belonged to him." The baptized "are made over to him."[4] Thus baptism in Jesus' name speaks of being brought into union with Jesus. It signifies a new relationship, a new lordship.

We can be quite sure that the "name" of Jesus meant not a formula, but the power or the reality of Jesus. By baptism one is brought into the story of which

Jesus Christ is center and into union with him. Certainly the baptismal name was not a historical reference to Jesus, the rabbi of Nazareth, but a declaration of the name of the exalted Christ, the *Kyrios*—the name of Jesus at which all things would eventually bow (Phil. 2:9-11). Was the name actually spoken at the moment of baptism? Acts 22:16 suggests that the name might be spoken by the person who was baptized, while James 2:7 suggests that it was pronounced over the candidate. But these passages are no more than hints; they do not tell us what was said or when or by whom.

Baptizing in the name of Jesus is not what a reader of Matthew 28:18-20 would expect. There the risen Jesus directs his followers to baptize in the triadic name. But no such baptismal practice appears in Acts or in the Pauline churches. Evidently the ending of Matthew expresses the mind and perhaps the practice of one part of the first-century church rather than an unmistakable command by the risen Lord.

However, at least from the second century, a fuller statement came into use, and the church has baptized in the triadic name. The earliest reference outside of Matthew 28:19 to use of the threefold name at baptism is the *Didache* which twice directs that baptism be made "in the name of the Father and of the Son, and of the Holy Spirit" (*Didache* 7:1, 3). Yet a little later, in speaking of "the Eucharist," it says: "You must not let anyone eat or drink of your Eucharist except those baptized *in the Lord's name*" (*Didache* 9:5). Perhaps the two styles of naming were in use side by side, and the writer of the *Didache* may have regarded them as virtual equivalents.

A few sectarian groups today follow the book of Acts literally and baptize only in the name of Jesus. Since the church describes baptism as normatively in the triune name (BCP, pp. 313, 859) it is an ecumenical puzzle to know how to regard baptisms that follow scripture literally but that disregard this early and continuous tradition of the threefold name. Such baptism does what the church once did, but does it do what the church does?

(4) Several accounts in Acts speak of the baptism of households.

Two conspicuous instances of the baptism of households are when Lydia and her household are baptized, 16:15, and when the Philippian jailer is baptized *with all his family* (16:33). The baptism of the family of Crispus is implied (18:8). In none of these cases is it said who made up the household.

The "household" (the Greek term is *oikos*; the Latin term is *familia*) was regarded in the ancient world, and especially among Jews, as an indissoluble unit of life The *oikos* would have included, at a minimum, a husband and wife and their children and their house slaves. It was inconceivable that part of this unit could be in the new life in Christ and all of it not be. When the convert who was baptized was the head of a household, the *oikos* was regarded as effectively evangelized, and all its members were baptized.

This practice is not exactly "infant baptism." It did not focus on small children, although it obviously did not exclude them. A few years ago Clinton Morrison suggested that at the time of the New Testament, infant baptism was not a distinct concept. "While the church may have been baptizing children all along, it had not yet considered the practice a special kind of baptism. This sort of refinement often has to await controversy; but until then. . .there simply was no theme of infant baptism, even if children were being baptized."[5]

Rather, what we see in the New Testament is something more like "family baptism." Hippolytus (writing c. 215 CE) gives some terse directions for family groups at the water. He says: "Baptize the little ones first. All those who can speak for themselves shall do so. As for those who cannot speak for themselves, their parents or someone from their family shall speak for them. Then baptize the men, and lastly the women" (chapter 21). While the family entered the new life together, one must make what one can of Hippolytus' order of children first, then the men and the women.

Then and later this practice created a painful problem when one member of a marriage became a Christian and the other did not. What then of the children? Some Christian wives were evidently driven out of the home by their unbelieving husbands. Paul counsels (1 Cor. 7:12-16) that when the parents are divided in faith, the believing parent sanctifies the children, no doubt implying that they might be included in baptism.

Although it is clear that when parents were baptized, their children were baptized with them, we do not know what Christian parents did about children who were born to them later. There is no evidence that such children were baptized, but neither is there any evidence that they were not baptized but were held until a later ill-defined "age of accountability." One supposes that if the baptism of the children of believing parents had been postponed, this postponement would have raised pastoral problems that would have required regulation or left some marks of controversy. Presumably such children were baptized at an early age, but one cannot be certain.

(5) The accounts in Acts often relate baptism to the Holy Spirit, but in different ways.

Baptism in Acts and in Paul, as we have seen, is in the name (i.e. the reality) of Jesus Christ, or the Lord Jesus. One who is baptized is no longer one's own. It is clear also that in Acts the Holy Spirit is constitutive of baptism. Peter said at Pentecost: *"Repent, and be baptized every one of you in the name of Jesus Christ so that your sins may be forgiven; and you will receive the gift of the Holy Spirit"* (2:38).

These two realities—the name and the Spirit—although they are both essential to baptism, can be mentioned separately, and either can precede the other. A New Testament scholar, G. R. Beasley Murray, has said: "Both Paul and the author of Acts recognized the work of the Spirit before baptism, in baptism and after baptism, precisely as they saw the Spirit at work before conversion, in conversion and after conversion. We must beware of exaggerating distinctions in the various stages of what the New Testament writers probably saw as a unitary process."[6]

Rather than there being in Acts a single uniform pattern in the relation between water baptism and the gift of the Holy Spirit, the baptismal narratives suggest three patterns. Each must be seen in connection with its situation, and the situations must be seen in the light of the overall purpose of the book, which is not to give a model for sacramental practice, but to document the missionary expansion of the church as it moves from Judea to Samaria and to the ends of the earth (1:8).

To identify the three:

1. *The Pentecost pattern:* the Spirit takes the initiative.

> On the Day of Pentecost, as reported in 2:1-42, the Spirit falls dramatically on those who were *together in one place* (i.e. Peter, "the eleven," and others who were with them), but evidently not on the members of the crowd of hearers in Jerusalem (vss. 1-4). Peter, the spokesman, preaches from Joel that "this is the promised new day," i.e. the expected age of the Spirit (vss. 14-36); many persons believe and are baptized (vss. 37-42). By the Spirit a new thing is happening; persons believe, and baptism follows.

> The pattern of Pentecost is replicated at the house of Cornelius (chapter 10), where for the first time the gospel is carried to Gentiles. Peter goes to Cornelius' house and tells the news of Christ (vss. 34-43); while he is speaking, the Holy Spirit unmistakably falls on the hearers (vss. 44-45); they are baptized (vss. 47-48).

This is the Gentile Pentecost (although, unlike at Pentecost, the Spirit comes on the new believers rather than on Peter and those who came with him). Again a new thing is happening whose divine reality is witnessed by the initiative of the Spirit which Peter could not but acknowledge. *"Can anyone withhold the water for baptizing these people who have received the Holy Spirit just as we have?"* (10:47).

The phrase "baptism with the Holy Spirit" is mentioned in connection with these two incidents: First in the opening paragraph of Acts when, in an obvious anticipation of Pentecost, the departing Jesus tells his disciples *you will be baptized with the Holy Spirit not many days from now* (1:5); then when Peter, after he has visited Cornelius, returns to Jerusalem where he tells others what had happened (11:1-18). He says that while he was still speaking in Cornelius' house, *the Holy Spirit fell upon them just as it had upon us at the beginning* (11:15)—making a connection between the house of Cornelius and Pentecost. Peter says that he was reminded of a word of Jesus, *"John baptized with water, but you will be baptized with the Holy Spirit"* (11:16).

These are the only places in the New Testament that expressly identify an incident as *baptism with the Holy Spirit.* In these accounts it is not an individual experience nor a second experience—neither a moment of ecstasy nor a passage to some more intense life of faith. Rather, both of these occasions are corporate, belonging to the biography of the church, rather than the believer. Both are inaugural and unique—one at the church's beginning (2:1-47), and one as it moves to include Gentiles (10:1—11:18). The Spirit authorizes these crucial events in the earliest life of the church, and baptism follows.

2. *The Samaria pattern:* linking a new community with the old.

The account of the gospel at Samaria describes initiatory acts: (1) A water baptism, in which the Spirit is not given. The text simply says that when Philip went to Samaria and preached the gospel, many believed and were baptized. And (2) a subsequent laying on of hands by the apostles, which conferred the Spirit. The Samaritan believers only received the Holy Spirit when Peter and John came from Jerusalem and laid hands on them (8:4-17). This two-step pattern was shaped by its situation, but what was its situation?

Acts is organized around missionary expansion, showing how the church spread into new regions and yet remained one. Samaria was located between Judea and Galilee; its religion was close to Judaism, but was regarded with hostility by Jews. Samaria was, as Jews saw it, schismatic territory. When the Christian movement spread there, it seemed necessary to unite the new community of believers with the parent church at Jerusalem. Two apostles come from Jerusalem with a gesture of bonding and blessing. The Spirit ratifies the union.

[This account was read at Confirmation in the Prayer Books of 1892 and 1928, inevitably suggesting that the Samaria pattern gave biblical warrant for what the Episcopal Church did when baptism by a priest was followed at a later time by confirmation by a bishop, which act conferred the Holy Spirit (1928 BCP, p. 296). But this use of the story was misleading, and the 1979 Prayer Book does not appoint the Samaria story to be read *At Confirmation* (p. 929). The Samaria incident was not told in Acts to provide a model for sacramental initiation. As Reginald Fuller put it, "The separation of the laying on of hands in Acts 8 has nothing to do with the Western Medieval separation of Confirmation from Baptism but is due rather to Luke's redactional interest in subordinating each successive new stage in Christian mission to the Jerusalem church and its apostolate."[7]

Two-stage Christian initiation by infant baptism and adolescent confirmation traces no continuity to the New Testament and the early church. It arose in the Late Middle Ages and was developed in Catholic and Protestant churches in the modern period, and only in the West. Inevitably it suggested a division between Christ and the Spirit and tended to reduce water baptism virtually to a negative or pre-Christian rite.[8]]

The account of Paul's work at Ephesus (19:1-7), a passage which contains many puzzles, gives a partial parallel to the Samaria pattern. The believers at Ephesus knew of Jesus from Apollos, but they had only the baptism of John. John himself had said that his baptism of repentance would be superseded by a baptism with the Holy Spirit (Mk. 1:8 and parallels). Thus both the understanding and the experience of the Ephesians were incomplete. When they heard the full Christian message from Paul, *they were baptized in the name of the Lord Jesus* (whether by Paul or by someone else is not said). Then, *When Paul had laid his hands on them, the Holy Spirit came upon them, and they spoke in tongues and prophesied.*

This series of events is like Samaria inasmuch as the Spirit is given following baptism and by a laying on of hands—although, unlike Samaria, the giving of the Spirit by the laying on of hands follows immediately after baptism. The Ephesian experience is like Pentecost in that the reality of the Spirit is evidenced by speaking in tongues, although, unlike Pentecost, it is the baptized who speak in tongues. (When he says *tongues,* is the author thinking of the Pentecost phenomenon of people speaking in languages other than their own or of the Corinthian phenomenon of people speaking in sounds that are unintelligible unless there is an interpreter?)

In this pattern, evidenced at Samaria and less clearly at Ephesus, the order is baptism, followed by the Holy Spirit through a laying on of hands as a gesture of bonding and unity.

3. *A single action.*

A third pattern appears in the several instances of baptism in which there is no mention of a special action of the Spirit nor of a ministry of the apostles. Persons are just "baptized"—"the washing" said it all (8:36, 38; 16:15, 33; 18:8). In the baptism of Paul (9:17f), there is no separable Spirit-act. Ananias laid his hands on Paul for healing. He says that Paul will be filled with the Holy Spirit, but nothing in the story connects the Holy Spirit with a specific act, probably implying that the Holy Spirit is given in baptism itself.

This pattern suggests that a simple, unitary baptismal action is ritually and theologically complete; water, forgiveness, Christ, church, and the Spirit are united. They do not all need to be named or to be expressed separately in order to be effectively enacted. To state the theology of the matter: God is unitary and personal and human beings are unitary and personal. Baptism, however rudimentary or full its words and actions, unites all of God with all of a person. Nothing is left out that must be made up by another act at another time. One cannot be baptized into the divine name, be brought into the life of Christ and the communion of believers and somehow be missing the Holy Spirit.

Looking at these three patterns, both the Pentecost pattern and the Samaria pattern seem to be exceptional. (1) The Pentecost pattern belongs uniquely to the church's very beginning in Jerusalem—its baptism in the Spirit, its *clothing with power from on high* (Lk. 24:49). It is partially replicated at the house of Cornelius as, in a new beginning, the church which has originated in the spiritual soil of Judaism moves to include Gentiles. (2) The Samaria pattern met the situation of the church's spread to a neighboring rival population, demonstrating that the community of faith in Christ could exist in multiple locations and yet be one. At Ephesus the same pattern marks the unique moment when a small community moved from the baptism of John (sign of the old age) to baptism in the name of Jesus.[9]

While it is useful to observe the variety in the book of Acts, nothing should qualify the unity of Christian initiation. In the earliest days, to repent, to believe in Jesus, to have one's sins forgiven, to be in Christ, to receive the Holy Spirit, to be a Christian, to be baptized, to be a member of the church, were not distinct or sequential, but were elements of a single complex reality—entering the new life in Christ. In telling of entry into the new life, some elements might be emphasized on certain occasions and some might be diminished or omitted. But what was omitted in any instance of telling was present in the fullness of the baptismal reality whether it was stated or not. In some rites, certain parts of the complex meaning of baptism were enacted in words and gestures, and in other more simple, compact rites, they were not. Yet, enacted and explicit or not, Christ and the Spirit were (indeed, are) inseparably and actively present.

(6) There was little concern about who administered baptism.

Whereas the ritual washings of Judaism were self-administered, Christian baptism (following the model of John the Baptist) was received. It was administered *to* someone and administered *by* a person who represented the church. Who may administer baptism became a matter of regulation and controversy in later centuries, but at this early time there seems to have been little concern as to who might baptize. The apostles baptized, of course, but 1 Corinthians 1:14-17 indicates that Paul did not invariably baptize his own converts, and Acts 10:48 suggests that Peter was willing to delegate the role of baptizer. Philip baptized (4:12, 38), as presumably did other evangelists. Ananias baptized Paul (9:18). Was it understood that any Christian could baptize? Were there were some persons who might not baptize? Nothing in the record answers such questions.

(7) The baptisms used the water that was at hand.

The baptisms in Acts all have a somewhat improvisatorial sound. None takes place at a special time or in a special place, and none uses any special water.

The Ethiopian eunuch and Philip found a wadi alongside the road on which their chariot was traveling (8:36). Lydia and her friends met near a river (16:13). In the case of the Philippian jailer, the water may well have been that in the *impluvium*, a pool that ordinarily stood in the unroofed atrium of a Roman house (16:32-34).

Nothing in Acts indicates the mode of the baptism. How deep was the water into which Philip and the eunuch stepped? One cannot establish early baptismal practice from the Greek vocabulary. The principal New Testament terms—the verb "baptize" (*baptizein*), and the noun "baptism" (*baptisma*)—are forms of words that in secular and biblical Greek mean to immerse, to dip, or to deluge or douse. But the specific forms which are used in Christian texts seldom appear elsewhere—almost as though the church developed special terms for its rite and its unique meanings. The words mean what they mean in the texts that are precisely the texts in question, and they keep their own counsel.

An early Christian document, the *Didache* (late first or early second century), is the first known attempt to regulate in the matter of the baptismal water. It says: "Baptize in running water, 'in the name of the Father and of the Son and of the Holy Spirit.' If you do not have running water, baptize in some other. If you cannot in cold, then in warm. If you have neither, then pour water on the head three times, 'in the name of the Father, Son and Holy Spirit'" (*Didache* 7:1-3). Cold running water is preferred, but not necessary; "baptize" (which is not defined, but very likely means to immerse) is the preferred action, but pouring water on the head three times is acceptable.

In addition to the evidence of early practice that is provided by documentary sources, a number of early baptismal sites and pools have survived. The early baptisteries probably represent continuity, for the ways of carrying out a central ritual act are likely to maintain older customs. While some of the early baptismal pools are in ruins, many are solid structures which are quite well preserved. Generally they were large enough to stand in. A few seem to suggest that the person being baptized stood in the pool alone, while the baptizing minister remained outside it, but most pools were large enough so that persons who were being baptized and persons who were doing the baptizing would stand in the water together. They vary in depth from a foot or so to thigh-depth. At first most of the pools were recessed into the ground, and persons went down into them by several (often three) steps on one side, and then up on the opposite side. Later many baptismal pools were built above the floor. Many were octagonal in shape—the number eight suggested to the early Christians newness and the resurrection. Some were in the shape of a cross, and a few resembled a tomb. Some were of stone and quite plain, but many were covered by mosaic designs, often of great beauty.[10]

Early mosaics sometimes show the candidate stooping down in the water while the minister dashes water over him or her with a large bowl. The Romans took pleasure in what they could do with water, and in some places water seems to have poured into the pool from a spout, and persons stood under it.

For many centuries, the baptismal water was not located in the eucharistic room, but in a separate structure, often round or octagonal, built near to the church. Some of these baptisteries became quite grand, and their pools were very wide. For a long time only the bishop's church had a baptistery, where baptism was done, ordinarily once a year, on the Eve of Easter.

In the Middle Ages, a font which held only a small amount of water came to be located inside every parish church. Baptisms were performed locally and at any time of the year, usually within a few days of a child's birth. But this diminishment in the quantity and conspicuousness of the water was a late development, brought about partly by the loss of the catechumenate and infants being the subjects of baptism and partly by the movement of the church into the colder climate of Northern Europe. In difficult conditions, people, then as now, did what they could.

The accounts in Acts are still not very circumstantial. These early baptisms seem somewhat impromptu. It has been commented that they seem, by later standards, somewhat like emergency baptisms. Yet they show the vitality, the Spirit-led innovativeness and adaptability of a growing, preaching, baptizing community.

We do not read of the baptisms in Acts as though these accounts set a rule or limit as to what should always be done. While the book of Acts is our first word, it should not be our last. The puritan idea that church practice must always conform to the Bible—doing neither more nor less than can be justified by biblical precedent—would painfully limit Christian life and worship. The Spirit which led in the early years of the church continued to lead and still leads.

The rite had been simple—no doubt often almost starkly simple—at first. Under necessity it can still be externally simple, while being at the same time spiritually complete. However, the passage rite of becoming a

Christian had an essential meaning and structure to which the early Christians sought to give outward form.

Today's church is heir of the developments in Christian initiation that marked the first four or five centuries when the Christians were winning the pagan world to faith. And of course it is heir also of many losses, deformations and recoveries which have followed.

The revisions of baptismal liturgy that have been carried out in the twentieth century have begun with the New Testament and the early church, not admitting any sharp break between the apostolic generation and the generations that immediately followed it. Again, we can no more be literal in following the early church's models than we can be with those of the New Testament. Some things that the early church did would not suit the situation, the culture, or the sensibility of today, and some possibilities are open today that were not at earlier times. The aim is not to replicate the early models—even though they are a better guide than were the late-medieval model that had provided the basis for initiatory rites and customs in most of the West throughout the modern period. If we are free with respect to the past, we are free in a tradition of creativity and greatness from which we can and should benefit. In whatever developments are made—whether in fourth-century Jerusalem or in the twentieth-century ecumenical West—we baptize into the name, as the apostles did, and we give witness to the one church of Christ, holding and enacting the same vital, life-changing gospel.

CHAPTER 8

The Scriptures Appointed "At Baptism"

When a baptism takes place *at the principal service on a Sunday or other feast,* a rubric directs that *the Collect and Lessons are properly those of the day* (BCP, p. 300). However, whenever, for cause, a baptism is held at some other time, the same rubric says that the collect and readings *are selected from "At Baptism,"* that is, from Proper 10 in the votives on p. 928 of the Prayer Book. These passages are chosen solely for their pertinence to baptism. Several of them appear elsewhere among the baptismal scriptures, but not all.

This list begins with Ezekiel 36:24-28, a passage which is used at the Great Vigil. However, a rubric says that *any of the other Old Testament Lessons for the Easter Vigil may be substituted.* (The Vigil readings are discussed in chapter 3 above.) From the New Testament one may choose from three epistle and three gospel readings. One may select from the five psalms which are appointed.

Ezekiel 36:24-28

[This passage is appointed for the Great Vigil, and is commented on at p. 55.]

Romans 6:3-5

[This passage, Paul's central statement on baptism, is also appointed for the Principal Service of Easter Day (see pp. 62, 266).]

Romans 8:14-17

[This passage, which gives the heart of Paul's theology of the Holy Spirit, is also appointed for the Vigil of Pentecost, and is discussed on pp. 98 and 268.]

2 Corinthians 5:17-20

So if anyone is in Christ, there is a new creation: everything old has passed away; see, everything has become new! All this is from God, who has given us the ministry of reconciliation; that is, in Christ God was reconciling the world to himself, not counting their trespasses against them, and entrusted the message of reconciliation to us. So we are ambassadors for Christ, since God is making his appeal through us; we entreat you on behalf of Christ, be reconciled to God.

While this passage does not mention baptism, it describes what is true for *anyone who is in Christ.* Such a person is a new person living in a new order of reality, a *new creation.* The language of the NRSV seeks to suggest the abruptness of the Greek. As one steps into the life in Christ, the God who created and who in the end will create again is now in the midst of history making a fresh creative act. *If anyone is in Christ—new creation! Everything old has passed away; see, everything has become new!*

The central term in Paul's thought here is *reconcile,* which appears in several forms: *God has reconciled,* creating *the message and ministry of reconciliation,* in which Christians are ambassadors appealing to others to *be reconciled.*

Most of the terms and images that Paul uses for Christ and what he accomplished came from the Jewish scriptures, but he found his word *reconcile* not in the Bible, but in the everyday life of the cities in which he traveled. In every marketplace merchants offered goods at a higher price than they thought they could get, and buyers proposed paying less than they thought they would eventually have to pay. The parties were at odds, and until something yielded, nothing was sold or bought, and there was frustration all around. But after argument—no doubt often heated—the seller came down and the buyer went up, a bargain was settled, and the parties were *reconciled.*

Paul saw this event, which was repeated many times a day in the *agora* at Corinth and in every city, to be a picture of God's action in Christ. Without saying how it came to be, he thinks of God and humanity as estranged. Humanity was made for God, but there had come to be an unbridgeable gap between holy God and sinful humanity. Then Paul's gospel announces that in Christ a *reconciliation* is effected.

But he cannot use his metaphor from the marketplace without altering it significantly. In the case of God and humanity, the gap is not closed by a little giving and taking on both sides, but in a single, free act, and all from God's side. *All of this is from God. . .In Christ God was reconciling the world to himself.* The New Testament never entertains the idea that the work of Christ has won the favor of God, bringing offended divinity to a point of reconciliation. In Paul's terms, God, acting in utter grace, is the reconciler, not one who needs to be reconciled.

When a bargain is effected, the parties stop eyeing one another looking for advantage; hands are clasped, accounts and reckoning are over, and no one remembers the futile time in which it seemed that no agreement would be possible. Paul, who has observed the marketplace, says that God does not *count their trespasses against* a reconciled world.

If reconciliation is to be effective, an initiative must be taken by a party with the strength and authority to break the force of the estrangement. However, although this party has offered to restore the relationship, no reconciliation takes place until a response is made. A willingness to reconcile must be met by a willingness to be reconciled. What God has done for sinful humanity must be consented to. Effective consent is given in the inner act of faith and the outward gesture of baptism.

Paul must add that God's act of reconciliation is not merely something to be received and appreciated, it is also a message to be told. The church, a reconciled people, is given *the ministry of reconciliation.* Inevitably Christians will read Paul's image of ambassadorship in terms of mission. Since the reconciliation was for all—for *the world*— others must be invited into the reconciled community. But Paul's words do not refer primarily to the church appealing to an un-reconciled world. Rather, Paul is addressing Christians. God's appeal through Paul to *be reconciled* is made to the reconciled community—as though the task of reconciliation were never finished. The title of a recent volume catches the idea when it speaks of *Reconciliation: The Continuing Agenda.*[1] God's reconciling work in Christ is complete; we cannot repeat it or add to it. But it opens the never-ending task of addressing in his name all that remains unreconciled—to appeal to all to be reconciled to God, to be reconciled to the fact of their reconciliation.

[This Pauline theme of reconciliation through Christ is most fully developed in this passage, but it appears also in Romans 5:10f and

Colossians 1:19-22; and the idea without the term can be found in Ephesians 2:14-17.]

Mark 10:13-16

People were bringing little children to him in order that he might touch them; and the disciples spoke sternly to them. But when Jesus saw this, he was indignant and said to them, "Let the little children come to me; do not stop them; for it is to such as these that the kingdom of God belongs. Truly I tell you, whoever does not receive the kingdom of God as a little child will never enter it." And he took them up in his arms, laid his hands on them, and blessed them.

When people brought their children to Jesus for his touch of blessing, the disciples tried to keep them away, probably seeking to protect their master from a nuisance. The kingdom, as they saw it, was for knowledgeable adults. But Jesus rebuked them saying that the children should be allowed to come to him, for they have a place in the kingdom. Indeed, they are model for membership in the kingdom, which one must enter as a child or not at all. He took them in his arms and blessed them. (Mk. 9:37 has already told of Jesus identifying with children.)[2]

In this passage Jesus does not explain what it is about children that makes them the paradigm for membership in the kingdom of God. We must inquire on our own. The idea that he has humility in mind has been suggested, but by sentimentalists who have forgotten how demanding children can be. Perhaps Jesus is thinking of the sense of freshness and wide-eyed wonder that children exhibit—freshness and wonder that are lost in a jaded, self-enclosed, diminished adulthood and that must somehow be recovered. Adults think they have seen it all before, and it is hard to persuade them of the reality of grace and surprise. In some classic lines the seventeenth-century Anglican writer Thomas Traherne remembered his childhood:

All the World was mine, and I the only spectator and enjoyer of it. I knew no churlish proprieties, nor bounds, nor divisions: but all proprieties and divisions were mine: all treasures and the possessors of them. So that with much ado I was corrupted, and made to learn the dirty devices of this world. Which now I unlearn, and become, as it were, a little child again that I may enter the Kingdom of God.[3]

Ordinarily when adults try to become as a little child they become very affected. Yet in the midst of adult experience, we can become genuinely aware of the continued pertinence to us of the person we used to be and of the way life once looked to us. Remembering one's childhood can fill one with a sense of nostalgia, regret and loss, or even with acute pain. But Jesus is not speaking psychologically or in terms of life stages, but in terms of the kingdom—in categories of salvation. When Jesus speaks of becoming like a little child as the way to the kingdom, he is stating in a different idiom his appeal to set aside one's presumed sophistication and achieved place in the world, to seek a new mind (a *metanoia*) and to approach life as one of the *little ones*.

The story of Jesus and the children has been read in the baptism rite since the medieval and Reformation service books, for baptism was what the community did for children. In the Sarum Manual, it was read at the first part of the baptism rite, the part that represented the admission of persons to the catechumenate. From there, it was brought into the opening part of the baptismal rite of the 1549 Prayer Book. When in 1552 the two parts of the baptismal rite were unified, the story of Jesus and the children was retained. It remained as the principal scripture reading in the Prayer Book baptismal rite through the 1928 Prayer Book.

The legitimacy of using this gospel reading for this liturgical purpose has been questioned. After all, the evangelists are not talking about Christian baptism. Should we read these verses in the liturgy as though they were? But there are suggestions that baptism may have provided the background for this story of Jesus and the children. Much of the material in Mark's gospel seems to have been included because it was in some way relevant to the life of the first century church. Could this passage which speaks for the inclusion of children in the community of grace have been remembered, retold, and then included by the evangelist with baptism in mind? It is hard to say for what other situation in the first century church it might have been intended.

Moreover, Jesus' words to the disciples, *Do not stop them,* may give a clue from the text itself to the situation in life for which it was written. The New Testament scholar Oscar Cullmann observed that several New Testament accounts of baptism include something like an objection that had to be met before the baptism could proceed.[4] In Acts 8:36 the Ethiopian eunuch argues his own case, saying *"What is to prevent me from being baptized?"* In the house of Cornelius, Peter sees the evidence of the Spirit and asks *"Can anyone withhold the water?"* (Acts 10:47). When he retells the story in Jerusalem, he asks *"Who was I that I could hinder God?"* (Acts 11:17). Matthew's account of Jesus' baptism says that *John would have prevented him.* (Mt. 3:13). One must ask, In at least some of the earliest

Christian churches, did baptism include some such ritual objection? In all the instances cited here, the Greek word which is translated "prevent" or "forbid" is the same, and it is the word that is used in the synoptic gospels in the story of Jesus and the children. Was the story of Jesus and the children retold in the early church because it had a tie with baptism? The linguistic evidence cannot prove, but it can strongly suggest.

While this passage cannot demonstrate that infant baptism was first-century practice, it can be used to question any pattern of church life that would keep children from being included in full membership on the grounds that they lack sufficient intellectual grasp of the faith. The fine Scottish theologian H. R. Macintosh, speaking to the point, said some years ago, "Even for those who could not have understood his teaching Jesus nevertheless had a real gift; a gift he could impart and they could receive, namely his love."[5]

The early church often spoke of persons who were baptized as *neophytes,* persons, newly born. Most of these persons were fully grown, but, using terms of salvation rather than of chronological age, one does not ask whether or not infants are to be baptized, but one recognizes that all persons who are baptized are infants. Baptism is precisely where the church has to do with children.

[This story is also told in Matthew 19:13-15 and Luke 18:15-17, but only the Markan account is used in the lectionary.]

John 3:1-6

[This passage, with some additional verses included, is also appointed for Lent 2 in Year A. See p. 31.]

Psalm 15

This short psalm was sung by pilgrims, and it may have been used as a series of quasi-liturgical questions and answers. It describes the character that was expected in one who was going to the temple, which is spoken of as *your tabernacle* or *your holy hill.* The requirements for a pilgrim are largely things that are *not* to be done; one is to remain blameless. The moral negatives give the hymn a cautious and prudential tone. Yet the psalm depicts a life of godly integrity—one *who speaks the truth from his heart,* who *does no evil to his friend,* who *does not take back his word.* Such a person is stable and *shall never be overthrown.* As said or sung in the baptismal liturgy, connections can easily be drawn between this psalm and the life of faithfulness that is pledged in the promises of the Baptismal Covenant (BCP, pp. 304f).

Psalm 23

[This psalm is suggested for use in the baptism rite at the movement from the font, and it is discussed on p. 251.]

Psalm 27

In this quite personal psalm, life in relation with God is depicted in a variety of images (several of them quite warlike). Verses 1-4 say that God has been found trustworthy in times of distress and will be trusted in the future. In verse 5 the psalmist desires the temple as a sign of security that will hold in times of trouble. Beginning at verse 10, he speaks directly to God, expressing a somewhat troubled relation. God prompts the poet's heart to search for God (vs. 11), yet the psalmist fears that perhaps God will not be found (vss. 12f). The poet, torn between trust and uncertainty, speaks what is poetically a "lament" (vss. 11-17). In the final verse, he speaks to himself counseling a hopeful waiting.

This hymn mingles trust with a great deal of realism and an admission that life in relation to God can be bewildering and full of contradiction. Probably most persons of faith at times question God. This psalm gives them permission to do so. Even at baptism, one's idealism must not be naive. Persons in the biblical tradition, ancient and modern, have their times of darkness, bafflement, and lament. But the darkness does not have the final word.

Psalm 42:1-7

[This psalm is suggested for use in the baptism rite at the movement to the font (see p. 244).]

Psalm 84

The psalmist expresses a religious homesickness for the temple. He loves the temple and its life of devotion as a sign of the presence of God. *Happy are they who dwell in your house! they will always be praising you.* The poet, as he writes, is away from the temple—he does not say why. He expresses his longing eloquently. *For one day in your courts is better than a thousand in my own room.* The psalm closes with a glowing avowal of trust.

To catch the suitability of this psalm for baptism we may think of the experience of converts and imagine what this psalm celebrating the temple and its life of devotion would mean to someone who has, after struggle and with the thrill of discovery, come into the life of Christ and the church. Such persons, like most of the Jews who have said or sung this psalm, would never have seen the literal temple in Jerusalem; yet the temple, spiritualized and universalized, stands for the actuality and presence of God. It is a place in the spirit to which, after long exile, one had at last come home.

Canticle 9

In this canticle, from Isaiah 12:2-6, a prophet expresses trust in God. Like Hebrew poetry in general (and like a fair share of our hymns), it speaks, almost simultaneously, (1) of God and what God has done, and (2) of the quality of life that is opened to one who lives in faithful, grateful relation to such a God. The prophet says celebrationally that God is his salvation and his strength. As he speaks of God, he speaks of himself, saying that he will trust, rejoice, give thanks, call on God's name, speak of God's deeds, and sing God's praises. The passage ends with a voice calling Israel to sing or shout aloud for the Holy One is in the midst. It is as though the praise of God brought about human liberation and fulfillment. This mixture of what is true about God and what is consequently true for the community of faith accounts for the glow and vitality of the canticle.

A Vigil on the Eve of Baptism

The Book of Occasional Services contains a service that may be used *when it is desired to celebrate a vigil on the eve of the Bishop's Visitation or other occasion in preparation for the administration of baptism at a principal Sunday morning service* (pp. 131-35). The simple rite begins with the Service of Light (BCP, p. 109) and continues with readings. Eleven passages are listed, of which three or more are to be used. Each reading is followed by silence and a psalm, canticle, or hymn. A homily is preached. Then the candidates and their sponsors are called forward; the candidates kneel, the sponsors each place a hand on the shoulder of their candidate, and the celebrant lays a hand on the head of each in silence. A prayer is said, and the service ends with a blessing and dismissal.

All the appointed readings appear elsewhere in the scriptures for the baptismal occasions of the Prayer Book or *The Book of Occasional Ser-*

vices and have received comment elsewhere in this book. But they are listed here:

The story of the flood.	Genesis (7:1-5, 11-18); 8:6-18; 9:8-13; with Psalm 5:3-9 or Psalm 46.
The story of the covenant.	Exodus 19:1-9a, 16-20a; 20:18-20; with Canticle 2 or 13.
Salvation offered freely to all.	Isaiah 55:1-11; with Canticle 9.
A new heart and a new spirit.	Ezekiel 36:24-28; with Psalm 42.
The valley of dry bones.	Ezekiel 37:1-14; with Psalm 30 or Psalm 143.
Baptized into his death.	Romans 6:3-5.
or *We are children of God.*	Romans 8:14-17.
or *Now is the day of salvation.*	2 Corinthians 5:17-20.
The baptism of Jesus.	Mark 1:1-6.
or *You must be born again.*	John 3:1-6.
or *The resurrection and the Great Commission.*	Matthew 28:1-10, 16-20.

CHAPTER 9

Other New Testament Passages

A few New Testament passages which do not appear among the baptismal occasions of the Prayer Book fill out aspects of the New Testament understanding of baptism and provide a larger thematic context for the liturgical readings. We shall look at some of them in their New Testament order:

Mark 10:35-40 and Luke 12:50

[A parallel passage in Matthew 20:20-23 does not contain the reference to baptism.]

James and John, the sons of Zebedee, came forward to him and said to him, "Teacher, we want you to do for us whatever we ask of you." And he said to them, "What is it you want me to do for you?" And they said to him, "Grant us to sit, one at your right hand and one at your left, in your glory." But Jesus said to them, "You do not know what you are asking. Are you able to drink the cup that I drink, or be baptized with the baptism that I am baptized with?" They replied, "We are able." Then Jesus said to them, "The cup that I drink you will drink; and with the baptism with which I am baptized, you will be baptized; but to sit at my right hand or at my left is not mine to grant, but it is for those for whom it is prepared." [Mark 10:35-40]

"I have a baptism with which to be baptized, and what stress I am under until it is completed!" [Luke 12:50]

From the time that John the Baptist drops from the record, nothing is said in the synoptic gospels about baptizing. When Jesus sends out his disciples to extend his mission (as in Mk. 6:6a-13 and parallels), they preach and heal and cast out demons, but they do not baptize. The only evidence to the contrary comes in the isolated and equivocally stated passages in John (3:22-23; 4:1-2) that say that for a time John and Jesus led parallel, even rival, baptizing ministries. No one in the New Testament is spoken of as having been baptized by Jesus or by the disciples during Jesus' ministry. It seems unlikely that Jesus' mission included baptism.

Yet in two passages in the synoptic gospels, Jesus, speaking metaphorically, refers to the crisis of his mission, his coming passion, as his "baptism." In Mark 10:35-40, the saying occurs when two disciples make a request for places of honor, and Jesus replies by asking, *"Are you able to drink the cup that I drink, or be baptized with the baptism I am baptized with?"* In the partial parallel in Luke 12:50, Jesus' reference to baptism is not prompted by an incident, but speaks of the pressure that is placed on him by his mission, which he calls his "baptism," and the outcome of which he foresaw.

These texts may evidence a reading back into the gospels of later Christian ideas which connected baptism with Jesus' passion. However, the connection could have been made by Jesus himself, drawing on the Jewish scriptures. The *cup* he is to drink could have been suggested by such biblical images as the cup of judgment in Psalm 75:8 and Isaiah 51:17, 22, or the *cup of horror and desolation* in Ezekiel 23:33, or the bitter cup which is a sign of God's wrath in Psalm 11:6. His "baptism" could allude to the emphasis in the Jewish scriptures on water as a threat. The Jews were not at home on the sea, and they seem to have feared it. Adversity, persecution, and the dread of death were spoken of as being overwhelmed by deep waters. In Psalm 42:9b (NRSV 42:7b), *"All your rapids and floods have gone over me,"* and in Psalm 69:16-17 (NRSV 69:14-15; see also vss. 2-3 [NRSV vs. 2]) the psalmist cries to God: *"Save me from the mire; do not let me sink; let me be rescued from those who hate me and out of the deep waters. Let not the torrent of waters wash over me, neither let the deep swallow me up; do not let the Pit shut its mouth upon me."* In Jonah's prayer he says, with horror, *"The waters closed in over me; the deep surrounded me"* (Jon. 2:5). John the Baptist's mission had given baptism a radical eschatological interpretation, making it a sign of (virtually a ritual substitute for) the judgment to come. Thus the idea that drinking a cup and entering deep waters could symbolize suffering was present in the scriptures that both Jesus and his hearers would have known, and Jesus himself may have brought this image-material together around his own mission, creating the image of his coming passion as his "baptism."

[These verses are appointed for Proper 22, Year B, but not for any occasion that is expressly designated for baptism.]

1 Corinthians 6:11

. . .And this is what some of you used to be. But you were washed, you were sanctified, you were justified in the name of the Lord Jesus Christ and in the Spirit of our God.

This verse concludes a passage in which Paul has set forth some contrasts between the old life and the new. (Converts' minds run to contrasts.) He has given (in vss. 9-10) a list of social sins which would keep one from inheriting the kingdom of God. Then he says, in effect, to his readers, "Some of you used to be like that, but, in a great personal transformation, you have broken with your old way of life."

Paul identifies the new that had replaced the old by a series of three verbs:

You were washed,
*   you were sanctified,*
*   you were justified*
*   in the name of the Lord Jesus Christ*
*   and in the Spirit of our God.*

The references to being *washed,* to *the name of the Lord Jesus Christ,* and to *the Spirit of our God* all make it clear that Paul has baptism in mind. All three verbs—*washed, sanctified, justified*—are in a Greek tense which speaks of a definite past act and are in the passive voice—a "divine passive," implying that "God washed, sanctified, and justified you."

Paul's word *you were washed* draws on the most immediate practical function of water, its ability to cleanse. When he retells the story of his own baptism in Acts 22:16, he says that Ananias directed him, *"Get up, be baptized, and have your sins washed away, calling on his name."* To the idea of being washed, which might seem a negation, suggesting a cleansing from past sins, Paul adds the positive terms, *you were sanctified, you were justified,* which connect the imagery of the baptismal washing with the gifts of redemption. *Sanctified* is a term of Jewish cultic life where it speaks of being set apart for God—as the people are sanctified, the priest is sanctified, and the sabbath is sanctified. *Justified* means being set right with God. Being made holy and righteous are not human achievements, but are gifts from God in Christ (1 Cor. 1:30) which are secured to a believer through faith, and one's faith is enacted in baptism. Paul's three verbs do not speak of different actions, but rather of a single, complex action for which no single term is adequate.

In this passage, as in Romans 6, Paul speaks of a contrast between old ways of moral conduct and new by reminding his readers of their baptism. Their decisive turning away from a dissolute, destructive life and their entering a new life under a new lordship was signified in their baptism. By it they are no longer what they were.

The phrase *in the name of the Lord Jesus* suggests the early Christian practice, witnessed in Acts and Paul, of baptizing in the name of Jesus Christ. When Paul speaks of being baptized *in the Spirit of our God*, he seems to say (as he does also in 1 Cor. 12:13) that the Spirit is the very element in which one is baptized.

1 Corinthians 15:29

Otherwise, what will those people do who receive baptism on behalf of the dead? If the dead are not raised at all, why are people baptized in their behalf?

This isolated and puzzling verse should be noted even in this selective survey. Dozens of interpretations have been proposed. Evidently in the Corinthian congregation some form of vicarious baptism (Paul must mean Christian baptism) was performed for persons who had died. Was it done for Christian believers who had died before they could be baptized? Was it for family members who had died in unbelief? Had some of the Corinthians adopted a practice from one of the Hellenistic religions? These and other proposals are all conjectural, and there are arguments for and against any of them. There is no other New Testament reference to such a custom, which may have developed only in Corinth and only among a few members of the Corinthian community, as Paul's *those people* suggests. Baptism for the dead does appear among some marginal groups later in the early period, and it is a conspicuous practice in present-day Mormonism.

Paul speaks of this custom, neither approving it nor condemning it, but apparently using an *ad hominem* argument. Earlier in this chapter he had indicated that at least some members of the Corinthian congregation held that there was no resurrection (vss. 12ff.)—particularly no resurrection that had anything to do with the body (vss. 35-57). Yet if some of these same persons were practicing this *baptism on behalf of the dead*, Paul will point out their inconsistency, in effect saying: "Since you believe what you believe, why do you do what you do? If there is no resurrection, your action is futile. But since you do practice this vicarious baptism, you yourselves attest, in this awkward way, to the reality of the resurrection."

Several observations may be made: (1) The practice was so accepted and authoritative that, without subscribing to it himself, Paul can argue from it to persuade his readers of the reality of the resurrection. (2) The custom suggests, albeit in cryptic terms, the closeness that held between the living and the departed in the minds of the early Christians. (3) The verse and its mysteries indicate how little we know about Christian cultic life in the earliest years.

Galatians 3:27-28

As many of you as were baptized into Christ have clothed yourselves with
   Christ. There is no longer Jew or Greek,
   there is no longer slave or free,
   there is no longer male and female;
for all of you are one in Christ Jesus.

Having said that Christians are children of God through faith (3:26), Paul turns at once to baptism, saying, in effect, "As Christians, you are what you are through *faith* and through *baptism*." Both are active and effective; each requires the other. The Scottish writer James Denney once said, "Baptism and faith are but the outside and the inside of the same thing."[1]

Paul's saying that in baptism one "puts on" Christ, uses the image of clothing. In biblical idiom, clothing signifies character. One is what one wears. A prophet says that God has clothed him with the garments of salvation (Isa. 61:10). In baptism a Christian acquires new "clothing," i.e. a new character, a new self, through union with Christ.

The new condition has implications for the collective life. All the baptized are children of God. All wear the new clothing. All are made what they are in relation to this new reality. But this new reality is a revolutionary force from which a radically reconstituted human community is born, a community in which the divisions and rankings of a sin-structured social order are broken down. Citing the baptismal reunification formula (which we encountered earlier), Paul lists some of those divisions—divisions that on natural grounds seemed insurmountable.

♦ Paul was a Jew, and for him the religious division between the people of the covenant, the law and the promises, and those without the law must have seemed rooted in divine purpose. For the first part of his life he would have thought that this division could not be overcome, indeed that it was a matter of principle that it not be overcome.

♦ Nothing would seem more unbridgeable than the economic and social division between a person who was free and a person who was held as the property of another.

♦ Paul includes here (and in no other instance of the baptismal re-unification formula) the division between male and female—a division rooted in creation and physiology, and hence good, but deeply shaped into superior and inferior by long centuries of patriarchal culture.

It has sometimes been proposed that in this verse Paul may have been giving a Christian reply to a prayer said by a Jewish man, thanking God that he was not made a Gentile, a slave, or a woman. This prayer is in the Jewish tradition, and, while it cannot be shown to be as old as the first century, it nevertheless speaks to attitudes that run deep in the Jewish and Gentile traditions of Paul's time.

Paul's claim that deep social divisions are overcome in Christ should not be made to sound as though he were projecting an utterly egalitarian, undifferentiated community. Clearly to some extent the divisions of society are rooted in creation and providence. Even after a new Christian had believed and been baptized, ethnic, social, and sexual identities would remain as they had been. By becoming a Christian, one did not cease to be a Greek or a slave, and males remained males and females remained females.

What Paul means when he says, *All of you are one in Christ Jesus,* is that in the new community formed by baptism any advantage or disadvantage that had attached to one's former status is overcome. All persons now belong equally to the new shared life. All are equally open to the call and gifts of the Spirit; anyone can teach, and anyone can learn; can be forgiven and can extend forgiveness; can help and receive help. Any can be an *alter Christus* to any other. The socially disadvantaged are, in Christ, the free persons of God, while the socially advantaged are, in Christ, servants of all. This equality was for the earliest Christians a wonderful vindication of their message. Divided humanity is in potentiality made one in Jesus Christ; and the church, which is constituted in baptism, is the sign community of the race made new.

Paul Minear remarks on how thoroughly theological Paul's thinking is when he speaks of the abolition of inherited marks of kind and status: "It was not a matter of personal tolerance or a social flexibility in overcoming racism or sexism or elitism. It was matter of God's action in creating a 'new humanity.'"[2] If Paul were writing today about the community that is brought to birth in baptism, he would no doubt mention some divisions of society which have emerged since the first century and which deeply challenge the unifying power of the gospel. His always-pertinent message needs to be repossessed by the church in every new social setting. Moreover, it is not just a matter of the church speaking to the divisions of society around it. The church, as a baptized people, must be aware of its own well-demonstrated ability to allow itself to be captured by the divisions and inequalities of its society and watchful of its own tendency to overlook, internalize, or even justify, those divisions and inequalities.

[This passage is appointed for Proper 7 in Year C, but not for any occasion that is expressly designated for baptism.]

Ephesians 5:11-14

Take no part in the unfruitful works of darkness, but instead expose them. For it is shameful even to mention what such people do secretly; but everything exposed by the light becomes visible, for everything that becomes visible is light. Therefore it says,

> *"Sleeper, awake!*
> *Rise from the dead,*
> *and Christ will shine on you."*

The passage speaks in terms of darkness and light, urging Christians to keep a moral distinctiveness from the society around them. The world is darkened, and its works are "unfruitful." In becoming a Christian one abandons *the barren works of darkness*, steps into the light and thereafter lives in the light.

These words quite certainly make an indirect reference to baptism, which at an early time came to be referred to as "illumination." Earlier in the passage, the author had said to his readers: *Once you were darkness, but now in the Lord you are light* (Eph. 5:8). In coming into the life in

Christ, they had passed from darkness to light. The church today might be less confident than it was in its earliest days about identifying the realm of darkness and the realm of light, for quite a lot of light shines outside the church and quite a lot of darkness has invaded it. Yet the Christian gospel identifies the world as unmistakably darkened, and it points to Christ as its light—but also to the church, as the people of light, and to the light-filled life into which one steps by faith.

To round off his point, the author reinforces his contrast by some lines of poetry, which he introduces as a quotation, *Therefore it says*. However, there is no biblical or non-biblical passage to which the quoted words correspond. They are commonly taken to be a fragment of an otherwise unknown hymn, probably a baptismal hymn. The lines are addressed to the sleeper, the dead one—i.e. to the baptismal candidate. It has been suggested that the words may have been sung as a call to the candidate at the point of baptism. Metaphors are mixed; stepping from darkness into light is compared to awaking from sleep and rising from the dead. Inevitably these polar experiences—darkness and sleep and death versus light and waking and life—become connected as conveyors of spiritual, redemptive, and sacramental meaning.

Interestingly, the early Christian writer, Clement of Alexandria (c.150–c. 215) gives a text which reproduces the quotation in Ephesians on Christ as light, and then adds three more lines:

Awake, sleeper,
Rise from the dead,
And Christ will shine upon you:
The Sun of Resurrection,
He who was born before the dawn,
Whose beams give life.
   [Protrepticus 9:84]

Does Clement's text complete the original hymn, or does he include lines that were added by him or by a tradition he knew?

[This passage is read on Lent 4, Year A. It was mentioned in chapter 3 above, but discussion was postponed to this location, where the text could be quoted and fuller comment could be given.]

Colossians 2:8-15

See to it that no one takes you captive through philosophy and empty deceit, according to human tradition, according to the elemental spirits

of the universe, and not according to Christ. For in him the whole full-
ness of deity dwells bodily, and you have come to fullness in him, who is
the head of every ruler and authority. In him also you were circumcised
with a spiritual circumcision, by putting off the body of the flesh in the
circumcision of Christ; when you were buried with him in baptism, you
were also raised with him through faith in the power of God, who raised
him from the dead. And when you were dead in trespasses and the
uncircumcision of your flesh, God made you alive together with him, when
he forgave us all our trespasses, erasing the record that stood against us
with its legal demands. He set this aside, nailing it to the cross. He dis-
armed the rulers and authorities and made a public example of them,
triumphing over them in it.

This densely written passage holds puzzles of vocabulary, grammar and ideas for the interpreter, but its general thrust and its bearing on the understanding of baptism are clear enough. Evidently the Christians at Colossae were attracted by speculations concerning orders of spiritual re-ality and by the appeal of a kind of knowledge which was attained by ascetic practices (2:18). Such ideas, in the writer's judgment, traced to *philosophy* and to *human tradition* coming from the *elemental spirits* which controlled human life (2:8a). While such ideas offered an account of the human place in the universe, they did so by displacing Christ and his work (2:8b). Hence a running theme of this letter is the complete adequacy and finality of Christ and of God's work in him. All things are from Christ, through Christ, and for Christ (1:15ff). In him *all the treasures of wisdom and knowledge* are hidden (2:3). He is the one in whom *the whole fullness of deity dwells bodily* (2:9); he is *the head of every ruler and authority* (2:10). Moreover, the Colossian Christians had *come to fullness in him* (2:10). Nothing requires a supplemental redeemer or redemption.

The Christians had been caught up into Christ's saving work through identification with his death and resurrection. When they had been *dead in trespasses,* God had made them *alive together with him* (2:13). This iden-tification with the redeeming Christ had come through baptism in which they were *buried with him* and *raised with him through faith in the power of God* (2:12). In this argument, for reasons that no doubt traced to mis-leading claims that were being made at Colossae, the writer introduces a comparison between baptism and circumcision. In Jewish tradition, cir-cumcision (although it was only for males) was a sign of membership in the covenant (Gen. 17:10). It was not merely a physical act, but was mor-alized to signify a dedicated heart (Deut. 10:16). The author of Colossians draws contrasts, saying that baptism is *a spiritual* rather than a literal, physical *circumcision* (2:11). It is *a circumcision made without hands* (2:11, NRSV margin); that is to say, it is divinely administered. It *puts off* not a scrap of flesh, but *the body of flesh*—i.e. *the old self with its practices* (3:9). Baptism is not minor surgery, but a total personal, moral renovation as one is identified through faith with the death and resurrection of Jesus Christ.

In Christ, God had erased the record that had stood against a sinner, nailing it to his cross like the charge against a crucified criminal (2:14). Christ is a cosmic figure who has won a redemption for all. In him God had overcome the deluding powers of the universe and displayed them as prisoners in his triumphant procession (2:15). How could anyone who had been joined to such a redeemer think him inadequate and search for something other or something better?

[This passage is appointed for Proper 12 in Year C, but not for any occasion expressly designated for baptism.]

Colossians 3:8-17

This is a sustained passage of contrasts, with strong baptismal associations. The author urges Christians to "put away" and "put off" and to "put on." Again the biblical image of clothing is used; clothing is a sign of character, and changed clothing signifies a changed self.

An expanded paraphrase may bring out the connection of this passage with baptism:

> *Do not lie to one another* [a negative ethical demand; the community
> can only be united in truthfulness],
> *seeing that* [in the light of the great indicatives of the gospel]
> > *you have* [negatively] *stripped off* [the unclothing, "Do you
> > renounce?"] *the old self with its practices,*
> > *and* [you] *have* [positively] *clothed yourselves* [the image of
> > clothing] *with the new self, which is* [unlike the old self, which
> > is destined to die] *being renewed in knowledge according to the
> > image of its creator.*
> *In the renewal* [among you who, no credit to yourselves, have come to
> this new condition] *there is no longer* [as there had been in the
> past, social divisions and rankings, such as]:
> > > *Greek and Jew,*
> > > *circumcised and uncircumcised,*
> > > *barbarian, Scythian,*
> > > *slave and free;*
> > *but Christ is all, and in all!*

The contrasts spoken of are deeply moral. An *old self,* which is destined to die, is set over against a new nature, which is in the process of being renewed. The lost image of God is restored.

The baptismal reunification formula, which we have found in 1 Corinthians and Galatians, reappears in 3:11 in a somewhat different form; again it celebrates the new community in Christ, shaped by baptism, in which the old divisions are broken down. In the old life, people were identified by what made them unlike one another. In the new life, they are all being refashioned into the same image, the image of Christ—an image which is not captive of any ethnic or class group, but which can come to expression in the human material of any of them.

[This passage is appointed for Proper 13, Year C, but not for any occasion expressly designated for baptism.]

Titus 3:4-7

But when the goodness and loving kindness of God our Savior appeared, he saved us, not because of any works of righteousness that we had done, but according to his mercy, through the water of rebirth and renewal by the Holy Spirit.

This text is dense with theological content—about God, about salvation, about renewal by the Holy Spirit—suggesting that a liturgical formula or a confessional affirmation may lie behind it. The saving action arises from *the goodness and loving kindness* of God (probably referring to God the Father). When the writer says that the goodness of God *appeared* (Greek *epiphaino,* shone forth), he does not mention Christ expressly, but Christ is surely implied. Salvation is due to God's mercy, not to *works of righteousness that we had done.* Nothing done from our side was effective on God to secure salvation; rather it flows from the free communication of divine goodness. The appointed means of God's saving work is *the water of rebirth and renewal by the Holy Spirit,* words that clearly refer to baptism.

When the writer speaks of *rebirth* here, he does not use the "born again" language of John 3:3, 5 and 1 Peter 1:3, but a different word, *palingenesia,* which is only used in one other place in the New Testament, Matthew 19:28, where it speaks in an eschatological context of the rebirth of all things. While sacramental vocabulary speaks of persons as "born again" in baptism, this passage indicates that regeneration in baptism should not be thought of individualistically.[3] Rebirth of any individual stands within the prior cosmic renovation which God's goodness brings about in the last days, of which baptism is a foretaste. The *rebirth and renewal* are the direct work of God *by the Holy Spirit*. The Holy Spirit acts to bring new life to an alienated world (vs. 3), but the Spirit works through *the water of rebirth.*

[These verses are read on Christmas Day in all three lectionary years.]

Biblical Passages and Allusions in the Baptismal Rite

CHAPTER **10**

The presence of the scriptures is felt at baptismal occasions not only through biblical passages that are read or sung but also through biblical allusions that pervade the text of the rite. Here, as it often does, the Prayer Book weaves the Word of God into the fabric of prayer and praise by which it guides the church's reply to the Word of God.

THE OPENING VERSICLES AND RESPONSES

The rite of Holy Baptism adds to the accustomed opening dialogue of the eucharist a special set of versicles and responses which give a tone and a focus for what is to follow. (This dialogue is also used when the promises of baptism are formally renewed at Confirmation, Reception, and Reaffirmation—see BCP, p. 413. It is not used when baptism takes place at the Vigils of Easter, Pentecost, Epiphany 1, or All Saints.) The exchange is:

Celebrant *There is one Body and one Spirit;*
People *There is one hope in God's call to us;*
Celebrant *One Lord, one Faith, one Baptism;*
People *One God and Father of all.*

These lines come from Ephesians 4:2b-6, with the New Testament text slightly abridged and the letter-writer's *you* adapted to *us*. The text in Ephesians reads:

. . .bearing with one another in love, making every effort to maintain the unity of the Spirit in the bond of peace. There is

> *one body and one Spirit,*
> *just as you were called to the one hope of your calling,*
> *one Lord, one faith, one baptism,*
> *one God and Father of all,*
>> *who is above all and through all and in all.*

A great theme of Ephesians is that in Christ the broken human community has been made one. This oneness which is given in Jesus Christ is for all; it is in principle true for all and is accessible to all. This oneness is known, by the Spirit, in the church, through which it is to be proclaimed and exhibited in history. The letter-writer urges the local community to demonstrate this unity in its common life. He appeals to his readers to show humility, gentleness, patience and forbearance—character traits that are needed if they are to *maintain the unity of the Spirit in the bond of peace* (4:3). The unity of Christians is a gift to be received and a task to be pursued.

Then in verses 4-6 the author, looking beyond the human task of maintaining oneness, holds before his readers the great objective realities that are constitutive of this new unity. He names them as: *one body and one Spirit,. . .one hope of your calling, one Lord, one faith, one baptism, one God and Father of all.* The oneness of the church is not first of all a goal to be brought about by human planning and effort, but is rather "a fact, given in the gospel, inherent in the nature of the church and its membership, guaranteed by the one Spirit who inspires it, the one Lord who governs it, and the one God who is source of its life."[1]

The author makes his point by means of a repeated, rhythmic "one" and a series of nouns. The passage can sound like a Christian expansion of the great summons, *Hear, O Israel: The LORD our God, the LORD is one* (Deut. 6:4 RSV; the liturgical *shema*), which stands at the heart of Jewish faith. Israel's vision of one God, one creation, one humanity, one history and one destiny is continued and developed by the Christian sense of one redemption, one Redeemer, one redemptive community and rite, and one familial relation with the divine.

There is one body and one Spirit: The church is the one body in which the one Spirit dwells. As an Lesslie Newbigin has said, "Christ has one body, not many."[2]

Just as you were called to the one hope of your calling: The given oneness is a dynamic factor, drawing believers forward. They are united in a summons which is also a destiny. In Christ they are given a common past and a common future.

One Lord, one faith, one baptism: The words speak of a shared faith in a single object of faith and a common rite of faith. The presence of baptism on this list is a remarkable indication of the importance of this rite in the mind of the first century community. The commentator G. B. Caird has restated the text so as to show the relatedness of these terms: *One Lord in whom all have believed and in whose name all have been baptized.*[3] The phrase "one baptism" has been perpetuated in the Nicene Creed, where it is a constant reminder that the church of Christ knows only one baptism, not many distinct and competing baptisms. When one is baptized, one is baptized not into a local community or into many local communities in aggregate, but into Christ and all his people.

One God and Father of all, who is above all and through all and in all: The climax of this list is in God. All is from the Father and in the Father. When the author concludes saying *one God and Father of all*, he continues, repeating his own word "all" in a somewhat liturgical-sounding close, *who is above all and through all and in all*, which the Prayer Book rite does not echo, perhaps thinking that it would sound too much like an ending, while the exchange on p. 299 is meant to provide an economical beginning.

By means of this biblically derived exchange, the liturgy opens the act of baptism declaring "the great unities" of the Christian faith.

BIBLICAL ALLUSIONS IN THE BAPTISMAL CREED

The creed, which forms the first part of the Baptismal Covenant, declares the faith into which one is baptized. By the late second century this brief confession, in substantially its present form, was used in question-and-affirmation form at the moment of baptism—its three-parts corresponding with the three-fold immersion. Somewhat later, the creed was taught in the catechesis that preceded baptism, the "giving" of the creed. Then at baptism, the candidate was asked, "Do you believe in. . .?" and answered "I believe. . ."—the "return" of the creed. This dual use continued through the medieval Service Books where the creed, declared in an opening part of the rite, at the church porch, corresponded with the early church's admission to the catechumenate; later, in a second part of the rite, within the church, the creed was used in interrogatory form and was followed by the baptism.

The creed was used in this two-part way in the 1549 Prayer Book in which the rite of Public Baptism began at the church door where the child to be baptized was signed with the cross on the forehead and given an exorcism; the gospel from Mark 10 was read, and the creed was given. Then the child was taken into the church where, at the font, after a brief exhortation, the renunciations were made followed by the creed and other promises, all in interrogatory form. Baptism was then administered.

This rite, combining, as it did, two originally separate actions, was thought to contain redundancies; and in the Prayer Book of 1552 the Ministration of Baptism all took place at the font, where, after the godfathers and godmothers made the renunciations, the creed was asked in one long question, and was affirmed in the name of the child. After further brief prayers the baptism was administered. Substantially this rite, with a single use of the creed, continued in the later Prayer Books of the Church of England.

In the Episcopal Church, the Prayer Books from 1789 to 1928 did not use the creed in either declaratory or interrogatory form, but only asked:

> Minister. *Dost thou believe all the Articles of the Christian Faith, as contained in the Apostles' Creed?*
> Answer. *I do.*
> Minister. *Wilt thou be baptized in this faith?*
> Answer. *I will.*

The drafters of the American Book intended that baptism would ordinarily be performed as it was in the English Prayer Books in the setting of morning prayer or evening prayer, at which the creed would be said, and this way of handling the creed may have been thought sufficient. Yet this summary submission of the creed was hardly satisfactory when private baptisms became common and the rite lost the context of the Offices. The revision of 1979 (which in this matter traces to Prayer Book Studies 18, 1970) has placed the creed, in interrogatory form, in the baptismal covenant, where it is said by the candidates, sponsors and the congregation.

The creed has roots in the apostolic church in the brief confessions of faith that are embedded in some of the first-century epistles. Evidently in the Pauline churches, the basic Christian confession was *Jesus is Lord.* Paul was convinced that no one could say *"Jesus is Lord"* truly unless prompted by the Spirit (1 Cor. 12:3). Thus this avowal, made with the whole self, was salvation: *If you confess with your lips that Jesus is Lord and believe in your heart that God raised him from the dead, you will be saved* (Rom. 10:9). This confession which is said now only by a small body of believers yet holds the final truth of things, and Paul envisions a time when, throughout the cosmos, *every tongue will confess that Jesus Christ is Lord* (Phil. 2:11). Everyone will know to be true what now the Christians know to be true.

The fuller declarations of faith that are preserved in the New Testament do not function as statements of doctrine, but are more like hymns or doxologies or blessings.

Some are quite Christocentric, as 1 Tim. 3:14:

The mystery of our religion is great:
> *He [Christ] was revealed in flesh,*
>> *vindicated in spirit,*
>>> *seen by angels,*
>> *proclaimed among Gentiles,*
>>> *believed in throughout the world,*
>>>> *taken up in glory.*

Some are two-part confessions, as 1 Corinthians 8:6:

For us there is one God, the Father,
> *from whom are all things and for whom we exist,*
and one Lord Jesus Christ,
> *through whom are all things and through whom we exist.*

And some have a triadic form, as 2 Corinthians 13:13:

The grace of the Lord Jesus Christ,
the love of God,
and the communion of the Holy Spirit be with all of you.

The triadic naming of God in Jesus' commission to baptize (Mt. 28:19; and see *Didache* 7:3) seems to have given the Apostles' Creed its threefold structure:

I believe in God, the Father almighty. . .
I believe in Jesus Christ, his only Son, our Lord. . .
I believe in the Holy Spirit.

In the Baptismal Covenant (BCP, p.304, 416f) the candidate, the sponsors and the congregation all affirm:

(1) *I believe in God the Father almighty,*
     creator of heaven and earth.

Since this creed is the baptismal affirmation, it speaks in the first-person singular, saying *"I."* As an act of commitment, it says not *"I believe that"* but *"I believe in."*

While the creed is a summary of the witness of the scriptures, it is selective. Much that is important in the Bible and in Christian faith, such as the human situation or the love of God or the history of Israel, goes unmentioned. The creed concentrates quite specifically and objectively on the saving divine action.

The creed speaks first of *God the Father almighty.* The Jewish scriptures speak a few times of God as father of Israel or of Israel's king, as in Isaiah 63:16; Jeremiah 3:4; or Psalm 2:7. The image, however, becomes central in the message of Jesus, who speaks of the Father's care (Mt. 6:25-34) and urges his hearers to be like the Father (Mt. 5:44f). In the highly christological gospel of John, the Father is spoken of almost exclusively in relation to the Son; Jesus speaks often of the exclusive mutual knowing and loving that persists between himself and his Father (Jn. 5:19-47 et passim).

The term *the Father almighty* echoes the Jewish scriptures which speak often of God's sovereignty over nature and history. In the earliest Christian writings, the actual term *almighty* is used most in the book of Revelation, where it speaks, usually in quasi-liturgical terms, of the power by which all things are finally judged and set right (Rev. 1:8; 4:8; 11:17; 15:3; 16:7, 14; 19:15; 21:22). Thus when the creed sets *fatherhood* and *almightiness* side by side, it speaks in paradox. God is near and yet transcendent; God's intimacy and compassion are held alongside God's power and justice.

When the creed says that God is the *creator of heaven and earth* it rejects some early heresies which held that the creation of the physical world was unworthy of God. The church's faith allows no division between creation and redemption. The Creator—and not some power other than or less than the Creator—redeems, and the Redeemer is the creator. In these words at the opening of the creed, Christians concur in the deep Jewish conviction, found in the creation stories and echoed in the Psalms and the prophets, that creation is from God, and hence good. God is a *faithful Creator* (1 Pet. 4:19), who continues to give life to the creation (Acts 17:25; 1 Tim. 6:13), sustains it and leads it toward its destiny (Rom. 8:19ff; Heb. 1:30; 2:10; 4:13).

> (2) *I believe in Jesus Christ, his only Son, our Lord.*
>   *He was conceived by the power of the Holy Spirit*
>   *and born of the Virgin Mary.*
>   *He suffered under Pontius Pilate,*
>   *was crucified, died, and was buried.*
>   *He descended to the dead.*
>   *On the third day he rose again.*
>   *He ascended into heaven,*
>   *and is seated at the right hand of the Father.*
>   *He will come again to judge the living and the dead.*

The second paragraph of the creed, by far its longest section, emphasizes verbs—*conceived, born, suffered, was crucified, died, was buried, rose again, ascended, is seated, will come.* The subject of these verbs is *Jesus,* a human name, united with the divine purpose to save by the title, the *Christ,* and related uniquely to God as *his only Son,* and set in a place of final lordship.

This portion of the creed is based on the preaching by which the apostles reached out to the non-Christian world. The form of their preaching was not moral counsel or ordered teaching, but rather summary narrative—a witness to events that had happened in time-place actuality (2 Pet. 1:16) but which were yet charged with divine significance. Paul, in 1 Corinthians 15:3ff, reminds his readers of what he had said when he had first come among them and handed on to them the tradition that he had first received:

> *I handed on to you as of first importance*
>   *what I in turn had received:*
>   *that Christ died for our sins in accordance with the scriptures,*
>   *and that he was buried,*
>   *and that he was raised on the third day in accordance with*
>   *the scriptures,*
>   *and that he appeared to. . . .*

A similar outline of the events of the evangelical history appears in the sermons that are reported in the book of Acts (e.g. 2:22-36; 10:36-43; 13:17-41). The early Christian witnesses had first heard the story of Jesus from those who were in Christ before them; then what they had heard they "handed on" faithfully.

This second paragraph of the creed turns this material of the apostolic preaching into Christian confession. What God has said in the redemptive saga as witnessed by the apostles is returned as the church makes its confession of faith.

1 Peter 3:18-22 contains a series of proclamatory statements that anticipate the baptismal creed: *Christ suffered for sins; he was put to death. . .*, but

was made alive; then, in a quite obscure reference, he preached to *the spirits in prison*; he *has gone into heaven and is at the right hand of God.* It seems significant that these christological affirmations come in a context that is clearly baptismal.

The creed begins with Jesus' conception and birth, which are told in their different ways by Matthew and Luke, but which are spoken in the creed in merest summary, emphasizing the supernatural features of the gospel accounts, saying that the Divine Word coming among us was an act of God.

The creed omits entirely the public ministry of Jesus. The verbs pass from *born of the Virgin Mary* to *He suffered under Pontius Pilate, was crucified, died and was buried,* naming in a few words the passion events which fill the last third or so of the gospel narratives. (Pilate, who is mentioned in the Christian creed, is mentioned in a somewhat similar way in Acts 3:13; 4:27; 13:28, and 1 Tim. 6:13. He is part of the creed because at a crucial point he became part of the gospel story.)

The clause *He descended to the dead* has long raised questions as to what it means and how it is related to the New Testament.[4] At one extreme, some commentators have regarded the words as a simple amplification of the foregoing statement of Jesus' death, but at the other extreme the tradition has given highly mythical accounts of Jesus' descent into hell and what it accomplished. Two intriguing but not entirely self-explanatory texts in 1 Peter may be the most pertinent New Testament references: 3:19 speaks of Christ, after his death, making a *proclamation to the spirits in prison*; and says that *the gospel was proclaimed even to the dead.* (Other texts, such as Eph. 4:19f and Acts 2:27, are also relevant; and apocryphal material may be an influence; but all these passages are obscure.) The credal affirmation may be taken to speak of the cosmic scope of Christ's conquest of disobedience.

The witness that *on the third day he rose again* appears first (among our extant sources) in 1 Corinthians 15:4, where Paul refers to the prior tradition that he had first received and then transmitted. It is affirmed also, of course, in the resurrection appearances in Matthew, Luke, and John. Beyond the stories of the empty tomb and Jesus' appearances to his followers, the conviction that Christ who died is now living pervades the faith of the New Testament. His resurrection is an event of significance for the race. *As all die in Adam, so all will be made alive in Christ* (1 Cor. 15:22). In Christ, death has been met and overcome.

That Jesus *ascended into heaven* is only narrated as an event in Luke's writings, where it concludes his account of Jesus' life (Lk. 24:50-53) and opens his narrative of the earliest church (Acts 1:1-11). It is spoken of in other places such as 1 Peter 3:22 and Ephesians 1:20. But, without using the term or the story of ascension, the New Testament faith and literature expresses the conviction that the Christ who died and rose again lives now with the Father and yet is in and with his church.

The vision of the living Christ *seated at the right hand of the Father,* is spoken of often in several of the varieties of the New Testament literature. (See Lk. 22:69; Acts 2:34f; Eph. 1:20; Col. 3:1; 1 Pet. 3:22; and especially Heb. 1:3, 13; 8:1; 10:12f; 12:2.) This Christian imagery drew most specifically on Psalm 110:1ff, a royal psalm, in which the king is set in honor by God's appointment: *The* [divine] LORD *said to my* [regal] *Lord, "Sit at my right hand, until I make your enemies your footstool."* The place at the right hand signifies honor and rule. The populace approaches the throne through the one at the right hand, and the monarch acts toward them through the one at the right hand. The early Christians adopted this image to speak of the royal yet mediatorial place of the risen Christ, who was not only with God, but through him God and humanity stood in deep mutual relation.

The affirmation that Christ *will come again to judge the living and the dead* has filled a large place in the myth world in which Christians have lived, giving rise to art, legends and visionary poetry, much of it moralistic and some of it terrifying. In the scriptural witness itself, Christ's "coming again" is spoken of in vivid, apocalyptic terms in the earliest-written New Testament book, 1 Thessalonians (4:15-18). However, Paul himself does not repeat that sort of description; his infrequent later references to Christ's "coming" or to "the day of Christ" are not at all pictorial, but they are expectant and comforting (as Phil. 1:6). Another type of New Testament thought changes the idiom radically. In John 14, the departing Jesus speaks of his going to the Father's house to prepare a place for friends he has left behind but not forgotten. He will *come again* to take them to be with him. Apocalyptic terms are replaced by almost domestic or familial terms.

The picture of Christ as judge of *the living and the dead* echoes most directly 1 Peter 4:5, which, in a quasi-credal passage, speaks of Christ *who stands ready to judge the living and the dead.* Paul in his address in Athens speaks of Christ as the final judge: *God. . .has fixed a day on which he will have the world judged in righteousness by a man whom he has appointed* (Acts 17:31). A last judgment is graphically described in the vision in Matthew 25:31-46 of the Son of Man, having come in his glory, judging from his throne all the nations. The most powerful source for the theme as it lodged in the Christian imagination was no doubt Revelation 20:11-15 (see also 20:4-10). The dead, both small and great, stand before the great white throne. Books are opened, and *the dead were judged according to their works.*

The theme of Christ as judge originated, no doubt, in part through the sense that even though Christ's resurrection, taking place in the midst of history, has pledged the end, yet most things go on as they had. Sin and suffering, folly and oppression continue. The new age, which anticipates the end, has begun; yet the old age persists. A great deal is not sorted out justly by the processes of history. Evil has more than gotten its innings, and much good has gone down to apparent defeat. The one who by his cross and resurrection dealt decisively with evil in the midst of history is the one who by God's appointment will set it right, justly and compassionately, at the end. The different idioms in which the New Testament presents this theme are witnesses to the fact that final judgment is not part of history and experience and hence cannot be described literally. It is profoundly real, but it is a reality only accessible through pictorial speech.

It seems important to note that the portions of the creed which follow the record of Jesus' death and burial all carry christology beyond the historical and empirical. In them it must be clear that when speaking of the relation between God and ourselves, i.e. between heaven and earth, everything must be expressed in symbol. Language of movement and place is used because as creatures of space and time, it is our only language. But "coming down" and "going up" and "the right hand of the Father" are not literal terms. Literal up is not good nor literal down bad. But we use language taken from our earthbound physicality to express many immaterial things as higher or lower, and we use this symbol-making capacity of the mind to express as well as we can the mystery of the work of God in and beyond history.

(3) *I believe in the Holy Spirit,*
  the holy catholic Church,
  the communion of saints,
  the forgiveness of sins,
  the resurrection of the body,
  and the life everlasting.

The third paragraph of the creed, comprising six noun phrases, identifies facts or conditions which are the result of the actions that have been named in the second paragraph.

The Holy Spirit, the immediate, personal presence of God in and to the church, comes as a consequence of the completion of Christ's earthly work (Jn. 16:7; Gal. 4:4-7). The Holy Spirit is the giver of divine life, truth, and power. Through the Spirit, the living Christ is actualized, and his gifts are imparted.

When in the creed the church says, "I believe in *the holy catholic church*," it professes belief in itself. The church, it is often remarked, is part of its own creed. The church's presence in history—even with its sin, compromise and failure—is an act in the divine saving work. It is *the household of God, which is the church of the living God, the pillar and bulwark of truth* (1 Tim. 3:15).

The phrase *the communion of saints* amplifies the foregoing words, expressing the sharing of life (the *koinonia*) that persists between Christ and the church (Jn. 15:1-6; Gal. 2:19f; Eph. 1:22; 4:15-16), among Christians, who are *members of one another* (Eph. 4:25), and between the church in history and the church in the life beyond.

The creed, which does nothing to analyze the human condition, to belabor sin, or to call persons to repentance, says, "I believe in. . .*the forgiveness of sins*." The emphasis is eloquent. To probe human failure and self-contradiction without knowing something that transcends sin's terrible negation can only lead to despair. Christians can look at sin courageously, for they know the reality of forgiveness. The first factor in forgiveness is God, who is a forgiving God (Neh. 9:17). God's forgiveness was extended in a great objective deed in Christ (2 Cor. 5:19). The church is a forgiven people engaged in a mission of extending in Christ's name forgiveness to all who will accept (Jn. 20:23f; Lk. 24:47; Acts 5:31; 10:43; 13:38f).

In the New Testament gospel, the resurrection of Jesus was not an isolated event, but a pledge that others would, through him, share in a life that transcends death, *Christ has been raised from the dead, the first fruits of those who have died* (1 Cor. 15:20). The direct biblical background for the credal affirmation of *the resurrection of the body* is Paul's argument in 1 Corinthians 15. When the apostle had declared the resurrection, he had to say more. It was inconceivable for one of Jewish training that human beings could be such and be purely spiritual. Humanity is constituted in embodiedness. In Paul's mind, to be disembodied would not be to be more than human, but to be less than human. So he says that the resurrection life will be in a *body* (Greek *soma*). But neither Paul nor anyone else can describe literally the conditions of a life other than the one we know. So Paul says that the resurrection body will not be a body like the present one. He illustrates by the way in which a developed plant is continuous with and yet radically unlike the seed which "died" to bring it forth (1 Cor. 15:36f). He speaks of a *spiritual body,* putting together in paradox two words, *spiritual* (Greek *pneumatikon*) and *body* (Greek *soma*), that do not ordinarily belong together. He speaks of a body that does not decay toward death.

With this venture—as remarkable for its reticence as for its vision—into what he calls a *mystery* (15:51), Paul has reached the limit of what he can say. There he leaves the subject, and there the creed leaves it. We can know nothing of any life beyond this one, but we can step into what may come next without fear, for we know one who has passed victoriously through this life and the death which follows it, and we can trust him.

The creed which began with creation and touched at its heart on suffering and death, ends with an affirmation of life: *and the life everlasting.* Once in an argument Jesus drew from the text "I am the God of Abraham, the God of Isaac, and the God of Jacob," the conclusion that since God was the God of the patriarchs, they lived, *He is God not of the dead, but of the living* (Mk. 12:26f). True life is life in relation to God. Whoever lives such a life lives in a life that human death cannot end. The theme is articulated in a different way by Paul, who thinks of humanity as made for life and of death as a terrible intruder, a spoiler, an enemy, whom Christ has overthrown in his dying and rising. Those who live in Christ now live by a risen life over which death has no power (1 Cor. 15:54-57).

The Johannine writings, using a different idiom, speak often of "eternal life," but they do not mean the indefinite continuance of life, but a different kind of life, from a different source, in a different governing relation, and toward a different goal. The Word, in whom was life (1:3b-4), became flesh to bring life, life abundant, to those held in death. That life can be had now. *Very truly I tell you, anyone who hears my word and believes him who sent me has eternal life, and does not come under judgment, but has passed from death to life* (5:24).

In a few words, the creed has carried the candidate and the baptized community from primal beginnings to final endings, catching up in its redemptive panorama our human life, suffering, and death—and doing so all through one central saving figure.

THE ALLUSION IN THE FIRST OF THE PROMISES THAT FOLLOW THE CREED

All the promises which follow the creed in the Baptismal Covenant have a generally biblical base, but the first promise draws on one quite specific passage:

> Celebrant *Will you continue in the apostles' teaching and fellowship,*
> *in the breaking of bread, and in the prayers?*
> People *I will, with God's help.*

This question adapts Acts 2:42 which describes the life of the Christian community in Jerusalem immediately after Pentecost.

> *They devoted themselves*
> *to the apostles' teaching and fellowship,*
> *to the breaking of bread*
> *and the prayers.*

This verse is one of several in the early chapters of Acts which summarize the life of the earliest Christian community, stressing its harmony, single-mindedness and the good opinion in which it was held by all (see also 4:32-37; 5:12-16). Later literature reports internal conflict and external opposition, suggesting that, at least to some extent, these summaries idealize the early community. Yet a great deal can be told about a group by how it idealizes itself.

The first fact of this summary is the community itself. The gospel is concretized in a face-to-face group, meeting in a place and around one faith. The life of the community is identified by four constitutive factors:

The apostles' teaching. This community is built around a message, an account of reality, a structure of truth (the Christian *didache*). It holds its own identity through a story it shares and through a growing understanding of the implications of this story for thought and conduct.

And fellowship. The word "fellowship" is the commonest translation of the Greek word *koinonia*. Regrettably, the word "fellowship" has come to suggest warm-hearted enjoyment of companionship and to project an air of human-initiated, easily incited, but superficial friendliness and good will. The word *koinonia* means "common life," and "communion" might be a preferred English equivalent. The term is filled in the New Testament by a rich evangelical content. It includes sharing in material things (vs. 44), but more deeply, *koinonia* speaks first of all of a community that shares in the divine life. Its oneness is God-given; it has its ultimate reference in the enduring relation with God. It is a commonness with Christ—his death and resurrection and his ascended life which he shares with his people, as they share their life with him. The *koinonia* is "the *koinonia* of the Holy Spirit" (2 Cor. 13:13).

Further, it is a *koinonia* of believers. Those who are members of Christ are also members of one another (Eph. 4:25). None of them is complete alone; they need and are needed. They love and care for one another; they practice patience and forgiveness; they weep with those who weep and rejoice with those who rejoice (Rom. 12:15).

To the breaking of bread. The community is sustained by common actions—principally by one common action. The term "the breaking of bread" draws on the Jewish custom of beginning each meal with the solemn breaking of a loaf, with thanksgiving. In the New Testament, the phrase is sometimes used of meals which were not in the specific sense the eucharist (as Acts 27:35), but it was also one of the first names for the specific Christian cultic meal (Acts 20:7; 1 Cor. 10:16). For Jews, every meal was sacred, and for the early Christians the distinction between ordinary food and the eucharist was not sharp. Clearly the *koinonia* in Jerusalem was expressed and sustained by the sharing in food, a token of the sharing in life.

And the prayers. This people was inwardly compelled to speak to the one to whom it owed its life. It was a community of prayer. One should not make too much of the presence in Acts 2:42 of the definite article: *the prayers.* But Jewish prayers, while they were "the prayer of the heart," were structured, and they were spoken in a formal way. The definite article may suggest that the Christians, too, drawing on this liturgical heritage, were using the prayers of the synagogue and beginning to shape their own formed, ordered life of prayer.

In the Prayer Book baptismal rite, this promise indicates that in becoming a Christian one commits oneself to a community, which is the space-time representation of the new life in Jesus Christ. In that community, one finds an account of saving truth, a body of people bonded to Christ and to one another, an elemental rite in which, by taking food, persons share the life of God and of each other, and the direction of life to God in an ordered life of prayer.

To speak in merest summary of the other questions of the Baptismal Covenant:

That Christians should resist evil suggests James 4:7, *Resist the devil, and he will flee from you,* and 1 Peter 5:8f. That Christians should confess their sins and seek restoration might be thought to trace to 1 John 1:8f.

A Christian's obligation to be a witness is supported by the missionary passages of the New Testament, such as Philippians 2:15f and Matthew 28:19.

Seeing Christ in all persons, as in the third question, traces to Matthew 25:40,45, *Just as you did it/did it not to one of the least of these who are members of my family, you did/did not do it to me.*

The fourth question is based on the deep conviction of the prophets that life in covenant requires commitment to justice, tempered by mercy (e.g., Mic. 6:6-8).

THE PSALM COMMENDED FOR THE MOVEMENT TO THE FONT: PSALM 42

[A rubric (BCP, pp. 312-313) suggests that when during the baptismal action there is a formal movement to the font, Psalm 42 might be said or sung in procession to the font, with Psalm 23 used on return from the font.]

Psalm 42 opens with an expression of deep religious longing, *My soul is athirst for God, athirst for the living God* (vs. 2). The speaker craves the living God as passionately, as obsessively as one who is thirsty craves water.

This psalm had early associations with Christian baptism. Basing their art on verse 1, *As the deer longs for the water-brooks, so longs my soul for you, O God,* some early Christians decorated their baptismal pools with mosaics depicting deer drinking at a stream. At baptism water is used externally; it is not drunk. However, the human experience of water cannot be neatly divided out, and meanings of birth, of dying and threat, of drinking, and of washing and restoration all pass easily into one another. The psalm, as interpreted by the early mosaics, speaks of life in relation to God as a source of wonderful refreshment.

The psalmist is evidently a temple official who led in the processions and the music (vss. 4-5). However, he is cut off from the exercise of his role (vs. 2b) and from the satisfaction it gave him as a service in the presence of God. He is desolate in his isolation—like a priest away from his or her altar or an organist away from her or his console and choir. Moreover, the psalmist is taunted by others (vs. 3) and is in despair. But in verses 6-7 he speaks to himself, easing his own disquiet and assuring himself that he will again give thanks to God.

The biblical allusions in the Thanksgiving over the Water

As the action turns to the baptismal element, the rubric says, *The Celebrant blesses the water* (BCP, p. 306), setting it apart for its sacramental purpose.

The tone and function of this prayer and the dialogue which introduces it cannot but remind one of "The Great Thanksgiving" that stands at the heart of the eucharistic action. But with the similarities, there are differences. The giving of thanks was so essential in both the Jewish meal and the sequence of the Christian eucharist which derived from it—taking, blessing, breaking, and giving—that a prayer of blessing was from the beginning firmly secured as a constitutive feature of communion. By contrast, none of the instances of baptism in the New Testament and none of the second-century sources mentions a blessing of the water. For that matter, the Prayer Book directions for Emergency Baptism (BCP, pp. 313f) indicate that a baptism may lack this blessing of the water and be a true baptism. Moreover, a prayer over the water is not listed among "the essential parts of Baptism" in the rubric for Conditional Baptism (BCP, p. 313). Clearly a baptism that lacks such a prayer of blessing but that contains the essentials would be a baptism; and in terms of its sacramental reality, every baptism is a first-class baptism.

Yet something that was, strictly speaking, non-essential became from an early time quite important. Our earliest circumstantial account of baptism, Hippolytus' *Apostolic Tradition*, c. 215 CE, says that when the baptizing party arrives at the water, "they shall first of all pray over the water" (chapter 21). Nothing is said as to the content of this prayer. Later, a prayer over the water became a part of the rites of baptism—its importance being influenced, no doubt, by analogy with the eucharist in which a prayer of consecration is not only essential, but came in time to be dramatized as the operative moment in the eucharistic action.

The medieval prayer for "the consecration of the font" was quite lengthy and full of biblical references. In the medieval West and in the Roman Church until modern times the baptismal water was consecrated only a few times a year. In the 1549 Prayer Book, the water was to be changed, with an appointed prayer, at least once a month. Under these regulations, most baptisms used water that had been previously consecrated, and the prayer would not have been heard very often. However, since the Prayer Book of 1552, Anglican baptismal rites have included a prayer at the water at each baptism. But over the generations the character of the prayer has changed.

The sixteenth-century continental reformers questioned the consecration of the baptismal water, knowing that holy water had often been put to superstitious uses; and they regarded the consecration of such water as a custom without scriptural warrant. The Calvinists held that grace works only in *persons*, hence they objected to the blessing of *things*. The baptismal rites that were prepared for the Protestant churches lacked a consecration of the water, and many of them as a matter of principle still lack it.

The prayer that was provided in the Prayer Book of 1549 for the times when the water was changed spoke (somewhat equivocally) of the sacramental use to which this water would be put. In the prayer made at the font just before the actual baptism in the 1552 book, no mention was made of the water itself. It was strictly a prayer for God's grace in the persons who would be baptized. (This prayer also dropped any mention of the types of baptism from the Jewish scriptures—although they were retained in an earlier prayer in the rite.) In the 1662 Prayer Book, the words *sanctify this water to the mystical washing away of sin* were added in the prayer, making it unmistakably a consecration. This was the prayer that was in use in the colonial Anglican churches through most of the 18th century and was taken up into the American Prayer Book.

The 1928 American book dropped the prayer that had contained the references to the types from the Jewish scriptures, and no such references appeared in the consecration of the water, thus the Episcopal Church had a baptism rite which made no use of the Genesis or later biblical typology.

The Thanksgiving over the Water of the 1979 Prayer Book has restored the allusions to the Jewish scriptures; it includes a rubric directing the celebrant to touch the water; and it reflects some altered understandings of consecration.

Following the lead of biblical and Jewish categories, consecration is understood as effected by a prayer of thanksgiving. By the giving of thanks, which is a performative action, some part of our tortured and abused world is brought out of its alienation or ambiguity and set in the right relation between God, the giver, and humanity, the receiver. God, the Original Blesser, blesses freshly (Gen. 1:4, 10, 12, 22, 25, 31; 1 Tim. 4:4f).

Thanksgiving prayers in the Jewish (and derivatively in the Christian) tradition set a present action in a context by rehearsing in the prayer itself the community's memory of past mercies. (A classic instance is the prayer at Firstfruits in Deut. 26:1-11.) What one seeks from God now is based on past divine goodness and faithfulness. Thus in the baptism rite, the Thanksgiving over the Water sets what we do here and now with this water in the context of God's creative and redemptive work. The prayer weaves together a selection of biblical allusions, telling the story of creation and redemption in terms of water:

Over it [water] *the Holy Spirit moved at the beginning of creation.* The summary of divine creative-redemptive action in this prayer begins with the biblical story of creation in which water and the Spirit are linked. The Genesis account speaks of a dark, formless void, *the deep*—a desolate potentiality. Then *a wind from God swept over the face of the waters* (Gen. 1:2 NRSV). The stir of this mighty wind, *ruach* (breath or spirit), over the water has suggested to Christian readers that the Holy Spirit, who was made known through Jesus Christ, but who from all eternity has been the Lord and giver of life, had been the active force in the primal creation. The account speaks of a world being stirred into order, light, and life by the *ruach elohim*. All begins with the water—but the water as acted upon by the Spirit. Speaking of the baptismal water, Ambrose once said, "You saw the water, but not all waters have curative power. . . .The water does not heal unless the Spirit descends and consecrates the water."[5]

Through it [water] *you led the children out of their bondage in Egypt into the land of promise.*   The anamnesis turns to the saga of Israel's emancipation from Egypt, and again water has mythic importance. The Red Sea was a barrier, indeed a trap. On one side of it were the pursuing Egyptians and certain destruction; on the other side was freedom in covenant and the promise of the land that had been pledged to the nation's ancestors. But how were the people to get through? In a way that indicated sovereign divine agency throughout, the Israelites passed through the sea on dry land and sang the victory of God on the other shore (Ex. 14:1-15:21). God, who had subdued the chaos (Gen. 1:1f), divided the waters of the Red Sea for the people. When one tells the gospel story in terms of water, this decisive, emancipating, summoning, people-making incident must be included.

The thanksgiving prayer has so far followed the sequence of the mighty acts at the Easter Vigil. But it uses no more from the Jewish tradition. The flood story comes next in the mighty acts that are recounted in the Vigil, but L. L. Mitchell comments: "It was apparently felt that the water in the flood story, in spite of its use as a type of baptism from the patristic period through Luther, did not fulfill the same function as the water in Christian baptism and would be inappropriately cited here."[6] The series passes to the Christian scriptures.

In it [water] *your Son Jesus received the baptism of John and was anointed by the Holy Spirit as the Messiah, the Christ.*   Jesus was baptized in the Jordan—the river by which Israel had long ago entered the land. The prayer speaks of Jesus' baptism as his anointing by the Holy Spirit to be the Christ—a theme implicit in the baptism narratives and clearly said in Acts 10:38.

In it [the water of baptism] *we are buried with Christ in his death. By it we share in his resurrection.*   The prayer turns to us. Having spoken of creation, of the exodus, and of Christ—it now speaks of the Christian in Christ. His death and resurrection for others are primary, but through the baptismal water we are identified with him and what he did. His death, burial and resurrection become ours (Rom. 6:3-11).

This prayer follows several New Testament texts (e.g. Acts 13:29; 1 Cor. 15:4) in mentioning specifically Jesus' burial. When the early Christians told the story of Jesus, the mention of his burial emphasized that he had really died, for burial is a way of recognizing the finality of death and marking closure. Paul's inclusion of Jesus' burial in his statements of baptismal meaning (Rom. 6:4; Col. 2:12) dramatized the identification of each baptized believer with Jesus' death. The baptismal creed repeats Paul it as it adopts the terms of the early Christian preaching: *He. . .was crucified, died, and was buried.*

Then the prayer, following the creed and the pattern of Paul's thought, turns to Jesus' resurrection, in which we share. It is sign and actualization of a new life.

Through it [the water of baptism] *we are reborn by the Holy Spirit.* The Holy Spirit is the very life of God, imparting itself to the human creation. The image of rebirth is most fully developed in John 3, but it is also found in 1 Peter 1:3, 23; 2:2. Titus 3:5, the text that is closest to the Prayer Book Thanksgiving prayer, speaks of the kindness of God, who *saved us, not because of any works of righteousness that we had done, but according to his mercy, through the water of rebirth and renewal by the Holy Spirit.*

Therefore in joyful obedience to your Son, we bring into his fellowship those who come to him in faith, baptizing them in the Name of the Father, and of the Son, and of the Holy Spirit. The prayer turns to this present ritual act. When it speaks of the baptizing church as obeying Jesus and when it speaks of baptizing in the triadic name, it obviously alludes to the conclusion of Matthew in which the risen Jesus commissions his followers to *make disciples of all nations* and to baptize *in the name of the Father and of the Son and of the Holy Spirit* (Mt. 28:19).

The biblical allusions that are woven into this not very long prayer are a reprise of themes from the history of salvation. They are all heard over the seasons in the lectionary readings for the baptismal occasions. This central prayer does not introduce novel ideas, but in a selective summary it declares the heart of the matter. In the lectionary readings the church hears in third-person terms the saga of what God has done and will do. However, in prayer—in this prayer specifically—the church turns such third-person discourse into second-person address: *We thank you, Almighty God.* The church asks new gifts from God on the basis of a history of grace.

THE ALLUSIONS IN THE CONSECRATION OF THE CHRISM

Eternal Father, whose blessed Son was anointed by the Holy Spirit to be the Savior and servant of all, we pray you to consecrate this oil, that those who are sealed with it may share in the royal priesthood of Jesus Christ; who lives and reigns with you and the Holy Spirit, for ever and ever. Amen.

This brief prayer refers to God's Son who was *anointed by the Holy Spirit to be the Savior and servant of all.* The petition for God to "consecrate this oil" is thus based in the anointing and the servanthood of Jesus himself. This consecration here and now is rooted in the prior consecration of Jesus Christ. We have seen that Jesus' baptism is spoken of, as is his anointing (implicitly in the baptism accounts, and expressly in Acts 10:35). Luke 4:18f, citing Isaiah 61:1, speaks of Jesus' anointing for his Messianic mission. The anointing of the Servant traces to Isaiah 42:1 (and we may remember the Servant allusion in the synoptic accounts of Jesus' baptism). In its petition, this prayer seeks that the oil and the action of anointing may unite Christian believers with the prior anointing of Jesus Christ.

When the prayer speaks of *those who are sealed with it,* it draws on the Pauline imagery of Christians as sealed (2 Cor. 1:21f; Eph. 1:13; 4:30; cf. Rev. 7:3; 9:4; 14:1 and the source of this imagery, Ezek. 9:4-6.)

In common use, a seal could be a mark or brand put on property as a sign of ownership or a seal or tattoo put on the hand or the arm or the forehead of soldiers or slaves to identify whose they were. In the New Testament, the image of a divine "seal" (Greek, *sphragis*) describes a Christian's relation to God; 2 Timothy 2:19 expresses the idea of belonging when it says that *God's firm foundation stands, bearing this inscription [seal]: "The Lord knows those who are his."* The seal of the Spirit cannot be seen, but it will be recognized by God. The New Testament itself nowhere speaks of baptism as a divine "seal," however, in later Christian generations, this term became an important part of the vocabulary of baptism.[7]

The prayer asks that those who are sealed with this oil *may share in the royal priesthood of Jesus Christ.* The words draw on the passages in 1 Peter 2:9f and Revelation 1:6; 5:10 in which the author speaks of Christians as *a royal priesthood.* These passages express a Christian claim to the role of Israel that had been spoken of in Exodus 19:6 and Isaiah 43:20f. Fr. Yves Congar, an eminent Roman Catholic theologian, has said, "We are all priests in the one high priest, Jesus Christ."[8]

THE ALLUSION IN THE FORMULA OF BAPTISM

The baptismal words:

> N., *I baptize you in the Name of the Father, and of the Son, and of the Holy Spirit.* Amen.

clearly trace to Jesus "commission" in Matthew 28:19 (cf. *Didache* 7:1, 3). The triadic terms in Matthew and in the *Didache* were not a prescription of words that must be used, but a naming of the divine reality into which persons are baptized. In the most concise way possible, they name the fullness of God as made known in the Christian revelation.

THE PSALM COMMENDED FOR THE MOVEMENT FROM THE FONT: PSALM 23

This familiar "Shepherd Psalm" was written from a pastoral people whose ancestors—Abraham, Jacob, Moses, David, Amos—had been shepherds, and no one was far from shepherding. Everyone understood the herder's responsibility to lead sheep to water and plentiful grass and protect them from danger. In a moment of illumination, some shepherd thought: As I am to my sheep, God is to me. This shepherd-poet developed the image expressing with simplicity and beauty his own trusting, grateful relation to God.

The psalm still makes a direct appeal, speaking of the support and provision of God even to readers who live far from sheep and pastures in a modern post-industrial world. As the psalm begins, it speaks *about* God (vss. 1-3) and has a tone of serenity; this third-person form of speech and this tone return at the end (vs. 6). But the central portion of the psalm (vss. 4-6a) is addressed *to* God and is somewhat more intense, mentioning *fear,* the *shadow of death,* and *my enemies.*

While Christians in any age can identify with the psalmist's depiction of divine care and support, in the early church the imagery of Psalm 23 held special associations with Christian baptism, for the early baptismal rite consisted of baptism in water, followed by an anointing with oil, and leading directly to feeding at the communion. The early Christians must have thought that this psalm—with its still waters, its anointing with oil, its overflowing cup, and a table spread by God—was divinely given comment on Christian baptism and the life which followed it. Ambrose of Milan said to those who had just been baptized: "Learn the nature of the sacraments you have received. Listen to what blessed David says who saw the mysteries beforehand in the Spirit. . . .How often have you listened to the Twenty-third Psalm without understanding it? See how fittingly it is applied to the heavenly sacraments."[9]

Psalm 23 figured heavily in the baptismal art of the early church. (It was often conflated with the imagery of John 10 about the Good Shepherd who knows his sheep and gives his life for them.) We have mentioned the wall painting at the house church in Dura Europos, p. 72 above. In addition to the presence of the Shepherd in representational art, Psalm 23 was

sung at baptism very widely in the early church, evidently in some places
by the newly baptized as they went from the baptistery to the eucharistic
room.

THE ALLUSION IN THE POST-BAPTISMAL
ACT AND THE PRAYER FOR THE SPIRIT

Immediately after the water baptism, the minister (if the minister is a bishop
or a priest) performs an act of consignation (using chrism if desired) using
language of "sealing." The act is followed by a prayer for the gifts of the
Spirit. The order of these actions may be reversed so that the prayer precedes the consignation (or anointing).

(1) *The consignation,* which may use oil, is accompanied by terms of
    sealing:

> N., *you are sealed by the Holy Spirit in baptism and marked as
> Christ's own forever.*

Commonly in ancient culture, a seal (*sphragis*) spoke of a mark or
brand that was put on property as a sign of ownership or of a seal or
tattoo that might be put on the hand or the arm or the forehead of
soldiers or slaves to identify whose they were.

The image of the divine seal (*sphragis*) is part of the vocabulary of
Christian identity, and hence of baptism. Paul sets the seal of the Spirit
in a cluster of eschatological ideas. The seal is given now, but as an
indelible pledge of future glory. *It is God who. . .has anointed us, by
putting his seal on us and giving us his Spirit in our heart as a first
installment* (2 Cor. 1:22). The word translated "first installment" is
arrabon, something given now which is real but which secures something fuller to come. The Holy Spirit as a seal pledges the future Christian inheritance and final redemption (Eph. 1:14). Christians, by the
seal of the Spirit, have been marked so that at the day of redemption
they will be known and identified as Christ's possession (Eph. 4:30; 2
Tim. 2:19). The Holy Spirit is the presence now of the power of the
Age to Come.

Revelation 7:3 adds a dramatic touch to the image of the *sphragis.*
In a heavenly vision, an angel holds back judgment, saying, *"Do not
damage the earth or the sea or the trees, until we have marked the*

servants of our God with a seal on their foreheads." The seal is a protection; the faithful who are sealed are not touched in a time of general destruction. (In this passage, *seal* may refer to baptism, but if so, the reference goes unstated.) The idea derives from Ezekiel 9:3-8 in which faithful persons are preserved in a time of travail by a *tau*, a T-shaped, cross marked on their foreheads.

The seal speaks of spiritual realities such as the Holy Spirit, bonding with God, divine ownership, and the certainty of God's promise—realities which lie in the circle of baptismal themes. However, in the New Testament there is no clear reference to baptism itself as the seal, and no outward action is associated with sealing. Yet it was the way of the early church to act out spiritual meanings, and very soon in some places an anointing was given at baptism, and it was sometimes referred to as the *seal*. However, the term *seal* was used flexibly. Sometimes it referred to the sign of the cross, and very commonly to the water and to baptism itself. All the initiatory actions took place within moments of one another and were parts of a unified ritual act, all of which was baptism, and all of which was *seal*.

Over the centuries in the West, the post-baptismal anointing came to be reserved to the bishop, and it was separated in time, usually by a number of years, from baptism. This second stage of initiation, which came to be called "confirmation," was understood in some special way to confer the Holy Spirit. With the seal separated from baptism, the unitary Christ-and-Spirit initiatory act of the New Testament and the early church had become obscured. The New Testament scholar Rudolf Schnackenburg has remarked: "One will seek in vain in the Pauline Letters to discover a peculiar sacrament of the Spirit alongside baptism."[10]

The term *seal,* after many generations of absence from the Prayer Book, is introduced in the initiatory rite of the 1979 revision, but it appears in the closest possible association with the water action. Immediately after the baptism, the bishop or, in the absence of a bishop, the priest prays over the newly baptized persons, asking for the gifts of the Spirit. Then the bishop or priest places a hand on the person's head (using chrism if desired) and says to each one: "N., *you are sealed by the Holy Spirit in Baptism and marked as Christ's own for ever."* While the words declare that the baptized persons are marked as "Christ's own" by the seal of the Spirit, they also make it clear that this sealing of the Spirit is not something over and above baptism, but is "in baptism." To be baptized is to be sealed. The post-baptismal prayer and laying on of hands with the sign of the cross (and anointing) explicates something which is true, but which since it is true needs to be said rather than taken for granted. The seal is a part of the complex but unified sign-action of baptism. It has no independent meanings. One is sealed by the Spirit "in baptism" even if (as is the case in some liturgies and in emergency conditions) nothing is done in the rite itself to enact that meaning. However, this implicit meaning is strong, and the Prayer Book liturgy, by these words and gestures, makes it explicit. As in the ancient world a person who belonged to another bore the seal of that other, each baptized Christian is "marked as Christ's own for ever."

(2) *The prayer* that is said after the baptism(s), and before or after the consignation, first gives thanks for the benefits of baptism; then it asks for the newly baptized:

> *Give* them [him, her] *an inquiring and discerning heart, the courage to will and to persevere, a spirit to know and to love you, and the gift of joy and wonder in all your works.*

These gifts of the Spirit trace to words of the prophet Isaiah who, looking forward with confidence, portrays a coming king, who, like David (1 Sam. 16:1-20), will have the abiding presence of the Spirit of God. Isaiah says in 11:2:

> *The spirit of the LORD shall rest upon him*
> *the spirit of wisdom and understanding,*
> *the spirit of counsel and might,*
> *the spirit of knowledge and the fear of the LORD.*

By the Spirit, the coming king will have the gifts and character required for his demanding role.

Isaiah speaks of six gifts, listed in three pairs: intellectual gifts of *wisdom and understanding*; practical gifts of *counsel and might*; and religious gifts of *knowledge and the fear of the LORD.* This passage became part of the description of the hoped-for Messiah, and in time the Christian church saw it as descriptive of Christ, who was the good royal figure foreseen by Isaiah and who by divine anointing possessed these gifts.

This passage very early found a place in baptismal liturgy. A post-baptismal prayer giving thanks for forgiveness and speaking of grace and the Spirit is found as early as Hippolytus' *Apostolic Tradition* (c. 215 CE). Later, when Ambrose of Milan (c. 339-97) explains the rites of Christian initiation to the newly baptized, he tells them that following the baptism (and also, in Milan, the washing of the feet of the newly baptized)

> The spiritual seal follows. . .when the Holy Spirit is infused at the priest's invocation: *"the Spirit of wisdom and understanding, the Spirit of counsel and strength, the Spirit of knowledge and piety, the Spirit of holy fear."* These might be called the seven "virtues" of the Spirit.[11]

Ambrose clearly refers to Isaiah's prophecy as he asks for "the seven virtues of the Spirit." The ancient world liked to have things in sevens, and the Greek version of the Jewish Bible, in translating this passage, gave seven gifts, rather than the six of the Hebrew text. The Latin tradition continued this list so that for many centuries the church spoke of "the sevenfold gifts of the Spirit," as in older hymns and devotional texts it still does.

A prayer for the Spirit's gifts followed baptism in some of the early Western sacramentaries. However, when, in the Middle Ages, by a series of unplanned steps, the bishop's blessing became detached from baptism (and in time became confirmation), the gifts of the Spirit were taken to be conferred, not at baptism, but in this post-baptismal episcopal action. A prayer by the bishop for the gifts of the Spirit was a part of the confirmation rite in the medieval service books, and the bishop's confirmation prayer was sustained in the English and American Prayer Books from 1549 through the American Prayer Book of 1928. For more than four hundred years Anglican bishops, at confirmation, prayed, in words that followed closely those of the 1552 Prayer Book:

> *Almighty and ever living God, who hast vouchsafed to regenerate these thy servants by Water and the Holy Ghost, and hast given unto them forgiveness of all their sins; Strengthen them, we beseech thee, O Lord, with the Holy Ghost, the Comforter, and daily increase in them thy manifold gifts of grace, the spirit of wisdom and understanding, the spirit of counsel and ghostly strength, the spirit of knowledge and true godliness: and fulfill them, O Lord, with the spirit of thy holy fear, now and for ever. Amen.*

Early in the process that led to the 1979 revision, it was decided that the action with water that speaks of Christ and forgiveness belongs together with the action of laying on of hands (or anointing) that speaks of the Holy Spirit, despite all the centuries in which they had been separated in the West. Any initiatory action that speaks of the Holy Spirit, rather than following baptism after a period of years and representing a different life-stage from that represented by baptism, must be within the baptismal action, for the seal is a part of the baptismal action. Thus in the 1979 Prayer Book a prayer for the gifts of the Spirit stands within the baptismal rite where it is the first thing done following the baptism in water.

The Prayer Book revision process also addressed the vocabulary of this prayer. Not only had the gifts of the Spirit become seven rather than six, but as over the centuries the Hebrew terms had been put into Greek and Latin and then into sixteenth-century English, the words that described the gifts of the Spirit had become rather homogenized, making the gifts sound too much alike. So for the first time since the Edwardian Prayer Books the terms of this prayer were examined, paying attention to the Hebrew of Isaiah 11:2, but at the same time seeking equivalences suited to twentieth-century society and faith.

Thus one of the oldest prayers in continuous use in the Western church remains in use. However, it is given fresh wording, and it is now the first prayer said immediately after the baptism, by the minister of baptism (who may be a bishop or a priest). It is in the ritual location in which it originated and in which it is liturgically and theologically coherent. The Holy Spirit is actively present in baptism whether the Spirit is named or not; but since the presence of the Spirit is constitutive of the reality of the sacrament, it is desirable that the Spirit's active presence be given clear expression in the rite itself.

As we have noted, this post-baptismal prayer arises from Isaiah's prophecy, with its tone of royalty and messianism. The gifts of the Spirit that were sought for a good and wise king who was to come were understood by Christians to have been given to Christ, God's Anointed. In the liturgy, these gifts are asked for every person who is baptized. Every Christian needs and is entitled to the interior gifts that in a plenary way were Christ's gifts. The use of Isaiah's words in this prayer for the Spirit says that every person who is baptized—whatever significance she or he may have by society's standards—is admitted to the ranks of royalty and is gifted accordingly.

BIBLICAL ALLUSIONS IN THE WELCOME OF THE BAPTIZED

Following the baptism, the congregation, bidden by the Celebrant, says to the newly baptized:

> *We receive you into the household of God. Confess the faith of Christ crucified, proclaim his resurrection, and share with us in his eternal priesthood.*

In these words a gathering-in comes first, a reception into the household of God; but the gathering-in leads at once to a call to share in common purposes. The phrase *the household of God* traces to several New Testament passages which speak of "the *oikos* of God." (See Eph. 2:19; 1 Tim. 3:15; Heb. 3:6; and 1 Pet. 4:17.) In the ancient world, and especially among Jews, the *oikos* was a unit of life whose members shared deep, lasting responsibility and caring. Each person stood within a small commonwealth in which much was received and much was owed. The congregation's welcome says that by baptism one enters an *oikos* which does not take its identity from biological relation or ethnic continuity, but it is called into being and held in being by an act of God. Like every *oikos*, it has a common history; it requires mutual bonding and loyalty among its members.

Having expressed its welcome, the congregation speaks to the newly baptized in the imperative mood. The words *confess the faith of Christ crucified* are not from the New Testament, but from the post-baptismal reception of the baptized that had been in the Prayer Book since the sixteenth century, which said: *We receive this Child (Person) into the congregation of Christ's flock; and do sign him (her) with the sign of the Cross, in token that hereafter he (she) shall not be ashamed to confess the faith of Christ crucified...* The life of faith is a life of confession lived in a confessing community.

The words *proclaim his resurrection* suggest 1 Corinthians 15:2, 4, 14. Writing to the Christians at Corinth, Paul reminds them of *the good news that I proclaimed to you, which you in turn received, in which you also stand.* This *good news* is that *Christ...was raised on the third day.* Moreover, this affirmation of Christ's resurrection is not one belief among many, but is crucial to the life of faith. All else depends on it. *If Christ has not been raised, then our proclamation has been in vain and your faith has been in vain* (1 Cor. 15:14). Clearly the church's life derives from an apostolic *proclamation* which traces to an *event* of universal significance. Yet that saving divine *event* only becomes effective as it is *proclaimed*. This welcome by the congregation says that as the life of the newly baptized derives from a resurrection proclaimed, the baptized, who owe everything to prior proclamation, are called to be in their turn apostolic proclaimers.

The congregation invites the new Christian(s) to *share with us in his eternal priesthood.* Christ is frequently referred to as priest in the New Testament and the Christian tradition, even though Jesus was not a priest in the literal sense, but stood in the tradition of Jewish rabbis or teachers. The image of him as priest did not grow from his ministry of teaching and healing in Galilee and Judea, but from Christian reflection on his death and resurrection and the restoration they effected of the human relation to God.

The theme of Christ as priest is developed principally in the Letter to the Hebrews, in which Jesus' redemptive work is explained through the actions of the high priest on the Day of Atonement. The fundamental description of a priest on which this comparison is based is expressed in Hebrews 5:1, *Every high priest chosen from among mortals is put in charge of things pertaining to God on their behalf, to offer gifts and sacrifices for sins.* A priest is representative—one of us, but chosen to deal, through the sacrificial system, with the god-ward side of life. Christ is a compassionate high priest because he knew human life and suffering first hand (Heb. 2:10, 17f; 4:15f; 5:7-10). In his highly original presentation, the author of Hebrews, in something of a paradox, says that Christ was not only priest, but sacrifice. His cross was his offering for human sin. This author thinks dualistically. Christ's priesthood and his sacrifice, while they were accomplished in acts in history, also are continuing acts carried out in the eternal order. What the high priest did each year in the tabernacle on the Day of Atonement, Christ did in heaven once for all. The author, quoting Psalm 110:4, has God, in effect, commission the Son, saying *"You are a priest forever"* (7:17, 21). Whereas the levitical sacrifices had to be repeated, Christ's sacrifice was final, *for all time a single sacrifice for sins* (10:12). Thus, using terms derived from the idiom of Hebrews, the Prayer Book speaks of *his eternal priesthood.*

This priesthood is fundamentally Christ's. He is uniquely and finally the Great High Priest. However, he not only acts for others, he brings others into association with himself. He creates a priestly people. In Israel's self-awareness, the priestly class was grounded in the priestly nation (Ex. 19:6). The early church considered itself heir of the prerogatives of Israel:

a chosen race, a royal priesthood, a holy nation (1 Pet. 2:9). In this Christian appropriation of Jewish material, metaphors are mixed. Christians are "living stones" built into a spiritual house, but at the same time they serve within the house as *a holy priesthood to offer spiritual sacrifices acceptable to God through Jesus Christ* (1 Pet. 2:5). The first priesthood is that of Christ. All other priestliness derives from his. But in him the church is made a priestly people, and each Christian participates in its priestly work of intercession and mutual self-giving. Hence the invitation of the congregation: *Share with us in his eternal priesthood.*

THE BIBLICAL BASIS FOR THE PEACE

After the baptism(s), the rite passes to the eucharistic action by way of bidding and exchanging the peace, an act which had a place in early Christian worship (Rom. 16:16; 1 Cor. 16:20; 1 Thess. 5:26; 1 Pet. 5:14). It is not just a gesture of friendliness. It is an expression of oneness that exists, and it is a call to a oneness that does not yet exist. *Shalom* speaks not of feelings and a state of mind, but of the right ordering of life between human persons and God, within the human community, and within oneself. It is a condition for which humanity was made, but a condition lost in sin and restored in Christ (Rom. 5:1; Eph. 2:14). *Shalom* is the term with which the risen Jesus greets his disciples (Jn. 20:19, 21). Indeed, it is opening greeting (2 Cor. 1:2; Gal. 1:3; Eph. 1:2; Phil. 1:2; Col. 1; 2; 1 Thess. 1:1; 2 Thess. 1:1; 1 Tim. 1:2; 2 Tim. 1:2; Philem. 1:3; 1 Pet. 1:2; 2 Pet. 1:2; Rev. 1:4), and it is closing benediction (1 Cor. 16:20; 2 Cor. 13:12; Eph. 6:23; Phil. 4:7; 2 Thess. 3:16; 1 Pet. 5:14).

CHAPTER 11

Images of Baptism

The scriptures do not explain baptism in an ordered, discursive way. Rather, they present it in a body of images which declare meaning by suggestion or indirection. When the New Testament speaks of both redemption and baptism in metaphoric terms, such terms are not second best, but are inevitable. God's work for humanity is something that is rich, authoritative and life-determining for a believer, but it is entirely non-empirical—something for which there is no literal language. When we speak of God or of the human relation to God, images or picture-talk are all we have. Such talk can be clear and precise, but as images are clear and precise.

The ways of images. Before looking at specific images, we may consider the ways of images.

The church's images of baptism derive from the scriptures, of course. But the image-talk of the scriptures grows in turn from deep, concrete human experience—from engagement with time, the body, other persons, earth, air, fire and water, and with a pre-existing image tradition. The general store of images from nature, social life, and the religious heritage is used by the New Testament writers, but heightened or altered or reconfigured under the pressure of a new reality.

Enduring images arise when common things are touched by revelatory encounter. Water, yes, but water whose natural evocative meanings serve Christ and the gospel. In the image-talk of the Bible everyday things have been seen from new vantage points and cast in new combinations. When believers have seen what they have through the eyes of faith, they seek to express it so as to make it intelligible and sharable—a struggle which is never more than partially successful. Thus the language by which baptism is described always has about it, along with clarity and communicativeness, a measure of dimness or opacity. It seeks to express a mystery that cannot be pointed to or brought fully under the categories of common language.

Human consciousness always makes images and is made by images. It is characteristic of religious symbols that as they seek to interpret the object of inquiry, they also interpret the interpreter. They reach into deep levels of consciousness, disclosing the self to itself. Each symbol that introduces us to the mystery of God in redemptive action introduces us at the same time to the mystery of ourselves. Christians who consider baptism deeply end by considering themselves deeply as well.

A religious image always uses the material of nature and culture—things we can see and point to—to speak of something that cannot be specifically pointed to in the world around us. Images therefore communicate meaning not by defining, but by suggesting or intimating. They are dense with possibilities. They can be seen now in one way and now in another. They contain meaning; they point to meaning; but they hold more meaning than one who is using an image is aware of at any one time. Thus we are never through with any image that holds authority for us—as though at a certain point we had extracted all the meaning it holds and could discard it and deal with the meaning directly. Metaphoric language does not explain; it always invites.

Having been articulated by the imagination, metaphors are understood by the sympathetic imagination. If we are to grasp biblical metaphors and let them inform our existence in faith, we must have our own receptive imaginations in working order—something that does not come easily in our literal-minded culture.

Although the Christian community derives its original, immediate insights from images, the mind cannot stop with image-talk. The community of faith makes its basic images an object of inquiry, reflecting on them, even while it lives from them. Persons who by gift and training are good at doing so ask questions and develop systematic, reasoned-out accounts of meaning. The church, for its own well-being, requires that the truth by which it lives be explored and developed rigorously. Faith needs to explain itself to itself and to the society in which it lives. Christianity has been called a "reason why" religion. However, all ordered statements of doctrine take their rise from prior symbolic speech; theologians begin their constructions with language whose first form is image. Symbols such as going up or coming down, water or light, redemptive sacrifice, reconciliation, or making whole, when they are caught up in the Christian revelation, give the mind work to do; they provide it with material to work with; and they set it going in certain directions. However, they open; they do not close the process of inquiry. Metaphoric speech comes first, and nothing is true in discursive theology that is not first true in the image-talk that arises from primary disclosure.

This order of things indicates that we do not go directly to meaning and then look for figurative ways of expressing it—ways suited perhaps to children, or at least to persons who cannot manage discursive thought. That way of looking at the matter—a fairly common way—reduces images to illustrations of something already known. No doubt, writers, teachers and preachers do look for illustrations which will explain, clarify or capture their auditors' imaginations; and they are pleased when they find good ones. But at the level of the baptismal images of the New Testament, the order is otherwise. Images are not contrived and secondary. They are not crutches for persons who cannot walk alone. They are primary occasions of original disclosure. The sign and the reality signified are grasped at the same time. The basic images of baptism (which are also images of redemption) lodge in the imagination, where they carry an impulse toward meaning. They inform life at a pre-rational level, and then they launch the mind on its never-ending questioning, differentiating, comparing, constructing work.

It is the way of images to mix. No image is literally true; and none is complete in itself. Each image reaches beyond itself to related images, all of them modifying and amplifying one another. We can say some things about Christ or about baptism by one image, but not all that needs to be said. Hence we bring images together, and we pass from one of them to another. The opening sentence of the first essay ever written on one of the sacraments, Tertullian's *On Baptism* (c. 210 CE), provides an example. Tertullian speaks of "that water of ours in which the sins of our original blindness are washed away and we are set at liberty unto eternal life."[1] In a few words Tertullian mixes images of water and washing, blindness and sight, confinement and liberty, and death and life. His metaphors are so compounded that a person of prosaic mind might find them unintelligible, but someone who is at ease with symbols and who is aware of the reality to which Tertullian refers would find his language clear enough.

The way of images persists. One need only look at Hymn 294 in the baptism section of *The Hymnal 1982*:

Baptized in water,
    sealed by the Spirit,
        cleansed by the blood of Christ our King:
heirs of salvation,
    trusting his promise,
        faithfully now God's praise we sing.

Baptized in water,
    sealed by the Spirit,
        dead in the tomb with Christ our King:
one with his rising,
    freed and forgiven,
        thankfully now God's praise we sing.

Baptized in water,
    sealed by the Spirit,
        marked by the sign of Christ our King:
born of one Father,
    we are his children,
        joyfully now God's praise we sing.[2]

This short hymn is little more than a series of image-terms describing baptism—eight or more of them, depending on how one counts and combines. Yet the hymn is not an incoherent jumble. With unconscious sophistication, churchgoers (some of whom in their weekday or professional life may be no-nonsense persons) think and speak in images, slipping from one picture to another, finding it all comprehensible and life-informing. To mix images in this way is a reminder that all are images. None is complete or final; all are asked to point beyond themselves—to be transparent to Christ and the gospel.

As our examination of the biblical material will have suggested, Christians from the beginning drew on natural things, on social roles, on common actions, and on the prior image-tradition of the scriptures, to develop a body of picture-talk to describe baptism. These early images, coined as they were in the original, creative insight of faith, have persisted. We still use them; we return to them. Indeed, it is not too much to say that, in an ultimate sense, they are all we have. They are images so closely bound up with the reality they represent that no substitutes have commended themselves, and no new coinages have claimed rival authority. At some times and among some groups, certain of the images for baptism have receded, while others have come to the fore. Images have been neglected and then rediscovered. (Even Paul's image of dying and rising with Christ has for periods of time been obscured.) Not all the classic images for baptism have remained equally accessible to modern readers, and those which have lost their original immediacy must now be explained. Some images that persist are perceived now in different senses than they were when they were coined, for the image-makers lived in their culture, and we, the perceivers, live in ours. A few traditional images are so shopworn that they pass by us awakening little attention or reflection. Familiarity has made us suppose that we understand them. Yet dulled though some of them may be, these metaphors can grow sharp again. Insofar as they carry the gospel in which our identity in faith is secured, we only lose appreciation for them when we lose appreciation for it.

Many of the biblical images—such as light and darkness; life and death; health and sickness—draw on the meaning-bearing character of common, elemental things. They ask us to look freshly at the ordinary and yet significant material that was available to the image-making community and remains available to us, the image-interpreting community. Some baptismal images have a base not in nature, but in time-bound, culture-specific acts such as ritual washing or anointing. And some grow from ordinary social interaction such as achieving agreement with someone. Often, when the things of common life are used to speak of the gospel of a crucified Messiah, the image-material is turned in unexpected directions.

With these somewhat theoretical observations in mind, we turn to the baptismal vocabulary of the New Testament, identifying several clusters of related images:

Air, breath and life; water, birth and death.   One cluster of images uses language of birth and death, life and breath (the Spirit).

Life is familiar but elusive. It is irreducible, essential, and precious. It is the basis for all else. When conscious beings live, much is possible; but without life, there is nothing. Yet, basic though life is, it is mysterious. It always inheres in living things; hence, while we can identify signs of its presence or absence, we cannot isolate life itself, quantify it or put it in a test tube for analysis. We cannot make it. We can only receive it, treasure it, and transmit it. And, of course, we can reduce it and end it.

We enter life by the unique, mysterious, one-way passage out of non-being into being which we call birth. We live for nine months in water before we come into the strange world of air. The sign of our full arrival is that we breathe—as the cessation of breath signals that life has ended. Although we draw our life from prior life in the great continuity of living things, yet each life is an absolute beginning. Something, someone lives and breathes which did not live and breathe before.

But the air that moves within one's body is matched by the moving air around one. Persons who live outdoors, like herdsmen in tents, are aware of the wind and its unpredictable ways. It can be gentle, or terrifying, or suddenly altogether still. One can hear its sound and see its effects, but one does not see the wind itself or know whence it comes or where it goes.

Life is ours and yet not ours. Once we have it and cherish it we cannot hold it indefinitely. It passes over to death, which, as far as ordinary experience can tell us, is final, irreversible.

In the image-system of the Christian community, the Spirit, the divine breath, is the Lord and giver of life—the life of God which at creation stirs chaos into order and breathes life into that which does not live. Life originates in the living God; but life is transmissible. God makes life be where there is no life, or God restores life where there once was life, but where it has been hopelessly lost. Then where life is made to be, it can be shared and imparted to others.

Jesus' discourse in John 3 speaks of being "born again" or "born from above." The term implies the radical inadequacy of life as we know it, and it offers a new kind of life which must be entered, if it is to be entered at all, by a new kind of birth. This "born again/ from above" image of John 3 says nothing about dying to live or about turning away from a past. It speaks as though life began freshly. In the midst of Life A we are, or we must come to be, in Life B. This birth is an immediate divine act. 1 John speaks often of being *born of God* (2:29; 3:9; 4:7; 5:4, 18; some of these instances may mean "born of Christ").

The author of 1 Peter uses the image, saying as he opens his baptismal homily that God *has given us a new birth unto a living hope* (1:3). This birth is a beginning which pledges endings. While the image of birth is not prominent in Paul, a letter from the Pauline circle contains a baptismal allusion which says that God has given salvation *according to his mercy, through the water* [in Greek literally, *the washing*] *of rebirth and renewal by the Holy Spirit* (Titus 3:5).

New birth speaks of life brought out of non-life. But the biblical literature, in an even more drastic style of thought, pictures life returning where it had been, but where it had ended in the irreversible fact of death. In Ezekiel's vision, the spirit of the Lord set him *in the middle of a valley; it was full of bones. He led me all around them; there were very many lying in the valley, and they were very dry.* The prophet was asked the unpromising question *Can these bones live?* Then as the divine word is spoken, the bones are stirred to life. *And the breath came into them, and they lived, and stood on their feet, a vast multitude* (Ezek. 37:1-10). God brings life, not out of prior life, but out of death.

It is part of the fascination of water that it speaks of both life and death. We cannot live without water, but neither can we live in it. Water in sufficient quantity and under control supports life, but too much water out of control can be a terrifying threat. Water is danger and a sign of death as truly as it is refreshment and life. The New Testament meanings of baptism take some of their suggestive power from this duality of water.

Drawing on this ambiguity, 1 Peter 3:18-22 says that baptism is prefigured by the story of Noah's ark *in which a few, that is, eight persons, were saved through water.* Most readers would think that the water in the flood story in Genesis 6-8 speaks of judgment and destruction rather than of rescue or salvation. Yet the water that destroyed also saved. The homilist reads the flood account as the story of the preservation of Noah and his family and the restoration of the covenant with humanity and nature. It is a story of good news. The homilist says: As Noah and others were saved from or by the water, baptism now saves you.

Paul, as we have seen, unites his baptismal theology with his essential gospel by the imagery of death and resurrection. His way of seeing things has been revolutionized by Jesus Christ, and he speaks in paradox. Whereas life regularly passes over to death, Paul speaks of a life that begins in death or of a death that passes over to life. *If we have been united with him in a death like his, we will certainly be united with him in a resurrection like his* (Rom. 6:5).

It is of interest that Paul uses the imagery of death and resurrection, while (unless the Titus 3:5 text is allowed) he makes no use of "rebirth" imagery. The Johannine literature, by contrast, uses the "born again/from above" image of a new beginning, with no mention of a prior dying. Paul says that living persons must die in the creative death of another so that they may rise to new life. John says that living persons must live, i.e. they must be born into a new kind of life. The minds of the two great theologians of the New Testament are informed by different image-systems. However, the eclectic Christian imagination disregards such distinctions and conflates death/resurrection and rebirth imagery quite easily.

Family, father, children.   The New Testament describes redemption and baptism, its sign, as bringing one into a family and giving one a divine parent and many human sisters and brothers. This family is a gift, yet, as families do, it carries obligation.

The familial imagery of Father and children appears in two forms:

(1) Some texts and writers use biological terms of birth. In the natural imparting of life, one is brought into life and a social setting out of non-being, non-life. Birth speaks of radical newness.

(2) Other texts and writers use legal terms and speak of adoption. In adoption one who is already alive and existing in one social context is, by an intentional act, given new parents and new siblings; one is set in a new family with all the rights of a naturally born member.

Both of these images are anticipated in language concerning God and Israel in the Jewish scriptures: Israel is spoken of as God's firstborn son (Ex. 4:22) and God's child (Deut. 14:1; see also Isa. 1:2ff; 30:1-9; Jer. 3:14—and Num. 11:12, where the imagery is that of God as Israel's mother, rather than its father). In the language of adoption, Hosea 1:9 and 2:23 (cited in Rom. 9:24f and 1 Pet. 2:10) speak of God calling people to be his people who had not been his people.

Both of these family images speak of grace, a life into which persons are brought by divine gift, saying that we are made what we become only through divine initiative. No one either comes to birth or is adopted into a family by one's deliberate act.

This father-and-child cluster of figures inevitably suggests the idiom of Jesus, who in his teaching in the synoptic gospels used familial imagery pervasively and powerfully. He addresses his audiences as children of the Father; they do not have to become children of God; it is their existing condition. Jesus urges them, since they are God's children, to live as becomes children of the Father. They are to depend on the Father (Mt. 6:25-34), to ask the Father for good things (Lk. 11:9), and to be like the Father (Mt. 5:43-48). They are to act as what they are. Yet surprisingly, formative though Jesus' words must have been among the early Christians, no other idiom of New Testament speech continues this thought idiom.

Rather, the theologians of the first-century Christian community do not assume that all persons are, by reason of their humanity, children of God. Rather, they assume that persons are not children of God but must become such.

The imagery of entering God's family by *birth* is developed largely in John, who says that one enters God's family by a new birth, a fresh divine act of which baptism is a sign. This birth is grace. In birth, the one who is being born is entirely dependent. A parent gives life to a child: a child receives life from a parent.

In the New Testament, this divine birth is very different from the mythological stories of the ancient world in which heroes or founders of nations are begotten by matches between gods. Similarly, unlike ordinary birth into the human family, which requires two parents to bring one new person into being, the New Testament speaks of a birth from God. There is no other with whom God must or could interact in order to beget life. Persons are given *power to become children of God, who were born, not of blood or of the will of the flesh or of the will of man, but of God* (Jn. 1:12f). As we have noted, 1 John speaks often of birth as an immediate divine act (2:29; 3:9; 5:1, 4, 18); 4:7 says, *Because love is from God, everyone who loves is born of God.* But in the thought of 1 John, this birth from God sets one in a family with other children: *Everyone who believes that Jesus is the Christ has been born of God, and everyone who loves the parent loves the child* (5:1). *Those who love God must love their brothers and sisters also* (4:21).

The image of entering God's family by *adoption* is from Paul. In the Roman world, one person could adopt another by a legal process of making a payment before witnesses. Using these terms, Paul describes being brought into the divine family by an intentional act. *You did not receive a spirit of slavery to fall back into fear, but you have received a spirit of adoption. When we cry "Abba! Father!" it is that very Spirit bearing witness with our spirit that we are children of God, and if children then heirs, heirs of God and joint heirs with Christ* (Rom. 8:15-17). This image can express Paul's message of divine grace, for adopted children are wanted children.

We must pause over Paul's use of the term *sons.* Following the tradition, Paul refers to Christ as *the Son* (Greek *huios*); and then, in speaking of baptism, he says that Christians are made sons (plural, *huioi*) in the Son (*huios*). *When the time had fully come, God sent forth his Son. . .to redeem those who were under the law, so that we might receive adoption as sons. And because you are sons, God has sent the Spirit of his Son into our hearts, crying "Abba! Father!" So through God you are no longer a slave but a son, and if a son then an heir* (Gal. 4:4-7, RSV). Although he uses the word for a male child, clearly Paul is referring to all Christians and means to be inclusive, not sex-specific. The NRSV seeks to be faithful to his intention by translating *huioi* as "children" or "sons and daughters." But before Paul's masculine terms are set aside in loyalty to his clear intention, it may be noted that his image of Christians as adopted sons was influenced by the legal structures of his day. In both Galatians and Romans, he connects adoption with inheritance: *We are children of God, and if children, then heirs, heirs of God* (Rom. 8:16f). In Paul's society, generally speaking, inheritance passed to sons. By Jewish law, the firstborn son received a double portion. (Deut. 21:17.) So when Paul says to his readers, *you are all [male and female Christians alike] sons* [huioi] (Gal. 3:26, 28 RSV), he is not perversely referring to Christian women as sons, but he is declaring the gospel, using the legal structures of his time in order to overturn them. He means that "you are all [male and female Christians alike] adopted children, and as such full members of the family and heirs, heirs of God, and, indeed, co-heirs with Christ." Paul implies that if women are held in second-class status in the social and legal structures of the Jewish and Hellenistic world, in the new community created by grace and faith and signified by baptism, men and women are together heirs of eternal life.

The Prayer Book uses both of these images: In the rite itself we thank God that through the water of baptism *we are reborn by the Holy Spirit* (p. 306). A prayer after the actions of reaffirming the promises of baptism thanks God *for adopting us as your own children* and making us worthy to be heirs (p. 311). The catechism says that *Holy Baptism is the sacrament by which God adopts us as his children and makes us members of Christ's Body, the Church, and inheritors of the kingdom of God* (BCP, p. 858).

Light, darkness.   Light is a profound factor in human experience—one that can easily be taken for granted. We do not see light, although it is through light that we see anything at all. Light gives us a world. Yet we seldom attend to light, for we are busy attending to what light makes possible.

In the ancient world, the daily passing from darkness to light would have had a power it has largely lost today. Through almost all of human history, light was not in human control, and darkness was not the minor and temporary inconvenience it is for most people today. The rhythms of life depended on the alternation of daylight and dark, and the human ability to modify the natural daily giving and withholding of light was quite limited. When the last campfire went out, darkness made the strongest persons helpless and often fearful. Without light, there is no depth, no color, no dimension, no intelligible world. In the dark, sighted persons grope and stumble as blind persons often do in the daylight. When darkness came, it was quite total and unrelieved, and when the light came, it was a daily gift. The religious use of light/darkness imagery drew on an elemental mystery.

The imagery of baptism as a passage by divine mercy out of night and into day derived its power from this human limitedness in the face of darkness and this human dependence on the gift of sunlight. *Once you were darkness, but now in the Lord you are light* (Eph. 5:8). We still, even in our comfort-filled, incandescent, fluorescent world, have enough experience of being plunged unexpectedly into total darkness or of stepping from darkness into light so that the images retain their power.

The fundamental, world-making fact of light is encountered in the first act of creation: *"Let there be light."* This primal divine giving of light was available to be drawn on in the consciousness of Israel. The prophets, especially Ezekiel and Isaiah, saw the divine glory in terms of light. The return of Israel after the exile was as the breaking day (Isa. 60:1f).

In the New Testament, Christ is the eternal light (Jn. 1:4). He is the world's light in which others may walk (Jn. 8:12; 9:5) and whose children others may become (Jn. 12:35, 46). The primal light shines in the gospel, and in Christian hearts where it gives *the light of the knowledge of the glory of God in the face of Jesus Christ* (2 Cor. 4:4-6). Christians *share in the inheritance of the saints in light* (Col. 1:12).

However, light imagery, which is used frequently in the New Testament for Christ and the gospel, is seldom used with clear reference to baptism. We have noted Ephesians 5:8f: *Once you were darkness, but now in the Lord you are light. Live as children of light*, and the hymn quotation in 5:14, probably from a baptismal setting, which plays with the theme of light, resurrection, and being awakened. The references in Hebrews 6:4 to *those who have once been enlightened* and in 10:32 to the suffering that came *after you had been enlightened* both probably speak of baptism.

Soon after the New Testament period, however, "illumination" (or "enlightenment") became a favorite term for baptism. Justin Martyr, writing about 150 CE, tells his pagan reader, "This [baptismal] washing is called illumination, since those who learn these things are illumined within."[3] Later, Basil the Great (d. 379 CE) said, "The one who is not baptized is not illuminated. And without illumination the eye cannot see its proper objects and the soul cannot contemplate God."[4] The Christians of the early centuries used the light imagery of the story of Jesus healing the man born blind (Jn. 9) to speak of baptism as naturally as they used the water imagery of the story of the lame man healed at the pool (Jn. 5:1-18).

Some critics have thought that when the early Christians used the language of light in the ways they did, they were borrowing from Hellenistic religions in which illumination often referred to an inner gnosis that united members of an elite with the basic order of things and that was imparted to them after they underwent the necessary disciplines. But in early Christian light imagery, the "illuminated" were not a select group. Since baptism was "illumination," to be a Christian at all was to be among the "illuminated." Moreover, the terms in which early Christian writers explained illumination were not taken from cosmological systems, but were rooted in the Bible and the story of grace. They quoted the affirmation *God is light and in him there is no darkness at all* (1 Jn. 1:5). They referred to the unapproachable light in which God dwells (1 Tim. 6:16) and the light on the first day of creation, the pillar of fire in the wilderness, the glory of Moses on Sinai, the Eternal Word as light and life (Jn. 1:4, 8f), the dazzling light of the transfiguration, and the light of the knowledge of the glory of God in the face of Jesus Christ (2 Cor.4:5f). They quoted Isaiah's summons, *Arise, shine, for your light has come* (Isa. 60:1), and his good news that *the people who sat in darkness have seen a great light* (Isa. 9:1f, quoted in Mt. 4:15f). Since it is the way of light to spread, to communicate itself, the light imagery which spoke of Christ spoke also of Christians who have been called *out of darkness into his marvelous light* (1 Pet. 2:9). They are to *walk in the light* (1 Jn. 1:7; 2:9), to live as children of light (Eph. 5:8), and, indeed, to be *the light of the world* (Mt. 5:14-16). The coming of Jesus Christ was as the bursting of daylight on a darkened world, and in baptism one who had been confined in that darkness was called into the light.

Clothing, reclothing.   Common sense might suggest that becoming a Christian could be described in terms of putting off old clothing and putting on new—especially in a society in which what one wore was often a sign of one's class or occupation. But the image draws depth from an idiom of the Jewish scriptures in which clothing is an expression of character; one is what one wears. God is robed in majesty and girded with strength (Ps. 93:1) and is urged to *put on strength* (Isa. 51:9). In a passage that anticipates the Christian's "armor of God" in Ephesians 6:10-17, God puts on *righteousness like a breastplate, and a helmet of salvation on his head* (Isa. 59:17). A psalmist wants his opponents to be clothed with shame and dishonor (Ps. 35:26). The redeemed are clothed with *the garments of salvation* (Isa. 61:10; for the idiom, see also Job 29:14; Zech. 3:4.) In anticipation of Pentecost, Jesus tells the disciples that they will be *clothed with power from on high* (Lk. 24:49).

Clothing is expressive. A penitent or one in deep sorrow puts on sackcloth (Joel 11:13). When a wandering son is welcomed home, the best robe is put on him (Lk. 15:22). So close is the association between clothing and the person that to injure a garment was to violate the one whose garment it was (1 Sam. 24:4-6).

There is much wisdom in this biblical idiom. If our clothing expresses what we are, it also can influence us to become something we are not. Persons may think of themselves or their task differently when they put on an athlete's uniform or a judge's robe or an actor's costume. If one is what one wears, a change of clothing can prompt an inward change.

The earliest Christians adopted the idiom of old clothes and new to speak of salvation, baptism, and the baptismal life. We have noted Paul's comment *as many of you as were baptized into Christ have put on Christ* (Gal. 3:27) and the "put off/put on" language of the baptismal passage in Colossians 3:9-17 (which is echoed in Eph. 4:22-24). The image carries implications for ethics: *clothe yourselves with compassion, kindness, humility, meekness, and patience* (Col. 3:12; see also 2:11; 3:9). Augustine was converted when his eye fell on Romans 13:14, *put on the Lord Jesus Christ, and make no provision for the flesh.* A passage in some little-known early Christian baptismal hymns says, "I forsook the folly which is cast over the earth; and I stripped it off and cast it from me: and the Lord renewed me in His raiment" (*Odes of Solomon* 11:9-10). Among some later writers, "garment" became a term for baptism itself.

In the early rites of baptism, when the candidates came to the water, they disrobed and were baptized in the nude. Clothing was a sign of a way of life that they were decisively leaving. At first, after their baptism, they simply resumed their street clothes, but at least as early as the fourth century, the newly baptized were given a special white garment. Cyril interprets this robe through Isaiah 61:10, "He has clothed me with the garment of salvation, and with the robe of gladness he has covered me."[5]

Our clothing can be a self-affirmation or a self-negation. The imagery of baptism uses this elemental human trait to speak of grace.

Scented oil and anointing. The important cluster of baptismal images around the figure of anointing (*enchristing*, so to speak) needs explaining today, for, unlike the biblical periods, modern American society anoints hardly anyone. We put people into office by words, verbal affirmations and speeches, and we may expect them to raise their right hand. We honor persons with a ribbon or a medal or an academic hood, but we are uncomfortable with more than a few restrained tactual, bodily actions. (The coronation rite for the British monarch, among its archaic touches, continues to use anointing.) But in the ancient world, persons and things—priests, kings, prophets, altars—were set apart by an anointing with (usually scented) oil. It was a designation and a sign of divine empowerment. The exuberance of ancient anointing is suggested in Psalm 133:2 in which the oil which is poured on the head runs down over the beard and shoulders and clothing. In the incident in John 12:1-7, the house is filled with the fragrance of the perfume with which Mary of Bethany anointed Jesus' feet. Important guests were anointed in a gesture of honor or devotion (Mt. 26:6-13). Anointing also represented healing (Lk. 10:34) and joy. Oil makes a cheerful countenance (Ps. 104:16). The king was anointed with the oil of gladness (Ps. 45:8). Athletes, especially wrestlers, were anointed. Bathing was often rather formalized and comprised several stages, sometimes described as "bathing and oiling."

The New Testament image of anointing is first of all christological. The word "Christ," *christos*, is not a name, but a title which means "the anointed." It is the equivalent of the Hebrew term "Messiah," which gathers up the long Jewish saga of history and promise. When (in Hebrew or in Greek form) it was used of Jesus it relates him to the hope, disappointment and yearning of Israel and to the purpose of God to redeem (Lk. 4:18-21; Heb. 1:9). Jesus was identified with the Servant of God who in the first of the Servant Songs of Isaiah is spoken of as anointed by the Spirit of God for a mission (Isa. 42:1). Jesus' baptism (which was his anointing, Acts 10:38) identified him as the one on whom that long expectation came to rest. His anointing was for his redemptive work (Lk. 4:18; and see Jn. 12:1-8).

The church, in Christ, is a community of the anointed, *It is God who. . .has anointed us, putting his seal on us* (2 Cor. 1:21f). Rather than anointing being for a select few and their special tasks, each Christian is an anointed person. *You have been anointed by the Holy One, and all of you have knowledge* (1 Jn. 2:20). The Christian's anointing is derivative—one is an anointed member of a people which is anointed in the Anointed One. Christians as sharers in Christ's anointing are claimed by God as kings and priests.

In the early church (although not clearly in the New Testament) water baptism was followed by an anointing (*chrisma*) with oil. Cyril of Jerusalem, speaking to the newly baptized about 340 CE, found in the act a link between Christians (the anointed ones) and Christ (the Anointed). He said to them, "You have become christs by receiving the mark of the Holy Spirit."[6]

Sealing, being sealed. We have seen that the New Testament speaks of Christians as sealed by God. To carry someone's seal was a mark of ownership. The baptismal seal identified one as God's protected property. Basil the Great warns, "Unmarked treasure can easily be stolen by thieves. Unbranded sheep can safely be raided."[7] Those who carried the seal would be known as God's own possession when the time came for them to be claimed.

The seal (Greek *sphragis*) of the Spirit is described in Ephesians 1:14 as *the pledge* (Greek *arrabon*) *of our inheritance*. It is a present grasp of the future—a *now* which looks to a *not yet*, a taste of grace now which is a foretaste of glory to come. The seal is a present gift which links one to the powers of the age to come. The same word, *arrabon*, is translated "first installment" in 2 Corinthians 2:21f: *It is God who establishes us with you in Christ and has anointed us, by putting his seal on us and giving us his Spirit in our hearts as a first installment.* Something is firmly in hand now which is wonderful in itself, but which secures to one the yet more wonderful reality which will ultimately be possessed. The future pledged in the Spirit's seal is not uncertain, *God has given us the Spirit as a guarantee* (again, *arrabon,* 2 Cor. 5:5).

The New Testament speaks of the "seal" as an act or gift of God, who by the Holy Spirit sets this mark on or establishes this bond with those who are special objects of divine care. Yet within a century, an anonymous Christian homily known as Second Clement turned the image around and asked Christians to regard the seal as placing upon them a divinely given obligation. God gives the seal, to be sure, but the recipient must value it and cherish it. The homilist speaks of *those who have not guarded the seal* (7.6) and urges his hearers to *keep. . .the seal undefiled.* (6.9)

In the book of Revelation the seal is protection: the faithful who are sealed are not touched in a time of destruction. (See especially Rev. 7, in which the seal may refer to baptism.) This image derives from Ezekiel 9:3-8 in which faithful persons are preserved by a *tau*, a T-shaped cross marked on their foreheads.

Even though, in the biblical writings, it is not clear that the "seal" refers to an act that was performed at baptism, it does picture what it means to belong to Christ, and within a short time, "sealing" became an important part of baptismal vocabulary and baptismal ritual.

Drinking, tasting.　　　Since in religion and culture many of the symbolic uses of water gather around thirst and refreshment, it is surprising that the baptismal texts of the New Testament make so little use of images of drinking, especially since the Bible was written in lands where water is scarce. We have encountered Paul's single but important reference to drinking of one Spirit in

1 Corinthians 12:13 (which we have proposed may have been suggested by the water from the rock in the wilderness which the thirsty Israelites drank). The Gospel of John refers to Jesus himself as the water of life (Jn. 4:7-15) and as the source of the Spirit which he offers to the thirsty (Jn. 7:37-39). None of these Johannine passages refers unmistakably to baptism, but the Fourth Gospel supplied symbols of water and drinking which the mind of the early church inevitably referred to baptism. We have noted the use that the early Christians made in hymns and art of Psalm 23 and its still waters and of the opening of Psalm 42 and its deer at the waterbrook.

A small touch in 1 Peter might easily be overlooked. In 2:2a the homilist urges the newborn, i.e. the newly baptized, *Long for the pure spiritual milk so that by it you may grow into salvation.* They need nourishment. Then in verse 2b the subject continues, but it also changes. The homilist adds: *if indeed you have tasted that the Lord is good.* The homilist has commended *pure spiritual milk* that will give the newborn nourishment and will help them grow. Then at once, within the same thought, he passes to a related idea—*if indeed you have tasted that the Lord is good.* The words are an echo of Psalm 34:8, *Taste and see that the LORD is good,* a psalm verse which Cyril indicates was used in the fourth century at the baptismal eucharist when he says to the newly baptized: "After this you hear the Cantor inviting you in sacred song to participate in the holy mysteries. His words are: *Taste, and see that the Lord is good.*"[8] In 1 Peter 2:2, the Greek words for "tasted" and for "good" both suggest the pleasure in food or drink. The homilist turns from what is good for the newly born (2:2a) to the enjoyment of a new and thrilling flavor (2:2b). The "spiritual milk" is not only nourishing; it has an additional advantage; it is delicious. Drawing on the experience of tasting, the homilist says, in effect, "Taste, for the Lord is satisfying, pleasing." Taste is self-authenticating; it is only known by experience. No amount of description will impart an unknown flavor. Taste is validated by tasting, as God is validated by believing.[9]

It seems possible that the link in 1 Peter 2:2 between the imagery of birth and the imagery of feeding was suggested by the baptismal eucharist. If so, 1 Peter would be our earliest witness to the direct link between baptism and eucharist, a link which soon became all but universal.

At the baptismal eucharist described by Hippolytus, c. 215 CE, a special chalice of water was given, presumably symbolizing inward cleansing and inward life. The baptismal imagery of the *Odes of Solomon* speaks of water for drinking: "Speaking water touched my lips from the fountain of the Lord plenteously: and I drank and was inebriated with the living water that doth not die" (Ode 11).

Washing, bathing. Since baptism uses water, inevitably it will draw on meanings of washing, cleansing, or purifying. In telling of his baptism, Paul says that Ananias instructed him, *Get up, be baptized, and have your sins washed away, calling on his name* (Acts 22:16).

The theme has a natural base in the human experience of dirt or soiledness and in the ability of water to restore one's hands, one's whole body, one's clothing or one's soiled utensils to acceptability and use. The biblical uses have a cultic base in the washings that were required among the Jews for purifying after ritual pollution or before approaching the holy. At Sinai, before the giving of the Covenant, God said to Moses, *"Go to the people and consecrate them today and tomorrow. Have them wash their clothes and prepare"* (Ex. 19:10). In the sacrificial system, when a taboo was broken, one became soiled or impure, as though a kind of contamination had been contracted; and an appointed cleansing was required. While in detail much of the priestly ritual of cleansing by ablutions or by sacrifice seems remote today, it held before Israel a powerful religious reality. One who speaks of sin as a stain or contamination takes it to be a condition rather than a succession of misdeeds. What one needs is not so much exhortation to do better from here on, but a means of being made pure and restored to one's place in the covenant community and before God. This message of divine cleansing reached to areas of the consciousness of guilt that could not be dealt with by calls for moral reform, saying that however deep the stain, a cleansing is available for sinners.

Inevitably the use of water for cleansing was spiritualized or moralized. In the most profound reaches of Israel's religion, the image stood for inward reality, as in the repentant psalmist's plea, *Wash me through and through from my wickedness and cleanse me from my sin* (Ps. 51:2), or in Isaiah's report of God's offer of washing from sin and injustice (Isa. 1:18), or in Zechariah's pledge of a fountain opened for sin and impurity (Zech. 13:1). Psalm 24:4a links clean hands with a pure heart. In 1 Peter the homilist says, *Baptism. . .now saves you—not as a removal of dirt from the body, but as an appeal to God for a good conscience, through the resurrection of Jesus Christ* (3:21). This passage is notoriously difficult. (The crucial Greek word which is translated "appeal" occurs nowhere else in the New Testament, and it is variously understood.) But clearly the homilist intends a similarity and a contrast. Bodily washing is effective automatically; when water is applied, one is cleansed whether one wants to be or not, as when a parent bathes a dirty child. But baptism—which the writer has spoken of as an effective act (vs. 21a)—does not cleanse apart from the inward consent which establishes a right relation with God. The rite is a call for moral commitment and for loyalty to God, without which it is not saving. This new life is effected by the power that was at work in Jesus' resurrection (vs. 21b).

The image in the book of Revelation which speaks of making one's robes white by washing them in the blood of the Lamb, strikes many modern readers as bizarre at best and gruesome or immoral at worst. But it was no doubt convincing to persons familiar with priestly and sacrificial terms. Paradoxically, blood rather than being a stain, provides the one adequate cleansing from inward stain.

It is often remarked that although the imagery of washing became important—indeed, dominant—in the church's understanding of baptism, it is relatively infrequent in the New Testament passages on baptism. There are a few instances of it. After Paul has described the formerly dissolute ways of some of the Corinthian converts, he says, *But you were washed* (1 Cor. 6:11). In telling of his own baptism, he says that Ananias told him, *Be baptized and have your sins washed away* (Acts 22:16). The (probably) deutero-Pauline letter to Titus says that God has given salvation *according to his mercy, through the water [the washing] of rebirth and renewal by the Holy Spirit* (Titus 3:5). Hebrews, which is full of cultic references, speaks of approaching the heavenly sanctuary *in full assurance of faith, with our hearts sprinkled clean from an evil conscience* (Heb. 10:22). And Ephesians 5:26 speaks of Christ making the church holy, cleansing it *with the washing of water by the word,* while 2 Peter 1:9 speaks of persons who are *forgetful of the cleansing of past sins.* John the Baptist proclaims that Jesus is *the Lamb of God who takes away the sin of the world* (Jn. 1:29). These instances all speak of the redemptive work of Christ as the world's or the church's or the Christian's washing, and many of them refer, clearly or by inference, to baptism. When redemption was spoken of as a washing, baptism, the water-sign of redemption, was inevitably suggested.

Since this symbolic vocabulary speaks of *transformation*, many of the images are paired, expressing contrasts, describing an interior revolution by naming simultaneously an old condition and a new: darkness and light, death and life, blindness and sight, soiledness and cleanness, old clothes and new. In repentance, one estimates one's own past differently and turns

away from false gods, from destructive conduct and from the social solidarities that had informed and supported it. In faith one comes to a new life
by way of a new birth. In Eucharistic Prayer B these paired images are
expressed in words that are particularly suited to a baptismal eucharist: *In
him* [in Christ], *you have brought us out of error into truth, out of sin into
righteousness, out of death into life.* (BCP, p. 368).

These images have been identified and discussed here separately, or at
least in related clusters. They draw on different parts of human experience,
and they refer to different aspects of redemption and baptism. They can be
looked at individually. Yet each only suggests part of what it means to
become a Christian. The images reach out toward one another, and they all
finally arise from and refer back to one rich, but unitary thing. They will be
misunderstood and they will lead to misconstruction of baptism unless
they are held together in their complementarity and interaction.

In a great oration about baptism (which he called "illumination") Gregory of Nazianzus showed the delight he took in these images and in as-
sembling them for his hearers:

> As Christ the giver of it [of illumination] is called by many various names,
> so too is this gift, whether it is from the exceeding gladness of its nature
> (those who are very fond of a thing take pleasure in using its name), or
> that the great variety of its benefits has reacted for us upon its names.
>
> We call it, the gift, the grace, baptism, unction, illumination, the cloth-
> ing of immortality, the laver of regeneration, the seal, and everything that
> is honorable.
>
> We call it the gift, because it is given to us in return for nothing on
> our part; grace because it is conferred even on debtors; baptism because
> sin is buried with it in the water; unction, as priestly and royal, for such
> were they who were anointed; illumination because of its splendor; cloth-
> ing, because it hides our shame; the laver, because it washes us; the seal
> because it preserves us, and is moreover and indication of dominion.
>
> In it the heavens rejoice; it is glorified by angels, because of its kin-
> dred splendor. It is the image of the heavenly bliss. We long indeed to
> sing out its praises, but we cannot worthily do so.[10]

CHAPTER 12

Some Running Themes

In following the biblical material through the lectionary, the baptismal rite, and the book of Acts, we have given attention largely to separate passages, often removing them from their order and contexts. We identify here some topics and themes that may indicate the coherence of the biblical presentation of baptism.

Baptism is integral to New Testament thought and the gospel

What the New Testament says about baptism tends to be embedded in passages that are principally about something else. It is seldom itself the focus of attention. Rather, writers focus on doctrinal, ethical and pastoral matters, but they do so from a point of view which assumes baptism to be constitutive of Christian identity and to form a bond among Christians and between an author and his readers.

In a sense, there is no specific "baptismal theology" in the New Testament. Baptism is transparent to the gospel—a carrier of the central New Testament understandings of Christ, church, Holy Spirit, forgiveness, and the redemptive purpose of God. Since the images of baptism are at the same time images of Christ and redemption, it is understood as they are understood. Baptism must be discussed as part of the fabric of New Testament truth—a part which gives access to the whole. Each baptism enacts the divine Good News. In it the church encounters freshly its own foundational event, its own central message; and through it a new life is enclosed by grace.

The specialness of baptism consists in its special function rather than in a special meaning. The distinctiveness of baptism is a consequence of its initiatory character. Baptism stands for birth, newness, for leaving an old life and entering a new. It marks one's beginning-place in the life of Christ and the church, and it is not repeated. No matter when and under what circumstances it is administered, any true baptism is an enactment of divine grace which cannot be added to and is not withdrawn. Baptism declares in one's behalf at the beginning the whole meaning of God's gracious self-giving and the whole meaning of one's response in faith—meanings which one must live into in the time that follows.

Baptism came into being along with, and not subsequent to, the church itself. There seems to have been no discussion leading to a decision that the church would be a baptizing community. From the beginning, consent to the gospel was sealed by baptism. Apart from the transitional stage in the early church when one was a catechumen (a stage whose equivocal character the early writers often recognized) there was no such thing as an unbaptized believer.

The way in which the story of Jesus is told in the gospels and referred to in Acts suggests that the earliest Christians would have traced their baptism not to initiatory rites in the Hellenistic religions, nor to sectarian Judaism, nor to proselyte baptism, but to Jesus' baptism by John, following which he stepped into public life as a man anointed for a redemptive vocation (Lk. 4:18-21). His calling was a "baptism" which led him to a cross (Mk. 10:35-40; Lk. 12:50).

Christian baptism unites believers with that redemptive death and with the resurrection that followed. Thus baptism is an enactment of the gospel —and the New Testament will not let us settle for narrow views of either the gospel or of baptism. In Western Christianity, especially in its American version, baptism tends to be thought of individualistically. We ask: What does it do about my sins? or for me? or for this small child? However, baptism, while it is administered personally and by name, is not just an event for an individual person nor for a local congregation, but an event for the Great Church, and it is set in the context of the long-laid redemptive purpose of God in and beyond history. Moreover, the creation emphasis in the baptismal liturgy asks us to locate baptism beyond even its fullest ecclesial context and in the setting of a cosmic celebration. My baptism relates not just to my past or present sins, or my faith, or my religious affiliation, but to my fundamental humanity, to my life in the world. When Paul discussed baptism in the context of his Adam-and-Christ theme, he indicated the universal bearing of the act. Baptism signals the restoration of a humanity gone wrong; it places one within the new collective life; it is the sign of the new aeon of forgiveness, life and glory. Some early Christian writers spoke of the sacrament as restoring the baptized to the paradise from which our first parents had been banished. Further, the new creation of which the baptismal scriptures speak is not only future; it has begun. *Everything old has passed away; see, everything has become new!* (2 Cor. 5:17). Through baptism and the Spirit, one participates now in *the freedom of the glory of the children of God* (Rom. 8:19-21) for which the whole creation waits. Thus baptism is a sign in our flesh that we are caught up in the sweep of the Christian message from creation, through sin and redemption, to new creation.

Baptism is from God

Christian baptism is undeniably a human act, witnessing to our faith. It is carried out through our more or less wise pastoral judgments; it enrolls one in the well-intentioned, but very imperfect community of the church; and it involves commitments of life that are as informed and wholehearted as they can be. Yet, while such human responsibility and consent are constitutive of the act of baptism, it should be understood that we are not baptized into our faith, our understanding, our conversion, or our experience.

Before baptism is an act of human witness, it is a gift lodged in divine freedom. As such, it is received by the church and by the Christian with gratitude and administered with reverent joy. Just as salvation is of God and of grace, so baptism, the sign of salvation, is God-given. *"He [God] saved us. . .according to his mercy, through the water of rebirth and renewal by the Holy Spirit"* (Titus 3:5). Baptism is a celebrational recognition of the God who reconciles, restores, and makes alive. *All this is from God* (2 Cor. 5:18).

The centrality of God in baptism can be seen in the place that is held by the divine name. We cannot tell from the New Testament or the second century writings how the name may have been used in the early years in the actual performance of baptism. But we can be quite sure that the name was not a formula, but rather a mode of presence or of instrumentality. In biblical idiom, persons are as their names; the name stands for the person. Persons act and are acted on through their names. To know the name is to be given access to the person. One can be represented by and be dealt with through one's name. Thus, the name of Christ conveys the reality of Christ.

Christian baptism in both Acts and Paul was, as we have seen, *in the name of the Lord Jesus* (Acts 8:16; 19:5), or *of Jesus Christ* (Acts 2:38; 10:48), or *of the Lord Jesus Christ* (1 Cor. 6:11). To be baptized in the name of Jesus Christ means to be brought into union with Jesus Christ. As the Lutheran theologian Robert Jenson recently put it, "Whatever new reality the neophyte enters by this rite of passage, is named *Jesus'* reality."[1]

Although the New Testament presentation of baptism is highly Christocentric, christology is not self-sustaining. C. F. D. Moule once wrote, "In the last analysis, a Christology is itself impossible without the confession of God as Creator and as the Father of our Lord Jesus Christ."[2] If not from the very beginning, then at least within the first generation of the church, baptism had come, if not everywhere at least in some regions, to use the triadic name which we observed in Jesus' "Great Commission" (Mt. 28:19) and in the late first or early second century *Didache* (7:1, 3). This triadic naming, which was to become all but universal practice, was and is a way of affirming that to be baptized means to be bound into the strong name of the Trinity. In baptism we use the name of the triune God; but more profoundly, in baptism the divine name reaches out to enclose us within its compassion and power.

Christ and baptism

The English Baptist writer, Neville Clark, has said, "We must derive our basic understanding of baptism from the Christ-event. We must think christologically."[3] In baptism one is identified with Christ, but the name or title "the Christ" which speaks of the present, reigning Christ who is known in the church, speaks at the same time of the historical Jesus, the crucified. Baptism unites the baptized person with Christ and with the redemptive work he carried out—anointed with the Spirit as he was anointed, dying in his death, buried with him, rising in his resurrection, sharing in his victory over sin and death, ascended with him, entering on a new life in him, joined in his redemptive mission, and awaiting him.

However, Christ's union with humanity stands prior to the union of human lives with God through him. When in 1 Corinthians 1:13, Paul asks somewhat sarcastically, *Was Paul crucified for you? Or were you baptized into the name of Paul?* he is saying that it was Christ, not Paul, who first died for the Corinthians, and it was into his name that they were baptized. Priority lies in his saving initiative. As Paul put it in a later epistle: *We are convinced that one has died for all; therefore all have died. And he died for all, so that those who live might live no longer for themselves, but for him who died and was raised for them* (2 Cor. 5:14a-15). Rudolf Schnackenburg summarizes, "Christ died for the Corinthians. He acquired them for himself, and in baptism they are made over to Him."[4]

Some writers have spoken of a "general baptism," meaning that Christ's death and resurrection are the world's baptism. In a notable essay, the late J. A. T. Robinson argued that the *one baptism* that is spoken of both in Ephesians 4:5, *one Lord, one faith, one baptism*, and in the Nicene Creed does not refer to Christian baptism, but to the baptism of humanity that was accomplished in principle in the work of Christ. An individual's baptism is a baptism into this general baptism.[5]

Using a different idiom, an ecumenical document, now a few years old, speaking of the exchange between Christ and his people through baptism, said:

> For Jesus baptism meant that he was consecrated as Messiah. For us baptism means that we are consecrated as members of a messianic people. The baptism of Jesus meant that the righteous One took upon himself the sin of the many and became one with them. Our baptism means that we, the many, are incorporated into him and become one with him and in him.[6]

While baptism speaks of what has been done, it speaks to a Christian's present as well, for in Christ one lives freely and joyfully in a relationship with God which sin had broken but which is now restored. However, baptism also reaches to the future, for Christ's death and resurrection are described in the New Testament as the inauguration of the Age to Come; they are promise. Christian baptism, by its connection with Easter, does not simply look to a victory past, but it looks forward to the final kingdom that is pledged in Christ and demonstrated in his triumph over death and is coming into being in the church. It is a sacrament not just of memory, but of hope. Jürgen Moltmann has said, "Christian baptism is eschatology put into practice. It. . .is Christian hope in action."[7]

The Holy Spirit in baptism

The new life which is inaugurated in baptism is the actualization in a believing person of the Holy Spirit—the self-imparting divine vitality. If baptism is deeply Christocentric, it is also virtually "Pentecostal." It is spoken of as an anointing by the Spirit through which Christians are admitted to a royal or priestly life and community. Baptism is a "sealing" by the Spirit, marking one as God's own. It is an anointing which creates a community of prophets, those who know (1 Jn. 2:20). The new birth or fresh start in the midst of life's tired continuities is by water and the Spirit (Jn. 3:5), i.e. by cleansing and the immediate power of God.

The New Testament writers are not naive, but are aware of many spirits—true and counterfeit, divine and demonic. *Beloved, do not believe every spirit, but test the spirits to see whether they are from God* (1 Jn. 4:1). What are the insignia of God's Spirit?

In Acts, at the two inaugural events, first at Pentecost and then at Cornelius' house as the church moved to include Gentiles, the Spirit is a divine power whose "coming upon" or "descent" is evidenced by ecstatic phenomena.[8] These startling signs witness that God is not in human control, and the bursting of the divine life into human experience may well stretch the bounds of the linear, the rational and the ordered. Yet such experience should not be regarded as a normative way of validating the actuality of the Spirit. If the Spirit is sometimes demonstrated in moments of illumination and power that go beyond common logic, decorum, and grammar, such ecstatic experience cannot be equated with the Spirit. Ecstasy is a widespread religious and cultural phenomenon, and it can easily be induced. In itself ecstasy is full of ambiguity, and it may mislead. In Acts itself, the presence of the Spirit is not regularly equated with excitement. The Spirit, who may at times be irruptive and paranormal, is also described in the New Testament as a continued, gentle, sustaining, ordering, community-building presence. The church enjoys *the comfort of the Holy Spirit* (Acts 9:31).

In other strata of New Testament thought, the ecstatic does not figure in the experience of the Spirit. The Fourth Gospel says that the Spirit *descends and remains* on Jesus (Jn. 1:32f), and Jesus says to the disciples (i.e. to the church) that the Paraclete will *be with you forever* as a resident teacher and guide (Jn. 14:16, 26; 16:13). The author of 1 John assures his readers that *the anointing that you received from him abides in you*, giving you knowledge (1 Jn. 2:27). In the Johannine writings, the Spirit is a steady, informing divine presence.

When Paul wrote about worship at Corinth (1 Cor. 11-14), his "yes and no" argument concerning manifestations of the Spirit indicates the struggle in the Corinthian congregation (and evidently to some extent in Paul's own sympathies) between freedom and control. He affirms the gifts which are given to each Christian by the Spirit's own determinations (12:4-11), and he claims them for himself (14:18). However, in Corinth the gifts of utterance had been used for display and had led to personal vanity which subverted community. Paul argues that in the Christian assembly the gifts and their free exercise cannot be made an excuse for disorder. The prophets must not all talk at once nor interrupt one another. The Spirit's gifts are in the community and for the building up of the community—hence the paean to love in chapter 13. When Paul says, *The spirits of prophets are subject to the prophets,* he is saying that in the Christian assembly no one can be discourteous or inconsiderate and claim that he or she was made so by the Spirit, *for God is a God not of disorder but of shalom* (14:32). Decency, courtesy, intelligibility and order are of the Spirit. In Paul's mature letters, the Spirit is ethicalized, so that *the fruit of the Spirit is* not spectacular modes of utterance, but such modest, yet powerful community-binding forces as *love, joy, peace, patience, kindness, generosity, gentleness, and self-control* (Gal. 5:22f). The Spirit, who can begin the life of the gospel in the alienated human community by exceptional, shattering, demonstrative manifestations of divine presence and power, ordinarily creates and sustains the gospel-formed community in free, loving and joyful orderedness.

There is a recurrent tendency in the church to introduce some separation between Christ and the Spirit—as though baptism into Christ represented an ordinary level of faith and belonging, while true life in the Spirit is something more, reserved for special souls. But the New Testament speaks of the Spirit as the Spirit of Christ—the one through whom Christ is actualized in the church and in each believer. The Paraclete, the Johannine Jesus said, *will not speak on his own, but. . .will take what is mine and declare it to you* (Jn. 16:12-15). Christ acts and is effective through the Spirit, and the Spirit is Christ acting and speaking. Schnackenburg put it, "The *Pneuma* [the Spirit] proceeds from the risen Lord (cf. 1 Cor. 15:45; 2 Cor. 3:17), who thus continues his work through the Spirit and through Him creates his own Body, the Church. The Spirit stands in closest connection with Christ and carries on his work."[9] The matter can be put in two ways: Through Christ one has the Spirit; and only through the Spirit one has Christ.

Baptism, sin and forgiveness

In baptism God deals with human alienation and sin. The Nicene Creed says, *We acknowledge one baptism for the forgiveness of sins* (BCP, p. 359). In the baptismal rite itself, the Thanksgiving over the Water speaks of those who are to be baptized as *here cleansed from sin* (p. 307), and the post-baptismal prayer identifies *the forgiveness of sin* among the effects of baptism (p. 308; see also BCP catechism, p. 858). This theme in the Prayer Book witnesses to a strong ecclesiastical tradition. In the West, the understanding of baptism as an act of divine cleansing has been closely linked with the Christian analysis of sin.

The church has been convinced that baptism brought forgiveness because it finds the theme in the New Testament. The most prominent instance is no doubt the one that stands at the very beginning of the baptismal tradition, Peter's invitation on the Day of Pentecost, *Repent, and be baptized every one of you in the name of Jesus Christ so that your sins may be forgiven* (Acts 2:38).

Yet, the proposition that baptism is for the remission of sin, stated so directly, has given some conscientious persons pause. It seems to make forgiveness through baptism automatic, perhaps even magical, giving control in spiritual things too much into ecclesiastical hands. An external act is said to bring spiritual, eternal results. The caution must be taken seriously. Baptism is a performative sign only insofar as it is transparent to the great act of divine mercy which centers in Jesus Christ.

The mission of Jesus took its beginning from John the Baptist, who proclaimed *a baptism of repentance for the forgiveness of sins* (Mk. 1:4). His baptism was a judgment against sin and at the same time a deliverance from it. As Jesus ministered, he forgave (Mk. 2:5; Lk. 5:20). He carried his forgiving work even to the cross itself (Lk. 23:34). Jesus also taught others to forgive (Mt. 6:12ff; 18:21-35; Lk. 7:47ff; 17:3f). Far more is said about forgiveness by Jesus in the synoptic gospels than is said by anyone else in any other part of the New Testament. In his death (anticipated in his baptism) he stood with and for sinful humanity, restoring, by self-giving, the relation that sin had broken. Christ's cross is witness that sin matters; it matters to God. It is not dealt with by sweeping it away or quietly ignoring it. The cross is divine judgment on sin. Yet at the same time, the cross takes up the pain and cost of sin into the adequacy of infinite mercy. Thinking of Jesus' self-giving for the world's sake, he is *the Lamb of God who takes away the sin of the world* (Jn. 1:29). Forgiveness is in his name (Acts 2:38; 10:43; 13:38; 1 Jn. 2:12). All forgiveness traces to him.

To speak of Jesus as *the Lamb of God* uses the idiom of the Jewish sacrificial system. The Levitical sacrifices were, as Israel saw them, good news for sinners, for they were given by God. *For the life of the flesh is in the blood; and I have given it to you for making atonement for your lives on the altar* (Lev. 17:11). Christians, drawing on this heritage, saw Jesus as the one great, divinely provided sacrifice for sin and themselves as beneficiaries of its grace, *In him we have redemption through his blood, the forgiveness of our trespasses* (Eph. 1:7).

But divine forgiveness in Christ must reach where it is needed, and it does so through the witness of the church (Lk. 24:47). Jesus commissions his people, as the Father had commissioned him. They are, by the Spirit, to forgive sins, assured that the forgiveness they minister will be effective (Jn. 20:21). The baptizing church is the continuance of the freeing, forgiving mission of Jesus, *proclaiming release to the captives* (Lk. 4:18). What the risen Christ will be to the world, he will be through the church. And the church's offer of Christ is extended through the offer, in his name, of baptism. This outward rite is forever bound up with the gospel—the water united with the Word.

Of course, the Word reaches persons inwardly. One consents to it in repentance and faith. By repentance, one makes a radical re-evaluation of oneself, accepting the judgment on sin that was rendered in Christ's cross; and by faith one turns gratefully to Jesus Christ, putting one's whole trust in his grace and love (BCP, p. 302).

However, faith and repentance, while they are deeply inward, must be signified outwardly. They are shown in a reordered life, of course; but the appointed sign of repentance and faith is baptism. Where the inward response to the Word is present, baptism is not a "mere sign," for when God acts in forgiveness and when a repentant and believing person looks to God, the appointed sign is effective, accomplishing the reality it signifies. Christian baptism is not just a sign pointing to an act; it is itself an act, but an act which is an extension of, an actualization of the one great Act. Thus it is audacious, but not reckless when apostolic writers say, *Baptism now saves you* (1 Pet. 3:21), and *God our Savior. . .saved us. . .through the water of rebirth* (Titus 3:6).

Baptism and church

Christian baptism is an action of a community, bringing an individual into the shared life of a people—a life as intimately bound up with the living Christ as one's body is with one's personhood and identity. There is no private relation with Christ; to stand in relation with Christ is at the same time to belong to his people. This people is sign of the new humanity in Christ made accessible to all. It is the societal form of the gospel. This community, bound as it is to the gospel itself, can be an indispensable support in the life of faith. Yet it dare not be sacralized, for it is a very human and fallible community which may be the cause of most of the misgivings that one may have about faith.

Before the church is a baptizing community, it is a baptized community, and it is baptized by Christ who *loved the church and gave himself up for her, in order to make her holy by cleansing her with the washing of water by the word* (Eph. 5:26). The words describe the church as a whole as acted upon by Christ; he himself washes it, and the washing is his self-giving in its behalf.

Baptism which bonds one with Christ bonds one at the same time with others in a coinherence of giving and receiving, listening and speaking, forgiving and seeking forgiveness, of helping and being helped. In the exchanges of face-to-face community one acquires and practices the modest but endlessly difficult skills of membership: the skills of patience, reliability, truth-telling, serving.

Like a family when a new child arrives, when the church, through baptism, incorporates a new life, the church is changed. The South African writer Peter Hinchcliff said a few years ago that in each baptism "the whole relationship of God and humanity (in both the corporate and the individual sense) has been made explicit. And the church will never be the same again."[10]

The catholic community of faith includes great human variety, and within it there will be genuine differences in perception of the common Lord and diverse idioms of expression and ministry. Yet its members share one life and one destiny. The "one baptism" asks them to discover and bring to apprehensibility the unity that is at work even in the differences.

The church into which one is brought by baptism is always a community in process. Drawing its vitality from Christ, the church *grows with a growth that is from God* (Col. 2:19), as each member grows into Christ (Eph. 4:11-16). In its uneven life in history, the church has times of vitality and times of decadence. But God indwells it and leads it, through struggle into a new life, coming from a new source, and fashioned on a new model. In Christ, it *grows into a holy temple in the Lord* in which all the baptized *are built together spiritually into a dwelling place for God* (Eph. 2:21f).

Baptism and eschatology

In the New Testament proclamation, the resurrection of Jesus is not something that happened on a past date to a remarkable individual so much as it is the inauguration of a new age and the pledge of the final consummation. Since Christ was a representative person, one who carried in himself the many, what happened in him was of significance for the race. Christ's death and resurrection signaled the closing off of the old age of sin and death and the actualization in one person of the new life of glory that is promised in him for all (1 Cor. 15:20-23). Yet the old age persists, even though its defeat is pledged by Christ's victory. The church is a people which in the midst of sin and death knows and lives under the sign of that victory. It is a people of the new aeon—a witness to what is true, but unseen; to what will be, but is not yet. Baptism says that, in Karl Barth's words, "He is the Victor and we in Him are those who are awaiting the victory."[11]

One is joined to the life of the new age through faith and through baptism, faith's sign. Thus while baptism reaches to our deep past and touches our present, it also looks forward. While it gives much now, it is an act of promise. Neville Clark has said, "Baptism is a sacrament of inaugurated eschatology."[12] At the beginning of one's life in Christ the church speaks of eternal life and of glory. That which will be claimed at the end is declared at the start.

In the liturgy of Hippolytus (early third century), at the baptismal eucharist, there was (in addition to the chalice of wine and the chalice of water which we noted earlier), a chalice of milk and honey. This chalice was sometimes spoken of as representing the food of children, and the newly baptized have just been born. But it was also explained as the food of the promised land, "a land flowing with milk and honey." This chalice said to the newly baptized that even though they had just begun in the life of Christ and his people and had unknown struggles ahead of them, the promises were theirs. At the beginning, they could lay claim to the end.

Baptism and ethical commitments

Baptism necessarily and essentially carries moral implications. When Paul says that in baptism the body of sin is destroyed (Rom. 6:6f, 11-14), one might paraphrase: The self which was devoted to sinning has died. From baptism follows a new way of life, revised ethical priorities, a commitment to holiness, righteousness, truthfulness. Baptism, to be sure, speaks not of demand but of grace. It conveys the divine promise; it enacts God's "yes" to us. Then, the promise having been accepted, the life which begins in baptism is a believer's answering "yes" to God. This new life calls out moral discipline and moral vision. Properly understood, baptism is not an act that lasts only a few minutes; it is continued in the life which follows it. The English Methodist, Philip Watson, has said, "Baptism. . .is not merely an act of initiation. It has reference to the whole of the Christian life, which consists of an ever-renewed dying with Christ and rising with Him."[13]

The connection between baptismal gift and baptismal responsibility can be seen in the contour of Romans 6. Paul first speaks of the baptismal event in the indicative mood, telling what has been done, *We have been baptized into Christ Jesus. . .buried with him. . .united with him in a death like his. . .crucified with him* (vss. 3-6). Then as he continues and moves to a Christian's union with Christ's resurrection, he begins to speak of the baptismal life in imperatives: *Consider yourselves dead to sin and alive to God . . .do not let sin exercise dominion in your mortal bodies. . .present yourselves to God as those who have been brought from death to life* (vss. 11, 12, 13). While baptism is a gift of grace, it brings each baptized person into a covenanted life of obligation. As Paul puts it elsewhere: *One has died for all; therefore all have died. And he died for all, so that those who live might live no longer for themselves, but for him who died and was raised for them* (2 Cor. 5:14). The writer of Colossians appeals to baptism as the foundation for a new way of living: *If with Christ you died to the elemental spirits of the universe, why do you live as if you still belonged to the world?. . .If you have been raised with Christ, seek the things that are above. . ., for you have died, and your life is hidden with Christ in God* (Col. 2:20-3:4).

These New Testament passages speak in general terms about such things as righteousness of conduct, the old self and the new, the conquering of sin and death, and living for Christ. But ethical conduct is made up of particular actions and decisions. Perhaps early Christian converts had been tutored in the ways of their new faith, and non-specific terms served as "code words" which conveyed shared moral understandings and guided them in their difficult world. In his first extant letter, Paul reminds his readers of the instructions (*parangelias*) he had given them and urges them to continue in what they had been taught (1 Thess. 4:1f, and see 3:11—4:12).

The character of the ethics that arise from the New Testament gospel is somewhat surprising. The Christian message seems to require an inward revolution, a new self, a new life. It is put forward in a context of eschatological urgency; Christians should make a radical break with a perishing world. However, when specific morality is described, the persons made new in Christ are committed, not to a life of heroism or spiritual asceticism, but to doing on the whole quite modest things—being faithful, patient, kind, forgiving, compassionate in the spirit of Christ, speaking the truth in love, honorable in their dealings with their associates and obedient to civil authority. But a life of this kind can represent its own sort of quiet heroism.

By the early second century (and possibly sooner than that) baptism came, as we have seen, to be preceded by a period of probation and instruction, which soon became quite long and demanding. The first evidence of instruction before baptism is the *Didache* (late first or early second century) which opens with an account of "the two ways"—the way of life and the way of death. The document then says that baptism should proceed only after candidates have been instructed in these things (*Didache* 7:1). The pattern of negatives and positives may trace to Paul. Speaking in contrasts, he urges "put off the old, and put on the new;" in Gal. 5:16-26 he sets in two tables the works of the flesh and the fruit of the Spirit, and in 1 Corinthians 6:9-11 he contrasts what his readers were and what they have been called to be. (See also Col. 3:5-17.)

Early Christian ethical guidance can also be found in the easily remembered codes for ordering Christian households (Col. 3:18-4:1; Eph. 5:21-6:9; 1 Tim. 5:4, 8, 9-16; and 1 Pet. 2:18—3:7). While in proportion and detail these household tables differ, their roughly similar form suggests that they are instances of a common way in which the church could let new Christians know the implications of their baptism for life in the structures of intimate relationships.

The New Testament, to a great extent, puts forward an ethic of character. It is more concerned about what sort of people Christians are than it is in guiding specific conduct. When the early Christians speak specifically, they necessarily speak to the issues of their time. Hence, the biblical passion for a new life in the risen Christ needs to be repossessed as new situations require new ethical analysis and fresh guidance. But through the changes of time and circumstance, the fundamental character of the baptized life remains constant. As Gustaf Wingren put it, "Baptism brings the baptized into union with Christ's death and in so doing points to a life which is lived for the good of others."[14]

Baptism and mission

Baptism stands at the frontier between church and not-church. Existing at this church/world meeting-point, it is the act by which the church reaches into the world and by which the world ceases to be world and becomes church.

Even after many years of analyzing their own deeply habituated false priorities, churches remain to a great extent introverted. They live for themselves—turned inward so much that they can shelter church members from the world and its trauma, making it hard for them to discover a redemptive vocation in it. The church is preoccupied with the church, and baptism is seen largely in terms of church continuity or church growth—a bringing in, not a sending out.

A church which is truly informed by baptism is, by contrast, turned toward the world, engaged with the world—sometimes witnessing and serving, and sometimes judging and leading, and occasionally standing against the world for the sake of the world. It is a "worldly church" (in a proper sense) in the name of God who is at work in the church and in the life of each Christian, but who is at the same time at work in the world and in the life of each human being. And the divine work is one, all of it centered in Christ, the eternal Creative Word.

In baptism one is joined to that redemptive stream of history of which Jesus Christ is the center.[15] The background of that vocation traces to the Servant (i.e. Israel) who is given to be "a light to the nations" (Isa. 49:1-6). Jesus is anointed to proclaim God's Year of Jubilee—the release of captives, the forgiving of debts, the freeing of the oppressed (Lk. 4:16-21). But the Messiah dies. Yet his death and resurrection create a people. A person who receives Christian baptism shares in Christ's life-through-death, not only as a beneficiary of it, but as one who is committed to the redemptive purpose for which he lived and died and now lives. The mission which is first of all the *missio Dei*, and is then the mission of Jesus Christ, and then the church's mission, becomes the mission of the individual baptized Christian. We are baptized into the Christ whose life was a life for the world.

Thus baptism is a profoundly revolutionary act. Persons who had thought themselves to be self-sufficient and to be living in a self-sufficient society come to recognize that they are dependent and that life is grounded in grace. Their truest selfhood is given to them as they expend themselves for others in witness and service.

Christians live a paradoxical existence. By baptism they are brought into a new order of things, yet they continue in the old order, for the new interpenetrates the old. But now they are set in the old order to be in its midst a witness simultaneously for and against it. In the Baptismal Covenant, the candidate is asked, *Will you proclaim by word and example the Good News of God in Christ?* The candidate, joined by the congregation, replies, *I will, with God's help.*

Endnotes

Notes to chapter 1
Baptism and Experience

1. Martin Luther, *The Babylonian Captivity of the Church* (many editions). The quoted words come early in the section on baptism.

2. Gustaf Wingren, *Gospel and Church* (Philadelphia: Fortress Press, 1964), 131.

3. C. K. Barrett, *From First Adam to Last: A Study in Pauline Theology* (New York: Charles Scribner's Sons, 1962), 108.

4. J. G. Davies, *The Spirit, the Church and the Sacraments* (London: Faith Press, 1954), 162.

Notes to chapter 2
The Scriptures and Baptism

1. On the "baptismal pattern," see C. F. D. Moule, "The Nature and Purpose of I Peter," *New Testament Studies* 3 (1956): 4, "The early Church writers continually had the 'pattern' of baptism in mind, and often cast the Gospel into that dramatic form. The sacraments were vehicles of the Gospel and the Gospel was sacramental, and the two were virtually inseparable." Neville Clark, *An Approach to the Theology of the Sacraments,* Studies in Biblical Theology 17 (Chicago: Alec R. Allenson, 1956), 25, writing along a similar line, says, "Again and again when the word itself is not actually used baptism is in Paul's mind, though sometimes we have only an aorist tense to make plain that the reference is not to a period or a process but to an act at a point in time."

2. The literature on typology is not extensive. Three basic books on the New Testament use of the Old are C. H. Dodd, *According to the Scriptures,* (New York: Charles Scribner's Sons, 1953); Barnabas Lindars, *New Testament Apologetic: The Doctrinal Significance of the Old Testament Quotations* (Philadelphia: Westminster Press, 1961); and A. T. Hanson, *The Living Utterances of God: The New Testament Exegesis of the Old* (London: Darton, Longman and Todd, 1983).

   Much material on the early Christian use of types can be found in two books by Jean Danielou, *The Bible and the Liturgy* (South Bend, Indiana: University of Notre Dame Press, 1956), which has eighty pages on baptism; and *From Shadows to Reality: Studies in the Biblical Typology of the Fathers* (London: Burns and Oates, 1960).

Modern treatments of typology include A. G. Hebert, *The Throne of David* (London: Faber and Faber, 1941), which is valuable, but now old and perhaps insufficiently critical; and G. W. H. Lampe and K. Woolcombe, *Essays on Typology*, Studies in Biblical Theology 22 (London: SCM Press, 1957). There are fine theoretical insights in sections of Northrop Frye, *The Great Code: The Bible and Literature* (New York: Harcourt Brace and Jovanovich, 1982).

It may be useful to distinguish two areas of question: (1) how the two testaments are used in the structuring of a lectionary, and (2) how the lectionary material from the two testaments is used by preachers and teachers. There are useful insights along this line in Laurence Stookey, "Marcion, Typology, and Lectionary Preaching," *Worship*, 66 (1992): 3:251-62.

3 A semi-popular but serious study of the exodus theme is James Plastaras, *The God of Exodus* (Milwaukee: Bruce Publishing Co., 1966). David Daube in his *The Exodus Pattern in the Bible* (London: Faber and Faber, 1963), finds convincing parallels in the Jewish scriptures which other writers have missed. A. G. Hebert's small work, *When Israel Came Out of Egypt* (London: SCM Press, 1961) deserved to remain available longer than it did.

4 In Lampe and Woolcombe, op. cit., 28.

5 Cyril of Jerusalem, *Mystagogical Catecheses,* 1:3. The quotations from the fourth-century baptismal homilies in this present volume are from the texts in Edward J. Yarnold, *The Awe-Inspiring Rites of Initiation*, 2nd ed. (Collegeville, Minnesota: Liturgical Press, 1994).

6 Northrop Frye, op. cit., 79f.

7 The ecumenically prepared Revised Common Lectionary has addressed some of these matters. By a series of alternative readings, it provides a more sequential coverage of the Jewish scriptures. Although the results are commendable, any lectionary that combines the two testaments, giving two readings from the New and one from the Old, is up against a quantitative problem. The Jewish scriptures are more than three times as long as the Christian testament (more than that, if the apocryphal books are included). Any program of reading that is organized around the canonical Christian literature will necessarily slight in some way the Jewish sacred literature.

Notes to chapter 3
Scriptures for the Easter/Pentecost Complex

1 Some early steps in baptismal renewal were brought about in the fifties largely through pastoral and educational initiatives. The church was conceived as a redemptive fellowship into which one was brought by baptism. Baptism was brought out of the obscurity in which it had been lodged. Parents were prepared for baptisms more diligently than they had been. The corporateness of the church

was emphasized, and the image of the church as family was prominent (it was the fifties). These pastoral changes prepared the way for the liturgical texts which began to appear in the seventies. Brief reference to this work is made here in chapter 6 (see p. 185).

2   Some material here follows passages in D. B. Stevick, "Lent," Carl Daw, ed., *Breaking the Word*, (New York: Church Hymnal Corporation, 1994), a chapter which contains some theological discussion of the season and further material on the Lenten scriptures.

3   Walter Brueggemann, *Genesis,* Interpretation Series (Atlanta, Ga.: Westminster John Knox Press, 1982), 187.

4   Samuel Terrien, *The Psalms and Their Meaning for Today* (New York: Bobbs-Merrill Co., 1952), 169.

5   Two essays that seek to set the Paschal observance within the New Testament period are F[rank] L[eslie] Cross, *I Peter: A Paschal Liturgy* (London: Mowbray, 1954); and Massey H. Shepherd, Jr., *The Paschal Liturgy and the Apocalypse* (Richmond, Virginia: John Knox Press, 1960). While in detail they have not persuaded most scholars, they contain fascinating insights.

6   Tertullian, *On Baptism*, ed. Evans, 19:41. Tertullian adds a few sentences later, "For all that, every day is a Lord's Day: any hour, any season, is suitable for baptism. If there is any difference of solemnity, it makes no difference to the grace." Other early writers make the same point. Baptism at special times had nothing to do with the reality of the sacrament, only with the expressiveness of the sign.

7   The formulation "light, word, baptism and eucharist" summarizes the second rubric of BCP, 284; but the exact words are from Kenneth Stevenson, *Jerusalem Revisited* (Washington, D. C.: The Pastoral Press, 1988), 79.

8   *Genesis I-XI*, Torch Bible Commentaries (London: SCM Press, 1953), 44.

9   Alexander Schmemann, *For the Life of the World* [also published as *Sacraments and Orthodoxy*] (Crestwood, New York: St. Vladimir's Seminary Press, 1973), 14. I have changed the author's pronouns to eliminate the generic "man."

10 There is an extended discussion of the typology of Noah and the flood in scripture and the early church in Jean Danielou, *From Shadows to Reality,* (London: Burns and Oates, 1960), bk. 2.

11 Some early Christian art shows the scene of Abraham and Isaac in such a way as to relate it to the cross and to the eucharist. See, for example, the mosaic in the presbytery of St. Vitale in Ravenna (where it is an iconic reference to the allusion to Abraham and Melchizedek in the Roman Canon of the Mass).

12 Northrop Frye, op. cit., 183.

13 A fairly recent study of the exodus as a metaphor of revolution and emancipation is Michael Walzer, *Exodus and Revolution* (New York: Basic Books, 1985). The author might have done more than he did with the New England Puritans or the Mormons, or with some other modern-day movements of liberation, but he should not be faulted for things he did not do, when what he did do, he did so well.

[14] David Stanley, "The New Testament Doctrine of Baptism," *Theological Studies* 18 (1957): 187.

[15] Claus Westermann, *Isaiah 40-66* (Philadelphia: Westminster Press,1969), 289.

[16] Joseph Blenkinsopp, *Ezekiel,* Interpretation Series (Louisville, Kentucky: John Knox Press, 1990), 167.

[17] *Present and Future* (South Bend, Indiana: University of Notre Dame Press, 1966), 105.

[18] Gordon Lathrop, *Easter,* Proclamation 6, Series A (Minneapolis: Fortress Press, 1996), 11.

[19] Some cautious exegetes (including the recent thorough commentary by Paul Achtemeier in the Hermeneia Series) are not persuaded that 1 Peter is a baptismal homily or related to a baptismal occasion. However, not all of the exegetes who see the work in a baptismal setting are incautious.

[20] G. R. Beasley-Murray, *The New Testament Doctrine of Baptism* (London: Macmillan, 1963), 255.

[21] John V. Taylor, *The Go-Between God* (Philadelphia: Fortress Press, 1973), 5.

[22] Tertullian, *On Baptism*, ed. Evans, 19:41.

[23] Reinhold Niebuhr, *Beyond Tragedy* (New York: Charles Scribner's Sons, 1937), 28. Although it was written sixty years ago, nothing on the subject sticks in the mind quite like Niebuhr's chapter, "The Tower of Babel."

[24] Neville Clark, op. cit., 34.

[25] *Readings in St. John's Gospel* (London: Macmillan, 1949), 384.

[26] Oscar Cullmann, *Early Christian Worship* (Chicago: Henry Regnery, 1953), 84ff., 93ff., 110ff.

[27] A. M. Ramsey, *Holy Spirit: A Biblical Study* (Boston: Cowley Press, 1992), 10.

[28] Walter Brueggemann, *The Message of the Psalms* (Minneapolis: Augsburg, 1984), 35.

Notes to chapter 4
The Scriptures for the Christmas/Epiphany Complex

[1] Gregory of Nazianzus, "Sermon on Holy Baptism," ed. A. Hamman, *Baptism: Ancient Liturgies and Patristic Texts* (New York: Alba House, 1967), 89.

[2] See Kilian McDonnell, *The Baptism of Jesus in the Jordan: The Trinitarian and Cosmic Order of Salvation* (Collegeville, Minnesota: Liturgical Press, 1996), esp. chapters 12-16; Gabriele Winkler, "The Original Meaning of the Prebaptismal Anointing and Its Implications," *Worship* 52 (1978): 24-45.

[3] Leo the Great, *Letter (16) to the Sicilian Bishops,* in Thomas M. Finn, *Early Christian Baptism and the Catechumenate: Italy, North Africa and Egypt* (Collegeville, Minnesota: Liturgical Press, 1992), 80-83. Another text of this

letter is in Hamman, ed., op. cit., 229-36. Thomas J. Talley, *The Origins of the Christian Year* (New York: Pueblo, 1986), 36f, 126f., cites a letter written in 385 CE from Himerius, a Spanish bishop, which mentions baptisms at Epiphany as well as feasts of martyrs. A reply came from Siricius, Bishop of Rome, strongly condemning such practices.

4   Ambrose, "Sermons on the Sacraments," 1:13.

5   Bo Reicke, *The Epistles of James, Peter, and Jude,* Anchor Bible Series (Garden City, New York: Doubleday, 1964), 111.

6   Heinrich Schlier, *The Relevance of the New Testament* (New York: Herder and Herder, 1968), 242. Schlier's chapter 13, "The Baptism of Jesus as Presented by the Gospels," is very fine.

7   Emil Schuerer, *A History of the Jewish People in the Time of Jesus Christ* (New York: Charles Scribner's Sons, n.d.), 2:2:163.

8   The material here on the dove imagery and the voice from heaven largely follows C. K. Barrett's careful study of Jesus' baptism in chapter 3 of *The Holy Spirit and the Gospel Tradition* (London: SPCK, 1966). Barrett is cautious, remarking about the dove, "It is reasonable to suppose that this symbolism had a particular significance for those who used it. Unfortunately it is impossible now to discover certainly what that significance was" (35).

9   Krister Stendahl, *The School of Matthew* (Philadelphia: Fortress Press, 1968), 144.

10 *Testament of Levi,* 18:6-7, Charlesworth, ed., *Apocrypha and Pseudepigrapha,* 1:795. The closing words which are shown in brackets are widely taken to be a Christian interpolation based on the story of Jesus' baptism.

Notes to chapter 5
The Scriptures for the Vigil for All Saints and All Saints' Day

1   The *Martyrdom of Polycarp*, section 18, remains an early, valuable, and moving witness.

2   H. Boone Porter, *The Day of Light: The Biblical and Liturgical Meaning of Sunday* (New York: Seabury Press, 1960), 67.

3   Hippolytus, *Apostolic Tradition,* section 19. A very satisfactory edition is G. J. Cuming, ed., *Hippolytus: A Text for Students* (Bramcote, Nottinghamshire, U. K.: Grove Books), 1979.

4   Robert W. Jenson, *Visible Words: The Interpretation and Practice of Christian Sacraments* (Minneapolis: Fortress Press, 1978), 131. Jenson adds, "We are commanded to baptize simply insofar as we take the command to preach repentance in Jesus' name as addressed also to us."

5   *The Paschal Liturgy and the Apocalypse,* Ecumenical Studies in Worship (Richmond, Virginia: John Knox Press: 1960), 90.

Notes to chapter 6
Sunday as a Baptismal Day

[1] Abraham Joshua Heschel, *The Sabbath: Its Meaning for Modern Man* (New York: Farrar, Straus and Giroux, 1951), 8.

[2] *Christian Initiation: Baptism in the Medieval West* (London: SPCK, 1965), 107.

[3] See Daniel B. Stevick, *Baptismal Moments, Baptismal Meanings* (New York: Church Hymnal Corporation, 1987). Chapter 6, "Persistent Issues: (3) First Communion," pp. 91-114, discusses the relation between baptism and eucharist. After some history, pp. 104-14 consider the relation as its is set forth in the Prayer Book.

[4] Hippolytus, *Apostolic Tradition,* section 20.

[5] Talley, op. cit., 37.

[6] Porter, op. cit., 72f.

[7] George Herbert, *A Priest to the Temple,* chapter 22, quoted in John N. Wall, ed., *George Herbert,* Classics of Western Spirituality Series (New York: Paulist Press, 1981), 85. Some sixteenth- and early-seventeenth-century episcopal articles and injunctions seek to enforce baptisms on Sundays or Holy Days, with a congregation present. But their tone indicates that the authority of this practice was weakening.

[8] Porter, op. cit., 81.

[9] Gordon W. Lathrop, *Holy Things: A Liturgical Theology* (Minneapolis: Fortress Press, 1993), 39.

[10] Willy Rordorff, *Sunday: The History of the Day of Rest and Worship in the Earliest Centuries of the Christian Church* (Philadelphia: Westminster Press, 1968), 275.

[11] S. Anita Stauffer, *On Baptismal Fonts: Ancient and Modern* (Bramcote, Nottinghamshire, U. K.: Grove Books, 1994). The author gives good information on early baptismal sites, and her descriptions of and criteria for modern fonts are the best we have. This small book supplements the fuller work by J. G. Davies, *The Architectural Setting of Baptism* (London: Barrie and Rockliff, 1962).

The reference in the inscription to "eight niches" is to small cubicles, undoubtedly used as changing rooms, that were often built along each interior wall of the baptistery building.

Notes to chapter 7
How the Earliest Christians Baptized: Acts

[1] On the eunuch's exclusion from Israel, I have used the words of R. S. Paul, *The Atonement and the Sacraments* (Nashville, Tennessee: Abingdon Press, 1960), 336.

2   W. F. Flemington, *The New Testament Doctrine of Baptism* (London: SPCK, 1957), 49.

3   R. P. C. Hanson, *The Acts* (Oxford: At the Clarendon Press, 1967), 111.

4   Rudolf Schnackenburg, *Baptism in the Thought of St. Paul* (New York: Herder and Herder, 1964), 20.

5   Clinton Morrison, "Baptism and Maturity," *Interpretation* 17:4 (October 1963): 389.

6   G. R. Beasley-Murray, op. cit., 96.

7   Reginald Fuller, "Christian Initiation in the New Testament," John Gallen, ed., *Made, Not Born* (South Bend, Indiana: University of Notre Dame Press, 1974), 14. See also J. E. L. Oulton, "The Holy Spirit, Baptism and Laying on of Hands," *Expository Times* 66 (1955): 236-40; O. C. Edwards, "The Exegesis of Acts 8:4-25 and its Implications for Confirmation and Glossolalia," in *Anglican Theological Review,* supplemental series, 2 (1973): 100-12.

8   For a rapid historical summary, see D. B. Stevick, op. cit., 14-18. For some theological and pastoral argumentation, see idem, op. cit., chapter 5, "Persistent Issues: Confirmation," 54-90.

9   Even though the Pentecost and Samaria patterns seem to belong to specific situations in the church's earliest years, it is possible that in some way they continued in the divergent sacramental traditions that developed in the early centuries. The early Syrian churches (and others) anointed candidates before baptism, but not after baptism. It is not certain that these churches understood this anointing to signify the Holy Spirit, yet the sequence does suggest the Pentecost/Cornelius pattern—the Spirit before the water. In most other parts of the early church, baptism was followed by an anointing, performed by the minister of baptism, which was taken to signify the Holy Spirit. Did this sacramental tradition follow the Samaria/Ephesus pattern, in which the water came before the Spirit? T. W. Manson considered this link between Acts and the early liturgical traditions in "Entry into Membership of the Early Church," *Journal of Theological Studies* 48 (1947): 25-33.

10 See S. Anita Stauffer, op. cit.

Notes to chapter 8
The Scriptures Appointed "At Baptism"

1   Robert J. Kennedy, ed., *Reconciliation: The Continuing Agenda* (Collegeville, Minnesota: Liturgical Press, 1987).

2   The discussion of Jesus and the children owes a debt to the splendid article, cited above, by Clinton Morrison, "Baptism and Maturity," *Interpretation* 17:4 (October 1963): 387-401.

3   Thomas Traherne, *Centuries of Meditations,* 3:3.

[4] Oscar Cullmann, "Traces of an Ancient Baptismal Formula in the New Testament," *Baptism in the New Testament* (Chicago: Henry Regnery, 1950), 71-80.

[5] H. R. Macintosh, "Thoughts on Infant Baptism," *The Expositor* 13 (1917): 199, an old, but still a very good article.

Notes to chapter 9
Other New Testament Passages

[1] James Denney, *The Death of Christ* (New York: A. C. Armstrong and Son, 1902), 185.

[2] *Christians and the New Creation: Genesis Motifs in the New Testament* (Louisville, Kentucky: Westminster John Knox Press, 1994), 112.

[3] The expression "seeing now that this child [this person] is regenerate. . ." followed the actual baptism in the Prayer Book rites from 1552 on. These words seemed to some readers to skirt close to magic, and they occasioned disputes, trials, and schisms. While the ideas of new life in the Spirit and new birth are often expressed in the rite of the 1979 Prayer Book, the 1552–1928 words have been dropped. The long-standing Prayer Book use of "regeneration" in an individualistic sense could not be supported by the New Testament, and it caused needless misunderstanding.

Notes to chapter 10
Biblical Passages and Allusions in the Baptismal Rite

[1] G. B. Caird, *Paul's Letters from Prison* (Oxford: Oxford University Press, 1976), 71.

[2] Lesslie Newbigin, *A Faith for this One World?* (London: SCM Press, 1961), 81.

[3] Caird, op. cit., 73.

[4] At the founding of the Episcopal Church, this clause was debated. It was known that it came into the creed rather late, and its biblical basis seemed uncertain. Some members of the convention were prepared to drop it from the creed, but the English bishops, who had to approve the new church if they were to confer the episcopate, wanted the "integrity" of the creed to be respected. The creed was used in the Prayer Book of 1789, but with a rubric saying that any church (that is, the convention of any state) might omit it, and that "any Churches may, instead of the words, *He descended into hell*, use the words, *He went into the place of departed spirits*, which are considered as words of the same meaning in the Creed." This explanation apparently depended on reading *hell* as the Hebrew *sheol* of the Old Testament, a shadowy afterlife. Few congregations, if any, took advantage of this provision. Yet this rubric, a monument to eighteenth-century latitudinarianism, was continued in the revisions of 1892 and 1928.

5   Ambrose, *On the Sacraments,* 1:15. On the present passage, Yarnold comments, "Presumably Ambrose would have held that baptism with unconsecrated water was invalid."

6   L. L. Mitchell, "The Thanksgiving over the Water," *Initiation and the Churches* (Washington, D. C.: The Pastoral Press, 1991), 177-94. An informative essay on this central prayer. Also published in 1981 in an anthology edited by Bryan Spinks, entitled *The Sacrifice of Praise.*

7   The clarity with which the Prayer Book rite says that baptism is the seal—*N., you are sealed by the Holy Spirit in Baptism* (BCP, p. 308)—may be somewhat clouded by the bishop's prayer for the Consecration of the Chrism (BCP, p. 307), which asks that God will consecrate the oil *that those who are sealed with it may share in the royal priesthood of Jesus Christ,* seeming to say that the anointing is the seal. This difference should not be pressed; both are in a sense true. The two actions (baptism and anointing) stand close to one another in time, and the two meanings (baptism and sealing) are really one.

8   Yves Congar, *Lay People in the Church* (Westminster, Maryland.: Newman Press, 1957), 125.

9   Ambrose, *On the Sacraments,* 5:13. Other early texts indicate that in many places this psalm was sung at the eucharist.

10 Schnackenburg, op. cit., 91.

11 Ambrose, *On the Sacraments,* 3:8.

Notes to chapter 11
Images of Baptism

1   Tertullian, *On Baptism,* 1.1 (ed. Evans, p. 5).

2   Michael Saward, lyrics, hymn 294, *The Hymnal 1982* (New York: Church Hymnal Corporation, 1985). The mixed metaphors of Ephesians 5:14 have already been noted.

3   Justin, *Apology,* section 61.

4   Basil the Great, *Protreptic on Holy Baptism,* section 1 (ed. A. Hamman, op. cit., 76).

5   Cyril of Jerusalem, *Mystagogical Catecheses,* 4:8.

6   Ibid., 3:1.

7   Basil, *Protreptic on Holy Baptism,* section 4 (ed. A. Hamman, op. cit., 81).

8   Cyril of Jerusalem, *Mystagogical Catecheses,* 5:20.

9   See D. B. Stevick, "A Matter of Taste: 1 Peter 2:3," *Review for Religious* 47 (1988): 5:707-17.

10 Gregory of Nazianzus, *Sermon on Holy Baptism,* ed. A. Hamman, op. cit., 89.

Notes to chapter 12
Some Running Themes

[1] Robert Jenson, op. cit., 130.

[2] C. F. D. Moule, *Worship in the New Testament* (Richmond, Virginia: John Knox Press, 1961), 51.

[3] N. Clark, op. cit., 72.

[4] Schnackenburg, op. cit., 20.

[5] J. A. T. Robinson, "The One Baptism," *Twelve New Testament Studies* (Naperville, Ill.: Allenson, 1962), 158-75. Robinson gives credit for the origin of his thesis to Cullmann, especially his *Baptism in the New Testament.*

[6] *One Lord, One Baptism* (Minneapolis: Augsburg, 1961), 56. This report now seems like a tryout for *Baptism, Eucharist and Ministry,* but it has its own excellences and deserves to be remembered, as do many other documents and reports from Faith and Order.

[7] Jürgen Moltmann, *The Church in the Power of the Spirit* (New York: Harper and Row, 1977), 235.

[8] The incident at Ephesus also mentions that the Spirit was evidenced by speaking in tongues. But it is not clear whether we are to understand known languages, as at Pentecost, or unintelligible speech requiring an interpreter, as at Corinth. This story in Acts contains a number of puzzles, of which this is only one. It is best not to build too much on what happened at Ephesus.

[9] Schnackenburg, op. cit., 28.

[10] Peter Hinchliff, "Baptism: The Third Dimension," *Theology* 73 (1970): 488 [pronouns altered].

[11] Karl Barth, *Christ and Adam* (New York: Macmillan, 1968), 46.

[12] Neville Clark, "Baptism and Redemption," Basil Moss, ed., *Crisis for Baptism* (London: SCM Press, 1965), 74.

[13] Philip Watson, *The Concept of Grace* (Philadelphia: Muhlenburg Press, 1959), 23.

[14] G. Wingren, op. cit., 190.

[15] See Alexander Ganoczy, *Becoming Christian: A Theology of Baptism as the Sacrament of Human History* (New York: Paulist Press, 1976), 23: "Baptism. . .is much more than a simple ecclesiastical initiation rite or an act of Christian pedagogy. It is the sacrament of human historicity, centered on the God of history, made flesh in Jesus of Nazareth."

Some further resources

The biblical material in this study has followed the configurations that are offered in the lectionary and the Prayer Book rite. Several valuable studies have examined the early baptismal material, keeping to the structure of the gospels and the epistles, or distinguishing the types of New Testament thought, or following New Testament motifs into the early church. The following titles are a selection of this literature:

Beasley-Murray, G. R. *Baptism in the New Testament*. London: Macmillan, 1963. An almost encyclopedic work by an eminent English Baptist exegete; authoritative and detailed; Baptist polemics intrude only occasionally, although the final chapter is a vigorous defense of "believers' baptism."

Cullmann, Oscar. *Baptism in the New Testament*. London: SCM Press, 1950. A brief seminal study, with many original insights.

———. *Early Christian Worship*. London: SCM Press, 1953. The second half of this book tests how much can be said for the place of sacraments in John's gospel.

Danielou, Jean. *The Bible and the Liturgy*. South Bend, Indiana: University of Notre Dame Press, 1956. An authoritative study of the way in which the early liturgical texts and explanations of the liturgy used the scriptures; there is much emphasis on baptism.

———. *From Shadow to Reality*. London: Burns and Oates, 1960. An informative study of early Christian typology, with substantial chapters on the patristic use of the flood, the sacrifice of Isaac, and the exodus.

Dillistone, F. W. *Christianity and Symbolism.* Philadelphia: Westminster Press, 1955. A theological study of symbol and of several basic symbols.

Eastman, A. Theodore. *The Baptizing Community: Christian Initiation and the Local Congregation.* Rev. ed. Wilton, Conn.: Morehouse Publishing, 1991. A fine guide to the Christian parish as a community that is in the business of bringing persons into the life of Christ and his people.

Finn, Thomas M. *Early Christian Baptism and the Catechumenate: West and East Syria.* Collegeville, Minnesota: Liturgical Press, 1992.

———. *Early Christian Baptism and the Catechumenate: Italy, North Africa, and Egypt.* Collegeville, Minnesota: Liturgical Press, 1992.

Flemington, W. F. *The New Testament Doctrine of Baptism.* London: SPCK, 1957. A good, very approachable work; slightly dated, since it was written before the texts of the Dead Sea Scrolls had become widely available.

George, A., et al. *Baptism in the New Testament.* Baltimore: Helicon, 1964. A symposium by Roman Catholic scripture scholars.

Jackson, Pamela E. J. *Journeybread for the Shadowlands: The Readings for the Rites of the Catechumenate, RCIA.* Collegeville, Minnesota: Liturgical Press, 1993. Well-written comment on the scriptures appointed in the Roman liturgy for the stages of preparation for adult baptism, which the author presents as a journey. Serious patristic scholarship lies behind these attractive meditations.

Jennings, Theodore W. *Loyalty to God: The Apostles' Creed in Life and Liturgy.* Nashville, Tennessee: Abingdon Press, 1962. A fine modern study of the creed.

Jeremias, Joachim. *Infant Baptism in the First Four Centuries.* Philadelphia: Westminster Press, 1962. A classic presentation of the available evidence.

Kelly, J. N. D. *Early Christian Creeds.* London: Longmans Green and Co., 1952. A classic historical study of the creeds; for this present inquiry, see especially chapter 2, "Creeds and Baptism," pp. 30-61.

Mitchell, Leonel L. *Initiation and the Churches*. Washington, D. C.: The Pastoral Press, 1991. A gathering of valuable articles, some historical and some topical.

Moule, C. F. D. *Worship in the New Testament*. Richmond, Virginia: John Knox Press, 1961. The chapter on baptism gives wise judgments on most of the issues of fact and interpretation.

Porter, H. Boone. *The Day of Light: The Biblical and Liturgical Meaning of Sunday*. New York: Seabury Press, 1960. A valuable study, even though it was necessarily keyed to the 1928 Prayer Book.

Schlink, Edmund. *The Doctrine of Baptism*. St. Louis: Concordia, 1972. A very good Lutheran theological study which stays close to biblical sources.

Schnackenburg, Rudolf. *Baptism in the Thought of St. Paul*. New York: Herder and Herder, 1964. A splendid book by an outstanding Roman Catholic biblical scholar; written at an advanced level—the first half would be difficult for readers with no Greek.

Stanley, David M. "The New Testament Doctrine of Baptism: An Essay in Biblical Theology." *Theological Studies* 18 (1957): 169-215. A lengthy article by an able Roman Catholic exegete which surveys the New Testament material.

Stauffer, Anita S. *On Baptismal Fonts: Ancient and Modern*. Alcuin/GROW Liturgical Study 29-30. Bramcote, Nottinghamshire, U. K.: Grove Books, 1994. Brief, but informative.

Stevenson, Kenneth. *Jerusalem Revisited: The Liturgical Meaning of Holy Week*. Washington, D. C.: Pastoral Press, 1988. A popular, but solid summary of the heart of liturgy.

Stevick, Daniel B. *Baptismal Moments: Baptismal Meanings*. New York: Church Hymnal Corporation, 1987. A study of the historical, theological, pastoral, and liturgical backgrounds of the initiatory rites of the 1979 Prayer Book; contains substantial argumentation on infant baptism, confirmation, and first communion.

Stookey, Lawrence H. *Baptism: Christ's Act in the Church.* Nashville, Tennessee: Abingdon Press, 1982. A good work by a Methodist liturgical scholar.

White, R. E. O. *The Biblical Doctrine of Initiation.* Grand Rapids, Michigan: William B. Eerdmans, 1960. A large, thoroughly argued book by an English Baptist; good description and analysis of the biblical material; somewhat more aggressively Baptist than Beasley-Murray's similar book listed above.

Yarnold, Edward. *The Awe-Inspiring Rites of Initiation.* 2nd ed. Collegeville, Minnesota: Liturgical Press, 1994. An informative introduction to the fourth-century baptismal lectures; all the quotations from this patristic material in the present book use this edition.

Index of biblical passages

[This index omits references in which a biblical text is no more than mentioned. The entries in italics are principal lectionary readings or places that are given fairly extended discussion in the foregoing pages.]